Sun Certified System Administrator for Solaris™ 8 Study Guide

Peter H. Gregory

Sun Certified System Administrator for Solaris 8 Study Guide

Sun Microsystems Press
A Prentice Hall Title

Library of Congress Cataloging-in-Publication Data

Gregory, Peter H.
Sun Certified System Administrator for Solaris 8 study guide / Peter H. Gregory.
p. cm.
Includes bibliographical references and index.
ISBN 0-13-040933-2 (pbk.)
1. Electronic data processing personnel—Certification. 2. Operating systems (Computers) Certification—Study guides. 3. Solaris (Computer file) I. Title.

QA76.3 .G753 2001
005.4'469—dc21 2001049432

The publisher offers discounts on this book when ordered in bulk quantities.
For more information, contact: Corporate Sales Department, Phone: 800-382-3419; Fax: 201-236-7141; E-mail: corpsales@prenhall.com; or write: Prentice Hall PTR, Corp. Sales Dept., One Lake Street, Upper Saddle River, NJ 07458.

Editorial/production supervision: *BooksCraft, Inc.*
Cover design director: *Jerry Votta*
Cover designer: *Anthony Gemmellaro*
Manufacturing manager: *Alexis R. Heydt-Long*
Marketing manager: *Debby vanDijk*
Acquisitions editor: *Gregory G. Doench*
Editorial assistant: *Brandt Kenna*
Project coordinator: *Anne R. Garcia*
Sun Microsystems Press publisher: *Rachel Borden*

10 9 8 7 6 5 4 3 2 1

ISBN 0-13- 040933-2

Sun Microsystems Press

A Prentice Hall Title

To Corinne, Alana, Alexis, and Regan –

for lovingly pulling me back to the center where I belong.

To the New York City, Washington, D.C.,

and Pennsylvania terrorist victims and their families.

CONTENTS

CHAPTER 7

vi Editor *167*

CHAPTER 8

Disks *185*

PREFACE

Why Certification?

What is all the commotion about technical certifications? Is it just hype? Is it just 21st Century snake oil? Or is there really something to it? What is the true value of a certification? In the quest for competitive advantage among IT professionals, certification is rapidly becoming key to distinguishing between potential job candidates. Here is what industry analysts are saying:

- *Certification in leading technologies (such as Solaris) is a key to higher pay.*[1] This reflects a trend where companies are paying more for knowledge, rather than just experience.
- *Certification is becoming the new standard for professionalism in business.* Although the college degree is still very important, the technical certification is evidence of proficiency with a particular technology or product. Certification is an independent, objective verification of knowledge.
- *Having a certification may be the difference in getting invited to the interview.* Technologists need differentiators—not just accomplishments, but objective measures of technical proficiency—to stay competitive and stand out from the crowd of wannabe's.
- Managers value certification because it increases quality and productivity of work.[2]
- *Solaris is the market leader in the UNIX space.*[3] UNIX is the leader in the server OS space. Solaris does the heavy lifting on Wall Street, in compute-intensive engineering and biotechnology, and in E-commerce.

You need a certification if you want to stay ahead of the competition. This book will guide you to Solaris certification.

---

1. "Sorting Out Certifications," by Steve Alexander, *Computerworld*, December 13, 1999.
2. Gartner/Dataquest, Inc. Perspective report.
3. "Sun, About to Unveil Unix Server, Leads Market," by Amy Newman, Managing Editor, *ServerWatch*, September 25, 2000.

Intended Audience

This study guide is intended for experienced UNIX administrators who wish to prepare for the Sun Certified System Administrator for the Solaris 8 Operating Environment, Part I exam.

This book does not teach system administration, nor is it a substitute for systems administration classes taught by Sun Microsystems or its affiliates. Although this book may be a little "teachy" here and there, its purpose is to provide review material to help candidates prepare for the exam.

If you wish to take the exam but feel that you need to learn more, contact Sun Education at http://suned.sun.com/. There you can find out about training materials and classes in your area. You can also contact Sun Education at:

Sun Education
UBRM12-175
500 Eldorado Blvd.
Broomfield, CO 80021
Phone: (800) 422-8020, or (303) 464-4097
Fax: (303) 464-4490

Registering for the Exam

Follow these steps to register for the exam:

1. Purchase a Certification Voucher by calling Sun Education at 1-800-422-8020. Outside the U.S., contact your local Sun Education office. If you do not know the location of your local Sun Education office, you can find it at:

   http://suned.sun.com/USA/certification/global_contacts/index.html.

   The exam costs U.S. $150.00.

   You will be given a voucher number, which will be the letters "SE" followed by eight digits; for example, SE01470053. Save this number—you will need it to schedule the examination.
2. Schedule your examination by visiting the Prometric Services Web site at http://2test.com/.
   a. Select *Information Technology Certifications*. You'll then be taken to a login page; you must log in to continue (you will have an opportunity to create a login if this is your first visit to the site).

- **b.** After logging in, you will see the *Certification Program* page; select *Sun Education* from the pull-down menu.
- **c.** Select the country where you will take your exam.
- **d.** Select 310-011 SUN CERTIFIED SYSTEM ADMINISTRATOR FOR SOLARIS 8 PART I from the pull-down menu. Select the state or province if this appears on your screen.
- **e.** The exam is available only in English.
- **f.** Select the exam location and the schedule most suitable for you.
- **g.** You'll be given a confirmation, which includes more numbers that you will need in order to take the exam. For U.S. locations, you can also print a map showing the exam location.

Be sure to understand the policy for changing your exam date and time in case you need to reschedule your exam. Also be sure you understand any time limitations regarding the starting time for your exam. If you are late, you may not be able to take your exam. Restrictions and penalties for cancellations and/or late arrivals may apply. Carefully read all of the terms and conditions printed on your exam confirmation.

Taking the Exam

Allow plenty of time to travel to the exam site, including finding a parking space and the location of the exam building and room. It may be advisable to call in advance if you are not familiar with the exam site.

No food or beverages are allowed in the exam room. You must check in any computer, laptop, PDA, calculator, recorder, or cell phone you bring in with you. The exam center will supply pencils and one sheet of paper for you to make calculations, draw diagrams, and so on, and you will have to surrender that piece of paper at the end of the exam. You are not allowed to take any written notes with you out of the exam.

You will probably be monitored on a closed-circuit television while you take the exam. An exam center I recently visited had a TV monitor out in the lobby. You will be taking the exam on a GUI-type workstation. You will need to log in, and you will need to furnish information from your exam confirmation in order to do so.

First you will be shown the Pre-Test Agreement. You must read and understand the agreement, and state whether you agree or disagree. *If you disagree with the first question in the Pre-Test Agreement, you will not be allowed to take the exam* (you will receive a refund). A sample Pre-Test Agreement appears in Appendix C.

Next, you will be presented with instructions and a sample exam question. This ensures that you are familiar with the exam format and the method for marking answers. You may skip the sample exam question if you wish and proceed to the exam itself.

You will have 90 minutes to take the exam. That's about one and a half minutes per question. The 90-minute time limit will begin once you start taking the exam. The amount of time remaining is always visible on the screen.

You may take a restroom break if you wish (according to rules at the testing center), but the time clock will continue counting.

Exam Questions

The exam contains 57 questions, which are a combination of multiple choice, free answer, and drag-and-drop. There is more than one version of this exam. Each version has questions that were carefully selected from a much larger pool of questions, so that each version of the exam covers the same subject area and has an equivalent degree of difficulty.

The process for developing the exam questions is not trivial. Exam questions are carefully written according to a strict set of guidelines and then tested. There is a whole field of study called *psychometrics* that is used to measure and evaluate each question. Only after passing careful scrutiny will an exam question ultimately find its way onto the exam.

Questions will appear on the screen one at a time. You will see each question and, in the case of multiple-choice questions, you will see all of the possible answers. In some longer questions, you can scroll down to see these.

If you are not sure of the answer, you may skip the question and return to it later. You can also "mark" any exam question that you wish to review later.

Multiple-Choice Questions

The exam contains two types of multiple-choice questions: some with one correct answer, and some with two or more correct answers. Multiple-choice questions with one correct answer will present radio buttons for selecting your answer, allowing you to select only one answer. If two answers appear to be similar, be very careful since only one answer is correct.

Multiple-choice questions with more than one correct answer will specify the number of correct answers. You must select *all* of the correct answers in order to get credit for the question. These questions present checkboxes that allow you to select more than one answer.

Here are two sample multiple-choice questions. Figure 1 shows a question with one correct answer; Figure 2 shows one with multiple answers.

Free-Answer Questions

Free-answer questions require that you type the correct answer into a blank text field. You must be very careful that you get the answer exactly right. But what about the order of options in a command? The exam is smart enough to figure this out—the exam knows about all possible

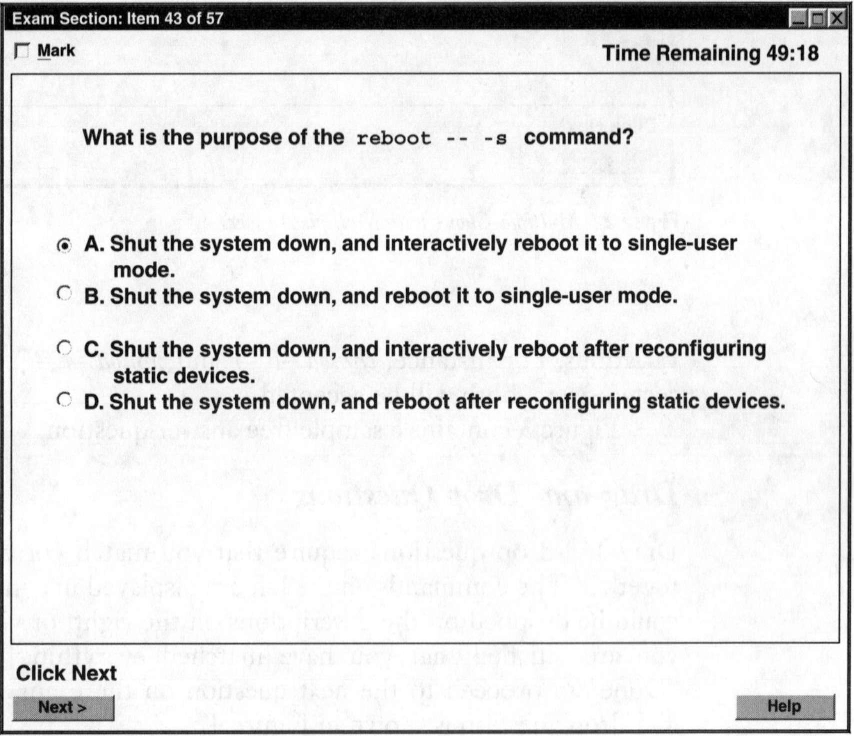

Figure 1 *Multiple-Choice Question with One Correct Answer*

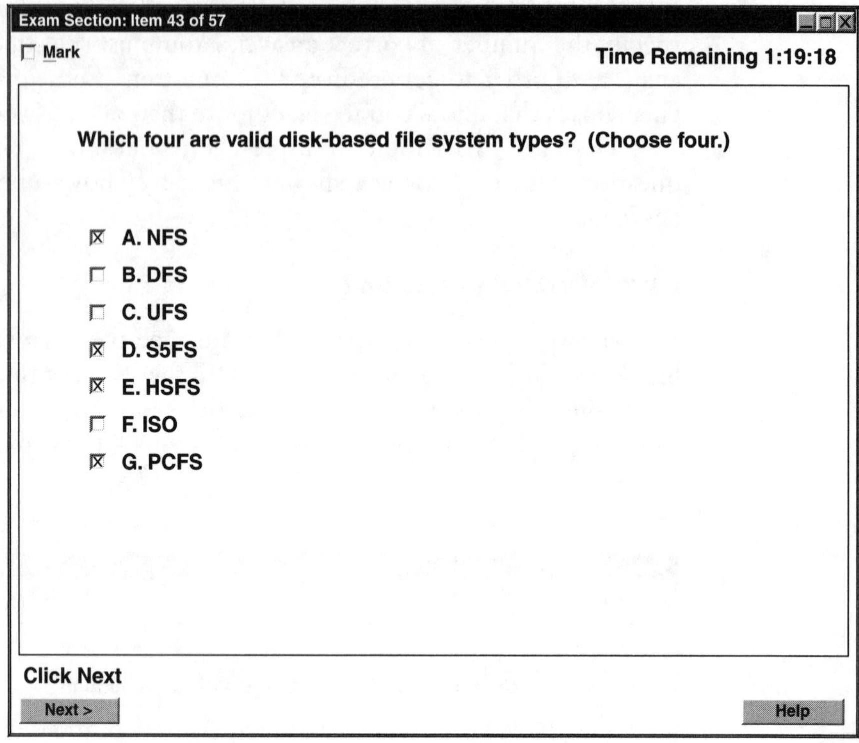

Figure 2 *Multiple-Choice with Multiple Answers*

variations. For instance, *chmod –F –r* and *chmod –r –F*; if both are correct answers, both will be accepted.

Figure 3 contains a sample free answer question.

Drag-and-Drop Questions

Drag-and-drop questions require that you match corresponding items together. The commands on the left are displayed in a movable icon that could be dropped on the descriptions on the right, or vice versa. When you are satisfied that you have matched everything correctly, press "Done" to proceed to the next question on the exam. A sample drag-and-drop question is shown in Figure 4.

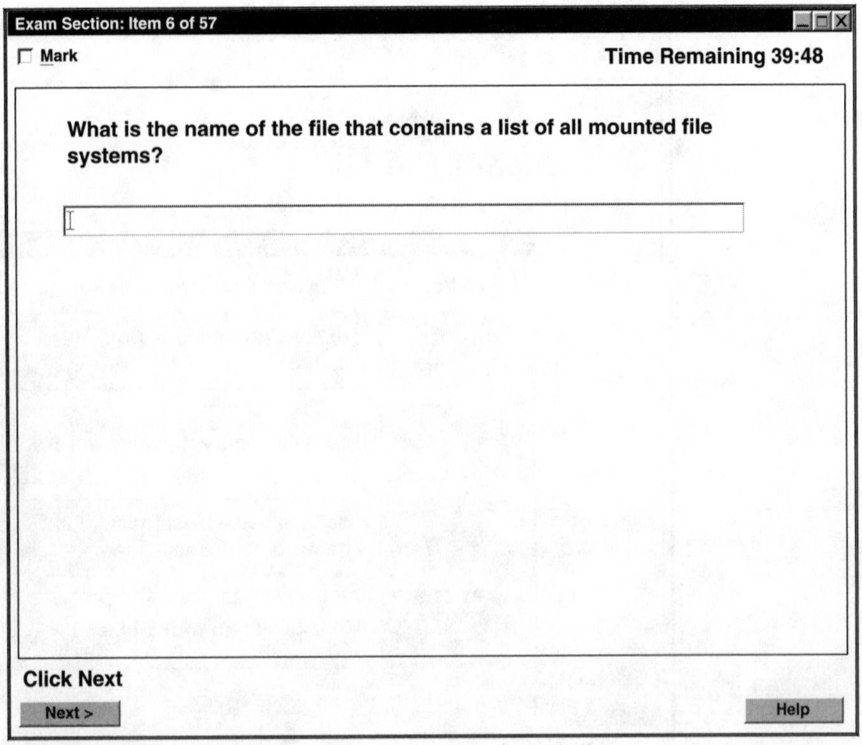

Exam Section: Item 6 of 57

Mark

Time Remaining 39:48

What is the name of the file that contains a list of all mounted file systems?

Click Next

Next >

Help

Figure 3 *Free Answer Question*

Reviewing Test Answers

After you have answered all of the questions, you will see a list of all the exam questions and the answers you selected (or filled in). Each question will have a special marking if you marked it for later review.

You may start at the beginning and review each question, you may review questions you marked earlier, or you may just skip around and check questions in any order you wish. You may unmark questions you marked, and you may mark other questions. You are free to review questions, change answers, and mark and unmark questions until time runs out or you finish the exam early.

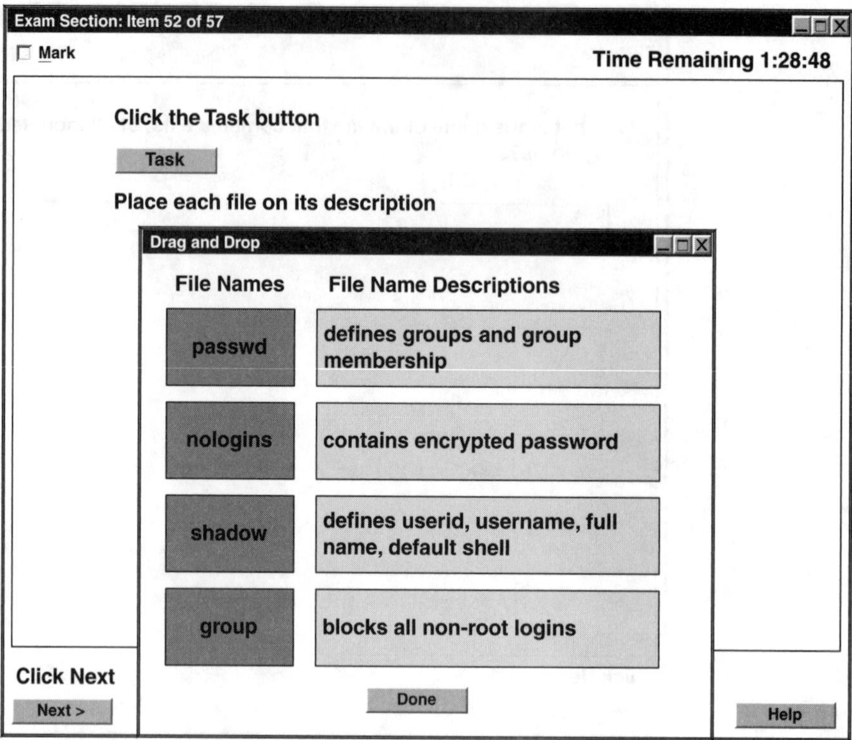

Figure 4 *Drag-and-Drop Question*

Scoring the Exam

Once you have finished the exam, it will be scored immediately. You must answer at least 66% of the questions correctly, which is at least 38 of the 57 questions.

You will receive a temporary certificate showing whether you passed or failed the exam. The certificate will include your name and the number of questions you answered correctly. A chart on the lower half of the certificate will indicate how you scored on each subject area. You will not know how you did on any individual question.

Retaking the Exam

If you failed the exam, you may take it again in as little as two weeks, but you cannot take the exam more than three times in a calendar year. You must register and pay for another examination. You can be assured that the version of the exam will not be the same one you took previously.

Conduct

You may not discuss the details of the exam with any other individual. You may not offer or accept help of any kind. A full explanation of conduct may be found in Appendix D.

How This Book Is Organized

Each chapter begins with a list of exam objectives. These objectives were developed by Sun Microsystems; they define the subject matter covered by the certification exam and this book. Here is an example exam objective:

- Using absolute or relative pathnames, select valid command strings to move between specified points within a given directory tree.

All of the certification objectives appear in Appendix B, along with the chapter number associated with each objective. This will allow you to quickly find the technical information behind each objective.

File names, commands, the names of systems, users and groups, and other terms, appear in italics in paragraphs and lists. For instance, the user *pmidey* on system *wallace* uses the *vi* command to edit the */etc/hosts.equiv* file.

Commands are explained in a consistent format throughout the book. The purpose of the command is briefly explained, its syntax shown, options and examples explained. For instance:

The *ps* command is used to view processes on a system. The syntax of the *ps* command is *ps [options]*. The options for *ps* are explained here.

- *-a*. List information about all processes most frequently requested: all those except process group leaders and processes not associated with a terminal.
- *-A*. List information for all processes.
- *-c*. Print information in a format that reflects scheduler properties as described in the *priocntl* command man page. The *-c* option affects the output of the *-f* and *-l* options.

Some examples of the *ps* command follow.

```
# ps -ef
     UID   PID  PPID  C    STIME TTY      TIME CMD
    root     0     0  0 05:32:00 ?        0:00 sched
    root     1     0  0 05:32:04 ?        0:00 /etc/init -
    root     2     0  0 05:32:04 ?        0:00 pageout
    root     3     0  0 05:32:04 ?        0:00 fsflush
```

Examples from real sessions appear in courier font, as in the example above. Text that is typed in by the user is always underlined.

Notes and warnings are enclosed in boxes so that they will stand out.

You will be challenged to ponder real-life scenarios that apply concepts that are discussed. For instance,

EXAM NOTES

THINK ABOUT IT . . .

Help! I just renamed a directory with important contents to the name of another directory that already exists. I meant to rename the directory, but because the target existed, my original directory is gone. Where did my original directory go?

Here is what happened. You meant to change the name of a directory to a new name, but unexpectedly the new name was the name of a directory that exists. You moved your directory underneath the existing directory.

Each chapter ends with a Chapter Summary and a Test Yourself section where there are ten multiple-choice and two free-answer questions. Because the exam contains few drag-and-drop questions, no sample drag-and-drop questions appear in this book.

The answers for test questions from all of the book's chapters are found in Appendix A.

Feedback

Despite the presence of reviews and controls at every level, from executive direction to copy editing, some mistakes are bound to slip through. That, or an unannounced change in behavior or functionality in Solaris itself, is bound to create a discrepancy between this book, the exam, and reality.

If a mistake is found in this book, all is not lost. Changes in the way books are published these days lead to the fact that this book will undergo several printing runs, each of which represents an opportunity to fix a mistake here and there.

Please send us feedback about any mistakes you find in this book, or about any ideas or comments you may have for future editions of this book.

Prentice Hall PTR
Attn.: Editor, Sun Microsystems Press
One Lake Street
Upper Saddle River, NJ 07458

We also publish an errata list online. Please visit us at
ftp://ftp.prenhall.com/pub/ptr/Sunsoft_books.w-053/Gregory/

Disclaimer

This is a book about Solaris 8. Every reasonable effort has been made to ensure that this book is as complete and accurate as possible. This book is offered as-is, and no warranty is implied. Neither the author nor Prentice Hall PTR should be held liable or responsible to any person or entity regarding any loss or damages that may arise as a result of the information contained in this book.

Acknowledgments

The author owes many thanks to:

- Geoff Carrier, an instructor at Sun Education, England, for high-quality feedback, great suggestions, and attention to the tiniest detail. Quality knows no bounds.

- Jennifer Blackwell, a great development editor at Prentice Hall Professional Technical Reference, for constructive engagement, and that keen eye toward consistency across the entire book. I hope we get to work on a project again soon.
- Diane Hudlin, of Sun Education, for her hospitality and for loaning me a conference room and access to her staff while I pored over the beta certification exams last winter, and for reviewing the book's layout and format, as well as the Preface.
- Steve Moore, of Sun Education, for a very thorough review of all of the sample exam questions.
- Evelyn Thompson, of Sun Education, for tracking down some hard-to-find exam information.
- Debby vanDijk, Marketing Manager at Prentice Hall Professional Technical Reference.
- Several at BooksCraft: Eric Sampson, for a really thorough copy-editing job, Bill Hartman for typesetting, Grechen Throop for production editing, and Sandi Schroeder for correcting and completing my indexing.
- Greg Doench, of Prentice Hall Professional Technical Reference, and Rachel Borden, of Sun Microsystems Press, for overall direction and access to other resources named above.
- Roger Santo and Gary McAllister for loaned (and returned!) equipment. I want to thank others of you who, for legitimate reasons, chose not to be mentioned in print; you know who you are.
- Gordon Marler, for help on Solaris packaging; and Rani Sandoy-Brown, for hints on taking CDE screenshots.
- My wife, Corinne, for elbowing me after I've pressed the snooze alarm at 4:00 A.M., and for help reviewing the Preface.
- Maurice J. Bach, author of The Design of the UNIX Operating System, for permission to use an illustration from the book.
- Capresso and Starbucks, for liquid sunshine during the dark Seattle winter months.

CHAPTER 1

System Concepts

After completing this chapter, you'll be able to meet the following Solaris Administration Exam objectives:

- Match selected system administration terms to their respective definitions: for example, daemons, shell, file system, kernel, operating system.
- Define the effect of using various main command options when viewing online manual pages.
- List the commands that display information for all active processes on the system.
- State the effect of sending a specified signal to a process.
- List the commands used to terminate an active process.

To fulfill these objectives, this chapter discusses:

- Operating system basics such as processes, programs, signals, file system, and the kernel;

- Tools used to view and control processes;
- Descriptions of the character and windows user interfaces;
- Basic features of the Common Desktop Environment (CDE); and
- Basic CDE controls and customization mechanisms.

1.1 Operating System

The Solaris operating system consists of the following components.

- Hardware control—this part of the kernel communicates directly with the hardware and handles interrupts generated by the hardware.
- Device drivers—these control the operation of all peripheral hardware devices. Block I/O devices are the system's random-access devices—that is, the disks. All other devices are character devices. There are both block and character device drivers for the system's disks.
- Buffer cache—this is a temporary storage area that functions as a performance optimizer. It stores (in memory) recently read and written disk data. For example, recently read disk blocks that are still in the buffer are available for rereading should another process in the system wish to read the same block.
- File subsystem—this handles all I/O requests to and from file systems.
- Process and control subsystem—this part of the kernel is responsible for creating and scheduling processes, interprocess communications, and process memory management. It communicates with the file subsystem to retrieve program files from the disk and load them into memory; it also reads and writes files requested by running programs. Memory management oversees the management of the system's RAM and virtual memory.
- System call interface—user and application programs access the file subsystem and the process control subsystem via a set of system calls.

Figure 1-1 illustrates the different parts of the kernel and their relationships with each other, with user programs, and with the system's hardware.

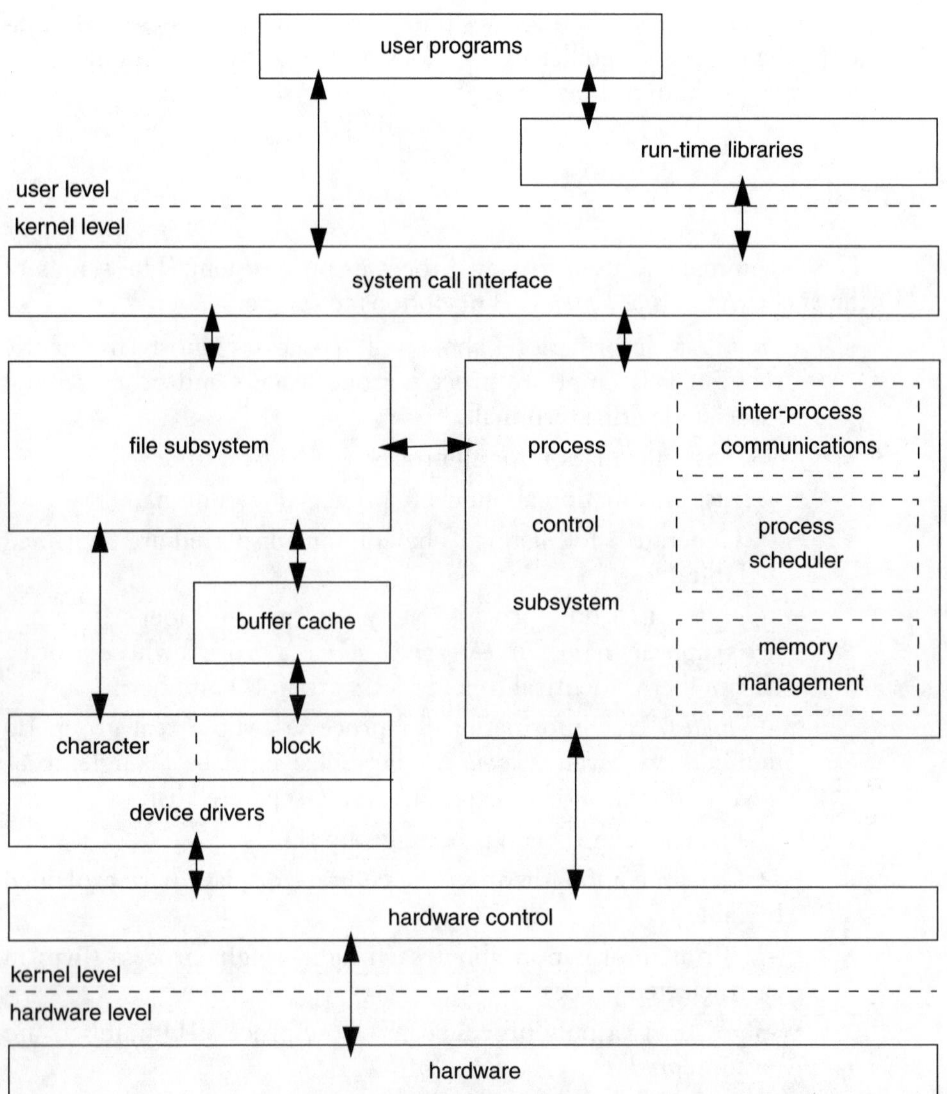

Figure 1–1 *Illustration of Kernel Components (Reprinted with permission from* The Design of the UNIX Operating System, *by Maurice Bach, Prentice Hall, 1986)*

1.2 Programs and Processes

A *program* is a file containing machine instructions that perform some specific task. A *process* is an instance of a program that is executing on a system. On a UNIX system, several processes can exist simultaneously; this is called multiprogramming or multitasking.

The *process scheduler* allocates time to runnable processes on the system. The process scheduler uses various parameters to determine which processes run and for how long.

The *ps* Command

The *ps* command is used to view processes on a system. The syntax of the *ps* command is *ps [options]*. The options for *ps* are:

- *-a.* List information about all processes most frequently requested. Exempt are process group leaders and processes not associated with a terminal.
- *-A.* List information for all processes; identical to *-e*.
- *-e.* List information about every process now running.
- *-f.* Generate a full listing. The columns displayed are explained in Table 1.1.
- *-g grplist.* List only process data whose group leader's ID number(s) appears in *grplist*. (A *group leader* is a process whose process ID number is identical to its process group ID number.)
- *-G gidlist.* List information for processes whose real group ID numbers are given in *gidlist*. The gidlist must be a single argument in the form of a blank- or comma-separated list.
- *-j.* Print session ID and process group ID.
- *-l.* Generate a long listing. The columns displayed are explained in Table 1.1.
- *-L.* Print information about each light-weight process (lwp) in each selected process.
- *-p proclist.* List only process data whose process ID numbers are given in *proclist*.
- *-P.* Print the number of the processor to which the process or lwp is bound, if any, under an additional column header, PSR.
- *-s sidlist.* List information on all session leaders whose IDs appear in *sidlist*.
- *-t term.* List only process data associated with *term*. Terminal identifiers are specified as a device file name and an identifier. For example, *term/a* or *pts/0*.
- *-u uidlist.* List only process data whose effective user ID number or login name is given in *uidlist*. In the listing, the numerical user

ID will be printed unless you give the *-f* option, which prints the login name.

- *-U uidlist*. List information for processes whose real user ID numbers or login names are given in *uidlist*. The uidlist must be a single argument in the form of a blank- or comma-separated list.
- *-y*. Under a long listing (*-l*), omit the obsolete F and ADDR columns and include an RSS column to report the resident set size of the process. Under the *-y* option, both RSS and SZ (see Table 1.1) will be reported in units of kilobytes instead of pages.

The fields displayed under the different display options are listed in Table 1.1.

Table 1.1 ps *Command Display Columns*

FIELD	OPTIONS	DESCRIPTION
F	-l	Flags (hexadecimal and additive) that are associated with the process. These flags are available for historical purposes; no meaning should currently be ascribed to them.
S	-l	The state of the process: O—process is running on a processor. S—sleeping; process is waiting for an event to complete. R—runnable; process is on run queue. Z—zombie state; process terminated and parent not waiting. T—process is stopped, either by a job control signal or because it is being traced.
UID	-f, -l	The effective user ID number of the process (the login name is printed under the *-f* option).
PID	all	The process ID of the process (this is the value used to kill the process).
PPID	-f, -l	The process ID of the parent process.
C	-f, -l	Processor utilization for scheduling (obsolete). Not printed when the *-c* option is used.
CLS	-f, -l	Scheduling class. Printed only when the *-c* option is used.
PRI	-l	The priority of the process. Without the *-c* option, higher numbers mean lower priority; with the *-c* option, higher numbers mean higher priority.
NI	-l	Nice value, used in priority computation. Not printed when the *-c* option is used. Only processes in the certain scheduling classes have a nice value.
ADDR	-l	The memory address of the process.
RSS	-l	The resident set size of the process, in kilobytes.
SZ	-l	The total size of the process in virtual memory, including all mapped files and devices, in pages.

Table 1.1 ps *Command Display Columns (Continued)*

FIELD	OPTIONS	DESCRIPTION
WCHAN	-l	The address of an event for which the process is sleeping (if blank, the process is running).
STIME	-f	The starting time of the process, given in hours, minutes, and seconds. (A process begun more than 24 hours before the *ps* inquiry is executed is shown in months and days.)
TTY	all	The controlling terminal for the process (the message, ?, is printed when there is no controlling terminal).
TIME	all	The cumulative execution time for the process, expressed in hh:mm:ss format.
CMD	all	The command name (the full command name and its arguments, up to a limit of 80 characters, are printed under the *-f* option). A process that has exited and has a parent, but has not yet been waited for by the parent, is marked <defunct>.
PGID	-j	The process ID of the process group leader.
SID	-j	The process ID of the session leader.
LWP	-L	The lwp ID of the lwp being reported.
NLWP	-L, -f	The number of lwp's in the process.

Some examples of the *ps* command follow.

```
# ps -ef
     UID   PID  PPID  C    STIME TTY      TIME CMD
    root     0     0  0 05:32:00 ?        0:00 sched
    root     1     0  0 05:32:04 ?        0:00 /etc/init -
    root     2     0  0 05:32:04 ?        0:00 pageout
    root     3     0  0 05:32:04 ?        0:00 fsflush
    root   285     1  0 05:33:02 ?        0:00 /usr/lib/saf/sac -t 300
    root   212     1  0 05:32:51 ?        0:00 /usr/lib/utmpd
    root   174     1  0 05:32:48 ?        0:00 /usr/sbin/cron
    root    45     1  0 05:32:11 ?        0:00 /usr/lib/devfsadm/
devfseventd
    root    47     1  0 05:32:11 ?        0:00 /usr/lib/devfsadm/devfsadmd
    root   107     1  0 05:32:44 ?        0:00 /usr/sbin/in.routed -q
    root   122     1  0 05:32:45 ?        0:00 /usr/sbin/rpcbind
    root   125     1  0 05:32:45 ?        0:00 /usr/sbin/keyserv
    root   217     1  0 05:32:51 ?        0:00 /usr/sadm/lib/wbem/
cimomboot start
    root   151     1  0 05:32:46 ?        0:00 /usr/sbin/inetd -s
    root   152     1  0 05:32:47 ?        0:00 /usr/lib/autofs/automountd
    root   155     1  0 05:32:47 ?        0:00 /usr/sbin/in.named
```

```
   root   296      1  0 05:33:08 ?        0:00 /usr/openwin/bin/fbconsole
-d :0
   root   168      1  0 05:32:48 ?        0:00 /usr/sbin/syslogd
   root   190      1  0 05:32:49 ?        0:00 /usr/lib/lpsched
(remainder of output suppressed)
#

# ps -lunobody
F S UID   PID  PPID C PRI NI ADDR     SZ  WCHAN     TTY TIME CMD
8 S 60001 3359 3357 0 40  20 70874058 271 7037608c  ?   0:00 httpd
8 S 60001 3360 3357 0 40  20 70864060 271 70861dec  ?   0:00 httpd
8 S 60001 3451 3357 0 40  20 70ab0f00 271 708617ac  ?   0:00 httpd
8 S 60001 3449 3357 0 40  20 70ab07d8 271 70861b6c  ?   0:00 httpd
8 S 60001 3452 3357 0 40  20 70ab00b0 271 70354b4c  ?   0:00 httpd
8 S 60001 3453 3357 0 40  20 70ad1630 271 70861fcc  ?   0:00 httpd
#
```

In the first example, the *-e* and *-f* options are used. This tells *ps* to show all running processes (*-e*) and to provide a "full" listing (*-f*). In the second example, a long (*-l*) listing of all processes running under the userid "nobody" (*-unobody*) is shown.

EXAM NOTES

THINK ABOUT IT . . .

A process on the system is spawning too many child processes. How would you find and subsequently kill it?

First, you could issue a *ps –el* command, and watch for the excess child processes. Note the values in the PPID column; these are the parent processes' ID. This parent process is the one you will need to kill (details on the *kill* command appear later in this chapter).

Note: Normally child processes are killed before parent processes to avoid so-called zombies. But in this case that is not feasible.

The *prstat* Command

The *prstat* command is used to dynamically display process statistics. The syntax of the *prstat* command is *prstat [options] [interval] [count]*, where *interval* is the time in seconds for display refresh (the default is five seconds), and *count* is an optional field telling *prstat* to display *count* times before exiting. By default, *prstat* will run forever.

The options for *prstat* are:

- *-a*. Report information about processes and users. In this mode, *prstat* displays separate reports about processes and users at the same time.
- *-c*. Print new reports below previous reports instead of overprinting them. This would be useful for recording output into a logfile or to a printer.
- *-C psrsetlist*. Report only processes or lwp's that are bound to processor sets in the given list. Each processor set is identified by an integer as reported by the *psrset* command.
- *-L*. Report statistics for each light-weight process (LWP). By default, *prstat* reports only the quantity of lwp's for each process.
- *-m*. Report microstate process accounting information. In addition to all fields listed in *-v* mode, this mode also includes the percentage of time the process has spent processing system traps, text page faults, data page faults, waiting for user locks, and waiting for CPU (latency time).
- *-n nproc[,nusers]*. Restrict number of output lines. The *nproc* argument determines how many lines of process or lwp statistics are reported, and the *nusers* argument determines how many lines of user statistics are reported if the *-a* or *-t* options are specified. By default, *prstat* can display as many lines of output as will fit within a window or terminal.
- *-p pidlist*. Report only processes whose process ID is in the given list *pidlist*.
- *-P cpulist*. Report only processes or lwp's that have most recently executed on a CPU in the given list *cpulist*. Each CPU is identified by an integer as reported by the *psrinfo* command.
- *-R*. Put *prstat* in the real time scheduling class. When this option is used, *prstat* is given priority over time-sharing and interactive processes. This option is available only for superuser.
- *-s key*. Sort output lines (i.e., processes, lwp's, or users) by key in descending order. Only one key can be used as an argument. There are five possible key values:
  - *cpu*—sort by process CPU usage. This is the default.
  - *time*—sort by process execution time.

    - *size*—sort by size of process image.
    - *rss*—sort by resident set size.
    - *pri*—sort by process priority.
- *-S key*. Sort output lines by key in ascending order. Possible key values are the same as for the *-s* option. See *-s*.
- *-t*. Report total usage summary for each user. The summary includes the total number of processes or lwp's owned by the user, total size of process images, total resident set size, total CPU time, and percentages of recent CPU time and system memory.
- *-u euidlist*. Report only processes whose effective user ID is in the given list *euidlist*. Each user ID may be specified as either a login name or a numerical user ID.
- *-U uidlist*. Report only processes whose real user ID is in the given list *uidlist*. Each user ID may be specified as either a login name or a numerical user ID.
- *-v*. Report verbose process usage. This output format includes the percentage of time the process has spent in user mode, in system mode, and sleeping. It also includes the number of voluntary and involuntary context switches, system calls, and signals received.

The columns displayed by *prstat* are described in Table 1.2.

Table 1.2 prstat *Command Display Columns*

FIELD	DESCRIPTION
PID	The process ID of the process.
USERNAME	The real user (login) name or real user ID.
SIZE	The total virtual memory size of the process, including all mapped files and devices, in kilobytes (K), megabytes (M), or gigabytes (G). The resident set size of the process (RSS) in kilobytes (K), megabytes (M), or gigabytes (G).
STATE	The state of the process: Cpu*N*—process is running on CPU *N*. Sleep—sleeping: process is waiting for an event to complete. Run—runnable: process in on run queue. Zombie—zombie state: process terminated and parent not waiting. Stop—process is stopped.
PRI	The priority of the process. Larger numbers mean higher priority.
NICE	Nice value used in priority computation. Only processes in certain scheduling classes have a nice value.

Table 1.2 prstat *Command Display Columns (Continued)*

FIELD	DESCRIPTION
TIME	The cumulative execution time for the process.
CPU	The percentage of recent CPU time used by the process.
PROCESS	The name of the process (name of executed file).
LWPID	The lwp ID of the lwp being reported.
NLWP	The number of lwp's in the process.
THE FOLLOWING COLUMNS ARE DISPLAYED WHEN THE *-v* OR *-m* OPTION IS SPECIFIED	
USR	The percentage of time the process has spent in user mode.
SYS	The percentage of time the process has spent in system mode.
TRP	The percentage of time the process has spent in processing system traps.
TFL	The percentage of time the process has spent processing text page faults.
DFL	The percentage of time the process has spent processing data page faults.
LCK	The percentage of time the process has spent waiting for user locks.
SLP	The percentage of time the process has spent sleeping.
LAT	The percentage of time the process has spent in latency (waiting for the CPU).
VCX	The number of voluntary context switches.
ICX	The number of involuntary context switches.
SCL	The number of system calls.
SIG	The number of signals received.

Some examples of the *prstat* command follow. Some of the blank lines that would actually appear on your screen are removed from these examples.

```
# prstat -L -U daemon
   PID USERNAME  SIZE   RSS STATE  PRI NICE      TIME  CPU PROCESS/LWPID
   235 daemon     16M   12M run      0    0   0:00.12  44% dwhttpd/4
   235 daemon     16M   12M sleep   59    0   0:00.00 0.0% dwhttpd/3
   235 daemon     16M   12M sleep   58    0   0:00.00 0.0% dwhttpd/2
   235 daemon     16M   12M sleep   58    0   0:00.00 0.0% dwhttpd/1
   234 daemon   9704K 2560K sleep   59    0   0:00.00 0.0% dwhttpd/3
   234 daemon   9704K 2560K sleep   28    0   0:00.00 0.0% dwhttpd/2
   234 daemon   9704K 2560K sleep   18    0   0:00.00 0.0% dwhttpd/1
```

```
Total: 2 processes, 7 lwps, load averages: 0.00, 0.01, 0.03

# prstat -p151,152
   PID USERNAME  SIZE   RSS STATE  PRI NICE      TIME  CPU PROCESS/NLWP
   152 root     2952K 1912K sleep   58    0  0:00.00 0.0% automountd/5
   151 root     2104K 1392K sleep   45    0  0:00.00 0.0% inetd/1

Total: 2 processes, 6 lwps, load averages: 0.00, 0.00, 0.01

# prstat -L -p151,152
   PID USERNAME  SIZE   RSS STATE  PRI NICE      TIME  CPU PROCESS/LWPID
   152 root     2952K 1912K sleep   59    0  0:00.00 0.0% automountd/7
   152 root     2952K 1912K sleep   59    0  0:00.00 0.0% automountd/6
   152 root     2952K 1912K sleep   58    0  0:00.00 0.0% automountd/3
   152 root     2952K 1912K sleep   53    0  0:00.00 0.0% automountd/2
   152 root     2952K 1912K sleep   58    0  0:00.00 0.0% automountd/1
   151 root     2104K 1392K sleep   45    0  0:00.00 0.0% inetd/1

Total: 2 processes, 6 lwps, load averages: 0.00, 0.00, 0.01
#
```

In the first example, *prstat* is displaying processes and lwp's for all processes owned by the user *daemon*. In the next example, *prstat* is displaying process numbers 151 and 152. In the last example, *prstat* is displaying processes and lwp's for processes 151 and 152.

EXAM NOTES

THINK ABOUT IT . . .

You suspect a performance problem on a system due to a process that is consuming a lot of CPU time. How could you locate and observe this process?

You could first issue the *ps -ef* command, looking for processes that have large values in the TIME field. If, for example, two suspect PIDS are 151 and 23462, run the command *prstat -p151,23462* and watch these processes over a period of time.

Signals

Signals are one of several methods that UNIX provides for processes to communicate with one another (others are messages, semaphores, and shared memory). A signal is an event that one process sends to another for a specific, and usually prearranged, purpose.

Some processes are written so that they perform specific tasks when a signal is sent to them. For instance, if a process sends the DNS daemon process in.named a SIGIOT signal, in response in.named dumps statistical data into the file /var/tmp/named.stats.

Two signals have universal use: SIGTERM and SIGKILL. The signal SIGTERM is used to terminate a process; the process is allowed to "clean up"—such as closing files and perhaps announcing its departure to other processes—before exiting. The signal SIGKILL is used to terminate a process immediately. In fact, a process has no choice but to instantly stop everything and exit.

The primary difference between SIGTERM and SIGKILL is that a program can be written to include special instructions—called an error handler—to run when it receives a SIGTERM signal. However, a process cannot shield itself against SIGKILL: the death of the process is instantaneous with no cleanup of any kind.

The command used to deliver signals to processes is discussed in the next section.

Terminating an Active Process

The *kill* command is used to send a signal to a process. The syntax of the *kill* command is *kill [options] processid...*, where *options* takes the form *-s* signal or *-signal*, and where *processid* is either a process (or list of processes) or process group (when a process group, the number is preceded by a minus sign). If the signal is not specified, then SIGTERM is implied.

Signals can be furnished in numeric or symbolic form. Table 1.3 equates numeric and symbolic signals.

Some examples of the *kill* command follow.

```
# kill -9 152
# kill -KILL 20452
# kill -1 -173 14544
# kill 149
# kill -STOP 850
# kill -CONT 850
```

In the first example, the SIGKILL signal is sent to process number 152. In the second example, the SIGKILL signal is sent to process number 20452. In the third example, the SIGHUP signal is sent to process group number 173 and process number 14544. In the fourth example, the SIGTERM signal (by default) is sent to process number 149. Finally, process number 850 is stopped (-STOP) and continued later (-CONT).

Table 1.3 *Selected Signal Numbers, Names, and Descriptions*

NUMERIC	SYMBOLIC NAME	DESCRIPTION
1	SIGHUP	hangup
2	SIGINT	interrupt
3	SIGQUIT	quit
4	SIGILL	illegal instruction
5	SIGTRAP	trace or breakpoint trap
6	SIGABRT	abort
7	SIGEMT	emulation trap
8	SIGFPE	floating point exception
9	SIGKILL	killed
10	SIGBUS	bus error
11	SIGSEGV	segmentation violation
12	SIGSYS	bad system call
13	SIGPIPE	broken pipe
14	SIGALRM	alarm clock
15	SIGTERM	terminated
16	SIGUSR1	user signal 1
17	SIGUSR2	user signal 2
18	SIGCHILD	child status changed
19	SIGPWR	power fail or restart
20	SIGWINCH	window size change
21	SIGURG	urgent socket condition
22	SIGPOLL	pollable event
23	SIGSTOP	stopped (signal)
24	SIGTSTP	stopped (user)
25	SIGCONT	continued

The *kill* command is by no means the only way for a process to be sent a signal. Processes can send signals to each other. The operating system kernel itself can also send a signal to a process; this occurs most frequently when the process encounters an unrecoverable error condition. For instance, if a process is writing to or reading from a pipe, and the pipe breaks (if the file system where the pipe resides runs out of disk space), the kernel will send the associated process a SIGPIPE signal. Unless the process(es) have specific error-handling code for this signal, the process will abort.

EXAM NOTES

THINK ABOUT IT . . .

A user has requested that you kill one of his or her processes. What should you do?

First, confirm that it is appropriate to terminate the process. If you determine that the process can be killed, then first send a SIGTERM signal to the process; this gives the process an opportunity to exit gracefully (if it has such instructions). If the process does not respond to a SIGTERM in a reasonable period of time (usually less than a minute), then send a SIGKILL signal to the process.

If, for example, the process ID of the user's process is 28429, then the first command issued would be *kill -TERM 28429*; the subsequent command, if necessary, is *kill -KILL 28429*. These can also be entered as *kill -15 28429* and *kill -9 28429*, respectively.

The pkill *Command*

The *pkill* command can be a more convenient way to kill processes, since it will both find and send a signal to one or more processes matching criteria. Without *pkill*, it would be necessary to first issue the *ps* command (to find the process ID), and then the *kill* command.

The companion command to *pkill* is *pgrep*. The *pgrep* command is similar to *pkill* except that it merely displays process numbers instead of sending signals to them. *pgrep* can be used to verify the syntax of *pkill*.

The syntax of the *pkill* and *pgrep* commands, respectively, is *pkill options pattern* and *pgrep options pattern*. The options for *pkill* are explained here. These options are valid for both *pkill* and *pgrep* unless stated otherwise.

- *-d delim*. Specifies the output delimiter string to be printed between each matching process ID. If no *-d* option is specified, the default is a newline character. The *-d* option is valid only when specified as an option to the *pgrep* command.
- *-f*. The regular expression pattern should be matched against the full process argument string (obtained from the *pr_psargs* field of

the */proc/nnnnn/psinfo* file). If no *-f* option is specified, the expression is matched against only the name of the executable file (obtained from the *pr_fname* field of the */proc/nnnnn/psinfo* file).

- *-g pgrplist*. Matches only processes whose process group ID is in the given list *pgrplist*. If group 0 is included in the list, this is interpreted as the process group ID of the *pgrep* or *pkill* process.
- *-G gidlist*. Matches only processes whose real group ID is in the given list *gidlist*. Each group ID may be specified as either a group name or a numerical group ID.
- *-l*. Long output format. Prints the process name along with the process ID of each matching process. The process name is obtained from the *pr_psargs* or *pr_fname* field, depending on whether the *-f* option was specified (see previous). The *-l* option is only valid when specified as an option to the *pgrep* command.
- *-n*. Matches only the newest (most recently created) process that meets all other specified matching criteria.
- *-P ppidlist*. Matches only processes whose parent process ID is in the given list *ppidlist*.
- *-s sidlist*. Matches only processes whose process session ID is in the given list *sidlist*. If ID 0 is included in the list, this is interpreted as the session ID of the *pgrep* or *pkill* process.
- *-t termlist*. Matches only processes that are associated with a terminal in the given list *termlist*. Each terminal is specified as the suffix following "/dev/" of the terminal's device pathname in the */dev* directory. For example, *term/a* or *pts/0*.
- *-u euidlist*. Matches only processes whose effective user ID is in the given list *euidlist*. Each user ID may be specified as either a login name or a numerical user ID.
- *-U uidlist*. Matches only processes whose real user ID is in the given list *uidlist*. Each user ID may be specified as either a login name or a numerical user ID.
- *-v*. Reverses the sense of the matching. Matches all processes except those which meet the specified matching criteria.
- *-x*. Considers only processes whose argument string or executable file name exactly matches the specified pattern to be matching processes. The pattern match is considered to be exact when all characters in the process argument string or executable file name match the pattern.

- *-signal*. Specifies the signal to send to each matched process. If no signal is specified, SIGTERM is sent by default. The value of *signal* can be one of the symbolic names defined in *signal* (man pages section "3HEAD") without the SIG prefix, or the corresponding signal number as a decimal value. The *-signal* option is only valid when specified as the first option to *pkill.*
- *pattern*. Specifies an Extended Regular Expression (ERE) pattern to match against either the executable file name or full process argument string. See the *regex* man page (Section 5) for a complete description of the ERE syntax.

Some examples of the *pkill* and *pgrep* commands follow.

```
# pgrep -n lp
191
#

# pkill -HUP -x in.named
#

# pkill -t pts/3
#

# pgrep -l snmp
  282 snmpdx
  290 snmpXdmid
#
```

In the first example, *pgrep* returns the list of all process numbers whose commands include the string "lp." In the second example, the SIGHUP signal is sent to all processes whose commands are "in.named." In the third example, the SIGTERM signal (by default) is sent to all processes associated with the device pts/3. In the last example, pgrep displays a long listing of all processes whose commands contain the string "snmp."

EXAM NOTES

THINK ABOUT IT . . .

You have network problems and need to kill all sendmail processes. How would you do this?

You could first issue the *pgrep –x sendmail* command to see which processes are listed. If you are satisfied with the results of the *pgrep* command, you could then issue the *pkill –x sendmail* command. This would send a SIGTERM signal to all processes where the command line includes "sendmail."

1.3 Daemon Processes

A *daemon* process is one that is not associated with a user session or screen. Instead, it is running quietly in the background. A daemon process typically starts when the system is booted, and runs for the life of the system. Examples of daemons include: sendmail (the email transport daemon), in.named (the DNS server), and nfsd (the NFS server).

Daemon processes have several unique characteristics:

- They ignore the SIGHUP (hangup) signal. This signal is usually sent to a process when its parent—usually a user session—exits.
- They run in a process group separate from any user session. This makes daemon processes immune to any actions that affect a user's process group.
- Their file descriptors STDIN (standard input), STDOUT (standard output), and STDERR (standard error) are closed.
- They are not associated with a physical or pseudo terminal.

Chapter 6, Files and Directories, describes in more detail standard input, standard output, and standard error.

1.4 The File System

A *file system* is the logical organization of directories, subdirectories, and files, all of which (usually) reside on a hard disk drive. A file system is hierarchical, with a top-most directory called its *root*. The root directory contains one or more files and/or directories. Those directories, in turn, contain one or more files and/or directories.

A *directory* is an entity that contains zero or more files or other directories. A *subdirectory* is a directory, which resides within a directory. The terms *directory* and *subdirectory* are nearly synonymous, except that the top-level directory is *never* called a subdirectory. A *file* is a collection of data containing zero or more characters and given a name.

The root directory of a file system is symbolized by a slash character ("/"). The slash character is also used as a delimiter between directory names in a path. A path, or pathname, is a hierarchical description of a file or directory within a file system.

Figure 1-2 shows an example of a file system's hierarchy.

The file system in Figure 1-2 contains the root directory at the top, shown with the "/." The root directory contains four subdirectories: *usr*, *etc*, *export*, and *tmp*. The subdirectory *usr* contains two subdirectories, *bin* and *local*.

For most purposes the terms "directory" and "subdirectory" are interchangeable. In the case of a file system's root directory, the terms directory and subdirectory are *not* interchangeable, since the root directory is *not* a subdirectory. Using the file system notation, the directory usr can be expressed "/usr". The subdirectory local is expressed "/usr/local"; the subdirectory bin (the one inside local) is expressed "/usr/local/bin".

EXAM NOTES

THINK ABOUT IT . . .

How are multiple instances of a subdirectory name (such as bin) appearing in a file system distinguished from one another?

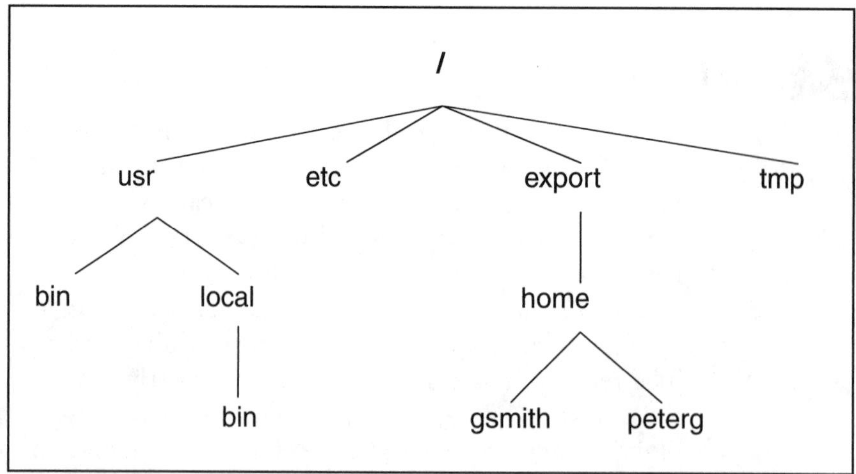

Figure 1–2 *File System Hierarchy*

1.5 Getting Help

Man Pages

The *man pages* is the name of the online command reference guide. Man pages are available through character or graphical interfaces. On a graphical interface (CDE or OpenWindows), it is necessary first to open a terminal window.

The syntax for man pages is *man [options] name...* . The following options are supported:

- *-a*. Shows all manual pages matching name within the MANPATH search path environment variable. Manual pages are displayed in the order found.
- *-d*. Debug mode. Displays what a section-specifier evaluates to, method used for searching, and paths searched by man.
- *-f file* . . . . Man attempts to locate manual pages related to any of the given files. It strips the leading pathname components from each file, and then prints one-line summaries containing the resulting basename or names. This option also uses the windex database, which is explained later.
- *-F*. Forces man to search all directories specified by MANPATH or the *man.cf* file, rather than using the windex lookup database. This is useful if the database is not up to date. If the windex database does not exist, this option is assumed.
- *-k keyword* . . . . Prints out one-line summaries from the windex database (table of contents) that contain any of the given keywords. The windex database is created using the catman command.
- *-l*. Lists all manual pages found matching names within the search path.
- *-M path*. Specifies an alternate search path for manual pages. *path* is a colon-separated list of directories that contain manual page directory subtrees. For example, if path is */usr/share/man:/usr/local/man*, man searches for name in the standard location, and then */usr/local/man*. When used with the *-k* or *-f* options, the *-M* option must appear first. Each directory in the path is assumed to contain subdirectories of the form man* or sman*, one for each section. This option overrides the MANPATH environment variable.

- *-r*. Reformats the manual page, but does not display it. This replaces the *man* - *-t* name combination.
- *-s section*…. Specifies sections of the manual for man to search. The directories searched for name are limited to those specified by *section*. Section can be a digit (perhaps followed by one or more letters), a word (for example, local, new, old, public), or a letter. To specify multiple sections, separate each section with a comma. This option overrides the MANPATH environment variable and the man.cf file. The section numbers are:
  - 1—user commands
  - 1M—system administration commands
  - 2—system calls
  - 3—library interfaces and headers, and library functions
  - 4—file formats
  - 5—standards, environments, and macros
  - 6—demos
  - 7—device and network interfaces
  - 9—device driver interfaces and driver-kernel interfaces
- *-t*. Man arranges for the specified manual pages to be troffed to a suitable raster output device (see the troff man page). If the *-t* flag is given, man updates the troffed versions of each named name (if necessary), but does not display them.
- *-T macro-package*. Formats manual pages using *macro-package* rather than the standard *-man* macros defined in */usr/share/lib/tmac/an*.

The *windex* database mentioned earlier is a three-column list consisting of a key word, the reference page that the key word points to, and a line of text that describes the purpose of the utility or interface documented on the reference page. The windex database is created using the *catman -w* command. It need not be re-created, unless the contents of the man pages database itself has changed.

The MANPATH environment variable can be used to specify other directories to be searched for man pages. Entries in MANPATH are separated by colons (":"). If MANPATH is not defined, the directory */usr/share/man* is the only one searched. If the man pages for a third-party software package installed its man pages in */export/tools/draw/man*, then MANPATH should be set to */usr/share/man:/export/tools/draw/man*.

Some examples of the *man* command follow.

```
# man -l signal
signal (3c) -M /usr/share/man
signal (3head) -M /usr/share/man
signal (3ucb) -M /usr/share/man
# man -s 3c signal
(output suppressed)
# man signal
(output suppressed)
# man man
(output suppressed)
# man -s4 shadow
(output suppressed)
# catman -w
# man -k quota
edquota       edquota (1m)     - edit user quotas for ufs file system
quota         quota (1m)       - display a user's ufs file system disk
                                 quota and usage
quotacheck    quotacheck (1m)  - ufs file system quota consistency
                                 checker
quotactl      quotactl (7i)    - manipulate disk quotas
quotaoff      quotaon (1m)     - turn ufs file system quotas on and off
quotaon       quotaon (1m)     - turn ufs file system quotas on and off
repquota      repquota (1m)    - summarize quotas for a ufs file system
rquotad       rquotad (1m)     - remote quota server
#
```

In the first example, *man* displays which man pages are available for signal. In the second example, the man page for signal in section 3c will be displayed. In the third example, *man* displays the first section found for signal (in this case, it will be section 3c). In the fourth example, the man page for the *man* command itself will be displayed. In the fifth example, the man page for the shadow file will be displayed. In the sixth example, the windex database is created with the *catman –w* command. Then, summaries from the man pages table of contents is printed for entries having to do with quotas.

A disadvantage of the man pages is that you must remember the name of the command or file before you can learn how it is used.

AnswerBook

The Answerbook is the entire collection of Solaris documentation available online on the system. The Answerbook contains the entire command reference—that is, the man pages—plus all of the other manuals that have been installed on the system.

Answerbook is available only in the OpenWindows or CDE graphical environments; it is not available in the character-only environment.

To start the Answerbook in OpenWindows, select Programs from the Workspace Menu, then select Answerbook2 from the Programs menu.

To start the Answerbook in CDE, select Help from the Workspace Menu, then select Answerbook2 from the Help menu.

Answerbook will display all of the online manuals installed on your system. The top of each Answerbook screen contains a search field; in this field, you can type in any command name or key word. Answerbook will show all sections containing that keyword; selecting one of the choices will show the part of the manual section containing the keyword.

Figure 1-3 shows a sample Answerbook session.

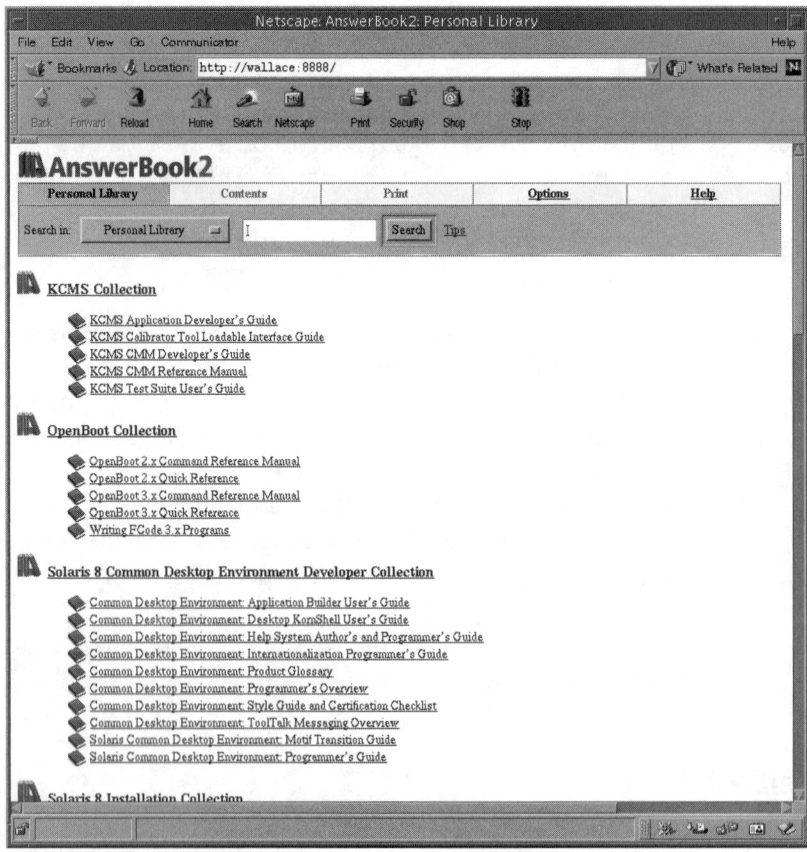

Figure 1–3 *Answerbook Session*

CHAPTER SUMMARY

The Solaris operating system consists of the kernel and the file system. The kernel manages system resources, and the file system manages storage on disks. A program is a set of machine instructions; a process is an instance of a program running on a system. The process scheduler manages the scheduling of processes that want to run.

The *ps* and *prstat* commands are used to display information about processes.

Signals are one method for processes to communicate with one another. The *kill* and *pkill* commands are used to send a signal to a process. Processes cannot ignore the SIGKILL signal.

Daemon processes run in the background; they are usually started at system boot time and run for the life of the system.

The file system is a collection of directories, subdirectories, and files. A file system is a hierarchical organization. Pathnames are used to describe directories and files.

Users get help by issuing man page commands to view command reference materials. The Answerbook is a graphical help system that contains Solaris documentation, including the command reference found in man pages.

TEST YOURSELF

MULTIPLE CHOICE

1. Given:

```
# kill -15 162
```

What is the result?

A. The SIGTERM signal is sent to process 162.
B. The SIGKILL signal is sent to process 162.
C. The KILL signal is sent to process 15, and the TERM signal is sent to process 162.
D. The SIGTERM signal is sent to process 162 fifteen times.

2. Which two are used to list processes? (Choose two)
   A. *plist*
   B. *lp*
   C. *ps*
   D. *prstat*
   E. *pstat*

3. What is the purpose of the MANPATH environment variable?
   A. It describes the location of the *man* command.
   B. It determines the location of temporary files used by the *man* command.
   C. It determines whether man displays the pathname to commands displayed.
   D. It determines which directories are searched by the *man* command.

4. Given the output:

```
PID USERNAME  SIZE   RSS STATE  PRI NICE      TIME  CPU PROCESS/NLWP
152 root     2952K 1912K sleep   58    0   0:00.00 0.0% automountd/5
151 root     2104K 1392K sleep   45    0   0:00.00 0.0% inetd/1

Total: 2 processes, 6 lwps, load averages: 0.00, 0.00, 0.01
```

   What can be said about process 152? (Choose four)
   A. It is running the *automountd/5* command.
   B. It is sleeping.
   C. It has five lightweight processes.
   D. Its parent process ID is 151.
   E. It is running at a higher priority than process 151.
   F. It is running at a lower priority than process 151.
   G. It is not possible to tell whether its priority is higher or lower than process 151.

5. Which command can you use to observe process 15489 for a while?
   A. `prstat -p15489`
   B. `ps -fp 15489`
   C. `prstat -L 15489`
   D. `prstat -P 15489`

6. Which four are functions of the Solaris kernel? (Choose four)
   A. Memory management
   B. File system quotas
   C. Hardware control
   D. Syslog buffering
   E. Process scheduling
   F. Process ordering
   G. Program compilation
   H. Stack tracing
7. Which three are characteristics of a daemon? (Choose 3)
   A. Runs in the background
   B. Always runs as root
   C. Always runs as setuid root
   D. Usually started at boot time
   E. Runs at a higher priority than user processes
   F. Is bound to a CPU on SMP systems
   G. STDIN, STDOUT, and STDERR are closed
   H. STDIN, STDOUT, and STDERR are mapped to syslog
8. Which is an example of a relative pathname?
   A. `/export/home`
   B. `/export/home/`
   C. `export/home`
   D. `-export/home`
9. Given the output:

```
 UID   PID  PPID  C    STIME TTY         TIME CMD
root   151     1  0   Feb 09 ?           0:00 /usr/sbin/inetd -s
```

   Which statement describes the command used to generate it?
   A. `ps -fudaemon`
   B. `ps -fp151`
   C. `ps -ft\?`
   D. `ps -ludaemon`

10. Which command is used to kill all processes associated with userid lp?
    A. `pkill -U lp`
    B. `pkill -v -n lp`
    C. `pkill -x lpsched`
    D. `pkill -t lp`

Free Response

11. What is the command used to send the SIGHUP signal to process number 1512?
12. What is the command used to display the man page for the *passwd* file?

CHAPTER 2

Installation

After completing this chapter, you'll be able to meet the following Solaris Administration Exam objectives:

- Describe the sequence of steps required to perform the Solaris 8 Operating Environment software installation on a networked standalone system.
- Identify the function of the following package administration commands: *pkgadd*, *pkginfo*, *pkgchk*, and *pkgrm*.
- Identify the steps required to install a patch, verify which patches are currently installed, and remove a patch using the *patchadd*, *patchrm*, or *showrev* commands.

To fulfill these objectives, this chapter discusses:

- Planning a Solaris operating system installation;
- Installing Solaris on a new system;

- Upgrading Solaris on an existing system;
- Installing Solaris and third-party software packages;
- Checking and removing software packages; and
- Installing and managing Solaris patches.

2.1 Installation Planning

Before Solaris can be installed on a system, some planning steps must take place. The success of an installation depends upon decisions made before the operating system is installed.

First, you need to determine whether your hardware is supported. Solaris 8 (SPARC edition) runs on systems listed in the Solaris 8 Sun Hardware Platform Guide found in the Solaris 8 on Sun Hardware Collection documentation at http://docs.sun.com/ or in your site's Answerbook (see Chapter 1 for more information about Answerbook).

You should also read the Solaris 8 (SPARC Platform Edition) Release Notes found in the Advanced Installation Guide to check on any other hardware or software compatibility or support issues.

Memory

A SPARC or Intel system must have at least 64MB of memory to install and run Solaris 8.

Disk Space

Next, you need to decide what software groups you will install; the software groups and their disk space requirements are found in Table 2.1.

Table 2.1 *Software Groups Disk Space Requirements*

SOFTWARE GROUP	DISK SPACE REQUIRED
End User System Support	1.6GB
Developer System Support	1.9GB
Entire Distribution	2.3GB
Entire Distribution Plus OEM Support	2.4GB

These estimates include swap space requirements; Solaris allocates 512KB (0.5GB) of swap space by default.

You also need to consider space required by any third-party applications and their data, plus home directories used by any users of the system.

Software Clusters

The Software Groups listed in Table 2.1 are also known as Software Clusters. They are:

- *End User System Support* contains *Core System Support* plus end user support such as the OpenWindows windowing system and the related DeskSet application files; this cluster includes the recommended software for an end user.
- *Developer System Support* contains *End User System Support* (plus the libraries), "include files," and tools needed to develop software in the Solaris 8 operating environment. Compilers and debuggers are not included in the Solaris 8 operating environment.
- *Entire Distribution* contains the entire Solaris 8 environment.
- *Entire Distribution plus OEM Support* contains the entire Solaris 8 release, plus additional hardware support for OEMs. This software group is recommended when installing Solaris software on SPARC-based servers.

Network Information

If the system to be installed is on a network, the information listed in Table 2.2 is also required. This should be available from the site's network or system administrator.

Note

If the system to be installed is *not* on a network, then *only* the Host Name from Table 2.2 is required.

If the system is connected to a network but is *not* part of a DNS, NIS, or NIS+ domain, then only the Host Name, IP Address, Subnet Mask, and Default Router are required.

Table 2.2 *Network Installation Information*

ITEM	DESCRIPTION/EXAMPLE
Host name	Assigned system name. On a running system that will be upgraded, type `uname -n`.
IP address	Example: 192.168.24.16. On a running system, type `ifconfig -a`.
Subnet mask	Example: 255.255.255.0. On a running system, type `ifconfig -a`.
Default router	Example: 192.168.24.1. On a running system, examine the file */etc/defaultrouter*.
Name service	This will be: none, DNS, NIS, or NIS+. On a running system, examine the file */etc/nsswitch.conf*.
Domain name	Example: *eng.yourcompany.com*. On a running system, type `domainname`.
Name server name	For NIS or NIS+, type `ypwhich`.
Name server IP address	For DNS, examine /etc/resolv.conf. For NIS, type `ypwhich <name server name>.hosts`. For NIS+, type `nismatch <name server name> hosts.org_dir`.

Release Media

You must have the following release media in order to install Solaris.

- Solaris 8 Installation English SPARC Platform Edition (for installation in English)
- Solaris 8 Installation Multilingual SPARC Platform Edition (for installation in Chinese, English, French, German, Italian, Japanese, Korean, Spanish, or Swedish)
- Solaris 8 Software 1 of 2 SPARC Platform Edition (for installation in all languages)
- Solaris 8 Software 2 of 2 SPARC Platform Edition (for installation in all languages)
- Solaris 8 Languages SPARC Platform Edition (only if you use the Multilingual Edition)

2.2 Software Installation on a New System

Solaris Web Start is the name of the program that is used to install Solaris on a system.

Solaris Web Start first detects whether a Frame Buffer (display adaptor) is found on the system. If so, the graphical interface is used;

otherwise, a character interface is used. The content and sequence of information in the graphical and character interfaces are generally the same. Examples of both are shown by Figures 2-1 and 2-2, respectively.

Installing from CD-ROM

The following is a synopsis of the steps taken to install Solaris from CD-ROM. The first six steps are displayed in character mode.

1. Insert the Solaris 8 Installation English SPARC Platform Edition or Solaris 8 Installation Multilingual SPARC Platform Edition CD into the system's CD-ROM drive.

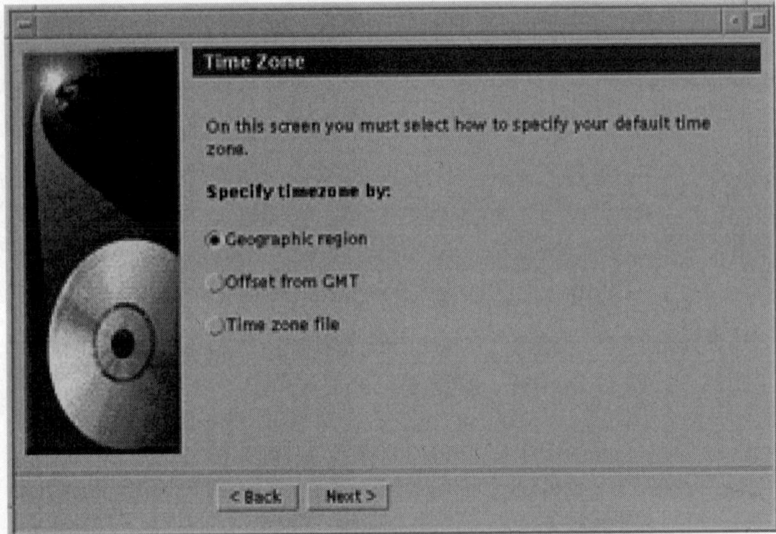

Figure 2–1 *Solaris Web Start Graphical Interface*

```
Please select how to specify your default time zone.
 Specify Time Zone by:
 1. Geographic region
 2. Offset from GMT
 3. Time zone file
    Please enter the number corresponding to how you
    would like to specify the time zone [1]:_
```

Figure 2–2 *Solaris Web Start Character Interface*

2. If this is a new system, turn the system on.
3. If this is an existing system, go to the "ok" prompt (by typing `halt` as root or by pressing both the Stop and A keys at the same time), and then type `boot cdrom`.
4. If you are using the Multilingual Edition, you will be asked to select which language you wish to use.
5. The system asks if this is a new installation or an upgrade. Select New Installation.
6. The system asks for confirmation that the boot disk is about to be formatted, queries for the size of the swap partition, and then asks whether the swap partition should start at the beginning of the disk.

The system then installs a "mini-root" OS on the swap partition and boots from it. If a frame buffer was detected on the system, the rest of the installation takes places in graphical mode. The following phase of the installation is used to gather some basic facts about the new system.

7. The system asks questions about network connectivity: host name, IP address, subnet mask, whether or not the system is a DHCP client, whether or not it needs IPv6, what kind of a name service is used (DNS, NIS, NIS+), and the time zone.
8. The system asks for the root password, whether Power Management should be used, and whether a Web browser needs to use a proxy server.
9. The installation software configures the system with information entered thus far, then ejects the CD-ROM and asks for the next CD-ROM, Solaris 8 Software 1 of 2 SPARC Platform Edition. Insert this CD-ROM.
10. The Solaris Web Start Installation Kiosk is started and displayed. This is a local Web page that you can use later to install Sun or third-party software. It will not be used yet. The next phase of the installation is used to determine which Solaris software is to be installed. In the next step, you can choose a Default or Custom installation. Custom Install enables you to install additional Solaris and third-party products from a CD, from a local or network file system, or by downloading from a Web page displayed in the Kiosk. The system first asks if a Default or Custom installation is desired. If you choose a Default installation, skip to Step 14.
11. The custom installation asks for Localizations (other language modules for other geographic locales) you might wish to install.
12. The custom installation displays a list of the available Solaris operating system modules, and lets you choose which ones you want to

install. Custom installation will also set up 64-bit support and printer selection. You can also choose to select software packages from the Web Start Installation Kiosk. Depending upon your choices, you might be asked to remove the Solaris 8 Software 1 of 2 SPARC Platform Edition CD and insert another.

13. The custom installation will ask you to specify the names and sizes of disk partitions that should be built on the boot disk.
14. The Solaris Operating System software will now be installed from CD. When installation from the Solaris 8 Software 1 of 2 SPARC Platform Edition is completed, a summary of installed software is displayed.
15. If additional software is to be installed, a dialogue box will appear and ask you to insert the appropriate media. Otherwise, the system will pause and wait for you to allow the system to reboot itself.
16. The system will now reboot and display a login prompt. Solaris OS installation is complete.

Operating system installation is complex, and there are many variables, some of which may not have been foreseen. Thus, it is important that you always verify the installation by checking the operating system installation logs in */var/sadm/install/logs*.

EXAM NOTES

THINK ABOUT IT . . .

Here is a scenario. Your system install is taking unusually long to complete, and the system appears to have stopped or hung. What should you do?

You can reboot the system from the release CD-ROM and examine the log files in */var/sadm/install/logs*. You may find that an error occurred—you should try the installation again.

2.3 Software Installation on an Existing System: Solaris Upgrade

When considering upgrading Solaris on an existing system, you have two fundamental choices: You can perform an upgrade of the existing OS or you can do a new install over it. Table 2.3 explores the merits of both approaches. Ultimately, you will need to decide which is best for your system.

Table 2.3 *Solaris Upgrade Versus Install*

ITEM	ADVANTAGES	DISADVANTAGES
Upgrade OS	Local changes intact	Takes much longer and there is potential for lingering issues
New install	Pristine installation; no old OS "leftovers"	All previous local changes destroyed

Preparing for an Upgrade

Follow these steps prior to upgrading a system.

1. Read the Solaris Release Notes to ensure that your hardware is supported by the new release.
2. Acquire any mandatory patches for the new release; check the site http://sunsolve.sun.com/ for patches and information.
3. Back up the system. Should an error or mishap occur during the upgrade, your system may be in an unstable state requiring a full or partial recovery.
4. Gather the following information from your system:
   - host name
   - IP address
   - subnet mask
   - default router IP address
   - domain name
   - type of name service used (DNS, NIS, NIS+)
   - IP address of name server

   You are now ready to perform the upgrade.

When upgrading Solaris on a system running one or more applications, a test system with the application should be upgraded first, and the application tested to ensure that it functions properly with the upgraded Solaris operating system. It is not recommended that a production system be upgraded without prior testing.

Upgrade Procedure

Note: The system should be backed up before the upgrade is performed. A hardware or software malfunction during the upgrade could result in an unusable system.

The following is a synopsis of the steps taken to upgrade an existing system. The first six steps are displayed in character mode.

1. Insert the Solaris 8 Installation English SPARC Platform Edition or Solaris 8 Installation Multilingual SPARC Platform Edition CD into the system's CD-ROM drive.
2. If this is a new system, turn the system on.
3. If this is an existing system, go to the "ok" prompt (by typing `halt` as root or by pressing both the Stop and A keys at the same time), and then type `boot cdrom`.
4. If you are using the Multilingual Edition, you will be asked to select which language you wish to use.
5. The system asks if this is a new installation or an upgrade. Select Upgrade.
6. The system searches for the swap partition and asks if it should be used for the "mini root" installation. This is the recommended choice. If, however, you do not want to use the swap partition, you'll have to find another; whichever partition you choose will be destroyed during the upgrade.

The system installs a "mini-root" OS on the partition you have chosen, and then boots from it. If a frame buffer was detected on the system, the rest of the installation takes place in graphical mode. The following phase of the installation is used to gather some basic facts about the system.

7. The system asks questions about network connectivity: host name, IP address, subnet mask, whether or not the system is a DHCP client, whether or not it needs IPv6, what kind of name service is used (DNS, NIS, NIS+), and the time zone.
8. The system asks for the root password, whether Power Management should be used, and whether a Web browser needs to use a proxy server.
9. The installation software configures the system with information entered thus far, then ejects the CD-ROM and asks for the next CD-ROM, Solaris 8 Software 1 of 2 SPARC Platform Edition. Insert this CD-ROM.

The Solaris Web Start Installation Kiosk is started and displayed. This is a local Web page that you can use later to install Sun or third-party software. You will not use it yet.

10. The system asks if you wish to perform an Upgrade Install or a New Install.

An Upgrade Install will upgrade an already installed Solaris operating system. A New Install will perform a fresh Solaris operating system installation.

The reason for the distinction at this point is that a system with several non-OS partitions will remain intact while a fresh OS is installed on the system. Installing Solaris as though it were a new system destroys all non-OS partitions.

For this illustration we will assume that you are upgrading the Solaris OS in place.

11. The system next asks if a Default or Custom Installation is desired. If a Default Installation is chosen, skip to Step 14.
12. The Custom Installation asks for Localizations (other language modules for other geographic locales) you might wish to install.
13. The Custom Installation displays a list of the available Solaris operating system modules, and lets you choose which ones you want to install. Custom Installation will also set up 64-bit support and printer selection. You can also choose to select software packages from the Web Start Installation Kiosk. Depending upon your choices, you might be asked to remove the Solaris 8 Software 1 of 2 SPARC Platform Edition CD and insert another.
14. The Solaris Operating System software will now be installed from CD. When installation from the Solaris 8 Software 1 of 2 SPARC Platform Edition is completed, a summary of installed software is displayed.
15. If additional software is to be installed, a dialogue box will appear and ask you to insert the appropriate media. Otherwise, the system will pause and wait for you to allow the system to reboot itself.
16. The system will now reboot and display a login prompt. Solaris OS installation has completed.
17. Examine the upgrade notes, */var/sadm/system/logs/upgrade_log*.
18. Examine the upgrade log, */var/sadm/system/data/upgrade_cleanup*. This file contains any unresolved local changes that the upgrade software could not merge with the new version of Solaris. You will have to examine these entries carefully and make any additional changes to ensure the system performs as expected.

It is strongly recommended that you back up your system *again* after the upgrade is completed, before you begin to make additional changes and before you begin to use the system.

Operating system upgrades are complex, and there are many variables, some of which may not have been foreseen. Success is not a given with upgrades. It is important that you always verify the upgrade by checking the operating system installation logs in */var/sadm/install/logs*.

EXAM NOTES

THINK ABOUT IT . . .

Here is a scenario. You want to upgrade your Solaris system, but there is not enough room in the root partition. What should you do?

First, you should carefully check the root partition for any unnecessary files that are consuming space, such as large core files. Next, if any files or programs were installed in the root partition, you should consider moving them to another file system.

At the very worst, you may have to back up the system, and perform a fresh install of Solaris with better disk partition sizes, and then restore the application programs and/or files afterwards.

2.4 Installing Software Packages

This section describes the steps used to install Solaris or third-party software. The commands associated with package installation and administration are `pkgadd`, `pkginfo`, `pkgrm`, and `pkgchk`. It is important for UNIX administrators to be familiar with these procedures since most environments experience a lot of changes—for example, addition of new software and upgrades to existing software—which require the package installation commands.

pkgadd Command

The *pkgadd* command is used to install software packages on a system. The syntax of the *pkgadd* command is `pkgadd [options] [pkgid...]`

where pkgid is a list of one or more packages to install. The options for *pkgadd* are explained here.

- *-a admin.* Define an installation administration file, admin, to be used in place of the default administration file. The word *none* overrides the use of any admin file and forces interaction with the user. If a full pathname is not given, pkgadd first looks in the current working directory for the administration file. If the specified administration file is not in the current working directory, *pkgadd* looks in the */var/sadm/install/admin* directory for the administration file.
- *-d device.* Install or copy a package from *device*. Device can be a full pathname to a directory or the identifiers for tape, floppy disk, or removable disk (e.g., */var/tmp* or */floppy/floppy_name*). It can also be a device alias (e.g., */floppy/floppy0*).
- *-M.* Instruct pkgadd not to use the */etc/vfstab* file for determining the client's mount points. This option assumes the mount points are correct on the server and it behaves consistently with Solaris 2.5 and earlier releases.
- *-n.* Installation occurs in noninteractive mode. The default mode is interactive.
- *-r response.* Identify a file or directory that contains output from a previous pkgask session. This file supplies the interaction responses that would be requested by the package in interactive mode. *response* must be a full pathname.
- *-R root_path.* Define the full pathname of a directory to use as the *root_path*. All files, including package system information files, are relocated to a directory tree starting in the specified *root_path*. The *root_path* may be specified when installing to a client from a server (e.g., */export/root/client1*).
- *-s spool.* Write the package into the directory *spool* instead of installing it.
- *-v.* Trace all of the scripts that get executed by pkgadd, located in the *pkginst/install* directory. This option is used for debugging the procedural and nonprocedural scripts.
- *-V fs_file.* Specify an alternative *fs_file* to map the client's file systems. For example, used in situations where the */etc/vfstab* file is nonexistent or unreliable.

Some examples follow.

```
# pkgadd -d /cdrom/s8ap/components/Sun_Enterprise_Authentication_
Mechanism/sparc/Packages
The following packages are available:
  1  SUNWkr5ad      Kerberos V5 Administration Tools
                    (sparc) 5.8.0,REV=99.12.09.18.58
  2  SUNWkr5cl      Kerberos V5 clients
                    (sparc) 5.8.0,REV=99.12.09.18.58
  3  SUNWkr5ma      Kerberos V5 Master KDC
                    (sparc) 5.8.0,REV=99.12.09.18.58
  4  SUNWkr5mn      SEAM Manual Pages
                    (sparc) 5.8.0,REV=99.12.09.18.58
  5  SUNWkr5sl      Kerberos V5 Slave KDC
                    (sparc) 5.8.0,REV=99.12.09.18.58
  6  SUNWkr5sv      Kerberized Network Services
                    (sparc) 5.8.0,REV=99.12.09.18.58
Select package(s) you wish to process (or 'all' to process
all packages). (default: all) [?,??,q]: 4
Processing package instance <SUNWkr5mn> from
</cdrom/s8ap/components/Sun_Enterpise_Authentication_Mechanism/sparc/
Packages>
SEAM Manual Pages
(sparc) 5.8.0,REV=99.12.09.18.58
Copyright 2000 Sun Microsystems, Inc. All rights reserved.
Using </> as the package base directory.
## Processing package information.
## Processing system information.
   1 package pathname is already properly installed.
## Verifying package dependencies.
## Verifying disk space requirements.
## Checking for conflicts with packages already installed.
## Checking for setuid/setgid programs.
This package contains scripts which will be executed with super-user
permission during the process of installing this package.
Do you want to continue with the installation of <SUNWkr5mn> [y,n,?] y
Installing SEAM Manual Pages as <SUNWkr5mn>
## Installing part 1 of 1.

Installation of <SUNWkr5mn> was successful.
The following packages are available:
  1  SUNWkr5ad      Kerberos V5 Administration Tools
                    (sparc) 5.8.0,REV=99.12.09.18.58
  2  SUNWkr5cl      Kerberos V5 clients
                    (sparc) 5.8.0,REV=99.12.09.18.58
  3  SUNWkr5ma      Kerberos V5 Master KDC
                    (sparc) 5.8.0,REV=99.12.09.18.58
  4  SUNWkr5mn      SEAM Manual Pages
```

```
                     (sparc) 5.8.0,REV=99.12.09.18.58
  5   SUNWkr5sl      Kerberos V5 Slave KDC
                     (sparc) 5.8.0,REV=99.12.09.18.58
  6   SUNWkr5sv      Kerberized Network Services
                     (sparc) 5.8.0,REV=99.12.09.18.58
Select package(s) you wish to process (or 'all' to process
all packages). (default: all) [?,??,q]: q
#

# pkgadd -n -d /cdrom/s8ap/components/PPP/sparc SUNWpppk
Copyright 2000 Sun Microsystems, Inc. All rights reserved.
adding ppp.

Installation of <SUNWpppk.2> was successful.
#
```

In the first example, the SEAM man pages package is installed from CD-ROM. In the second example, the ppp package is installed non-interactively from CD-ROM.

EXAM NOTES

THINK ABOUT IT . . .

You need to install some software packages on several systems on the network that do not have CD-ROM drives. You do not have an external CD-ROM drive available to take from system to system. What can you do?

You can install your packages over the network. Insert the CD-ROM on a system and make it available over the network with the `share` command. Then, mount the CD-ROM over the network with the `mount` command. Next, you can install the software packages on each network client from the mounted directory.

An advantage of this strategy is that you can install on several systems at once. Installations will take a little longer, though, since several systems might be accessing the CD at once, not to mention that installing over the network is likely to be slower than directly from a CD drive.

pkginfo Command

The *pkginfo* command is used to display a list of installed packages on a system. The syntax of the *pkginfo* command is `pkginfo [options]` `pkginst`, where `pkginst` is the name of an installed software package. The options for *pkginfo* are explained here.

- *-a arch*. Specify the architecture of the package as *arch*.
- *-c category*. Display packages that match *category*. Categories are defined with the CATEGORY parameter in the pkginfo file. If more than one category is supplied, the package needs to match only one category in the list. The match is not case specific.
- *-d device*. Defines a device, *device*, on which the software resides. Device can be an absolute directory pathname or the identifiers for tape, floppy disk, removable disk, and so forth. The special token spool may be used to indicate the default installation spool directory (i.e., */var/spool/pkg*).
- *-i*. Display information for fully installed packages only.
- *-l*. Specify long format, which includes all available information about the designated package(s).
- *-p*. Display information for partially installed packages only.
- *-q*. Do not list any information. Used from a program to check whether or not a package has been installed.
- *-r*. List the installation base for relocatable packages.
- *-R root_path*. Defines the full pathname of a directory to use as the *root_path*. All files, including package system information files, are relocated to a directory tree starting in the specified *root_path*.
- *-v version*. Specify the version of the package as *version*. The version is defined with the VERSION parameter in the *pkginfo* file. All compatible versions can be requested by preceding the version name with a tilde (~). Multiple white spaces are replaced with a single white space during version comparison.
- *-x*. Designate an extracted listing of package information. The listing contains the package abbreviation, package name, package architecture (if available) and package version (if available).

The `-p` and `-i` options are meaningless if used in conjunction with the `-d` option. The options `-q`, `-x`, and `-l` are mutually exclusive.

Some examples follow:

```
# pkginfo
application NSCPcom         Netscape Communicator
application SMCgcc          gcc
application SMClsof         lsof
```

```
application SMCnmap       nmap
application SMCtcpdu      tcpdump
application SMCtcprep     tcprelay
application SMCtracer     traceroute
application SMCwuftp      wu-ftpd
system      SUNW1251f     Russian 1251 fonts
application SUNWaadm      Solaris 8 System Administrator Collection
system      SUNWab2r      AnswerBook2 Documentation Server
system      SUNWab2s      AnswerBook2 Documentation Server
system      SUNWab2u      AnswerBook2 Documentation Server
application SUNWabe       Solaris 8 User Collection
application SUNWabsdk     Solaris 8 Software Developer Collection
system      SUNWaccr      System Accounting, (Root)
system      SUNWaccu      System Accounting, (Usr)
system      SUNWadmap     System administration applications
system      SUNWadmc      System administration core libraries
[remainder of output suppressed]

# pkginfo -l
   PKGINST:  NSCPcom
      NAME:  Netscape Communicator
  CATEGORY:  application
      ARCH:  sparc
   VERSION:  20.4.70,REV=1999.10.13.17.54
   BASEDIR:  /usr
    VENDOR:  Sun Microsystems, Inc.
      DESC:  This package contains the application and configuration
             files of Netscape Communicator 4.7 supporting
             International security.
    PSTAMP:  alnitakm13175452
  INSTDATE:  Apr 04 2000 21:51
   HOTLINE:  Please contact your local service provider
    STATUS:  completely installed
     FILES:    219 installed pathnames
                 5 shared pathnames
                30 directories
               186 executables
             45367 blocks used (approx)
[remainder of output suppressed]

# pkginfo -l SUNWaccu
   PKGINST:  SUNWaccu
      NAME:  System Accounting, (Usr)
  CATEGORY:  system
      ARCH:  sparc
   VERSION:  11.8.0,REV=2000.01.08.18.12
```

```
   BASEDIR:  /
    VENDOR:  Sun Microsystems, Inc.
      DESC:  utilities for accounting and reporting of system activity
    PSTAMP:  humbolt20000108182539
  INSTDATE:  Apr 04 2000 22:39
   HOTLINE:  Please contact your local service provider
    STATUS:  completely installed
     FILES:     47 installed pathnames
                 4 shared pathnames
                 6 directories
                39 executables
                 1 setuid/setgid executables
               489 blocks used (approx)

#

# pkginfo -p
application SMCtcprep      tcprelay
#

# pkginfo -x
NSCPcom           Netscape Communicator
                  (sparc) 20.4.70,REV=1999.10.13.17.54
SMCgcc            gcc
                  (sparc) 2.95.2
SMClsof           lsof
                  (sparc) 4.49
SMCnmap           nmap
                  (sparc) 2.3BETA14
SMCtcpdu          tcpdump
                  (sparc) 2000_04_30
SMCtcprep         tcprelay
                  (sparc) 1.0
SMCtracer         traceroute
                  (sparc) 1.4a5
SMCwuftp          wu-ftpd
                  (sparc) 2.6.0
SUNW5ttf          Traditional Chinese BIG5 True Type Fonts Package
                  (sparc) 8.0,REV=1999.12.14.07.46
SUNW5xmft         Chinese/Taiwan BIG5 X Windows Platform minimum required
Fonts Package
                  (sparc) 8.0,REV=1999.10.12.16.31
SUNWaadm          Solaris 8 System Administrator Collection
                  (sparc) 8.0,REV=1999.10.12.16.31
[remainder of output suppressed]
#
```

In the first example, pkginfo lists the package names and short descriptions. In the second example, a long listing for all installed packages is shown. In the third example, a long listing for the SUNWaccu package is shown. In the fourth example, a listing of partially installed packages is shown. In the last example, an extracted listing (abbreviation, name, architecture [if available] and version) of installed packages is shown.

EXAM NOTES

THINK ABOUT IT . . .

You need to determine the version of an installed software product. How would you do this?

Use the `pkginfo -x packagename` command. This will show the name and version of each package installed on the system. The `pkginfo -l packagename` command will show even more detailed information about the package.

pkgrm Command

The *pkgrm* command is used to remove one or more installed packages from a system. The format of the *pkgrm* command is `pkgrm [options] [pkgid...]`, where `pkgid` is a list of packages to remove. The options for *pkgrm* are explained here.

- *-a admin.* Use the installation administration file, *admin*, in place of the default admin file. `pkgrm` first looks in the current working directory for the administration file. If the specified administration file is not in the current working directory, `pkgrm` looks in the */var/sadm/install/admin* directory for the administration file.
- *-A.* Remove the package files from the client's file system, absolutely. If a file is shared with other packages, the default behavior is to not remove the file from the client's file system.
- *-M.* Instruct `pkgrm` not to use the */etc/vfstab* file for determining the client's mount points. This option assumes the mount points are correct on the server and it behaves consistently with Solaris 2.5 and earlier releases.

- *-n.* Noninteractive mode. If there is a need for interaction, the command will exit. You must specify at least one package name to remove when using this option.
- *-R root_path.* Defines the full pathname of a directory to use as the *root_path*. All files, including package system information files, are relocated to a directory tree starting in the specified *root_path*.
- *-s spool.* Remove the specified package(s) from the directory *spool.* The default directory for spooled packages is */var/sadm/pkg*.
- *-v.* Trace all of the scripts that get executed by `pkgrm`, located in the *pkginst/install* directory. This option is used for debugging the procedural and nonprocedural scripts.
- *-V fs_file.* Specify an alternative *fs_file* to map the client's file systems. Used in situations where the */etc/vfstab* file is nonexistent or unreliable.

The `rm` command should *never* be used to remove package files; this will corrupt the software products database. If you really must remove a file that is part of a package, use the `removef` command, which will update the software products database as appropriate.

Some examples follow:

```
# pkgrm SUNW1251f
The following package is currently installed:
   SUNW1251f        Russian 1251 fonts
                    (sparc) 1.0,REV=1999.10.13.15.03
Do you want to remove this package? y
## Removing installed package instance <SUNW1251f>
This package contains scripts which will be executed with super-user
permission during the process of removing this package.
Do you want to continue with the removal of this package [y,n,?,q] y
## Verifying package dependencies.
## Processing package information.
## Removing pathnames in class <fontenc>
## Removing pathnames in class <Xupdate>
## Removing pathnames in class <none>

[...several lines of output not shown...]

/usr/openwin/lib/locale/ru.ansi-1251/X11/fonts/TrueType/fonts.upr
```

```
/usr/openwin/lib/locale/ru.ansi-1251/X11/fonts/TrueType/fonts.scale
/usr/openwin <shared pathname not removed>
/usr/bin/lp_1251
/usr/bin <shared pathname not removed>
/usr <shared pathname not removed>
## Updating system information.
Removal of <SUNW1251f> was successful.
#

# pkgrm -n SUNWcttf

Removal of <SUNWcttf> was successful.
#
```

In the first example, the package SUNW1251f is removed. In the second example, the package SUNWcttf is removed noninteractively.

2.5 Noninteractive Package Installation and Removal

Examples in the prior `pkgadd` and `pkgrm` sections cite instances of noninteractive installation and removal. If you will be performing noninteractive installs and removes (`pkgadd` and `pkgrm`, respectively) with regularity, then there are some things you need to be aware of and changes you will need to make.

- You will need to change some of the options in the pkgadd/pkgrm administration file, */var/sadm/install/admin/default*. This file contains information that determines the default behavior of `pkgadd` and `pkgrm`. The default values in this file make nearly all installs and removes interactive.
- You will need to use the `-n` option with `pkgadd` and `pkgrm` when you want them to run noninteractively.
- You may need to run the `pkgask` utility in order to build a "response file," a file that contains canned answers to questions that an installation will ask. A common type of response that is saved in a response file is a pathname (e.g., where a product will be installed) queried by `pkgadd`. The `pkgadd -r` option will specify the location of the response file.
- You may also have `pkgadd` or `pkgrm` read keyboard responses from standard input or from a file, for instance `pkgrm SUNWcttf < /tmp/keyinput`. This is somewhat less elegant than `pkgask` and `pkgadd -r`, but you may find it more suitable at times.

pkgchk Command

The *pkgchk* command is used to check the accuracy of—or information about—installed packages. The format of the *pgkchk* command is `pkgchk [options] [pkgid...]`, where `pkgid` is a list of packages to check. The options for *pkgchk* are explained here.

- *-a.* Audit the file attributes only and do not check file contents. Default is to check both.
- *-c.* Audit the file contents only and do not check file attributes. Default is to check both.
- *-d device.* Specify the *device* on which a spooled package resides. Device can be a directory pathname or the identifiers for tape, floppy disk, or removable disk (e.g., */var/tmp* or */dev/diskette*).
- *-e envfile.* Request that the package information file named as *envfile* be used to resolve parameters noted in the specified *pkgmap* file.
- *-f.* Correct file attributes if possible. If used with the `-x` option, this option removes hidden files. When `pkgchk` is invoked with this option, it creates directories—named pipes, links, and special devices—if they do not already exist. If the `-d` option calls out an uninstalled package, the `-f` option will take effect only if the package is in directory (not stream) format. All file attributes will be set to agree with the entries in the *pkgmap* file except that setuid, setgid, and sticky bits will not be set in the mode.
- *-i file.* Read a list of pathnames from *file* and compare this list against the installation software database or the indicated `pkgmap` file. Pathnames that are not contained in *file* are not checked.
- *-l.* List information on the selected files that make up a package. This option is not compatible with the `-a`, `-c`, `-f`, `-g`, and `-v` options.
- *-m pkgmap.* Check the package against the package map file, *pkgmap*.
- *-M.* Instruct `pkgchk` not to use the */etc/vfstab* file for determining the client's mount points. This option assumes the mount points are correct on the server and it behaves consistently with Solaris 2.5 and earlier releases.
- *-n.* Do not check volatile or editable files' contents. This should be used for most post-installation checking.

- *-p path*. Only check the accuracy of the pathname or pathnames listed. *path* can be one or more pathnames separated by commas (or by white space, if the list is quoted).
- *-q*. Quiet mode. Do not give messages about missing files.
- *-R root_path*. Define the full name of a directory to use as the *root_path*. All files, including package system information files, are relocated to a directory tree starting in the specified *root_path*. The *root_path* may be specified when installing to a client from a server (e.g., */export/root/client1*).
- *-v*. Verbose mode. Files appearing as part of the installed package are listed.
- *-V fs_file*. Specify an alternative *fs_file* to map the client's file systems. For example, used in situations where the */etc/vfstab* file is nonexistent or unreliable.
- *-x*. Search exclusive directories, looking for files which exist that are not in the installation software database or the indicated *pkgmap* file.

Examples of *pkgchk* follow.

```
# pkgchk SUNWabe
ERROR: /opt/answerbooks/english/solaris_8/SUNWabe/collinfo
    file size <156> expected <181> actual
    file cksum <12876> expected <15728> actual
ERROR: /opt/answerbooks/english/solaris_8/SUNWabe/socat
    file size <504> expected <654> actual
    file cksum <37303> expected <54415> actual
#
```

```
# pkgchk -v SUNWabe
/opt/answerbooks/english/solaris_8/SUNWabe
/opt/answerbooks/english/solaris_8/SUNWabe/booklist.txt
/opt/answerbooks/english/solaris_8/SUNWabe/books
/opt/answerbooks/english/solaris_8/SUNWabe/books/ADVOSUG
/opt/answerbooks/english/solaris_8/SUNWabe/books/ADVOSUG/ebt
/opt/answerbooks/english/solaris_8/SUNWabe/books/ADVOSUG/ebt/
ADVOSUG.dat
/opt/answerbooks/english/solaris_8/SUNWabe/books/ADVOSUG/ebt/
ADVOSUG.edr
/opt/answerbooks/english/solaris_8/SUNWabe/books/ADVOSUG/ebt/
ADVOSUG.tag
/opt/answerbooks/english/solaris_8/SUNWabe/books/ADVOSUG/ebt/search.tdr
/opt/answerbooks/english/solaris_8/SUNWabe/books/ADVOSUG/ebt/toc.tdr
```

```
/opt/answerbooks/english/solaris_8/SUNWabe/books/ADVOSUG/figures
/opt/answerbooks/english/solaris_8/SUNWabe/books/ADVOSUG/figures/
8031.epsi.gif
/opt/answerbooks/english/solaris_8/SUNWabe/books/ADVOSUG/figures/
Editor-vi.fig346.epsi.gif
/opt/answerbooks/english/solaris_8/SUNWabe/books/ADVOSUG/figures/
Files.fig153.epsi.gif
/opt/answerbooks/english/solaris_8/SUNWabe/books/ADVOSUG/figures/
Files.fig154.epsi.gif
/opt/answerbooks/english/solaris_8/SUNWabe/books/ADVOSUG/figures/
Transition_app.
fig746.epsi.gif
/opt/answerbooks/english/solaris_8/SUNWabe/books/ADVOSUG/figures/
black_icon.epsi.gif
[remainder of output suppressed]

# pkgchk -l SUNWabe
Pathname: /opt/answerbooks/english/solaris_8/SUNWabe
Type: directory
Expected mode: 0755
Expected owner: bin
Expected group: bin
Referenced by the following packages:
        SUNWabe
Current status: installed

Pathname: /opt/answerbooks/english/solaris_8/SUNWabe/booklist.txt
Type: regular file
Expected mode: 0644
Expected owner: bin
Expected group: bin
Expected file size (bytes): 522
Expected sum(1) of contents: 41406
Expected last modification: Dec 11 05:34:02 1999
Referenced by the following packages:
        SUNWabe
Current status: installed
[remainder of output suppressed]
```

In this first example, `pkgchk` is used to check the integrity of the SUNWabe package, which had errors. In the second example, all directories and files in the SUNWabe package are displayed. In the third example, `pkgchk` lists all files with expected ownership and permissions for the package SUNWabe.

EXAM NOTES

THINK ABOUT IT . . .

You need to remove a software package associated with a particular file. The file is large and you know that you do not need it or the package. How would you do this?

First, you will have to determine which package(s) is associated with the file. To do this, you will search for the file name in */var/sadm/install/contents*. The following command can be used.

```
# grep filename /var/sadm/install/contents
```

The package name will appear. You can confirm that the file is a part of the package by entering the *pkgchk -v pkgname* command and looking for the file. You can then remove the package with the *pkgrm* command.

2.6 Installing Patches

A patch is a collection of files intended to update a software program. A patch is packaged using a particular format so that it can be easily acquired, distributed, and installed.

Operating system and product patches are released with regularity, including Sun's Recommended and Security Patches. It is important for UNIX administrators to be familiar with patch installation procedures and patch management strategies so that their systems can be kept current.

The commands used to manage patches are *patchadd*, *patchrm*, *showrev*, and *pkgparam*. Each of these commands is explained in this section.

Patches are identified by number. The patch number format is nnnnnn-vv, where nnnnnn is the patch identifier, and vv is the version of the patch. Sun periodically updates patches, which is reflected in the patch version number.

Where to Obtain Patches

Patches are available from the following sources:

- http://www.sunsolve.com/ (follow the Patches link)
- http://metalab.unc.edu/pub/sun-info/sun-patches/
- ftp://sunsolve1.sun.com/ (provided by Sun Service)
- ftp://sunsite.unc.edu/ (public access)

At these Internet sites, there are always two files associated with each patch. The first is the patch file itself and the second is a README file associated with the patch. Because some patches are very large, you might first wish to read about the patch by downloading just the README file, and then if you still need the patch you can then download it afterwards.

Patch Installation

After you obtain a patch, you'll need to store it somewhere. If you are at a site with several Sun systems, you might consider creating a patch archive on a server with enough available space to store all mandatory patches, plus any specific patches you need for your site.

Decisions about Patches

It is recommended that patches are installed so that they can be later "backed out." This requires that the system have a lot of extra disk space to store the backout information. Only in special circumstances (e.g., very old systems with insufficient disk space) should patches be installed without the backout option.

Next, your site should adopt a policy that determines which patches are installed on a system. It is recommended that only Sun's "recommended" and "security" patches be installed, plus patches that address specific problems that you are actually experiencing. Under no circumstances should all available patches be installed on a system.

You should consider updating recommended patches that are updated (i.e., if patch 150786-15 is updated to 150786-16). However, you should read the patch README file to see if the circumstances related to the patch's upgrade warrant your taking the time to upgrade the patch on your systems.

No single policy is ideal for all organizations. Variations in security, availability, resources, application and system architecture, and system use all help to determine which patches are installed on which systems.

Installing a Patch

The *patchadd* command is used to install patches. The syntax of the *patchadd* command is `patchadd [options] patch_dir patch_id...`, where `patch_dir` is the directory containing patches, and `patch_id` is a list of one or more patches to install. Another syntax, `patchadd [options] patch_dir patch_list` can be used, where `patch_list` is a text file containing a list of patches to install. The options for *patchadd* are explained here.

- *-d.* Does not back up the files to be patched. The patch cannot be removed.
- *-p.* Displays a list of the patches currently applied.
- *-u.* Installs unconditionally, turns off file validation. Applies the patch even if some of the files to be patched have been modified since their original installation.
- *-B backout_dir.* Saves backout data to a directory other than the package database. Specify `backout_dir` as an absolute pathname.
- *-C net_install_image.* Patches the files located on the mini root on a Net Install Image created by `setup_install_server`. Specify `net_install_image` as the absolute pathname to a Solaris 2.6 or compatible version boot directory.
- *-M patch_dir patch_id . . . | patch_dir patch_list.* Specifies the patches to be installed. Specify patches to the `-M` option in one of the following ways:

  1. By directory location and patch number.
     To use the directory location and patch number, specify `patch_dir` as the absolute pathname of the directory that contains spooled patches. Specify `patch_id` as the patch number of a given patch. Specifying multiple patch_id's is allowed.
  2. By directory location and the name of a file containing a patch list.
     To use the directory location and a file containing a patch list, specify `patch_dir` as the absolute pathname of the directory containing the file with a list of patches to be installed. Specify `patch_list` as the name of the file containing the patches to be installed.

- *-R client_root_path.* Locates all patch files generated by `patchadd` under the directory *client_root_path*. *client_root_path* is the directory that contains the bootable root of a client from the server's perspective. Specify `client_root_path` as the absolute pathname to the beginning of the directory tree under which all patch files generated by patchadd are to be located. `-R` cannot be specified with the `-S` option.

- *-S service.* Specifies an alternate *service* (for example, Solaris_2.3). This service is part of the server and client model, and can only be used from the server's console. Servers can contain shared */usr* file systems that are created by Host Manager. These service areas can then be made available to the clients they serve. `-S` cannot be specified with the `-R` option.

Some examples follow.

```
# patchadd -M /var/spool/patch 108528-03
Checking installed patches...
Verifying sufficient filesystem capacity (dry run method)...
Installing patch packages...
Patch number 108528-03 has been successfully installed.
See /var/sadm/patch/108528-03/log for details
Patch packages installed:
  SUNWcar
  SUNWcarx
  SUNWcpr
  SUNWcprx
  SUNWcsr
  SUNWcsu
  SUNWcsxu
  SUNWhea
  SUNWmdb
  SUNWmdbx
  SUNWpmr
  SUNWpmu
  SUNWpmux
  SUNWsrh
  SUNWtnfc
  SUNWtnfcx
#

# patchadd -M /var/spool/patches/8_Recommended 108652-18 108875-07

Checking installed patches...
Verifying sufficient filesystem capacity (dry run method)...
Installing patch packages...

Patch number 108652-18 has been successfully installed.
See /var/sadm/patch/108652-18/log for details
```

```
Patch packages installed:
  SUNWxwfnt
  SUNWxwinc
  SUNWxwman
  SUNWxwplt
  SUNWxwplx
  SUNWxwpmn
  SUNWxwslb

Checking installed patches...
Executing prepatch script...

    NOTICE: The following file is being replaced by this patch

          /etc/security/audit_event

    A copy of it has been saved under the name:

          /etc/security/audit_event.04130110

    The saved file needs to be scrutinized for any customizations
    that may have been made.  Please merge these modifications
    into the new audit_event that was delivered by this patch.

Verifying sufficient filesystem capacity (dry run method)...
Installing patch packages...

Patch number 108875-07 has been successfully installed.
See /var/sadm/patch/108875-07/log for details
Patch packages installed:
  SUNWarc
  SUNWcarx
  SUNWcsl
  SUNWcslx
  SUNWcsr
  SUNWcstl
  SUNWcstlx
  SUNWcsu
  SUNWhea
#
```

In the first example, the patch 108528-03 is installed. The patch is installed from the directory */var/spool/patch*. In the second example, patches 108652-18 and 108875-07 are installed from the directory */var/spool/patches/8_Recommended*.

EXAM NOTES

THINK ABOUT IT . . .

You need to install a large patch, but you do not have sufficient disk space in */var* for saving backout information. You do not want to install the patch without the ability to back it out later. What can you do?

You can specify an alternate location for the backout information with the `-B` option of `patchinstall`.

Listing Which Patches Are Currently Installed

The `patchadd -p` command will show you which patches are currently installed on a system. An example follows.

```
# patchadd -p

Patch: 108528-03 Obsoletes: 109153-01 109656-01 109291-06 109663-01
109309-02 109345-02 Requires: Incompatibles: Packages:  SUNWcar
SUNWcarx SUNWcpr SUNWcprx SUNWcsr SUNWcsu SUNWcsxu SUNWhea SUNWmdb
SUNWmdbx SUNWpmr SUNWpmu SUNWpmux SUNWsrh SUNWtnfc SUNWtnfcx
Patch: 109137-01 Obsoletes:  Requires: Incompatibles: Packages:
SUNWcsu
Patch: 109320-01 Obsoletes:  Requires: Incompatibles: Packages:
SUNWpcu SUNWpsu
Patch: 108974-07 Obsoletes: 109343-04 Requires: Incompatibles:
Packages:  SUNWcarx SUNWcsr SUNWcsu SUNWcsxu SUNWhea
Patch: 108977-01 Obsoletes:  Requires: 108974-01 Incompatibles:
Packages:  SUNWcsr SUNWhea SUNWvolu SUNWvolux
Patch: 108968-02 Obsoletes:  Requires: 108974-01 108977-01
Incompatibles:  Packages:  SUNWcsr SUNWesu SUNWhea SUNWvolu SUNWvolux
Patch: 108975-03 Obsoletes:  Requires: 108968-01 108974-01 108977-01
Incompatibles:  Packages:  SUNWcsu SUNWvolu
Patch: 108875-07 Obsoletes:  Requires: Incompatibles: Packages:
SUNWarc SUNWcarx SUNWcsl SUNWcslx SUNWcsr SUNWcstl SUNWcstlx SUNWcsu
SUNWhea
Patch: 108652-18 Obsoletes:  Requires: Incompatibles: Packages:
SUNWxwfnt SUNWxwinc SUNWxwman SUNWxwplt SUNWxwplx SUNWxwpmn SUNWxwslb
Patch: 109783-01 Obsoletes:  Requires: Incompatibles: Packages:
SUNWcsu
```

```
Patch: 108985-02 Obsoletes:  Requires: Incompatibles: Packages:
SUNWcsu
Patch: 109277-01 Obsoletes:  Requires: Incompatibles: Packages:
SUNWcsu
#
```

The `showrev -p` command will also show which patches are currently installed on a system. An example follows.

```
% showrev -p
Patch: 108528-03 Obsoletes: 109153-01, 109656-01, 109291-06, 109663-01,
109309-02, 109345-02 Requires:  Incompatibles:  Packages: SUNWcsu,
SUNWcsr, SUNWcarx, SUNWcar, SUNWcpr, SUNWcprx, SUNWcsxu, SUNWpmu,
SUNWpmr, SUNWpmux, SUNWhea, SUNWmdb, SUNWmdbx, SUNWsrh, SUNWtnfc,
SUNWtnfcx
Patch: 109137-01 Obsoletes:  Requires:  Incompatibles:  Packages:
SUNWcsu
Patch: 108974-07 Obsoletes: 109343-04 Requires:  Incompatibles:
Packages: SUNWcsu, SUNWcsr, SUNWcarx, SUNWcsxu, SUNWhea
Patch: 108975-03 Obsoletes:  Requires: 108968-01, 108974-01, 108977-01
Incompatibles:  Packages: SUNWcsu, SUNWvolu
Patch: 108875-07 Obsoletes:  Requires:  Incompatibles:  Packages:
SUNWcsu, SUNWcsr, SUNWcslx, SUNWcsl, SUNWcarx, SUNWarc, SUNWcstl,
SUNWcstlx, SUNWhea
Patch: 109783-01 Obsoletes:  Requires:  Incompatibles:  Packages:
SUNWcsu
Patch: 108985-02 Obsoletes:  Requires:  Incompatibles:  Packages:
SUNWcsu
Patch: 109277-01 Obsoletes:  Requires:  Incompatibles:  Packages:
SUNWcsu
Patch: 108977-01 Obsoletes:  Requires: 108974-01 Incompatibles:
Packages: SUNWcsr, SUNWvolu, SUNWvolux, SUNWhea
Patch: 108968-02 Obsoletes:  Requires: 108974-01, 108977-01
Incompatibles:  Packages: SUNWcsr, SUNWesu, SUNWvolu, SUNWvolux,
SUNWhea
Patch: 108652-18 Obsoletes:  Requires:  Incompatibles:  Packages:
SUNWxwfnt, SUNWxwplt, SUNWxwplx, SUNWxwinc, SUNWxwman, SUNWxwpmn,
SUNWxwslb
Patch: 109320-01 Obsoletes:  Requires:  Incompatibles:  Packages:
SUNWpcu, SUNWp
su
#
```

Removing a Patch

The *patchrm* command is used to remove patches. The syntax of the *patchrm* command is `patchrm [options] patch_id`. The options for *patchrm* are:

- *-f.* Forces the patch removal regardless of whether the patch was superseded by another patch.
- *-B backout_dir.* Removes a patch whose backout data has been saved to a directory other than the package database. This option is only needed if the original backout directory, supplied to the `patchadd` command at installation time, has been moved. Specify `backout_dir` as an absolute pathname.
- *-C net_install_image.* Removes the patched files located on the mini root on a Net Install Image created by `setup_install_server`. Specify `net_install_image` as the absolute pathname to a Solaris 2.6 or compatible version boot directory.
- *-R client_root_path.* Locates all patch files generated by `patchrm` under the directory `client_root_path`. `client_root_path` is the directory that contains the bootable root of a client from the server's perspective. Specify `client_root_path` as the absolute pathname to the beginning of the directory tree under which all patch files generated from *patchrm* will be located. The `-R` cannot be specified with the `-S` option.
- *-S service.* Specifies an alternate *service* (e.g., Solaris_2.3). This *service* is part of the server and client model, and can only be used from the server's console. Servers can contain shared */usr* file systems that are created by Host Manager. These service areas can then be made available to the clients they serve. `-S` cannot be specified with the `-R` option.

Only patches installed with the backout option can be removed. You will need to restore the system from a backup tape if you must back out patches installed without the backout option.

Some examples follow.

```
# patchrm 104945-02
# patchrm -S Solaris_2.6 104945-02
# patchrm -C /export/Solaris_2.6/Tools/Boot 104945-02
```

In the first example, the patch 104945-02 is being removed. In the second example, patch 104945-02 is removed from a boot server's OS image, specifically from the Solaris 2.6 version on that server. In the last example, patch 104945-02 is removed from a Solaris install server, specifically from the Solaris 2.6 image.

EXAM NOTES

THINK ABOUT IT . . .

You want to install a newer version of a patch. How would you do this?

First, you should back out all prior versions of the patch with the `patchrm` command. Search for prior versions with the `patchadd -p` command. Then, install the new version of the patch with `patchadd`.

Note: It is recommended you back up your system before performing this procedure.

CHAPTER SUMMARY

Solaris operating system installations—whether fresh installations or upgrades—must be carefully planned. You need to make sure your hardware is supported by the new release and that you have sufficient disk space.

A SPARC system must have at least 64MB of memory and 1.6GB of space to run Solaris 8.

If you are doing a fresh install, you must decide which software cluster to install. If the system is to be connected to a network, you must obtain several pieces of information related to network configuration, such as IP address, subnet mask, and domain name. Finally, you must determine if you have all of the right media.

When you start a fresh installation, you'll be asked several questions regarding system and network configuration and which software to install. You can accept the default disk partitioning scheme or input your own. From time to time you'll be asked to change CDs.

It is recommended that you back up a system being upgraded prior to the upgrade, and then again afterwards.

When you begin an upgrade installation, you'll be asked several questions regarding system and network configuration. From time to time you'll be asked to change CDs.

Software packages are installed with the `pkgadd` command. The `pkginfo` command gives information about installed software packages. The integrity of installed software packages is checked with the `pkgchk` command. The `pkgrm` command is used to remove installed software packages.

Patches are updates to software components, and can be obtained from http://www.sunsolve.com/, http://metalab.unc.edu/pub/sun-info/sun-patches/, ftp://sunsolve1.sun.com/, and ftp://sunsite.unc.edu/. Patches are installed with the `patchadd` command, listed with the `patchadd -p` or `showrev -p` commands, and removed with the `patchrm` command. Patches can be installed with or without the ability to be later backed out.

TEST YOURSELF

MULTIPLE CHOICE

1. Given:

   `# patchadd -d 104945-12`

   What is the result?

   A. The patch 104945-12 is deleted from the system.

   B. The patch 104945-12 is applied to the system, and the patch cannot later be backed out.

   C. This displays status of patch 104945-12.

   D. The patch is distributed to patch clients on the local network.

2. Which will display a list of files contained in the SUNWbnu package?

   A. `grep SUNWbnu /var/sadm/installed`

   B. `pkgchk -v bnu`

   C. `pkginfo -l SUNWbnu`

   D. `pkgchk -v SUNWbnu`

3. What is the minimum hardware required for the Solaris 8 Operating System?
   A. 1 CPU, 16MB RAM, 1.6GB disk
   B. 1 CPU, 64 MB RAM, 1.6GB disk
   C. 16 CPU, 256MB RAM, 1.3G disk
   D. 1 CPU, 16MB RAM, 2.3G disk
4. Which four are required before a fresh Solaris installation can begin? (Choose four)
   A. Domain name
   B. IP address
   C. Collision rate
   D. Name server IP address
   E. UUCP domain
   F. MAC address
   G. Subnet mask
5. Which three release media CDs are required to perform a Solaris upgrade? (Choose three)
   A. Solaris 8 Installation English SPARC Platform Edition
   B. Solaris 8 Upgrade 1 of 2 SPARC Platform Edition
   C. Solaris 8 Upgrade 2 of 2 SPARC Platform Edition
   D. Solaris 8 Software 1 of 2 SPARC Platform Edition
   E. Solaris 8 Software 2 of 2 SPARC Platform Edition
   F. Solaris 8 Upgrade English SPARC Platform Edition
   G. Solaris 8 Upgrade Set SPARC Platform Edition
6. What is the purpose of the *pkginfo -p* command?
   A. Display information about installed patches.
   B. Display information about permanently installed software packages.
   C. Display information about partially installed software packages.
   D. Display information about partially installed patches.

7. Which is used to list the files and directories in an installed software package?

   A. `pkginfo -x`

   B. `pkgchk -v`

   C. `pkginfo -v`

   D. `pkgchk -i`

8. Given:

```
# patchadd -p

Patch: 108528-03 Obsoletes: 109153-01 109656-01 109291-06 109663-01
109309-02 109345-02 Requires: Incompatibles: Packages:  SUNWcar
SUNWcarx SUNWcpr SUNWcprx SUNWcsr SUNWcsu SUNWcsxu SUNWhea SUNWmdb
SUNWmdbx SUNWpmr SUNWpmu SUNWpmux SUNWsrh SUNWtnfc SUNWtnfcx
Patch: 109137-01 Obsoletes:  Requires: Incompatibles: Packages:
SUNWcsu
Patch: 109320-01 Obsoletes:  Requires: Incompatibles: Packages:
SUNWpcu SUNWpsu
Patch: 108974-07 Obsoletes: 109343-04 Requires: Incompatibles:
Packages:  SUNWcarx SUNWcsr SUNWcsu SUNWcsxu SUNWhea
```

   Which is true about patch 108974-07?

   A. Patch 108974-07 supercedes patch 109343-04.

   B. Patch 108974-07 should be installed on this system.

   C. Patch 109343-04 must first be removed before installing patch 108974-07.

   D. Patch 108974-07 is not required on this system.

9. Where are system installation logs located?

   A. `/var/install/logs`

   B. `/var/sadm/system/install/logs`

   C. `/var/sadm/install/logs`

   D. `/var/adm/log`

10. You need to upgrade a system from Solaris 7 to Solaris 8. What procedure should you follow?
    A. Back up the system, upgrade Solaris, then back up the system again.
    B. Upgrade Solaris from the release media.
    C. Enter the command `reboot -- -upgrade`.
    D. Back up the system, repartition the system boot disk, upgrade Solaris, and then back up the system again.

FREE RESPONSE

11. What command is used to show installed packages and their versions?
12. You need to install patch 109545-03 without saving backout information. What command is used to do this?

CHAPTER 3

The Boot PROM

After completing this chapter, you'll be able to meet the following Solaris Administration Exam objectives:

- State or recognize the combination of actions required to interrupt a nonresponsive system.
- State the command strings used to manipulate custom device aliases.

To fulfill these objectives, this chapter discusses:

- An overview of the Boot PROM;
- Boot PROM commands;
- Commands used to interrupt and restart a nonresponding system; and
- Commands that create a custom device alias.

3.1 Overview of the Boot PROM

The Boot PROM is a software package written into the NVRAM of a Sun workstation or server. The name of the software package is OpenBoot. The name OpenBoot refers to a standard called the *IEEE Standard 1275-1994, Standard for Boot Firmware*. The Boot PROM is also known as the OpenBoot PROM, or OBP. PROM stands for Programmable Read-Only Memory; this refers to the hardware technology used to store the OpenBoot software.

The PROM software performs four main functions:

1. tests and initializes the system hardware;
2. determines the system's hardware configuration;
3. boots the operating system from disk or the network; and
4. contains debug facilities for testing hardware and software.

These functions are performed at system startup, as well as any time the administrator manually enters the PROM while the system is running.

3.2 Accessing the Boot PROM

The Boot PROM can be accessed in three ways. If a feature called "auto-boot?" is not set, then the system will power up, display the BOOT prompt, stop, and await further instructions. A running system can be temporarily halted and the Boot PROM prompt displayed by pressing Stop A (on a terminal connected to the console serial port, this is done by sending a BREAK). Boot PROM environment variables can be read from and written to with the *eeprom* command. This chapter describes these three methods in detail.

Entering Boot PROM with Stop A or BREAK

A running or hung system can be temporarily put into the Boot PROM by pressing Stop A on the system console. To press Stop A, press and hold down the Stop key; while holding the Stop key, press the A key. Then release both keys together. When you press Stop A, you will see the Boot PROM prompt as follows.

```
Type 'go' to resume
ok _
```

The "type 'go' to resume" message is displayed as a reminder in case you pressed Stop A accidentally.

On a system with no console but with a terminal connected to the serial port, sending a BREAK has the same effect as a console pressing Stop A.

Pressing Stop A suspends a running system. Any other users on the system may think that the system has crashed. The integrity of application data is at risk if the system is not continued with the "go" command. This is because some writes to the disk may be yet uncommitted and still in the disk cache. This is *not* the correct procedure for halting a system.

By using a terminal concentrator it is possible to telnet to the console port on another system. If you are doing this at your site, remember that if you press Stop A in this telnet session you are stopping the *local* system, not the remote system to which you have connected. To interrupt the remote system to which you are connected via the concentrator, you will need to enter a command to instruct the concentrator to send a BREAK character to the console port. Refer to your concentrator's user manual for guidance and see Chapter 12 for more on connecting to remote systems.

A system can be configured to ignore Stop A. This is accomplished by adding an entry to */etc/system* that reads "set abort_enable = 0".

Entering Boot PROM at Powerup

If the Boot PROM's *auto-boot?* configuration variable is set to *false*, then the system will not boot from disk. Instead, the system will stop and display the Boot PROM prompt after powering up and running system diagnostics. At this point, any valid Boot PROM command can be entered.

3.3 Boot PROM Commands

This section describes some of the common Boot PROM commands. Table 3.1 lists common commands and their descriptions.

Table 3.1 *Boot PROM Commands*

COMMAND	DESCRIPTION
go	Continue execution of the operating system.
boot	Boot an operating system image from hard disk, CD-ROM, or from a boot server over the network.
reset	Perform a power-on reset. It will also boot the system if *auto-boot?* is set to *true*.
sync	Write unwritten filesystem writes to disk; write the system's memory image to the primary swap partition; then perform a power-on reset.
test	Test specified hardware.
printenv	Display the values of all Boot PROM configuration variables. You can also display the contents of a single configuration variable; for example, *printenv auto-boot?* will print the value of the *auto-boot?* configuration variable.
setenv	Set the value of a Boot PROM configuration variable. For example, *setenv auto-boot? true* will set the value of the *auto-boot?* configuration variable to *true*.
devalias	Display or change device aliases. Changes are in effect only until the next system reset or power cycle. For permanent changes, use *nvalias*.
nvalias	Permanently change device aliases. See also *devalias*.
probe-scsi	Diagnostic routine used to find all active SCSI devices on the system. This can be helpful when adding new hardware to a SCSI bus or when diagnosing a SCSI device hardware problem.
password	Used to set the PROM password.
set-default	Return a configuration variable to its factory setting. For example, *set-default auto-boot?* will return the *auto-boot?* configuration variable to its original factory setting.
set-defaults	Return most configuration variables to their factory settings.

The *probe-scsi* command should not be used on a running system, as the system may hang during the *probe-scsi* and not recover. You should always gracefully shut down a system and then perform a *probe-scsi* command.

EXAM NOTES

THINK ABOUT IT . . .

You need to change the system's default power-up behavior so that it stops at the PROM prompt instead of booting automatically. What should you do?

Change the *auto-boot?* PROM configuration variable to *false*. This will cause the system to stop at the PROM's "ok" prompt at power up.

3.4 Boot PROM Configuration Variables

This section discusses some of the Boot PROM configuration variables. All can be set with the *setenv PROM* command or the `eeprom` shell command (both are described in the next subsection). Table 3.2 lists some of the configuration variables and their functions.

Table 3.2 *Boot PROM Configuration Variables*

VARIABLE	TYPICAL DEFAULT	DESCRIPTION
auto-boot?	true	If true, boot automatically after power on or reset.
boot-command	boot	Command that is executed if *auto-boot?* is true.
boot-device	disk, net	Device from which to boot.
boot-file	empty string	Arguments passed to booted program.
diag-device	net	Diagnostic boot source device.
diag-file	empty string	Arguments passed to booted program in diagnostic mode.
diag-switch?	false	If true, run in diagnostic mode.
fcode-debug?	false	If true, include name fields for plug-in device FCodes.
input-device	keyboard	Console input device (usually keyboard, ttya, or ttyb).
nvramrc	empty	Contents of NVRAMRC.
oem-banner	empty string	Custom OEM banner (enabled by *oem-banner?* is true).
oem-banner?	false	If true, use custom OEM banner.

Table 3.2 *Boot PROM Configuration Variables (Continued)*

VARIABLE	TYPICAL DEFAULT	DESCRIPTION
oem-logo	no default	Byte array custom OEM logo (enabled by *oem-logo?* is true). Displayed in hexadecimal.
oem-logo?	false	If true, use custom OEM logo (else, use Sun logo).
output-device	screen	Console output device (usually screen, ttya, or ttyb).
screen-#columns	80	Number of onscreen columns (characters/line).
screen-#rows	34	Number of onscreen rows (lines).
security-#badlogins	no default	Number of incorrect security password attempts.
security-mode	none	Firmware security level (options: none, command, or full).
security-password	no default	Firmware security password (never displayed).
use-nvramrc?	false	If true, execute commands in NVRAMRC during system start-up.

Accessing Boot PROM Configuration Variables

The Boot PROM configuration variables are examined and changed with the *printenv* and *setenv* Boot PROM commands. The syntax of the *printenv* command is *printenv [variable]*, where *variable* is a PROM configuration variable. The syntax of the *setenv* command is *setenv [variable [value]]*, where *variable* is a PROM configuration variable, and *value* is a new value. Some examples follow.

```
ok printenv
Variable Name                  Value                      Default Value

tpe-link-test?                 true                       true
scsi-terminator-id             7                          7
keyboard-click?                false                      false
keymap
sbus-probe-list                e01                        e01
ttyb-rts-dtr-off               false                      false
ttyb-ignore-cd                 true                       true
```

```
ttya-rts-dtr-off              false                         false
ttya-ignore-cd                true                          true
ttyb-mode                     9600,8,n,1,-                  9600,8,n,1,-
ttya-mode                     9600,8,n,1,-                  9600,8,n,1,-
mfg-mode                      off                           off
diag-level                    max                           max
#power-cycles                 74
system-board-serial#          5012995040947
system-board-date
fcode-debug?                  false                         false
output-device                 screen                        screen
input-device                  keyboard                      keyboard
load-base                     16384                         16384
[remainder of output suppressed]
ok

ok printenv auto-boot?
auto-boot? =                  true
ok

ok setenv auto-boot? false
ok

ok printenv auto-boot?
auto-boot? =                  false
ok
```

In the first example, the *printenv* command entered with no arguments shows all configuration variables. In the second example, the *printenv* command displays only the configuration variable *auto-boot?*. In the third example, the *auto-boot?* configuration variable is set to *false* with the *setenv* command. In the last example, the *printenv* command again displays the configuration variable *auto-boot?*.

Accessing Boot PROM Configuration Variables from UNIX

The Boot PROM configuration variables can be examined and changed through the *eeprom* command. The syntax for the *eeprom* command is *eeprom [variable[=value]]*, where *variable* is any of the variables listed in Table 3.2. Some examples follow.

```
$ eeprom auto-boot?
auto-boot?=true
$ eeprom auto-boot?=false
```

```
eeprom: cannot open /dev/openprom: Permission denied
$ su -
Password: ********
Sun Microsystems Inc.   SunOS 5.8       Generic February
2000
# eeprom auto-boot?=false
# eeprom auto-boot?
auto-boot?=false
#
```

In the foregoing example, the *auto-boot?* variable is displayed. Next, an attempt is made to change the value of *auto-boot?*, which fails because the user is not root. After *su*'ing to root, *auto-boot?* is successfully changed to *false* and its value verified.

3.5 Boot PROM Security Levels

The Boot PROM has three security levels. The security levels allow the administrator to restrict which commands can be entered by a user, giving the administrator a greater degree of control over the system's integrity. Table 3.3 describes the security levels and their meaning.

Use care in setting the Boot PROM security level. If you set the security level to Full and subsequently forget the Boot PROM *and* root passwords, you will not be able to recover the root password or the Boot PROM password because the system will not boot from CD-ROM (a commonly used method for recovering the root password involves booting from CD-ROM, mounting the system's root file system, and resetting the root password by editing the */etc/shadow* file). The only recourse will be to physically replace the system's PROM.

Table 3.3 *Boot PROM Security Levels*

SECURITY LEVEL	DESCRIPTION
Full	Only the *go* command can be entered. All other commands require the PROM password.
Command	Only the *go* and *boot* (with no options) commands can be entered. All other commands require the PROM password.
None	All commands can be entered. No commands require the PROM password.

EXAM NOTES

THINK ABOUT IT . . .

Your organization needs to protect the integrity of your end-user UNIX workstations. You do not give out root passwords. Should you do anything with the Boot PROM security levels?

The Boot PROM security level on each workstation should be set to Command or Full. The Boot PROM password should be unique—and not easily guessed—for each workstation. This will prevent users from being able to modify configuration variables or boot from CD-ROM (and therefore be able to become root and/or make any desired system changes).

3.6 Devices and Device Aliases

The Boot PROM communicates directly with devices on the system. Similar to a device's naming convention in the file system (e.g., */dev/dsk/c0t0d0s0*), the Boot PROM uses a convention to describe devices.

For instance, a typical disk might be:

```
/sbus@1f,0/SUNW,fas@e,8800000/sd@3,0:a
```

This is described as:

- /sbus@1f,0—sbus on main system bus, bus address 1f,0.
- 0, 8800000—the sbus slot number (0) and an offset (8800000).
- fas—the FAS device driver.
- sd@3,0—SCSI bus target 3, logical unit 0.
- :a—partition "a" on the disk.

Knowledge of these complex device names is not usually needed because these devices have easy-to-remember aliases. The Boot PROM uses aliases to provide a consistent and simple assortment of device names on any hardware platform. The disk device name aliases available are:

- disk
- disk0
- disk1
- disk2
- disk3
- disk4

- disk5
- disk6
- cdrom
- floppy
- net
- tape
- tape0
- tape1

The preset aliases usually include all of the common hardware devices on a system, and this makes it uncommon for an administrator to have to type in long device names.

The *devalias* Command

The *devalias* PROM command is used to create and modify the device aliases listed earlier. The syntax of the *devalias* command is *devalias [alias [device]]*, where *alias* is the name of an alias, and *device* is the full name of a device. Some examples follow.

```
ok devalias
screen                        /SUNW,ffb@1e,0
net                           /sbus/SUNW,hme@e,8c0000
disk                          /sbus/SUNW,fas@e,8800000/sd@0,0
cdrom                         /sbus/SUNW,fas@e,8800000/sd@6,0:f
tape                          /sbus/SUNW,fas@e,8800000/st@4,0
tape1                         /sbus/SUNW,fas@e,8800000/st@5,0
tape0                         /sbus/SUNW,fas@e,8800000/st@4,0
disk6                         /sbus/SUNW,fas@e,8800000/sd@6,0
disk5                         /sbus/SUNW,fas@e,8800000/sd@5,0
disk4                         /sbus/SUNW,fas@e,8800000/sd@4,0
disk3                         /sbus/SUNW,fas@e,8800000/sd@3,0
disk2                         /sbus/SUNW,fas@e,8800000/sd@2,0
disk1                         /sbus/SUNW,fas@e,8800000/sd@1,0
disk0                         /sbus/SUNW,fas@e,8800000/sd@0,0
scsi                          /sbus/SUNW,fas@e,8800000
floppy                        /sbus/SUNW,fdtwo
ttyb                          /sbus/zs@f,1100000:b
ttya                          /sbus/zs@f,1100000:a
keyboard!                     /sbus/zs@f,1000000:forcemode
keyboard                      /sbus/zs@f,1000000
```

```
name                               aliases
ok

ok devalias disk
disk                               /sbus/SUNW,fas@e,880000/sd@0,0
ok

ok devalias disk7 /sbus/SUNW,fas@e,8800000/sd@4,3
ok

ok devalias disk
disk                               /sbus/SUNW,fas@e,8800000/sd@4,3
ok
```

In the first example, *devalias* shows all device aliases. In the second example, *devalias* shows the alias for *disk*. In the third example, *devalias* changes the alias for *disk*7. In the last example, *devalias* shows the alias for *disk* with its new value.

Aliases created with *devalias* are lost after a system reset or power cycle. To permanently create new or different aliases, use the *nvalias* and *nvunalias* commands discussed in the next section.

The *nvalias* and *nvunalias* Commands

The *nvalias* command is used to permanently configure device aliases on the system. With the *nvalias* command, device aliases are permanently configured. The syntax for the *nvalias* command is *nvalias [alias [device]]*, where *alias* is the name of an alias, and *device* is the full name of a device.

The *nvunalias* command is used to delete a specified alias from the system. *nvunalias* reverses the effect of *nvalias* (described earlier). The syntax for the *nvunalias* command is *nvunalias alias*, where *alias* is the name of the alias to remove.

The *use-nvramrc?* configuration variable must be set to *true* for aliases set by *nvalias* to take effect.

EXAM NOTES

THINK ABOUT IT . . .

You added a second SCSI controller and external disks to a system. One of those external disks will be your primary boot disk. The *devalias* command does not list the new disk. What can you do?

Use the *nvalias* PROM command to permanently create a new device alias, for instance *disk9*. Next, change the *boot-device* PROM configuration variable to make *disk9* the new default boot device.

3.7 Troubleshooting

System Boots from Wrong Device

Problem: The system is supposed to boot from the disk; instead, it boots from the network. There are two possible causes for this:

1. The *diag-switch?* configuration variable is set to *true*.
   Interrupt the booting process with Stop A. Type the following commands at the OK prompt:

   ```
   ok setenv diag-switch? false
   ok boot
   ```

   The system should now start booting from the disk.
2. The *boot-device* configuration variable is set to *net* instead of *disk*.
   Interrupt the booting process with Stop A. Type the following commands at the OK prompt:

   ```
   ok setenv boot-device disk
   ok boot
   ```

   Note that the preceding commands cause the system to boot from the disk defined as *disk* in the device aliases list. If you want to boot from another service, set the *boot-device* with *devalias* or *nvalias* as appropriate.

System Boots from a Disk Instead of from the Network

Problem: The *boot-device* configuration variable is not set to *net*.

Interrupt the booting process with Stop A. Type the following commands at the OK prompt:

```
ok setenv boot-device net
ok boot
```

System Boots from the Wrong Disk

Problem: you have more than one disk in your system. You want the system to boot from disk2, but the system is booting instead from disk1.

The *boot-device* configuration variable is not set to the correct disk.

Interrupt the booting process with Stop A. Type the following commands at the OK prompt:

```
ok setenv boot-device disk2
ok boot
```

System Will Not Boot from Disk

Two common problems are discussed in this section.

If you get the error message "*The file just loaded does not appear to be executable,*" then the boot block on the boot disk is missing or corrupted. You will need to install a new boot block.

If your error message reads, "*Can't open boot device,*" the disk may be powered down. If the boot disk is external, check its power cord and SCSI cable connections. If the boot disk is internal, it may be missing or faulty.

Nonresponsive System

Several situations can render the console unresponsive to input. These troubleshooting steps can help you diagnose the problem and lead to a solution.

1. Verify that the keyboard is plugged in.
2. Verify that the monitor is plugged in.
3. Try pressing Stop A to see if the system hardware responds.
4. If there is no response, the system may be assuming that the console device has been set to the serial device. Connect a terminal to the serial port to see if the system responds to keyboard input.
5. Send a BREAK from the terminal to see if the system hardware responds.
6. If the system does not respond to Stop A (or BREAK), power cycle the system and carefully observe the boot sequence.

If none of these fixes the problem, then the system may have a hardware problem.

CHAPTER SUMMARY

The Boot PROM (also known as the OpenBoot PROM, OBP, or the PROM) is accessible in three ways: at powerup (if the *auto-boot?* configuration variable is set to false); when shutting down the system; or when pressing Stop A on the console (or BREAK on a terminal connected to the serial port).

The Boot PROM has several commands used to display and modify configuration variables and device aliases, set the password and security level, test the hardware, and boot the system. The Boot PROM configuration variables determine the hardware settings for the console and serial ports, control boot behavior, and determine security settings.

The Boot PROM configuration variables are displayed and set with the *printenv* and *setenv* PROM commands, respectively, and also with the *eeprom* shell command. You must be root to change settings with the *eeprom* command.

The three Boot PROM security levels are: Full (where the only allowed command is "go"; all other commands require the PROM password); Command (where the only allowed commands are "go" and "boot"; all other commands require the PROM password); and None (all commands are allowed). The security level is set by changing the *security-mode* and *security-password* configuration variables.

Device aliases allow the convenience of addressing devices using short, easy-to-remember names, rather than their full and somewhat cryptic names. Device aliases are displayed and changed with the *devalias* PROM command. Changes made with *devalias* last only until the next system reset or power cycle. Permanent device alias changes are made with the *nvalias* command.

A system that boots from the wrong device may have its *diag-switch?* or *boot-device* configuration variables set incorrectly. A system that will not boot from disk may have a missing or corrupted boot block, or the boot disk may be powered down.

You can attempt to revive a nonresponsive system by pressing Stop A on the console (or BREAK on the console terminal). If the system does not respond, you should next power cycle the system, and carefully observe the boot sequence for errors. If the system is still nonresponsive, the system may have a hardware problem.

TEST YOURSELF

MULTIPLE CHOICE

1. What is the purpose of the *devalias* command?
   A. Display information about deviant aliases.
   B. Set and display temporary device aliases.
   C. Set and display permanent device aliases.
   D. Set and display device labels.

2. What is the purpose of the *nvalias* command?
   A. Display information about nondeviant aliases.
   B. Set and display temporary device aliases.
   C. Set and display permanent device aliases.
   D. Set and display device labels.

3. Which two commands will change the value of the *auto-boot?* configuration variable to false? (Choose two)
   A. `auto-boot?=false;export auto-boot?`
   B. `devalias auto-boot? false`
   C. `devalias auto-boot?=false`
   D. `setenv auto-boot? false`
   E. `eeprom auto-boot?=false`
   F. `eeprom auto-boot? false`

4. Your Solaris workstation is nonresponsive. Place the steps used to attempt to revive the system in the correct order.
   a. power-cycle the system
   b. boot the system
   c. press Stop A on the system console
   d. examine the kernel image
   e. ensure the system is connected to the network
   - A. e, c, d, b
   - B. a, c, d, b
   - C. c, a, b, e
   - D. e, c, a, b

5. What is the purpose of the *security-mode* configuration variable?
   - A. It determines which commands can be entered without having to supply the PROM password.
   - B. It determines whether every command—or just the *boot* and *go* commands—are logged in the event log.
   - C. It is used to store the PROM security password.
   - D. It determines whether the system may be booted from a device on the network.

6. Which four statements are true about the Boot PROM? (Choose four)
   - A. It is also called the OBP.
   - B. It performs hardware testing, debugging, and boots the system from disk or the network.
   - C. It has a set of configuration variables that are used to determine the system hardware settings and boot behavior.
   - D. Its settings are lost when the system is reset or power-cycled.
   - E. Its configuration variables can be accessed from the Boot PROM command line as well as from the UNIX shell.

7. Given:

```
ok printenv boot-device
boot-device =           disk net
ok printenv auto-boot?
auto-boot? =            false
```

Which is true about the system's boot behavior?

A. Upon powerup, the system will boot from disk.

B. Upon powerup, the system will stop at the Boot PROM prompt. When the *boot* command is entered, the system will boot from disk.

C. Upon powerup, the system will stop at the Boot PROM prompt. When the *boot* command is entered, the system will ask whether it should be booted from disk or over the network.

D. Upon powerup, the system will stop at the Boot PROM prompt only if the boot disk is not present or powered up. Otherwise, it will boot over the network.

8. What is the correct syntax of the *eeprom* command?

A. `eeprom variable=value`

B. `eeprom variable [=value]`

C. `eeprom variable [value]`

D. `eeprom [variable [=value]]`

9. You need to add a device alias for an external SCSI disk so that you can boot from it in case of emergency. What sequence of actions should you take?

A. Define the alias with the *devalias* command, and then use the *boot* command to boot from it when you need to.

B. Define the alias with the *devalias* command, and then set the *boot-device* variable to the new alias.

C. Define the alias with the *nvalias* command, and then use the *boot* command to boot from it when you need to.

D. Define the alias with the *nvalias* command, and then set the *boot-device* variable to the new alias.

10. Given:

```
# eeprom security-mode=none
#
```

What is the result?

A. Boot PROM audit logging is set to the lowest level; no security events will be recorded.
B. Any valid Boot PROM command may be entered without also having to enter the PROM security password.
C. The PROM security password will not be used when processing keyboard commands.
D. The system can be booted from any device that contains a valid boot image.

Free Response

11. What command is used to set the *boot-device* configuration variable to net?

12. You need to change the system boot behavior so that it will boot from device disk3. What command is used to do this?

C H A P T E R 4

Initialization and Shutdown

4.1 System Run Levels

4.2 The OpenBoot *boot* command

4.3 System Initialization

4.4 System Shutdown

After completing this chapter, you'll be able to meet the following Solaris Administration Exam objectives:

- Match the Solaris run levels to their intended functions.
- State the function of the following files or directories and the relationships between them: */etc/inittab*, */etc/init.d*, */etc/rc#* (where # is 0, 1, 2, 3, 5, 6, or S), or */etc/rc#.d* (where # is 0, 1, 2, 3, or S).
- Identify the commands used to change the run level of a system to a specified state.
- Match the *boot* command options to their respective functions.
- Select the command that reports the current run level of a Solaris system.
- Given a sample run control directory, differentiate between the basic activity in a script whose name begins with an uppercase S and a script whose name begins with an uppercase K.

To fulfill these objectives, this chapter discusses:

- System run levels and their usage;
- The command used to determine the system's current and previous run levels;
- The commands used to change system run levels;
- The system initialization mechanism; and
- The system termination mechanism.

4.1 System Run Levels

There are several *run levels* (also called *init states*) defined for Solaris systems. A run level describes the basic state of a running system and defines which services are running and available for users. A system can be in only one run level at a time. Run levels are defined in Table 4.1.

Table 4.1 *Run Levels and Init States*

RUN LEVEL	INIT STATE	DESCRIPTION
0	Power Down	Used to shut down the system so that power can be turned off.
s or S	Single User	System is running for a single user (console only) with all filesystems mounted. No network services are available.
1	Administrative	System is running in administrative mode. All file systems are mounted. No network services are available.
2	Multiuser	Normal operations. All filesystems are mounted; all network services are running. The NFS, Web, and DHCP servers are not running.
3	Multiuser	Normal operations. All filesystems are mounted; all network services are running, including NFS, Web, and DHCP servers.
4	(Not Used)	Not used. This could be administrator-defined (which exceeds the scope of this book).
5	Power Down	Used to shut down the system so that power can be turned off. On systems so equipped, power will be automatically removed when shutdown is complete.
6	Reboot	Used to shut down the system and then reboot it to the default run level defined in */etc/inittab*.

Figure 4-1 illustrates the relationships and functions of the run levels.

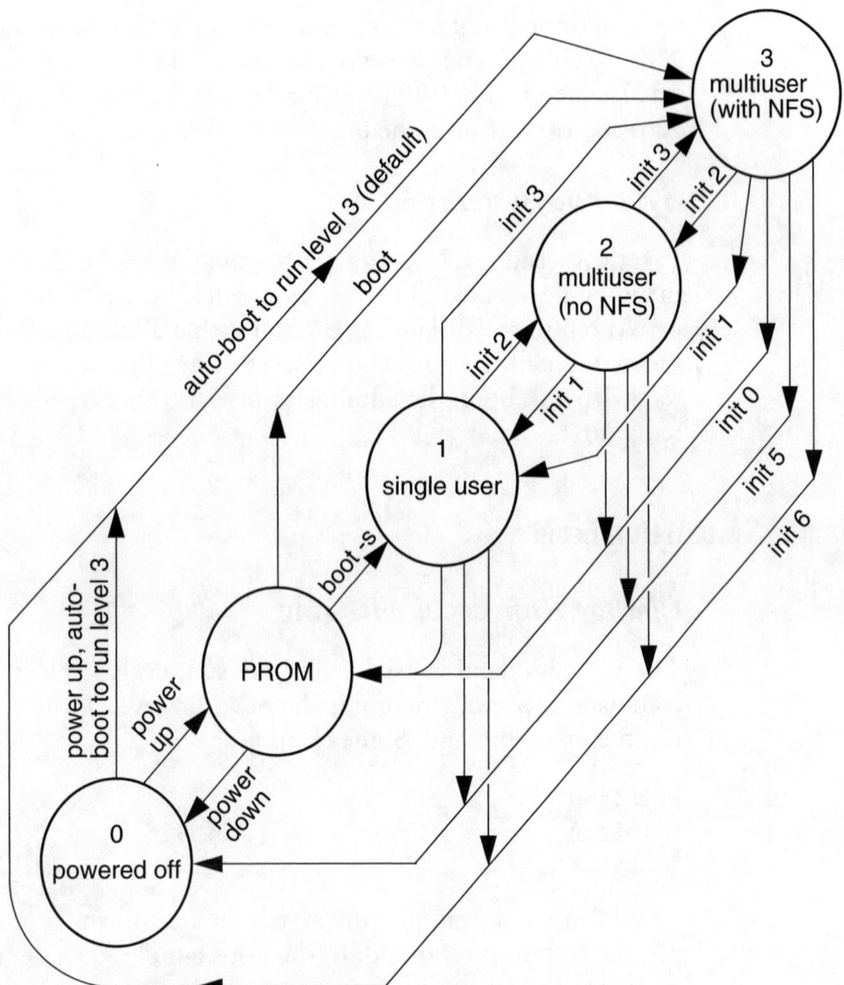

Figure 4–1 *Run Level State Transition Diagram*

Show System Run Level

The *who -r* command reveals which run level the system is currently running. An example follows.

```
# who -r
   .         run-level 3  Dec 11 04:21     3     0  S
#
```

In this example, the system is in run level 3, or multiuser mode with NFS, Web, and DHCP services running. The system entered run level 3 on December 11 at 04:21; since reboot it has been changed to run level 3 zero additional times; the previous run level was 0.

Sync File Systems

Before any run level change is attempted, it is advised that the *sync* command be performed. The *sync* command causes all unwritten buffers to be written to the disk(s). This ensures that all intended modifications to files and the file systems will be saved. The integrity of a system's file systems depends upon the administrator remembering to "sync the file systems" first.

Change System Run Level

Change Run Level with init

The *init* command is used to change run levels. The syntax for the *init* command is *init n*, where *n* is the new run level. Only the root user can run the *init* command. Some examples are:

```
# init 0
# init 6
# init s
```

In the first example, the system is shut down. In the second example, the system is rebooted. In the last example, the system is brought to single user mode.

Change Run Level with shutdown

The *shutdown* command is used like the *init* command to change system run levels. But before shutting the system down, the *shutdown* command sends warning messages to all logged-in users; this is particularly useful in situations where many people in different locations have logged in to a system, and where there are few other practical means for informing them that the system is about to be shut down.

The syntax of the shutdown command is *shutdown [options] [message]*, where *message* is a text message sent to users announcing the shutdown. The options for *shutdown* are:

- *-y.* Preanswer the confirmation question so the command can be run without user intervention.
- *-g grace-period.* Change the grace period in seconds from the 60-second default to *grace-period* seconds. This period is the delay between entering the command and *shutdown* commencing.
- *-i init-state.* If there are warnings, *init-state* specifies the state *init* is to be in. By default, system state 's' is used.

Some examples follow.

```
# shutdown

Shutdown started.    Thu Feb 22 04:31:58 PST 2001

Broadcast Message from root (pts/2) on wallace Thu Feb 22 04:31:58...
The system wallace will be shut down in 1 minute

Broadcast Message from root (pts/2) on wallace Thu Feb 22 04:32:29...
The system wallace will be shut down in 30 seconds

Do you want to continue? (y or n):  y
Broadcast Message from root (pts/2) on wallace Thu Feb 22 04:34:07...
THE SYSTEM wallace IS BEING SHUT DOWN NOW ! ! !
Log off now or risk your files being damaged

Changing to init state s - please wait
#
INIT: New run level: S
Print services stopped
Mar 22 04:34:29 wallace syslogd: going down on signal 15
Killing user processes: done.

INIT: SINGLE USER MODE:

Type control-d to proceed with normal startup,
(or give root password for system maintenance): ^D
ENTER RUN LEVEL (0-6, s or S) [3]: 3
[system startup messages omitted]

# shutdown -i0 -g0 "--- Emergency Maintenance ---"

Shutdown started.    Thu Feb 22 04:41:49 PST 2001
```

```
Do you want to continue? (y or n):   y
Broadcast Message from root (pts/2) on wallace Thu Feb 22 04:41:53...
THE SYSTEM wallace IS BEING SHUT DOWN NOW ! ! !
Log off now or risk your files being damaged
--- Emergency Maintenance ---
Changing to init state 0 - please wait
Print services stopped
Mar 22 04:41:02 wallace syslogd: going down on signal 15
The system is down.
syncing file systems… done
Program terminated
ok _
```

In the first example, the system is shut down to single-user mode with a one-minute grace period. Three standard messages are broadcast to users: the first ("`The system wallace will be shut down in 1 minute`") one minute from shutdown; the second ("`The system wallace will be shut down in 30 seconds`") 30 seconds from shutdown; and the final ("`THE SYSTEM wallace IS BEING SHUT DOWN NOW ! ! ! Log off now or risk your files being damaged`") immediately before shutdown. The system then enters run level "S," and a password prompt is displayed. In this example, the administrator then presses *Ctrl D* to resume run level 3.

In the second example, the system is being shut down to run level 0 immediately, with the special message "--- Emergency Maintenance ---" included in the messages sent to all users.

Change Run Level with reboot

The *reboot* command is essentially the same as the *init 6* command. The format of the reboot command is *reboot [options]*. The options for *reboot* are:

- *-d*. Force a system crash dump before rebooting.
- *-l*. Suppress sending a message to the system log daemon, syslogd, about who executed reboot.
- *-n*. Avoid the sync operation. Use of this option can cause file system damage.
- *-q*. Quick. Reboot quickly and ungracefully, without shutting down running processes first.
- *bootarguments*. These arguments are accepted for compatibility, and are passed unchanged to the *uadmin* function.

Some examples follow.

```
# reboot
syncing file systems... done

# reboot -- -r
syncing file systems... done
```

In the first example, the system is rebooted with reboot defaults. In the second example, the option *-r* is passed through to the boot program (this is signified by the "--" delimiter), where the *boot -r* option is used. The *boot* command is discussed later in this chapter.

Although *reboot* does by default perform a *sync* operation, system and application daemons are not gracefully shut down. Use this command only in circumstances when *shutdown* or *init 0* cannot be used.

Change Run Level with halt

The *halt* command is an emergency shutdown command, similar to *init 0*. *halt* should be used with care because it does not initiate the orderly shutdown of services or the clean dismounting of file systems. The syntax for the *halt* command is *halt [options]*. The options for *halt* are:

- *-d*. Force a system crash dump before rebooting.
- *-l*. Suppress sending a message to the system log daemon, syslogd, about who executed halt.
- *-n*. Prevent the sync before stopping.
- *-q*. Quick halt. No graceful shutdown is attempted.
- *-y*. Halt the system, even from a dialup terminal.

An example of the halt command follows.

```
# halt
syncing file systems... done
Program terminated
ok _
```

In this example, the system is immediately shut down to run level 0.

Although *halt* does by default perform a *sync* operation, system and application daemons are not gracefully shut down. Use this command only in circumstances when *shutdown* or *init 0* cannot be used.

Change Run Level with poweroff

The *poweroff* command is functionally equivalent to the *halt* command, except that power is removed from the system after it is halted. The options and usage are the same as the *halt* command.

EXAM NOTES

THINK ABOUT IT . . .

What is the best way to shut down the system?

It depends on your situation.

If you are doing routine maintenance, use the *shutdown* command with enough grace time to give users a chance to clean up and log off.

If you are on emergency power with only seconds of UPS reserve left, use the *poweroff* command. This will bring the system down quickly and remove power.

If you think the superblock is corrupted, try the *halt -n* command. This will force a halt without first syncing unwritten disk blocks (including the wrecked superblock, you hope).

Think you've finally caught that kernel bug? Use the *halt -d* command. This will force a crash dump before halting.

Are you about to run backups? Perhaps at your site you bring the system to single-user mode with *shutdown -i s* and back up your system while it's in single-user mode.

4.2 The OpenBoot *boot* Command

The *boot* command is issued at the PROM command prompt. The format of the *boot* command is *boot [OBP names] [file] [-afV] [-D default-file] [boot-flags] [--] [client-program-args]*. The options for *boot* are:

- *OBP names*. Specify the OpenBoot PROM (OBP) designations. Usually these are the device aliases such as *disk*, *net*, and *cdrom*. Unaliased device names are also allowed; for example, on Desktop SPARC–based systems, the designation */sbus/esp@0,800000/sd@3,0:a* indicates a SCSI disk (sd) at target 3, lun0 on the SCSI bus, with the esp host adapter plugged into slot 0.
- *file*. Name of a standalone program to boot. If a filename is not explicitly specified, either on the *boot* command line or in the *boot-file* NVRAM variable, *boot* chooses an appropriate default filename. On most systems, the default filename is the 32-bit Solaris kernel, */kernel/genunix*. On systems capable of supporting both the 32-bit and 64-bit kernels, the 64-bit kernel will be chosen in preference to the 32-bit kernel. *boot* chooses an appropriate default file to boot based on what software is installed on the system, the capabilities of the hardware and firmware, and on a user-configurable policy file.
- *-a*. The boot program interprets this flag to mean "ask me," and so it prompts for the name of the standalone program (in other words, the *file* specified earlier). The *-a* flag is then passed to the standalone program.
- *-V*. Display verbose debugging information.
- *-D default-file*. Explicitly specify the *default-file*. On some systems, *boot* chooses a dynamic default file, used when none is otherwise specified. This option allows the *default-file* to be explicitly set and can be useful when booting kadb (the kernel debugger) since, by default, kadb loads the *default-file* as exported by the *boot* program.
- *boot-flags*. The boot program passes all *boot-flags* to *file*. They are not interpreted by *boot*. The available *boot-flags* are:
    - *-a*. Interactively ask for configuration information, such as where to find the system file, where to mount root, and even override the name of the kernel itself. In the dialogue, default responses will be contained in square brackets ([]), and the user may simply enter RETURN to use the default response. To help repair a damaged */etc/system* file, enter */dev/null* at the prompt that asks for the pathname of the system configuration file.
    - *-r*. Reconfiguration boot. The system will probe all attached hardware devices and assign nodes in the file system to represent only those devices actually found. It will also configure

the logical namespace in */dev* as well as the physical namespace in */devices*.

- *-s*. Boot only to init level "s."
- *-v*. Boot with verbose messages enabled. If this flag is not given, the messages are still printed, but the output is directed to the system logfile.
- *-x*. Do not boot in clustered mode. This option only has an effect when a version of Sun Cluster software that supports this option has been installed.

- *client-program-args*. The *boot* program passes all *client-program-args* to *file*. They are not interpreted by *boot*.

Some examples follow.

```
ok boot net

ok boot cdrom

ok boot -r

ok boot -s

ok boot -as
Resetting ...
[some messages omitted]
Rebooting with command: boot -as
Boot device: /sbus/SUNW,fas@e,8800000/sd@0,0:a  File and args: -as
Booting the 32-bit OS ...

Enter filename [kernel/unix]: _____
Enter default directory for modules [/platform/SUNW,Ultra-1/kernel /
platform/sun4u/kernel /kernel /usr/kernel]: _____
Name of the system file [etc/system]: _____
root filesystem type [ufs]: _____
Enter physical name of boot device
[/sbus@1f,0/SUNW,fas@e,8800000/sd@0,0:a]: _____
configuring Ipv4 interfaces: hme0.
Hostname: Wallace

INIT: SINGLE USER MODE:

Type control-d to proceed with normal startup,
(or give root password for system maintenance): _

ok boot kernel/sparcv9/unix
```

In the first example, the system boots from a boot server over the network. In the second example, the system boots from a CD that is in the CD drive. In the third example, the system probes all hardware devices and rebuilds */dev* and */devices* when the system is booted. In the fourth example, the system boots into single-user mode. In the fifth example, the system is interactively booted into single-user mode (the entire dialogue is shown in the example). In the last example, the 64-bit kernel is explicitly booted.

See Chapter 3 for more information on *boot* and other PROM commands.

EXAM NOTES

THINK ABOUT IT . . .

How, in a single command line, could you reboot the system from a nondefault boot device?

Use the *reboot -- device* command. For instance, to boot from CD-ROM, enter *reboot -- cdrom*.

4.3 System Initialization

This section describes the mechanisms used to boot a system from the powered down state to multiuser mode. This description assumes that system defaults (auto-boot from PROM and boot to init level 3) have not been changed.

1. Upon powerup, the PROM displays the system identification and runs diagnostics to test the system hardware.
2. The PROM loads and runs the primary boot program, called *bootblk*. *bootblk* is used to find and load the secondary boot program located in the file system on the default boot disk.
3. *bootblk* loads the secondary *boot* program, *ufsboot*. *ufsboot* is used to load the kernel.
4. The kernel initializes and begins loading software modules. It uses *ufsboot* to read the modules off the disk until it is able to mount the root file system and read the modules itself; *ufsboot* is terminated.
5. The kernel creates the process table and starts the *init* process.

6. *init* reads its configuration file */etc/inittab* to see what to do next. In particular, the system's default run state is stored in a special entry in */etc/inittab* called the "initdefault" entry. This entry looks like the following:

   ```
   is:3:initdefault:
   ```

   In this example, the system's default run level is 3.
7. *init* starts the run control (rc) scripts, */etc/rc**. */etc/rc2* runs the scripts found in the directory */etc/rc2.d*; */etc/rc3* runs the scripts in */etc/rc3.d*. These scripts mount file systems and start all of the daemons, which perform system functions such as logging, network communications, and system services.
8. *init* starts the Service Access Controller (SAC) process, which governs access to the system's serial ports.
9. *init* starts the *ttymon* process, which displays the character-based login prompt on the system console.
10. The run control script */etc/rc2.d/S99dtlogin* displays a graphical login prompt on the system console. This overwrites the character-based login prompt described in Step 9.

The system is up and running, and ready to begin providing services.

EXAM NOTES

THINK ABOUT IT . . .

You want your system to be manually booted every step of the way by default. What changes could you make to accomplish this?

First, change the *auto-boot?* PROM configuration variable to *false* with the shell command *eeprom auto-boot?=false.* Next, change the system's default run level to S by changing the *initdefault* entry in */etc/inittab* from 3 to S. Finally, if you want to go all out, change the *boot-command* PROM configuration variable from "*boot*" to "*boot -a*" with the shell command *eeprom boot-command "boot -a"* (this last item is from Chapter 3).

4.4 System Shutdown

This section describes the mechanisms used to shut down a system from multiuser mode to powered off. This assumes that root has entered the *shutdown -y -i 5* command.

1. The *shutdown* command displays a warning message to all users, waits for 30 seconds, sends another warning message, and waits for 30 more seconds.
2. *shutdown* creates the */etc/nologin* file. This prevents anyone from being able to log on to the system.
3. *shutdown* displays one last warning, stating that the system is being brought down now.
4. *shutdown* runs the *init 5* command.
5. *init* starts the run control (rc) script */etc/rc0*. */etc/rc0* runs the scripts found in the directory */etc/rc0.d*. These scripts shut down all network services and system daemons.
6. */etc/rc0* kills all remaining processes and unmounts all file systems.
7. */etc/rc0* displays one last message stating that the system is down.
8. *init* runs the *uadmin 2 6* command.
9. *uadmin* kills all processes, flushes the buffer cache, dismounts the root file system, halts the processor, and removes system power.

   The system is now powered off.

Chapter Summary

System run levels determine the state of the system and what services are available. The *who* command is used to display the system's run level, and the *init* command is used to change it. The commands used to shut down the system are *shutdown*, *halt*, *reboot*, and *poweroff*.

The *boot* command issued from the PROM is used to boot the system from the default device or, optionally, from alternate devices such as the CD-ROM or over the network. Other boot options are *-r* (rebuild */dev* and */devices* directories if the system's hardware has been changed) and *-s* (boot to single-user mode).

The system initialization process begins when the PROM runs diagnostics and loads *bookblk*, which in turn loads *ufsboot*. *ufsboot* loads the kernel image. The kernel creates the process table and starts *init*, which upon reading */etc/inittab*—starts the run control scripts */etc/rc2* and */etc/rc3*. The *initdefault* entry in */etc/inittab* determines the system's default run level. These scripts run the shell scripts */etc/rc2.d/S** and */etc/rc3.d/S**, respectively. Finally, *init* starts the Service Access Controller and *ttymon*. The run control script */etc/rc2.d/S99dtlogin* displays a CDE login screen on the console.

The system shutdown process begins with the *shutdown* command sending out messages to all users warning of the impending shutdown. Then *shutdown* creates the */etc/nologin* file and runs the *init 5* command. The *init* process runs the */etc/rc0* run control script, which in turn runs the scripts */etc/rc0.d/K**, which shuts down all system services and daemons. All processes are killed, and all file systems are unmounted. Finally *uadmin* unmounts the root file system, halts the processor, and removes system power.

TEST YOURSELF

MULTIPLE CHOICE

1. Given the following */etc/inittab* file:

```
ap::sysinit:/sbin/autopush -f /etc/iu.ap
ap::sysinit:/sbin/soconfig -f /etc/sock2path
fs::sysinit:/sbin/rcS sysinit >/dev/msglog 2<>/dev/msglog </dev/console
is:3:initdefault:
p3:s1234:powerfail:/usr/sbin/shutdown -y -i5 -g0 >/dev/msglog 2<>/dev/
msglog
sS:s:wait:/sbin/rcS           >/dev/msglog 2<>/dev/msglog </dev/console
s0:0:wait:/sbin/rc0           >/dev/msglog 2<>/dev/msglog </dev/console
s1:1:respawn:/sbin/rc1        >/dev/msglog 2<>/dev/msglog </dev/console
s2:23:wait:/sbin/rc2          >/dev/msglog 2<>/dev/msglog </dev/console
s3:3:wait:/sbin/rc3           >/dev/msglog 2<>/dev/msglog </dev/console
s5:5:wait:/sbin/rc5           >/dev/msglog 2<>/dev/msglog </dev/console
s6:6:wait:/sbin/rc6           >/dev/msglog 2<>/dev/msglog </dev/console
fw:0:wait:/sbin/uadmin 2 0    >/dev/msglog 2<>/dev/msglog </dev/console
of:5:wait:/sbin/uadmin 2 6    >/dev/msglog 2<>/dev/msglog </dev/console
rb:6:wait:/sbin/uadmin 2 1    >/dev/msglog 2<>/dev/msglog </dev/console
sc:234:respawn:/usr/lib/saf/sac -t 300
co:234:respawn:/usr/lib/saf/ttymon -g -h -p "`uname -n` console login:
" -T sun
-d /dev/console -l console -m ldterm,ttcompat
```

What is the default run level of the system?

A. 5
B. 0
C. 3
D. S

2. Which three of the following commands will change the run level of a system? (Choose three)
   A. `init 0`
   B. `who -r`
   C. `poweroff`
   D. `reboot`
   E. `init -r`
   F. `takedown`

3. What is the purpose of the `reboot -- -s` command?
   A. Shut the system down, and interactively reboot it to single-user mode.
   B. Shut the system down, and reboot it to single-user mode.
   C. Shut the system down, and interactively reboot after reconfiguring static devices.
   D. Shut the system down, and reboot after reconfiguring static devices.

4. Your system is at the OK prompt. Which is the correct command to boot the system to run level "s"?
   A. `boot -r`
   B. `boot -s`
   C. `boot -- -r`
   D. `reboot -- -s`

5. You are rebooting your system in interactive mode (i.e., the Boot PROM command `boot -a`). Your */etc/system* configuration file is corrupted and you receive the following `boot -a` prompt:

```
Name of the system file [etc/system]:
```

   Which should you choose to boot the system?
   A. `^D`
   B. `dev/null`
   C. `/etc/system`
   D. `/dev/null`

6. What is the difference between the *halt* command and the *poweroff* command?
   A. There is no difference; they have the same syntax.
   B. The *halt* command stops the system, while the *poweroff* command powers down the system.
   C. The *halt* command syncs the file system, while the *poweroff* command does not.
   D. The *halt* command halts the CPU, while the *poweroff* only removes power.

7. You are writing a script to power the system off each night, but it is sometimes possible that a user could be on the system when the script will run. Which command would power the system down after giving the user a warning and time to log off?
   A. `shutdown -L5 -g15`
   B. `shutdown -i5 -g0`
   C. `shutdown -i5 -g15`
   D. `shutdown -i0 -t15`

8. Given:

```
# who -r
   .        run-level 3  Dec 11 04:21     3      0  S
#
```

   What is the current run level of the system?
   A. 3
   B. "."
   C. 0
   D. S

9. Given:

```
# who -r
   .          run-level 3  Dec 11 04:21     3      0  S
#
```

What is the previous run level of the system?

A. 3
B. "."
C. 0
D. S

10. You need to change your system's default run level from 3 to 2. What is the correct way to do this?

A. Change the `initdefault` entry in */etc/system* from 3 to 2.
B. Rename */etc/rc3* to */etc/rc2*.
C. Change the `initdefault` entry in */etc/inittab* from 3 to 2.
D. Rename */etc/rc3* to */etc/rc2*, after first saving a copy of */etc/rc2*.

FREE RESPONSE

11. State the command that is used to gently shut down the system and remove power.

12. What is the correct option to the *halt* command to force a crash dump before rebooting?

CHAPTER 5

User Administration

After completing this chapter, you'll be able to meet the following Solaris Administration Exam objectives:

- Identify the following login procedures: log into a system, log out of a system, and change login passwords.
- State the command used to identify which users are currently logged into the system.
- State the steps required to create user accounts on the local system using the *admintool* utility.
- State the command syntax to add, modify, or delete user/group accounts on the local system with the *useradd*, *groupadd*, *usermod*, *groupmod*, *userdel*, or *groupdel* commands.
- Given a user's login shell, list the shell initialization files used to set up a user's work environment at login.

To fulfill these objectives, this chapter discusses:

- User account configuration files;
- Adding, modifying, and deleting user accounts with Admintool;
- Adding, modifying, and deleting user accounts with shell commands;
- User shells; and
- User account commands.

5.1 Account Configuration Files

Three principal files define the identity of a user account: the password file, the shadow file, and the group file.

The Password File

The password file contains the basic identifying information for each user allowed to access a system. The system location of the password file is */etc/passwd*. The format of the password file is:

```
username:password:uid:gid:gcos-field:home-dir:login-shell
```

These fields are:

- username—the name that identifies the user account.
- password—in Solaris 8 an "x" in this field signifies that the corresponding shadow file contains the encrypted password string.
- uid—the unique numerical ID assigned to the account. The maximum value for UID is 2147483647, but administrators are urged to use values less than 60,000 to ensure compatibility with all of the tools that are used to manage accounts or display information that includes usernames.
- gid—the primary (default) numerical group ID assigned to the account. Like the UID field, the maximum value for GID is 2147483647, but a maximum of 60,000 is preferable.
- gcos-field—this is the user's real name (the term "gcos-field" is the historical term for this field).
- home-dir—the directory where the user is placed after logging in; this usually contains the user's own files and directories.

- login-shell—the initial shell that is started on behalf of the user upon logging in. If this field is blank, then */usr/bin/sh* is used.

The password file can be read by anyone on the system. There is no information that must be kept secret in this file. A sample password file looks like this:

```
root:x:0:1:Super-User:/:/sbin/sh
daemon:x:1:1::/:
bin:x:2:2::/usr/bin:
sys:x:3:3::/:
adm:x:4:4:Admin:/var/adm:
lp:x:71:8:Line Printer Admin:/usr/spool/lp:
uucp:x:5:5:uucp Admin:/usr/lib/uucp:
nuucp:x:9:9:uucp Admin:/var/spool/uucppublic:/usr/lib/uucp/uucico
listen:x:37:4:Network Admin:/usr/net/nls:
pete:x:100:4:Peter Gregory:/export/home/pete:/bin/sh
nobody:x:60001:60001:Nobody:/:
```

Fields in the password file are delimited by colons (":"), and blank fields are signified by two adjacent colons ("::"). For instance, note that the account name field for *daemon* is blank—just two colons. Also, daemon has no shell entry, so the last character for daemon is the colon delimiter.

The colon delimiter is also used in the shadow and group files, which are discussed in a later section.

It is possible and permissible to create more than one username in the password file with the same UID. Each username will have its own unique password. However, tools such as *ls* and *ps*, when used with options displaying username, will display the first username found in the password file matching the UID.

When a new account is added, changed, or removed with the *useradd*, *usermod*, or *userdel* commands (which are discussed later in this chapter), the system creates a backup copy of the password file, called */etc/opasswd*.

The Shadow File

The shadow file contains each user account's encrypted password, as well as specific per-account parameters governing "password aging." The system location of the shadow file is */etc/shadow*. The format of the shadow file is:

```
username:password:lastchg:min:max:warn:inactive:expire:flag
```

These fields are:

- username—this is the same username found in the password file.
- password—a 13-character encrypted password. If this field contains a lock string (e.g., "locked" or "NP"), the account is inaccessible; if blank, the account has no password.
- lastchg—date of last password change (literally the number of days between January 1, 1970, and the date the password was last changed).
- min—minimum number of days allowed before the password can be changed.
- max—maximum number of days allowed before the password expires.
- warn—the number of days prior to expiration that the user is warned.
- inactive—the number of days of inactivity allowed for the account before the account is automatically locked.
- expire—the date when the user account is deactivated.
- flag—a field reserved for future use.

The shadow file is restricted so that only the system administrator can read it. This is because an intruder could perform a "dictionary attack," using guessable passwords in an attempt to determine the passwords for one or more accounts. Programs that "crack" account passwords are available for this purpose; thus, the shadow file is not publicly readable.

A sample shadow file looks like this:

```
root:Pe0iQfp2LcAig:10528::::::
daemon:NP:6445::::::
bin:NP:6445::::::
sys:NP:6445::::::
adm:nIP3GPx2FIZYQ:11053::::::
lp:NP:6445::::::
uucp:NP:6445::::::
nuucp:NP:6445::::::
listen:*LK*:::::::
pete:GSSUYVrJ8EKyA:11055::::::
nobody:NP:6445::::::
```

Note that some of the accounts in the example shadow file have "NP" ("no password") or "*LK*" (locked) in them. These are just two ways of signifying that the accounts are locked against login. There is nothing really magic about "NP" or "*LK*"—they are just one way of easily showing that these accounts are locked and going to stay that way. You could put other text in the password field to suit your needs; for instance, a helpdesk ticket number or a date.

When a user changes his or her password, the system creates a backup copy of the shadow file, called */etc/oshadow*. This also occurs if root changes a user's password.

EXAM NOTES

THINK ABOUT IT . . .

Why are encrypted passwords found in */etc/shadow* and not in */etc/passwd?*

For many commands (*ps, ls,* etc.) to work properly, */etc/passwd* must be world readable. Prior to the use of */etc/shadow,* all users' encrypted password strings were also publicly readable. This gave people with "password cracking" programs an opportunity to discover other users' passwords. By moving the encrypted password strings to */etc/shadow* (which can be read only by root), the ability to access encrypted passwords is eliminated.

First, a bit of history. Older versions of UNIX did not have a shadow file; instead, the encrypted password string was found in the password file, in the second field that is usually filled with an "x" in Solaris. Solaris still supports the encrypted password appearing in the password file, although this is not advisable, since the password file is publicly readable.

Older versions of UNIX with no shadow file also had no password-aging capability.

The Network Information System (NIS) subsystem was designed around the old shadow-less architecture; this explains why NIS has no shadow map, nor does it support password aging.

The Group File

The group file contains a listing of all of the groups on the system, along with each group's numeric groupid and a list of each of the usernames that are secondary members of each group. The location of the group file is */etc/group*. The format of the group file is:

```
groupname:password:gid:user-list
```

These fields are:

- groupname—this is the name of the group.
- password—this is an optional password for the group.
- gid—the unique numerical ID assigned to the group. The maximum value for GID is 2147483647, but administrators are urged to use values less than 60,000 to ensure compatibility with all of the tools that are used to manage accounts or display information that includes group names.
- user-list—a comma-separated list of users allowed in the group. These groups are users' secondary group IDs.

A sample group file follows.

```
root::0:root
other::1:
bin::2:root,bin,daemon
sys::3:root,bin,sys,adm
adm::4:root,adm,daemon
uucp::5:root,uucp
mail::6:root
tty::7:root,tty,adm
lp::8:root,lp,adm
nuucp::9:root,nuucp
staff:GSSUYVrJ8EKyA:10:pete
daemon::12:root,daemon
sysadmin::14:
nobody::60001:
noaccess::60002:
nogroup::65534:
```

Note the password field in the group "staff." Groups can be password protected by putting a password string into the password field.

Note, though, that this is a *completely* manual process; there are no tools provided to put the group password in for you.

Hint: You can take a password string from the shadow file and use the vi editor to splice it into the group file. The group password will be the same as the account password from the shadow entry where you took the password string.

When a group is password protected, anyone who is *not* a member of the group will be challenged for the group's password when they have entered the *newgrp* command.

Primary and Secondary Groupids

Each user account has one *primary* groupid—this is the group defined in the password file. When a user logs on, this is his or her associated groupid.

Each user account also has zero or more secondary groupids. A user's secondary groups are those group entries that include the username in their lists of members.

There are some useful limitations of groupids. For example, each user account can be in no more than 16 groups, and a line in the group file cannot exceed 512 characters (including the newline character).

What happens if you need to add so many members to a group that you exceed the 512-character entry limit? You simply create another duplicate group entry—same name and group number—and list the additional members there.

The primary and secondary groupids directly impact file system access permissions, which is explored fully in Chapter 10.

EXAM NOTES

THINK ABOUT IT . . .

What would be the effect if a username were added to a group file entry when that group was the user's primary group?

The additional entry would have no effect, since the user is already configured for the primary group membership in the */etc/passwd* file.

The Root Account

The root account has special privileges on a system: Root is permitted to read and write every file on a system, regardless of the file's ownership and permission settings. System administrators log in with the root account so that they can perform administrative tasks.

The root account gets its power and privilege from the value of its user number: Root is user number zero, defined in the password file.

EXAM NOTES

THINK ABOUT IT . . .

What would be the effects of changing an ordinary user's user number to zero? What advantage might there be of putting root's entry at the end of the passwd file (instead of the beginning)?

Changing an ordinary user's user number to zero gives the user root privileges.

One advantage of putting root at the end of the password file is that if an intruder is able to modify the password file to give another user root privilege (see the first question here), then output from commands such as *ls* and *ps* would show that other user as the owner of root processes and files.

5.2 Admintool

Admintool is the primary user account maintenance program. It is used by system administrators to create, modify, and remove user accounts.

The system administrator must log in as root to use Admintool. To start Admintool, type *admintool&* at a shell prompt. The Admintool program appears as shown in Figure 5-1.

This initial view shows the system's existing user accounts. Select the Browse menu to manage groups. Figure 5-2 shows a sample Browse menu.

Add User Account

To add a user, select the *Edit* menu, then *Add*. Fill in the userid in the *User Name* field, the user's name in the *Comment* field, and the home directory in the *Path* field. If the user is to belong to any other groups, add the

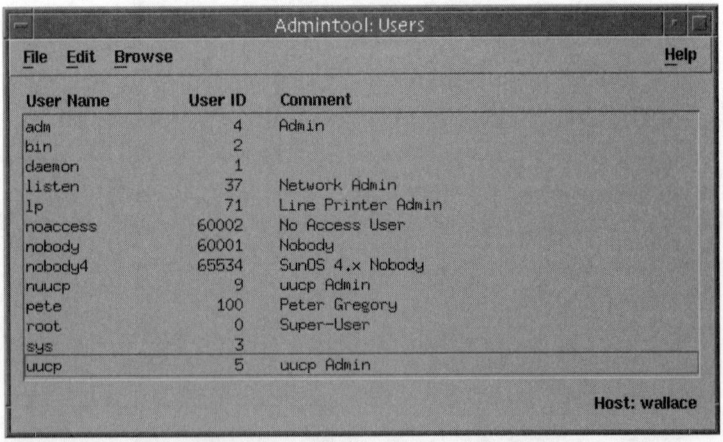

Figure 5–1 *Admintool*

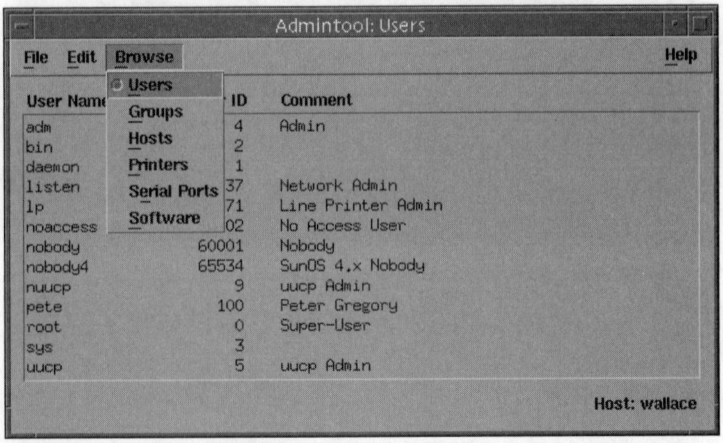

Figure 5–2 *Admintool Browse Menu*

group numbers in the *Secondary Groups* field. If you wish to impose password aging parameters, specify them in the *Min Change*, *Max Change*, *Max Inactive*, *Expiration Date*, and *Warning* fields. An example Add User screen is shown in Figure 5-3. Click OK or Apply to add the user.

Modify User Account

To modify a user account, select a user account in the main window by clicking on it. Then select the *Edit* menu, then *Modify*. An example *Modify User* screen appears in Figure 5-4.

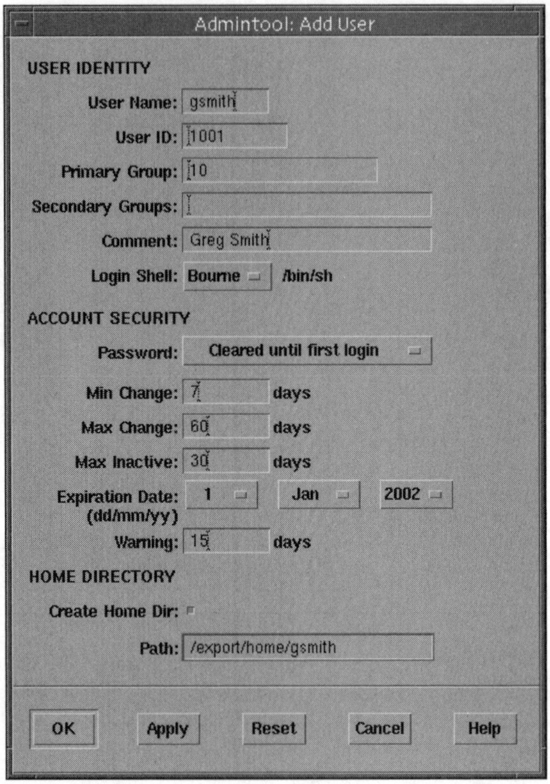

Figure 5–3 *Admintool Add User*

Lock User Account

Admintool can be used to lock a user account. This might be a useful alternative to removing an account (or changing its password) if you need to temporarily block access to the account. To lock a user account, modify it as you normally would, then in the *Password* pull-down, select *Account is Locked*. An example is shown in Figure 5-5.

Delete User Account

Admintool is also used to delete user accounts. To delete a user account, select a user account in the main window. Then select the *Edit* menu, then *Delete*. See Figure 5-6 for an example.

Figure 5–4 *Admintool Modify User*

Removing a user account destroys the record of its existence. The listed username for any files or directories that were owned by the user account will reflect the numeric user number of the prior owner. It is recommended that, instead of removing a user account, you lock it and add the word "Terminated" to the user's name field.

Add Group

Adding groups with Admintool is as straightforward as adding users. To add groups using *Admintool*, select the *Browse* menu, then *Groups*. The list of groups on the system then appears. See Figure 5-7 for an example.

To add a group, select the *Edit* menu, then *Add*. Type in the number and name of the new group, then press *OK*. An example is shown in Figure 5-8.

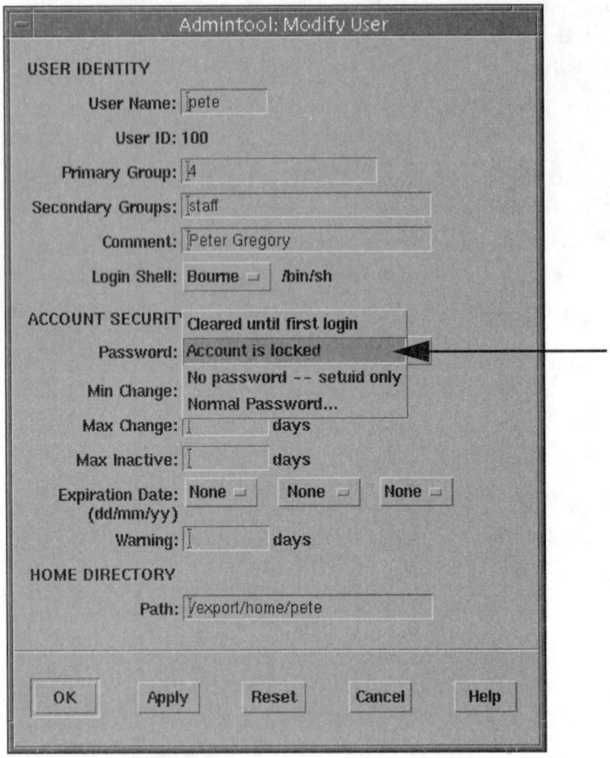

Figure 5–5 *Admintool Lock User*

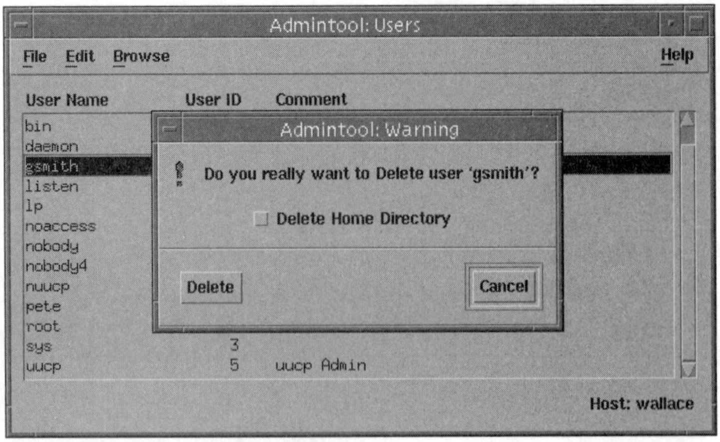

Figure 5–6 *Admintool Delete User*

Admintool: Groups

File Edit Browse Help

Group Name	Group ID	Members
adm	4	root,adm,daemon
bin	2	root,bin,daemon
daemon	12	root,daemon
lp	8	root,lp,adm
mail	6	root
noaccess	60002	
nobody	60001	
nogroup	65534	
nuucp	9	root,nuucp
other	1	
root	0	root
staff	10	pete
sys	3	root,bin,sys,adm

Host: wallace

Figure 5–7 *Admintool Groups*

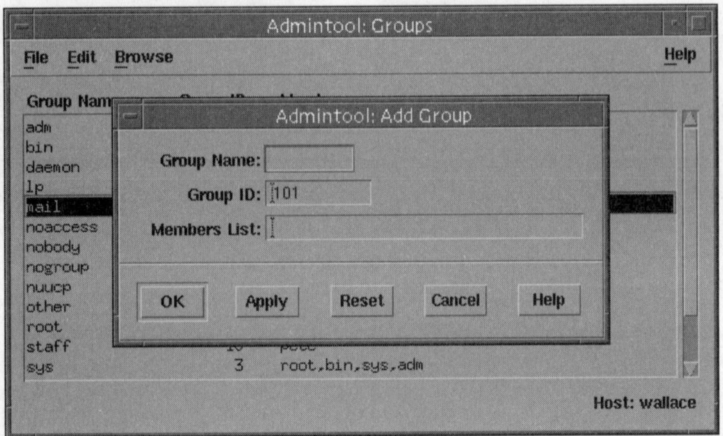

Figure 5–8 *Admintool Add Group*

Modify Group

Use the *Edit*, *Modify* group menu items to change the name or members of a group. Group members are listed by name, separated by commas. An example is shown in Figure 5-9.

Delete Group

Admintool is also used to delete groups. See Figure 5-10 for an example. To delete a group, select a group in the main window by clicking on it. Then select the *Edit* menu, then *Delete*.

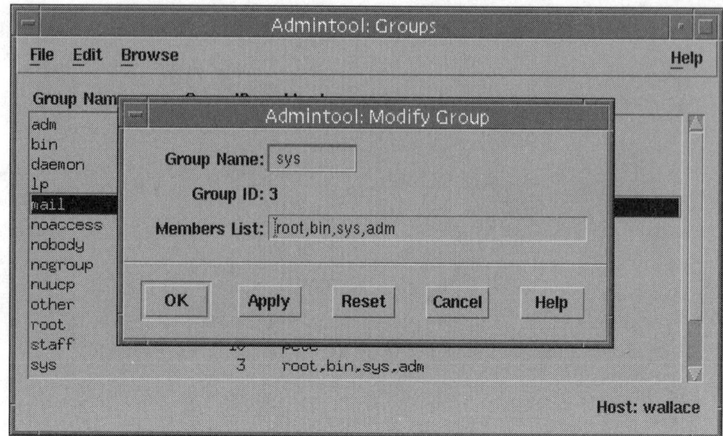

Figure 5–9 *Admintool Modify Group*

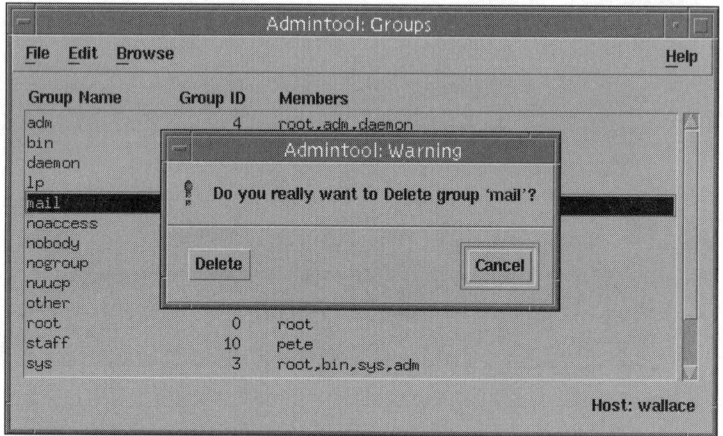

Figure 5–10 *Admintool Delete Group*

Removing a group destroys the record of its existence. The listed group name for any files or directories that were owned by the group account will reflect the numeric group of the prior owner. It is recommended that, instead of removing a group, you instead remove all users from its membership list and add the letters "LK" (short for "Locked") in the group's name field.

5.3 User Administration Shell Commands

In addition to the Admintool GUI program, there are also several shell commands that can be used to administer user and group accounts. The commands are *useradd*, *usermod*, *groupadd*, and *groupmod*.

These commands let you administer user and group accounts. Let's explore each of these in greater detail.

useradd Command

The *useradd* command is used to add a user account to the system. The syntax of the *useradd* command is *useradd [options] userid* where *options* is one or more *useradd* options, and *userid* is the name of an account to create. With no options specified, *useradd* will create an account with *useradd* defaults.

A second form of the command is *useradd –D [options]*. This form lets you view and, optionally, modify defaults.

The options for *useradd* are:

- *-A authorization*. One or more comma-separated authorizations defined in the */etc/security/auth_attrauth_attr* file. Only a user or role who has *grant* rights to the authorization can assign it to an account.
- *-b base_dir*. The default directory for the system if *-d dir* is not specified. *base_dir* is concatenated with the userid to define the user's home directory. If the *-m* option is not used, *base_dir* must exist. For example, *base_dir* would typically be something like */export/home*. If the account *jeffg* were being created, then the user's home directory would be */export/home/jeffg*.
- *-c comment*. This is generally a short description of the user account, and is currently used as the field for the user's full name. This information is stored in the user's */etc/passwd* comment (name) field.
- *-d dir*. The home directory. The default is *base_dir/account_name*, where *base_dir* is the directory for new login home directories, and *account_name* is the new login name.
- *-D*. Display the default values for *group*, *base_dir*, *skel_dir*, *shell*, *inactive*, and *expire*. When used with the *-g*, *-b*, *-f*, *-e*, *-A*, *-P*, or *-R* options, the *-D* option sets the default values for the specified fields. When used with no other options, the *–D* option displays all current defaults. The defaults are:

group=other (GID of 1)
base_dir=/home
skel_dir=/etc/skel
shell=/bin/sh
inactive=0
expire=Null
auths=Null
profiles=Null
roles=Null

- *-e expire*. Set the expiration date for the userid. The user cannot log in after this date. The *expire* option argument is a date entered using one of the date formats included in the template file */etc/datemsk*. Permissible formats include "10/5/2001" and "October 5, 2001" (dates including spaces must be quoted). A null value ("") defeats the status of the expired date. The *-e* option is useful for creating temporary logins.
- *-f inactive*. The maximum number of days allowed between uses of a login ID before that ID is declared invalid. Normal values are positive integers. A value of 0 defeats the status.
- *-g group*. An existing group's integer ID or character-string name. Without the *-D* option, it defines the new user's *primary* group membership and defaults to the default group. You can reset this default value by invoking *useradd -D -g group*.
- *-G group*. An existing group's numeric or character-string name. It defines the new user's *supplementary* group membership. Duplicates between group with the *-g* and *-G* options are ignored. No more than NGROUPS_MAX (a value defined in */usr/include/limits.h*, usually 16) groups can be specified. Multiple group names or numbers are separated by commas.
- *-k skel_dir*. A directory that contains skeleton information (such as *.profile*) that can be copied into a new user's home directory. This directory must already exist. The system provides the */etc/skel* directory that can be used for this purpose. Files such as .profile that are found in *skel_dir* will be copied into the user's home directory when the account is created.
- *-m*. Create the new user's home directory if it does not already exist. If the directory already exists, it must have read, write, and execute permissions by *group*, where *group* is the user's primary group.

- *-o*. This option allows a UID to be duplicated (nonunique). This will create an additional account with the same numeric UID as one that already exists. Normally, an error message will be generated advising that the new account cannot be created because of the duplicate.
- *-P profile*. One or more comma-separated execution profiles defined in the */etc/security/prof_attr* profiles configuration file.
- *-R role*. One or more comma-separated execution profiles defined in the */etc/user_attr* profiles configuration file. Roles cannot be assigned to other roles.
- *-s shell*. Full pathname of the program used as the user's shell. Its default is an empty field, causing the system to use */bin/sh*. The value of shell must be a valid executable file. Setting the shell to */bin/echo* will effectively prohibit the user from being able to log in to the account.
- *-u uid*. The numeric UID of the new user. This UID must be a non-negative decimal integer below MAXUID as defined in <sys/param.h>. The UID defaults to the next available (unique) number above the highest number currently assigned. For example, if UID's 100, 105, and 200 are assigned, the next default UID number will be 201. (UIDs from 0–99 are reserved for possible use in future applications.)

Some examples of *useradd* are shown here.

```
# useradd -D
group=other,1  basedir=/home  skel=/etc/skel
shell=/bin/sh  inactive=0  expire=  auths=
profiles=  roles=
#

# useradd -D -b /d1/export/home
#

# useradd jeffg
#

# useradd -s /bin/csh -u 14002 -c "Paul Graham" paulg
#
```

In the first example, *useradd –D* is used to display defaults. In the second example, the default home directory base directory has been changed to */d1/export/home*. In the third example, username *jeffg* has been created with all defaults. In the fourth example, the username *paulg* has been created; this user has the nondefault shell */bin/sh*, will be assigned UID 14002 (unless it exists already), and the string "Paul Graham" will appear in the account's comment field in */etc/passwd*.

EXAM NOTES

THINK ABOUT IT . . .

You import many files onto your system (perhaps from another system's backup tape); these files are owned by a nonexistent user, and you decide that it is easier to create a new userid associated with the files than to change the ownership of the files. How would this be done?

This is solved by creating a userid with a specific UID. For example,

```
# useradd engrtools -u 10082 -c "Engineering Tools"
#
```

EXAM NOTES

THINK ABOUT IT . . .

Your site adds its user accounts with *useradd* as part of a larger automated process. Different classes of users require different environments and, consequently, different initialization files (i.e., *.profile*, *.login*, etc.). How could you handle this easily with *useradd*?

You could create different "skeleton" directories, similar to the default */etc/skel*. Each of these skeleton directories would contain *.profile*, *.login.*, *.cshrc* (and others as applicable) files, each tailored for the specific class of user. Then, the *-k* option in *useradd* would be chosen as appropriate for each user added.

usermod Command

The *usermod* command is used to modify the account settings for existing userids on the system. The syntax of the *usermod* command is *usermod [options] userid*, where *options* is one or more *usermod* options, and *userid* is the name of an account to modify.

The options for *usermod* are:

- *-A authorization*. One or more comma-separated authorizations as defined in the */etc/security/auth_attr* file. Only a user or role who has grant rights to the authorization can assign it to an account. This replaces any existing authorization setting.
- *-c comment*. Specifies a comment string. *comment* can be any text string, generally a short description of the login, and is currently used as the field for the user's full name. This information is stored in the user's */etc/passwd* entry.
- *-d dir*. The new home directory of the user. It defaults to *base_dir/login*, where *base_dir* is the base directory for new login home directories, and *login* is the account name.
- *-e expire*. Specifies the expiration date for a login. After this date, no user will be able to access this login. The expire option argument is a date entered using one of the date formats included in the template file */etc/datemsk*. Permissible formats include "10/5/2001" and "October 5, 2001" (dates including spaces must be quoted). A null value ("") defeats the status of the expired date. The *-e* option is useful for creating temporary logins.
- *-f inactive*. Specifies the maximum number of days allowed between uses of a login ID before that login ID is declared invalid. Normal values are positive integers. A value of 0 defeats the status.
- *-g group*. Assigns an existing group's numeric or character name. It redefines the user's *primary* group membership.
- *-G grouplist*. Specifies an existing group's integer number or character string name. This redefines the user's *supplementary* group membership. Duplicates between group with the *-g* and *-G* options are ignored. No more than NGROUPS_UMAX groups may be specified as defined in */usr/include/param.h*. Multiple group names or numbers are separated by commas.
- *-l new_logname*. Specifies the new login name for the user. The *new_logname* argument must be a string no more than eight characters consisting of characters from the set of alphabetic characters, numeric characters, period (.), underline (_), and hyphen (-). The first character should be alphabetic and the field should contain at least one lowercase alphabetic character. A warning message will be written if these rules are not met. The *new_logname* argument must contain at least one character and must not contain a colon (:) or newline (\n).

- *-m*. Moves the user's home directory to the new directory specified with the *-d* option. If the directory already exists, it must have permission to read/write/execute by group, where group is the user's primary group.
- *-o*. This option allows a UID to be duplicated (nonunique). This will create an additional account with the same numeric UID as one that already exists. Normally, an error message will be generated advising that the account cannot be accessed because of the duplicate.
- *-P profile*. One or more comma-separated execution profiles defined in */etc/security/auth_attr*. This replaces any existing profile setting.
- *-R role*. One or more comma-separated execution profiles defined in the */etc/user_attr* profiles configuration file. Roles cannot be assigned to other roles.
- *-s shell*. Full pathname of the program used as the user's shell. It defaults to an empty field causing the system to use */bin/sh* as the default. The value of shell must be a valid executable file.
- *-u uid*. Specifies a new UID for the user. It must be a non-negative decimal integer less than MAXUID as defined in */usr/include/param.h*. The UID associated with the user's home directory is not modified with this option; a user may not have access to his or her home directory until the UID is manually reassigned using the *chown* command.

Some examples of *usermod* are shown here.

```
# usermod -s /bin/tcsh hamidf
#

# usermod -l shammer sgilbery
#

# usermod -G admins,backups jeffg
#
```

In the first example, the shell for userid *hamidf* is changed to */bin/tcsh*. In the second example, the userid is changed from *sgilbery* to *shammer*. In the last example, the user *jeffg* is added to the secondary groups *admins* and *backups*.

EXAM NOTES

THINK ABOUT IT . . .

What command would you use to change a user's home directory? Would any follow-up tasks be necessary?

Use the *usermod -m* command to change a user's home directory. You will also have to move the contents of the user's home directory to the new location and check to make sure that the permissions of the new home directory are correct.

EXAM NOTES

THINK ABOUT IT . . .

A group of people shares the same UID and account (they have different passwords since their usernames are different), and they work on files in the same home directory. One person in the group is given an additional role of occasionally working on confidential materials that the others in the group are not allowed to access. What change could be made to allow this person to continue working on the pool of files, but at the same time prevent others in the group from viewing the confidential files?

One way to solve this is to change the one person's UID to a new number, and change his or her groupid, but then to add those IDs to the group shared by the others. The command is:

```
# usermod -u 102 -g conf -G pool pbrown
#
```

In this example, the user's name is pbrown. Pbrown is given a new UID (102), a new group name (conf), and is added as a secondary member to the group *pool*.

userdel Command

The *userdel* command is used to remove a userid from the system. The syntax for *userdel* is *userdel [-r] userid*, where *userid* is the name of an account to be removed. The *–r* option, if specified, will remove the user's home directory from the system.

groupadd Command

The *groupadd* command is used to add groups to the system. The syntax for the *groupadd* command is *groupadd [options] groupid*, where *options* is one or more *groupadd* options, and *groupid* is the name of a group to add.

The options for *groupadd* are:

- *-g gid*. Assigns the group number for the new group. This groupid must be a non-negative decimal integer below MAXUID as defined in */usr/include/sys/param.h*. The groupid defaults to the next available (unique) number above the highest number currently assigned. For example, if groups 100, 105, and 200 are assigned as groups, the next default group number will be 201. Groupids from 0–99 are reserved by Solaris for future applications.
- *-o*. Permits duplicate group number.

Some examples of *groupadd* are:

```
# groupadd admins
#

# groupadd -g 300 backupadmins
#
```

In the first example, the group *admins* is created. In the second example, the group *backupadmins* is created as group number 300.

Exam Notes

Think About It . . .

After a disaster, you recover files from tape. Many files, however, are recovered with their old groupids. People cannot access these files because the groupid's have changed. You decide that it is easier to create a new group corresponding to the groupid on the recovered files than it would be to change the groupid of all of the recovered files. How would this be done?

Create a new group with *groupadd,* specifying the desired groupid. Then, add the required users to the new group with *usermod -G*. For example:

```
# groupadd -g 108 dbadmins
# usermod -G dbadmins paul
```

```
# usermod -G dbadmins mbowman
# usermod -G dbadmins sghani
#
```

groupmod Command

The *groupmod* command is used to modify existing groups. The syntax for *groupmod* is *groupmod [options] groupid*, where *options* is one or more *groupmod* options, and *groupid* is the name of a group to modify.

The options for *groupmod* are:

- *-ggid*. Specify the new numeric groupid for the group. This groupid must be a non-negative decimal integer less than MAX-UID, as defined in */usr/include/sys/param.h*.
- *-o*. Allow the GID to be duplicated (nonunique).
- *-nname*. Specify the new name for the group. The name argument is a string of no more than eight bytes consisting of characters from the set of lowercase alphabetic characters and numeric characters. A warning message will be written if these rules are not met. The *name* argument must contain at least one character and must not include a colon (:) or newline (\n).

Some *groupmod* examples are shown here.

```
# groupmod -nsysadmins admins
#

# groupmod -g201 admins
#
```

In the first example, the group *admins* is renamed to *sysadmins*. In the second example, the group number for the group *admins* is changed to 201.

EXAM NOTES

THINK ABOUT IT . . .

You have upgraded an application that now expects its primary groupid to be a different value. The impact of changing the groupids on all of the associated files would be too great; instead, you want to change the number of the existing group. How would you do this?

Use the *groupmod –g* command to change the group number of an existing group. For example:

```
# groupmod -g420 finance
#
```

groupdel Command

The *groupdel* command is used to remove a group from the system. The syntax for *groupdel* is *groupdel group*, where *group* is the existing group name to be deleted. An example is shown here.

```
# groupdel admins
#
```

In this example, the group admins is removed from the system.

EXAM NOTES

THINK ABOUT IT . . .

What are some of the advantages of using the *user* and *group* commands rather than Admintool?

You have more control with the *user* and *group* commands than with *Admintool*. Further, the *user* and *group* commands can be made part of shell scripts or custom programs, which can help to automate the process of adding, changing, and removing users. Also, repetitive changes can be put into a script (e.g., if the path to everyone's home directory has changed, then it would be easy to write a shell script to modify everyone's account very quickly; this would be very time consuming using *Admintool*).

5.4 Shells

A shell is a system-supplied, character-oriented program that accepts commands and displays the results of those commands.

The commonly used shells included with Solaris are the Bourne Shell (called "sh"), the C-Shell (called "csh"), and the Korn Shell (called "ksh"). Table 5.1 compares the features of each shell.

Table 5.1 *Shell Features Comparison*

FEATURE	BOURNE SHELL	C-SHELL	KORN SHELL
Aliases	Yes	Yes	Yes
Command-line completion	No	Yes	Yes
Command history	No	Yes	Yes
Environment variables	Yes	Yes	Yes
Job control	Yes	Yes	Yes
Systemwide login initialization file	/etc/profile	/etc/login	/etc/profile
User login initialization file	.profile	.login	.kshrc
Shell execution initialization file	.profile	.cshrc	.profile
Initialization file order at login	1. .dtprofile in home dir (if using CDE) 2. /etc/profile≈ 3. .profile in home dir	1. .dtprofile in home dir (if using CDE) 2. /etc/.login 3. .cshrc in home dir 4. .login in home dir	1. .dtprofile in home dir (if using CDE) 2. /etc/profile 3. .profile in home dir 4. .kshrc in home dir
User logout file	(none)	.logout	(none)

Bourne Shell

The Bourne Shell is the default shell in the Solaris environment. Like the other shells, the Bourne Shell has a scripting language capability; its scripting language is probably the most popular in the UNIX world. It has no command history or command-line completion capabilities.

Initialization Files

The global initialization file, */etc/profile*, is used to set environment variables for all Bourne Shell users. When a Bourne Shell user logs in, the user's shell executes */etc/profile* first. Then, the user's own initialization file, *.profile*, is executed. The *.profile* file is located in the user's home directory.

The order of execution of Bourne Shell initialization files is:

1. *.dtprofile* in home directory (if user logs into a console using CDE)
2. */etc/profile*
3. *.profile* in home directory

Environment Variables

Environment variables in Bourne Shell are defined using the *VARIABLE=value; export VARIABLE* syntax; an example follows:

```
$ TERM=xterm; export TERM
$
```

Aliases

The Bourne Shell user can predefine a command alias. An example alias follows.

```
rm () { /usr/bin/rm -i $* }
```

In this example, the *rm* command is aliased so that the *-i* option (manually verify the removal of each file) is used.

C-Shell

The C-Shell has a somewhat richer feature set than the Bourne Shell, specifically in that it has command history and command-line editing capabilities. Although C-Shell has its own scripting language, its syntax is quite different from the Bourne and Korn Shells, and is consequently less popular.

Initialization Files

The global C-Shell initialization file, */etc/.login*, defines environment variables for all C-Shell users on a system.

There are two user initialization files, *.cshrc* and *.login*. When a user logs in, both *.cshrc* and *.login* are executed. If, after logging in, the user starts another C-Shell, then just *.cshrc* is executed.

The order of execution of C Shell initialization files is:

1. *.dtprofile* in home directory (if user logs into a console using CDE)
2. */etc/.login*
3. *.cshrc* in home directory
4. *.login* in home directory

When the C-Shell user logs out, the *.logout* file in the user's home directory is executed.

The user files *.cshrc*, *.login*, and *.logout* are all located in the user's home directory.

Environment Variables

C-Shell environment variables are set using the *setenv VARIABLE value* syntax; an example follows.

```
% setenv TERM xterm
%
```

Aliases

C-Shell aliases are defined using the *alias* command. An example follows.

```
% alias rm "/usr/bin/rm -i \!*"
%
```

In this example, the *–i* option is always added whenever using the *rm* command.

Command History

The interactive C-Shell has a command history capability. The *history* command can be used to later recall these commands, and even to re-execute them without having to type them in again.

The history capability is deactivated by default; to permanently enable command history, put the *set history* command in your *.login* file.

Filename Completion

To use filename completion, the C-Shell variable *filec* must be set. To permanently enable filename completion, put the command *set filec* in your *.login* file.

Korn Shell

The Korn Shell is a superset of the Bourne Shell; that is, the Korn Shell has all of the Bourne Shell's features plus some of the built-in functions that the C-Shell is known for, including command-line completion and command history.

Initialization Files

The global initialization file, */etc/profile*, is used to set environment variables for all Korn Shell users. When a Korn Shell user logs in, the user's shell executes */etc/profile*. Next, the user's initialization file, *.profile*, is executed.

Many Korn Shell users also use a *.kshrc* file for Korn Shell–specific initialization commands. This capability exists so that Korn Shell users can use the Bourne Shell as needed. Login initialization for either Korn Shell or Bourne Shell can be placed in *.profile*, and Korn Shell–only commands placed in *.kshrc*.

To use *.kshrc*, the environment variable *ENV* must be set in the user's *.profile* (or in */etc/profile*) as follows:

```
ENV=$HOME/.kshrc;export ENV
```

The user files *.profile* and *.kshrc* are located in the user's home directory.

The order of execution of Korn Shell initialization files is:

1. *.dtprofile* in home directory (if user logs into a console using CDE)
2. */etc/profile*
3. *.profile* in home directory
4. *.kshrc* in home directory

Environment Variables

Korn Shell environment variables are set using the same syntax as that of the Bourne Shell: *VARIABLE=value; export VARIABLE*; an example follows.

```
$ TERM=xterm; export TERM
```

Aliases

Aliases are created using the *alias name=command* syntax. Our earlier example *rm alias* seen in the Bourne and C-Shells would be defined as follows:

```
alias rm="/usr/bin/rm -i $*"
```

The Korn Shell also supports Bourne Shell's function syntax.

Command-Line Editing

The Korn Shell uses a vi-like editing syntax that allows you to edit your command line while entering it. When you start entering a command, you are automatically placed in the vi "input mode." To enter command mode while on the command line, press ESC. You can then move about the command line using vi-like movement commands (left/right arrow, or the H or L keys), and enter input mode again by pressing ESC. If in command mode you press "v," the Korn Shell will start an actual vi session and give you full vi editing capabilities over your command line.

Command History

The Korn Shell keeps its command history in the file *.sh_history*, or in a different file as defined by the environment variable $HISTFILE. Up to 128 commands are stored there, unless the environment variable $HISTSIZE is set to a different value. The file .sh_history is assumed to be in the user's home directory.

Restricted Shells

A restricted shell is a shell with very limited capabilities that generally includes these features:

- the *cd* (change directory) command is disallowed;
- the $PATH environment variable cannot be changed;
- commands containing pathnames beginning with "/" are disallowed; and
- output cannot be redirected to a file (the use of > and >> in a command line is disallowed).

Restricted shells are available for circumstances that require a user to have a shell, but where the user's actions need to be more tightly controlled.

Two restricted shells are available: the restricted Bourne Shell and the restricted Korn Shell. The pathnames for these are */usr/bin/rksh* and */usr/lib/rsh*, respectively.

The restricted shell (*/usr/lib/rsh*) and the remote shell (*/usr/bin/rsh*) are easily confused. Because both */usr/lib/rsh* and */usr/bin/rsh* are shells, substituting one for the other may give you functional results, although not the results you intended.

5.5 User Account Commands

Let's explore some common account-oriented commands and functions that users can perform.

Finding Files by Username or Group

This section describes a few ways to find files on a system belonging to a specific user or group.

The *-l* option of the *ls* command shows the username and group name associated with files and directories. When *ls* shows the numeric value for a username or group, this is an indication that the username or group has been removed from the system. The *-n* option of the *ls* command shows the numeric userid and groupid.

The *find* command can be used to locate files on a system belonging to a particular user or group. The syntax of the find command is *find directory expression*, where *directory* is the place where *find* should start searching, and *expression* is one or more of the following:

- *-user username*. Search for files owned by *username*; *username* can be the actual username or the numeric userid.
- *-group groupname*. Search for files owned by *groupname*; *groupname* can be the actual group name or the numeric groupid.
- *-name filename*. Search for files named *filename*.
- *-print*. Find will list all files found matching criteria.
- *-exec command {}* \;. Execute *command* with the located file or files as arguments to *command*.
- *-type x*. Find files of type *x*, where *x* is one of: f (ordinary file), d (directory), b (block special file), c (character special file), D (door), l (symbolic link), p (named pipe), or s (socket).

Some examples of the *find* command follow:

```
# find /export/home -user mark -print
# find /tmp -user 1002 -exec ls -la {} \;
# find /export/tools -group toolmgr -name "*tmp" -exec rm
{} \;
```

In the first example, find will list all files owned by username *mark* in or below the directory */export/home*. In the second example, find will locate all "orphaned" files with userid 1002 in the directory */tmp* and perform an *ls –la* on each located file. In the last example, all files whose names end in "tmp" with groupid *toolmgr* in or below the directory */export/tools* are removed.

EXAM NOTES

THINK ABOUT IT . . .

What command syntax would be used to change the ownership of "orphaned" files to that of another user? The *find* and *chown* commands could be chained together. For example:

```
find / -user 1002 -print | xargs chown terry
```

What Users Are Logged In?

who *Command*

The *who* command is used to display which users are currently logged into the system. The format of the *who* command is *who [options]*. The options for *who* are:

- *-a*. Specify all (*-bdlpru*) options.
- *-b*. Show the system's boot time.
- *-d*. Show dead processes.
- *-H*. Print a header above output.
- *-l*. Show login processes waiting for someone to log in.
- *-n#*. Specify the number of users per line for the *-q* option.
- *-p*. Show active processes spawned by *init*.
- *-q*. Show just-logged-in usernames.
- *-r*. Show the system run level.
- *-s*. Short form of *who* (no time since last output or pid).
- *-u*. Show logged-in users.
- *-m*. Show information only about current terminal in *-u* format.
- *am i*. Show information about current terminal (same as *-m*).

Some examples follow.

```
# who
root        console       Sep 28 06:13     (:0)
```

```
pete         pts/2          Nov  6 05:23    (java)
mark         pts/6          Sep 28 06:13    (acorn)
# who -H
NAME         LINE           TIME
root         console        Sep 28 06:13    (:0)
pete         pts/2          Nov  6 05:23    (java)
mark         pts/6          Sep 28 06:13    (acorn)
# who -q
pete      root      mark
# users=3
# who am i
pete         pts/2          Jan 31 05:24    (java)
#
```

In the first example, *who* shows all logged-in users. The second example includes a heading. The third example shows all logged-in users in quick format.

The last example shows information about the current user. Note that root is running the *who am i* command, but that the output shows the user *pete*. The *who* command displays which users are logged in, but does not reflect whether any users have *su*'d to other accounts (including root).

The command *who am i* is frequently confused with a different command, *whoami*. The answers given by these two commands are essentially the same unless you have *su*'d from one account to another. In this situation, the *who am i* command will display the original logged-in username, while *whoami* will display the effective (*su*'d) username.

rwho *Command*

In environments with the *in.rwhod* feature enabled, the *rwho* command shows which users are logged in to all systems on the local network. The syntax of the *rwho* command is *rwho [-a]*, where the *-a* option will show only active users (those who have typed in commands in the past hour). An example follows.

```
# rwho
pete      grommit:pts/0 Nov  7 05:48
mark      wallace:pts/2 Nov  6 05:23
#
```

In this example, *pete* is logged into the system *grommit*, and *mark* is logged into the system *wallace*.

At large sites, *rwho* can create significant amounts of network traffic. This is because all systems running the *in.rwhod* daemon are frequently broadcasting their status to all other systems on the network. You can see why this feature is disabled by default.

rusers *Command*

In environments with the *rusersd* feature enabled, the *rusers* command shows which users are logged in to another system on the local network. The syntax of the *rusers* command is *rusers [-ahilu] hostlist*, where *hostlist* is a list of one or more host names. The options are:

- *-a*. Give a report for a machine even if no users are logged on.
- *-h*. Sort alphabetically by host name.
- *-i*. Sort by idle time.
- *-l*. Give a longer listing in the style of *who*(1).
- *-u*. Sort by number of users.

When the *–l* option is used, the *rusers* output resembles that of the *who* command; the output format is:

```
userid    hostname:terminal    login date    login time    idle time
login host
```

Some examples follow.

```
# rusers -l
Sending broadcast for rusersd protocol version 3...
pete         wallace:pts/2              Jan 31 05:24        7 (java)
gsmith       wallace:pts/3              Jan 31 05:29          (java)
mark         grommit:pts/0              Feb  1 04:04        7 (acorn)
Sending broadcast for rusersd protocol version 2...
#

# rusers
Sending broadcast for rusersd protocol version 3...
wallace          pete gsmith
grommit          mark
Sending broadcast for rusersd protocol version 2...
#
```

In the first example, the *rusers -l* command lists three users (*pete*, *gsmith*, and *mark*) on two systems (*wallace* and *grommit*), in the format resembling that of *who*. In the second example, the abbreviated *rusers* output lists the usernames who are logged into each system on the network.

finger *Command*

The *finger* command can be used to get information about other users on the system. The syntax of the *finger* command takes three forms:

```
finger [-bfhilmpqsw] [username]...
finger [-l] [ username@hostname 1 [ @hostname 2 .. .@hostname n]...]
finger [-l] [ @hostname 1 [ @hostname 2 .. .@hostname n]...]
```

In the first form, the available options are:

- *-b*. Suppress printing the user's home directory and shell in a long format printout.
- *-f*. Suppress printing the header that is normally printed in a short format printout.
- *-h*. Suppress printing of the *.project* file in a long format printout.
- *-i*. Force "idle" output format, which is similar to short format except that only the login name, terminal, login time, and idle time are printed.
- *-l*. Force long output format.
- *-m*. Match arguments only on username (not first or last name).
- *-p*. Suppress printing of the *.plan* file in a long format printout.
- *-q*. Force quick output format, which is similar to short format except that only the login name, terminal, and login time are printed.
- *-s*. Force short output format.
- *-w*. Suppress printing the full name in a short format printout.

In the second and third forms, the *-l* option forces long output format. Some examples follow.

```
# finger gsmith
Login name: gsmith                          In real life: Greg Smith
Directory: /export/home/gsmith              Shell: /bin/sh
On since Nov  7 06:18:59 on pts/17 from myclient
No unread mail
No Plan.
#

# finger -q gsmith
```

```
Login       TTY                 When
gsmith      pts/3        Wed Jan 31 05:29
#

# finger mark@grommit
[grommit]
Login        Name                 TTY         Idle    When     Where
pete     Mark Foster              pts/0              Thu 04:04  wallace
#

# finger @wallace
[wallace]
Login        Name                 TTY         Idle    When     Where
pete     Peter Gregory            pts/2              Wed 05:24  myclient
gsmith   Greg Smith               pts/3            1 Wed 05:29  myclient
#

# finger -l @wallace
[wallace]
Login name: pete                            In real life: Peter Gregory
Directory: /export/home/pete                Shell: /bin/sh
On since Jan 31 05:24:14 on pts/2 from myclient
Mail last read Thu Jun 29 04:23:10 2000
No Plan.

Login name: gsmith                          In real life: Greg Smith
Directory: /export/home/gsmith              Shell: /bin/sh
On since Jan 31 05:29:31 on pts/3 from myclient
2 minutes 11 seconds Idle Time
No unread mail
No Plan.
#
```

In the first example (finger gsmith), the username *gsmith* is logged in on the same system that executed the *finger* command. In the next example (finger –q gsmith), we see information about username *gsmith* but in quick format. In the third example (finger mark@grommit), we are querying specifically about the username *mark* on the system *grommit*. In the fourth example (finger @wallace), we are looking for short-form information about all users logged into the system *wallace*. In the last example (finger –l @wallace), we see long-form information about users logged into *wallace*.

In recent years many sites have disabled *finger* for security reasons. Check with your site administrator to see if this is the case in your organization. If *finger* is disabled on a system you're trying to reach, you'll get an error message that reads, "[system-name] connect: Connection refused".

Change Password

Root can change any user's account with the *passwd* command. The format of the *passwd* command is *passwd username options*. Allowable options include:

- *-d.* Deletes the password. Subsequent logins will not prompt for a password.
- *-f.* Forces the user to change passwords at the next login.
- *-l.* Locks the account, preventing further logins.
- *-n min.* Sets the minimum number of days between password changes.
- *-w warn.* Sets the number of days before password expiration that the user is warned about it.
- *-x max.* Sets the maximum number of days between password changes.
- *-s username.* Displays password attributes for username.
- *-a.* Displays password attributes for all users. Use only with the *-s* option.
- *-h username.* Changes the home directory for username.
- *-e username.* Changes the login shell for username.
- *-g username.* Changes the gcos-field (full name) for username.

Some examples follow.

```
# passwd -f mark
#

# passwd -s gsmith
gsmith  PS
#

# passwd -h gsmith
Default values are printed inside of '[]'.
To accept the default, type <return>.
To have a blank entry, type the word 'none'.

Home Directory [/export/home/gsmith]: /d2/home/gsmith
#
```

```
# passwd -e jhamid
Old shell: /bin/sh
New shell: /bin/csh
#

$ passwd
passwd:  Changing password for gsmith
Enter login password: *******
passwd(SYSTEM): Sorry: less than 7 days since the last change.
Permission denied
$

% passwd
passwd:  Changing password for gsmith
Enter login password: ******
New password: ******
Re-enter new password: ******
passwd (SYSTEM): passwd successfully changed for gsmith
%
```

In the first example, the account *mark* is forced to change passwords at the next login. In the second example, the password status for account *gsmith* is listed. PS means that the account has a password; NP means no password; and LK means the account is locked. In the third example, the home directory for account *gsmith* is changed to */d2/home/gsmith*. In the fourth example, the default shell for *jhamid* is changed from */bin/sh* to */bin/csh*. In the fifth example, a user attempts to change his password but is denied because the minimum number of days between password changes has not elapsed. In the last example, a user successfully changes his password.

Password Complexity

The *passwd* command also checks the "complexity" of the password that the user entered. By complexity we mean that all of the following rules must be met:

- The length of the password must be at least PASSLENGTH characters, where PASSLENGTH is a variable that is defined in the */etc/default/passwd* file. The default value is set to 6. Only the first eight characters are significant.
- The password must contain at least two lower- or uppercase letters and at least one numeric or special character.

- The password must be different from the userid and any reverse or circular shift of the userid. Upper- and lowercase letters are considered equal for this test. For example, user gsmith cannot change his password to GSMITH.
- The new and old passwords must differ by at least three characters. Upper- and lowercase letters are considered equal for this test.

Of the characterics listed, only PASSLENGTH can be changed. All of these characteristics can be bypassed if root is changing the password. This is discussed in the next section.

Root and Password Changes

The root user is permitted to change the password for any user. When root changes a user's password, the *passwd* command does not prompt for the old password. This permits root to "reset" a user's password in circumstances when the user has forgotten his or her password. This also permits root to lock a user's account by changing the user's password to a value that the user is unlikely to guess.

The password aging and complexity requirements are bypassed when the root user changes a user's password (or when root changes its own password). The danger of this feature is that a system administrator can set poor-quality passwords. Poor passwords are passwords that are short and/or easily guessed.

EXAM NOTES

THINK ABOUT IT . . .

Why should users change their own passwords?

First, the user will have a greater chance of remembering the password. This will lead to fewer sticky notes with passwords written down. Next, all of the quality rules about passwords (length, complexity, etc.) are enforced when users change their own passwords (no quality checking is performed when root changes a user's password). Finally, over time the user will have a better understanding of the password quality rules.

CHAPTER SUMMARY

Each person who uses a Solaris system is given a *user account*. The user account uniquely identifies the person; this allows the system administrator to tailor each user's working environment.

Account information is stored in the password file (*/etc/passwd*). Encrypted passwords and password aging information are stored in the shadow file (*/etc/shadow*). Group memberships are defined in the group file (*/etc/group*).

The user known as *root* has all system privileges. The attribute that gives root its power is its user number 0.

The system administrator uses the Admintool program to create, modify, and remove user accounts and groups. The *useradd*, *usermod*, *userdel*, *groupadd*, *groupmod*, and *groupdel* commands are command-line tools used to manage users and groups.

The system administrator has a choice of shells to choose from when setting up each new user. The various shells employ systemwide and per-user initialization files in order to customize each user's environment. The shells used in Solaris are the Bourne Shell, the C-Shell, and the Korn Shell. Restricted shells are available in instances where users need restricted capabilities.

There are a variety of commands available to see which other users are logged into the system or other systems on the network. They are *who*, *rwho*, *rusers*, and *finger*.

The user account is the sole means for associating an individual to a system. A system administrator creates a *username* for an individual. This username is a name that he uses to identify himself to the system. The administrator also assigns a secret password to the user account.

To use a system, the user must first *log in* with his or her userid and, later, the associated password as requested by the system. When the system is satisfied that the user has furnished the correct userid and password, the system admits the user.

The *-l* and *-n* options to the *ls* command list user/group names or user/group numbers, respectively. The *find* command can be used to find files owned by specific users or groups.

Users can change their password with the *passwd* command. The system will enforce password complexity policies, such as the length of the password and the number and type of characters in the password. These policies are not checked when root changes a user's password.

TEST YOURSELF

MULTIPLE CHOICE

1. Given the output:

```
root      console      Sep 28 06:13     (:0)
pete      pts/2        Nov  6 05:23     (java)
mark      pts/6        Sep 28 06:13     (acorn)
```

   Which statement correctly describes the command used to generate it?

   A. `who -u`
   B. `rusers`
   C. `rwhod`
   D. `ps -u`

2. Given:

```
# useradd -D skel_dir=/etc/skel
```

   What is the result?

   A. Existing users' *.profile* files are replaced by */etc/skel/.profile*.
   B. The *.profile* files used for all subsequently created accounts will be copied from */etc/skel/*.
   C. The default *.profile* files are deleted.
   D. Nothing. The command is invalid.

3. What command is used to search for files?

   A. `seek`
   B. `search`
   C. `find`
   D. `fs`

4. What is the purpose of the *rusers* command?
   A. List which local and remote users are logged on.
   B. Interactively remove user accounts.
   C. Bulk remove user accounts.
   D. List dormant user accounts.
5. Which three are valid expressions of the *find* command? (Choose three)
   A. `-exec`
   B. `-run`
   C. `-path`
   D. `-user`
   E. `-owner`
   F. `-groupid`
   G. `-list`
   H. `-print`
6. Given the passwd file entry:

   ```
   pete:x:100:4:Peter Gregory:/export/home/pete:/bin/sh
   ```

   What is this user's primary groupid?
   A. 100
   B. 4
   C. x
   D. It is NOT possible to tell.
7. Given the password file entry:

   ```
   pete:x:100:4:Peter Gregory:/export/home/pete:/bin/sh
   ```

   What is this user's first secondary groupid?
   A. 100
   B. 4
   C. x
   D. It is not possible to tell.

8. Given:

```
root::0:root
other::1:
bin::2:root,bin,daemon
sys::3:root,bin,sys,adm
adm::4:root,adm,daemon
uucp::5:root,uucp
mail::6:root
tty::7:root,tty,adm
lp::8:root,lp,adm
nuucp::9:root,nuucp
staff:GSSUYVrJ8EKyA:10:pete
daemon::12:root,daemon
sysadmin::14:
nobody::60001:
noaccess::60002:
nogroup::65534:
```

What is the effect of the user `mark` executing the *newgrp staff* command?

A. The *newgrp* command will create a new group called `staff`, overwriting the existing entry.

B. The *newgrp* command will attempt to create a new group called `staff`, but will be unable to because the group `staff` is password protected.

C. The user will be prompted for the password for the group *staff*.

D. The attempt will fail, because the group *staff* is locked by root.

9. Given the shadow file entry:

```
pete:NP:11055::::::
```

What is the meaning of the string `NP`?

A. The user selected a short password which encrypts to the string "NP".

B. The user's primary groupid is NP.

C. No password is required to log into the account.

D. The account is locked.

10. You need several people to log in to the same account to run an application, and you want files created by one person to be owned by all of the others. However, you do not wish to have the same password shared between all of the users. Which is the correct method to achieve this?
    A. Make all of the users members of the same group.
    B. Create all of the user accounts with the same user ID.
    C. Assign the same home directory for all of the users.
    D. Create one password file entry for all users, and one shadow file entry for each user.

FREE RESPONSE

11. What command is used to add a user account to the system?
12. You removed a user account from the system, but you did not check first to see if the user owned any files. What command and option should you use to locate files owned by that user?

CHAPTER 6

Files and Directories

After completing this chapter, you'll be able to meet the following Solaris Administration Exam objectives:

- Use absolute or relative pathnames and select valid command strings to move between specified points within a given directory tree.
- Select the metacharacter combinations necessary to construct pathname abbreviations for access to files and directories within the directory tree.
- State the commands needed to list the contents of directories and determine the file types within a directory.
- List the commands used to create or remove directories.
- State the commands used to copy, create, rename, or remove files.
- Identify how to search for regular expressions in the contents of one or more files.

To fulfill these objectives, this chapter discusses:

- Paths;
- Exploring the file system;
- Working with files; and
- Working with directories.

6.1 Paths

A *path* is the description of a file's location in the file system hierarchy. There are two ways to describe a file's location: an *absolute* path and a *relative* path. Each is explained in the following.

An *absolute* pathname begins with "/", the system's root, and is unambiguous. Examples of absolute pathnames are:

```
/etc/inet/inetd.conf
/export/home/gsmith/.profile
/var/adm/messages
```

Relative pathnames do not begin with "/", the file system's root. Instead, they begin with a directory name, or in the simplest case they can be just a filename. Relative pathnames are contextual; they are relative to a location in the file system. By itself, a relative pathname is ambiguous. Examples of relative pathnames are:

```
users.txt
log/loginlog
../gsmith/.profile
./go.sh
```

The first example is a simple filename. This file could be located anywhere in the file system.

The second example specifies the file *loginlog* that exists in the subdirectory *log*. Similar to the first example, we have no idea where the subdirectory *log* is.

A note on the notation in the third and fourth examples. The "../" means, "go up one directory," and "./" means "this directory."

Here is another example using this same notation:

```
../../../logs/install.log
```

This example states: Go up three subdirectories, down into the subdirectory *logs*, to the file *install.log*.

Path Metacharacters

In addition to the pathname notation described, the C-Shell and Korn Shell support an additional feature called *tilde expansion*.

One method of tilde expansion refers to the expansion of a userid to the userid's home directory. For example:

```
~gsmith
```

is expanded to:

```
/export/home/gsmith
```

Tilde expansion is used in the context of pathnames. Here are some additional examples of pathnames with tilde expansion:

```
~gsmith/.profile
~mhamid/bin/reload.sh
```

In these examples, the tilde and userids are expanded to the users' absolute home directory pathnames.

The Korn Shell also supports a tilde expansion corresponding to the current and previous working directory. The two notations are:

- ~+ expands to the current working directory ($PWD)
- ~- expands to the prior working directory ($OLDPWD)

For example, if the current working directory is */export/home/jgreen*, then the pathname *~+/bin/go.sh* is expanded to */export/home/jgreen/bin /go.sh*.

6.2 Exploring the File System

This section describes the commands used for file system navigation and exploration.

File System Navigation

The *pwd* command displays the current working directory. An example follows.

```
# pwd
/export/home/gsmith
#
```

In this example, the current working directory is */export/home/gsmith*.

The *cd* ("change directory") command changes your working directory to the one specified. Some examples follow.

```
# cd /var/adm
# cd local/bin
# cd ../lib
# cd ~gsmith/log
# cd ~-
```

Listing the Contents of Directories

The *ls* command is used to display the contents of directories. The syntax of the *ls* command is *ls [options] [file...]*, where *file* can be zero or more files and/or directories. The options for *ls* are:

- *-a*. Lists all entries, including those that begin with a dot (.), which are not normally listed.
- *-b*. Forces printing of nonprintable characters to be in the octal *\ddd* notation.
- *-C*. Multicolumn output with entries sorted down the columns. This is the default output format.
- *-d*. If an argument is a directory, lists only its name (not its contents); often used with *-l* to get the status of a directory.
- *-F*. Marks directories with a trailing slash (/), doors with a trailing greater-than sign (>), executable files with a trailing asterisk (*), FIFOs with a trailing vertical bar (|), symbolic links with a trailing at-sign (@), and AF_UNIX address family sockets with a trailing equals sign (=).
- *-g*. The same as *-l*, except that the owner is not printed.
- *-i*. For each file, prints the inode number in the first column of the report.
- *-l*. Lists in long format, giving mode, ACL indication, number of links, owner, group, size in bytes, and time of last modification for each file. If the file is a special file, the size field instead contains the major and minor device numbers. If the time of last modification is greater than six months ago, it is shown in the format "month date year" for the POSIX locale. Files modified

within six months show "month date time." If the file is a symbolic link, the filename is printed followed by "" and the path name of the referenced file.

- *-L*. If an argument is a symbolic link, lists the file or directory the link references rather than the link itself.
- *-q*. Forces printing of nonprintable characters in filenames as the character question mark (?).
- *-r*. Reverses the order of sort to get reverse alphabetic or oldest first as appropriate.
- *-R*. Recursively lists subdirectories encountered.
- *-t*. Sorts by time stamp (latest first) instead of by name. The default is the last modification time. (See *-u* and *-c*.)
- *-u*. Uses time of last access instead of last modification for sorting (with the *-t* option) or printing (with the *-l* option).
- *-x*. Multicolumn output with entries sorted across rather than down the page.
- *-1*. Prints one entry per line of output.

Some examples are shown here.

```
# ls
bin         lock.rs     Mail        src
# ls -F
bin/        lock.rs     Mail/       src/
# ls -a
.dt/        .exrc       .profile    bin         lock.rs
Mail        src
# ls -ail m*
    235659 -rw-r--r--   1 root    other    203264 Mar 16 09:01 m.tar
    235519 -rw-r--r--   1 root    other      2123 Apr 13 21:34 messages
    235408 -rw-r--r--   1 root    other      1241 Apr  6 05:04 messages.0
    235657 -rw-r--r--   1 root    other       553 Mar 31 07:46 messages.1
    235513 -rw-r--r--   1 root    other     47437 Mar 24 13:58 messages.2
    235529 -rw-r--r--   1 root    other    101656 Mar 16 09:44 messages.3
# ls -g m*
-rw-r--r--   1 other     203264 Mar 16 09:01 m.tar
-rw-r--r--   1 other       2123 Apr 13 21:34 messages
-rw-r--r--   1 other       1241 Apr  6 05:04 messages.0
-rw-r--r--   1 other        553 Mar 31 07:46 messages.1
-rw-r--r--   1 other      47437 Mar 24 13:58 messages.2
-rw-r--r--   1 other     101656 Mar 16 09:44 messages.3
#
```

In the first example, we discover that there are four files or directories (we cannot tell which is which): *bin*, *lock.rs*, *Mail* and *src*. In the second example, the *-F* option tells *ls* to append a "/" character next to each item that is a subdirectory. The items *bin*, *Mail*, and *src* are directories, and *lock.rs* is a file.

In the third example, the *-a* option tells *ls* to list all files, including those that begin with a period ("."). Without the *-a* option, *ls* will not show these files. We see that there are also two files, *.exrc* and *.profile*, plus the directory *.dt*.

Were we navigating in this example directory, we could subsequently *cd* to any of the subdirectories listed by typing *cd directoryname*; for example, *cd Mail*.

In the fourth example, we see a long listing of all files beginning with the letter m; the output includes inode numbers for each file. In the fifth example, we get a long listing (minus the name of each file's owner) of all files beginning with the letter m.

Determining File Size, Type, Owner, and Modification Date

The *-l* (long list) option of the *ls* command tells *ls* to list details about items in the directory. Consider this example.

```
# ls -l
drwxr-xr-x   3 pete     adm         1536 May 23 13:23 bin
-rw-r--r--   1 pete     adm       371935 Jul 25 20:40 lock.rs
drwxr-xr-x   3 pete     adm          512 May  4  2000 Mail
drwxr-xr-x   4 pete     adm          512 Jun 16 05:25 src
#
```

In this example, we see several details for each of the items *bin*, *lock.rs*, *Mail*, and *src*. These details are explained in the following for the first item, *bin*, as they appear from left to right.

- drwxr-xr-x—this is the permission string. This permission string notation is discussed in detail in Chapter 10.
- 3—this is the number of "links" to the directory "bin."
- pete—this is the owner of the directory "bin."
- adm—this is the groupid of the directory "bin."
- 1536—this is the number of characters contained in the directory "bin." (Note: For directories, this is not the number of characters contained in the files inside of the directory, but only in the directory entry itself.)

- May 23 13:23—this is the last-modified date.
- bin—this is the name.

The *file* Command

The *file* command is used to determine the type of a file. The syntax of the *file* command is *file [options] filename*..., where *filename* is a list of one or more files to be examined. The options are:

- *-h*. Do not follow symbolic links.
- *-f ffile*. *ffile* contains a list of the files to be examined.

Some examples follow.

```
# file /usr/bin/cp
/usr/bin/cp:     ELF 32-bit MSB executable SPARC Version 1,
dynamically linked, stripped
# file /tmp
/tmp:            directory
# file /etc/hosts
/etc/hosts:      commands text
#
```

In these examples, file displays the file type of */usr/bin/cp*, */tmp*, and */etc/hosts*.

6.3 Working with Files

Creating Files Using the *touch* Command

The *touch* command is used to create files or update the creation and/or modification date of a file or directory. *touch* creates an empty file; the basic syntax for *touch* is *touch filename*. The two allowable syntaxes for *touch* are *touch [-acm] [-r ref_file | -t time] file* ... , and *touch [-acm] [date_time] file* ... .

The options for *touch* are:

- *-a*. Change the access time of *file*. Do not change the modification time unless *-m* is also specified.
- *-c*. Do not create a specified file if it does not exist. Do not write any diagnostic messages concerning this condition.

- *-m*. Change the modification time of *file*. Do not change the access time unless *-a* is also specified.
- *-r ref_file*. Use the corresponding times of the file named by *ref_file* instead of the current time.
- *-t time*. Use the specified time instead of the current time. *time* will be a decimal number of the form: *[[CC]YY]MMDDhhmm [.SS]*, where each two digits represents the following:
  - *MM*—the month of the year [01–12].
  - *DD*—the day of the month [01–31].
  - *hh*—the hour of the day [00–23].
  - *mm*—the minute of the hour [00–59].
  - *CC*—the first two digits of the year.
  - *YY*—the second two digits of the year.
  - *SS*—the second of the minute [00–59].
  - Both *CC* and *YY* are optional. If neither is given, the current year will be assumed.

EXAM NOTES

THINK ABOUT IT . . .

You need to create a file that has the same creation date as an existing file. How is this done?

You should use the *-r* option of the *touch* command. For instance, to create the file log.txt that has the same creation time as the file *logWed.txt*, type *touch -r logWed.txt log.txt.*

Creating Files Using Output Redirection

A common method for creating files is to use output redirection from the command line or in a shell script. This refers to the ">" and ">>" syntax described in an earlier section. An example follows.

```
# ps -ef > /tmp/proc.txt
#
```

In this example, the file */tmp/proc.txt* is created and contains the output from the *ps –ef* command

Creating Files Using Copy

Users and administrators frequently need to copy one file to another, or to create a copy of a file. For instance, many would advise that a UNIX system administrator first make a copy of a configuration file before changing it.

The *cp* command is used to copy one file to another. *cp* can also be used to copy entire directories and their contents. The three allowable syntaxes of the *cp* command are:

- *cp [-fip] source_file target_file*. *cp* will copy the contents of *source_file* to *target_file*. If *target_file* already exists, it will be overwritten.
- *cp [-fip] source_file... target*. *cp* will copy one or more *source_files* to the directory *target*. *source_file* may not be a directory; *target* must exist and be a directory.
- *cp -r* | *-R [-fip] source_dir... target*. *cp* will copy one or more directories, including all files and directories contained in each *source_dir*, to *target*.

The options for *cp* are:

- *-f*. Unlink. If a file descriptor for a destination file cannot be obtained, attempt to unlink the destination file and proceed.
- *-i*. Interactive. *cp* will prompt for confirmation whenever the copy overwrites an existing target. A *y* answer means that the copy should proceed. Any other answer prevents *cp* from overwriting *target* or *target file*.
- *-r*. Recursive. *cp* will copy the directory and all its files, including any subdirectories and their files to *target*.
- *-R*. Same as *-r*, except pipes are replicated, not read from.
- *-p*. Preserve. *cp* will attempt to preserve a file or directory's owner, group, and permission settings.

Some examples follow.

```
# cp -p netmasks netmasks001118
# cp -i messages.* /tmp
cp: overwrite /tmp/messages (yes/no)? y
cp: overwrite /tmp/messages.0 (yes/no)? n
cp: overwrite /tmp/messages.1 (yes/no)? n
cp: overwrite /tmp/messages.2 (yes/no)? n
cp: overwrite /tmp/messages.3 (yes/no)? n
# cp -r /etc/inet /etc/inetsave
#
```

In the first example, the file *netmasks* is copied to the new (or existing) file *netmasks001118*; file ownership and permissions will be preserved. In the second example, several files are copied to the directory */tmp*; the *-i* option forces the user to decide for each file whether to overwrite the destination file or not. In the last example, the entire directory */etc/inet*—including any subdirectories—is copied to the directory */etc/inetsave*.

Moving Files

A file can be moved from one place to another, generally from one directory to another directory. This can be easier than copying and removing old copies, particularly if the file that needs to be moved is large; if available disk space is less than the size of the file, then you won't be able to make a copy of it on the same file system.

Moving files is done with the *mv* command; the syntax is *mv [options] source destination.* The options for *mv* are:

- *-f. mv* will move the file(s) without prompting even if it is writing over an existing target. Note that this is the default if the standard input is not a terminal. The *-f* option overrides the *-i* option.
- *-i. mv* will prompt for confirmation whenever the move overwrites an existing target. An affirmative answer means that the move should proceed. Any other answer prevents *mv* from overwriting the target.
- *source*. Filename to be moved.
- *target*. Destination file or directory. If *target* is a file and it exists, it will be overwritten. If *target* is a directory, then the name of the destination file will be the same as the name of the source.

Some examples follow.

```
# mv .profile OLD/.profile
# mv -i hostname.hme0 /tmp
mv: overwrite hostname.hme0 (yes/no)? y
# mv *.c ~geoff
#
```

In the first example, the file *.profile* is moved to the subdirectory *OLD*. In the next example, the file *hostname.hme0* is moved to the */tmp* directory; the *-i* option queries whether to overwrite the target file or not. In the third example, all files whose names end with ".c" are moved to username *geoff*'s home directory.

Renaming Files

The *mv* command is used to rename files; this is the same command used to move files. The only difference is in the way that the command is used. To rename a file, it is being "moved" to the same directory but to a different name, effectively renaming it. Some examples follow.

```
# mv .profile .profileOLD
# mv -i logfile logfileWed
mv: overwrite logfileWed (yes/no)? n
#
```

In the first example, the file *.profile* is renamed to *.profileOLD*. In the second example, the file *logfile* is renamed to *logfileWed*; because the *-i* option is used, the user is queried whether the file should be renamed or not.

EXAM NOTES

THINK ABOUT IT . . .

You have discovered that the two files, *log1.txt* and *log2.txt*, have their names switched. How can you switch them back?

Rename the first file to a temporary name: *mv log1.txt log1.tmp*. Then, rename *log2.txt*: *mv log2.txt log1.txt*. Finally, change the temporary file: *mv log1.tmp log2.txt*. Problem solved.

Removing Files

The *rm* command is used to remove files or directories. The two syntaxes of the *rm* command are *rm [-f] [-i] file...* and *rm -rR [-f] [-i] dirname... [file]...* The options for *rm* are:

- *-r*: Recursively remove directories and subdirectories in the argument list. The directory will be emptied of files and removed. The user is normally prompted for removal of any write-protected files. The write-protected files are removed without prompting, however, if the *-f* option is used or if the standard input is not a terminal and the *-i* option is not used. Symbolic links that are encountered with this option will not be traversed. If the removal of a nonempty, write-protected directory is attempted, *rm* will always fail (even if the *-f* option is used).

- *-R*. Same as *-r* option.
- *-f*. Remove all files (whether write-protected or not) in a directory without prompting the user. In a write-protected directory, however, files are never removed (whatever their permissions are), but no messages are displayed. If the removal of a write-protected directory is attempted, this option will not suppress an error message.
- *-i*. Interactive. With this option, *rm* prompts for confirmation before removing any files. It overrides the *-f* option and remains in effect even if the standard input is not a terminal.

The first form (*rm [-f] [-i] file...*) is used for removing one or more files. The *-f* option forces removal even if any of the files are read-only (otherwise, *rm* will ask if you are sure). The *-i* option, like the *-i* option in *mv*, gives you a chance to state yes or no to each eligible file removal.

The second form (*rm -rR [-f] [-i] dirname... [file]...*) is used for removing directories. The additional *-r* and *-R* options (which both do the same thing) permit recursive removal of a directory; this means that all subdirectories and their respective contents (and sub-subdirectories, and so forth) are removed. *The -f* and *-i* options in the second form have the same meaning as in the first form.

Some examples follow.

```
# rm .profileOLD*
rm: .profileOLD: override protection 444 (yes/no)? y
# rm -rf /tmp/logs
# rm -i message.*
rm: remove messages (yes/no)? n
rm: remove messages.0 (yes/no)? n
rm: remove messages.1 (yes/no)? n
rm: remove messages.2 (yes/no)? n
rm: remove messages.3 (yes/no)? y
#
```

In the first example, the file *.profileOLD* has 444 (read-only) permissions; *rm* asks if it should override the read-only file permissions and remove it anyway. See Chapter 10 for a complete discussion of file permissions.

In the second example, the subdirectory */tmp/logs* is removed, as well as any subdirectories or sub-subdirectories beneath */tmp/logs*. In the last example, all *messages.** files are removed, querying for each one found.

EXAM NOTES

THINK ABOUT IT . . .

You need to remove all files in */tmp* that are yours. How can you do this? Enter the command *rm -f /tmp/**. Files belonging to you will be removed; files owned by others will not be removed. You will see error messages, but *rm* will proceed until completed.

Displaying the Contents of Text Files

The *cat* and *more* commands are used to display the contents of text files. The *cat* command displays the entire contents of a file. The *more* command shows one screen full at a time, prompting you to press the spacebar to scroll forward to the next screen full, and so on until the end of the file has been reached.

Some examples follow.

```
# cat /tmp/names.txt
Peter
Jon
Michael
# more services
#ident "@(#)services  1.24  99/07/18 SMI"  /* SVr4.0 1.8 */
#
# Network services, Internet style
#
tcpmux          1/tcp
echo            7/tcp
echo            7/udp
discard         9/tcp           sink null
discard         9/udp           sink null
systat          11/tcp          users
daytime         13/tcp
daytime         13/udp
netstat         15/tcp
chargen         19/tcp          ttytst source
chargen         19/udp          ttytst source
ftp-data        20/tcp
ftp             21/tcp
telnet          23/tcp
smtp            25/tcp          mail
name            42/udp          nameserver
--More--(13%)
```

```
whois
domain          53/udp
domain          53/tcp
bootps          67/udp          # BOOTP/DHCP server
bootpc          68/udp          # BOOTP/DHCP client
hostnames       101/tcp         hostname
pop3            110/tcp                         # POP - V3
sunrpc          111/udp         rpcbind
sunrpc          111/tcp         rpcbind
imap            143/tcp         imap2           # v2
ldap            389/tcp                         # LDAP
ldap            389/udp                         # LDAP
ldaps           636/tcp                         #
ldaps           636/udp                         # LDAP
#
--More--(31%)
...
[remainder of output not shown]
```

In the first example, the contents of *names.txt* are displayed. In the second example, we are viewing the file *services* using the *more* command. After one screen full, *more* stops sending output, pauses, and displays the *--More--(xx%)* prompt. It is at this prompt where you can press the spacebar to continue scrolling through the file, or enter one of the other commands.

EXAM NOTES

THINK ABOUT IT . . .

Is there a way to create a small text file using the *cat* command?

Sure. Type *cat > filename*. You'll notice that you will not get a shell prompt back; *cat* is waiting for you to type in the contents of *filename*. Type a line or two, then press *Ctrl-D*. *cat* will create your file with the text you typed in, and you'll get your shell prompt back.

Searching for Text within Files

The *grep* command is used to search for text in a file. The syntax of the *grep* command is *grep [-bchilnsvw] pattern [filename]...* . The options for *grep* are:

- *-b*. Precede each line by the block number on which it was found. This can be useful in locating block numbers by context (first block is 0).
- *-c*. Print only a count of the lines that contain the pattern.
- *-h*. Prevent the name of the file containing the matching line from being appended to that line. Used when searching multiple files.
- *-i*. Ignore upper-/lowercase distinction during comparisons.
- *-l*. Print only the names of files with matching lines, separated by newline characters. Does not repeat the names of files when the pattern is found more than once.
- *-n*. Precede each line by its line number in the file (first line is 1).
- *-s*. Suppress error messages about nonexistent or unreadable files.
- *-v*. Print all lines except those that contain the pattern.
- *-w*. Search for the expression as a word as if surrounded by \< and \>.
- *file*. A pathname of a file to be searched for the patterns. If no file operands are specified, the standard input will be used.
- *pattern*. Specify a pattern to be used during the search for input. *pattern* may contain plain text as well as several special characters, including:
  - ^. This symbolizes the beginning of a line.
  - $. This symbolizes the end of a line.
  - . (period). This symbolizes any single character.
  - [n-m]. This symbolizes a single character whose value falls in the range beginning with the character *n* and ending with the character *m*. The range is determined by the characters' numeric ASCII value. The ASCII values of characters may be viewed in the "ASCII" man page.

  pattern frequently needs to be enclosed in double quotes if the characters searched for include spaces or characters that would be interpreted by the shell (e.g., | , * , ? , < , or >). When searching for characters with special meaning (e.g., ^ , $, . , [, or]), precede the character with a backslash ("\").

Some examples of the *grep* command follow.

```
# grep uucp passwd
uucp:x:5:5:uucp Admin:/usr/lib/uucp:
```

```
nuucp:x:9:9:uucp Admin:/var/spool/uucppublic:/usr/lib/uucp/uucico
# grep ^uucp passwd
uucp:x:5:5:uucp Admin:/usr/lib/uucp:
# grep csh$ passwd
pete:x:100:4:Peter Gregory:/export/home/pete:/bin/csh
gsmith:x:1001:10:Geoff:/export/home/gsmith:/bin/csh
# grep -v ":x:" passwd
daemon::1:1::/:
# grep 6000[0-9] passwd
nobody:x:60001:60001:Nobody:/:
noaccess:x:60002:60002:No Access User:/:
#
```

In the first example, the string "uucp" is located in the file *passwd*. Two lines are found.

In the second example, when found only at the beginning of a line, the string "uucp" is located in the file *passwd*. This time only one line is found.

In the third example, the string "csh," when located at the end of a line, is located in the file *passwd*. In the fourth example, lines not containing ":x:" are located in the file *passwd*. In the fifth example, lines containing "6000" followed by a number are located in the file *passwd*.

Other *grep* commands are described here.

- *fgrep*—this is a "fast grep" command that searches for patterns only without special symbols. This is useful for searching for plain text patterns in large files.
- *egrep*—this is similar to *grep*, except that *egrep* supports "full regular expressions" while *grep* supports "limited regular expressions." These refer to extended character searching syntax constructs that exceed the scope of this book.

6.4 Working with Directories

Creating Subdirectories

The *mkdir* command is used to create subdirectories. The syntax of the *mkdir* command is *mkdir [options] directory*. Absolute and relative pathnames are permitted in *directory*. Options for *mkdir* are:

- *-m mode*. Allows users to specify the mode to be used for new directories. Choices for modes can be found in the *chmod* command.

- *-p*. With this option, *mkdir* creates *directory* by creating all the nonexisting parent directories first.

Some examples follow.

```
# mkdir temp
# mkdir adm/local/lib
# mkdir /dev/flash
# mkdir -p /tmp/apps/ar/bin
```

In the first example, the subdirectory *temp* is created; it will be located beneath the current working directory when the *mkdir* command was executed.

In the second example, the subdirectory *lib* is created within the subdirectory *local*, which is located within the subdirectory *adm*. Note: If either *adm* or *local* do not exist as expected, *mkdir* will abort and the subdirectory *lib* will not be created.

In the third example, the subdirectory *flash* is created within the directory */dev*. This is an example of an absolute path. This command will work, regardless of the current working directory when *mkdir* is executed.

In the last example, the entire directory structure *apps/ar/bin* is created beneath the directory */tmp*. The *-p* option tells *mkdir* to create an entire structure at once. Without the *-p* option, it would be necessary to perform separate commands for each subdirectory (*mkdir /tmp/apps*, *mkdir /tmp/apps/ar*, and *mkdir /tmp/apps/ar/bin*).

EXAM NOTES

THINK ABOUT IT . . .

What will happen if you try to create a subdirectory with *mkdir* when that subdirectory already exists? Will *mkdir* overwrite and destroy your existing subdirectory?

mkdir will not destroy your subdirectory. Instead, it will return an error, complaining that the subdirectory already exists.

Renaming and Moving Directories

The *mv* command is used to rename and move directories. The syntax is *mv [options] source target*. The *mv* command works for directories in the same manner as for files. Where *source* and *target* are in the same directory, a directory's name is changed; if *target* is in a different directory, the directory *source* is moved to the location specified in *target*.

When a directory is moved, all of its contents are moved along with it. Thus, it is possible to move an entire directory tree with a single command. Absolute and relative pathnames are permitted for both *source* and *target*. You should be careful that the system will correctly interpret your intentions.

Some examples follow.

```
# mv logs/current logs/Nov
# mv /home /homedirs
# mv bin /local
# mv libs* OLD
```

In the first example, the subdirectory current beneath the subdirectory *logs* will be renamed to *Nov*. This is effectively a name change only. The pathnames in this example are relative to the current working directory when *mv* was executed.

In the second example, the directory */home* is renamed to */homedirs*. The pathnames here are absolute (they begin with a slash ("/")); this command works regardless of the current working directory.

In the third example, the subdirectory *bin* is moved to the */local* directory. This example is somewhat ambiguous, since it contains a mixture of absolute and relative pathnames; in this case, *bin* becomes a subdirectory of */local*, effectively creating */local/bin*.

In the last example, all directories named *libs** are moved to the subdirectory *OLD*.

EXAM NOTES

THINK ABOUT IT . . .

Help! I just renamed a directory with important contents to the name of another directory that already exists. I meant to rename the directory, but because the target existed, my original directory is gone. Where did my original directory go?

Here is what happened. You meant to change the name of a directory to a new name, but unexpectedly the new name was the name of a directory that exists. You moved your directory underneath the existing directory.

Removing Directories

The *rmdir* command is used to remove empty directories only. The syntax is *rmdir [options] directory*.... Options for *rmdir* are:

- *-p dirname*. Allow users to remove the directory *dirname* and its parent directories that become empty. A message is printed to standard error if all or part of the path could not be removed.
- *-s*. Suppress the message printed on the standard error when *-p* is in effect.

Some examples follow.

```
# rmdir /tmp/bin
# rmdir bin
# rmdir -p /tmp/apps/ar/bin
# rmdir */SCCS
```

In the first example, the subdirectory *bin* within the directory */tmp* is removed, only if the subdirectory *bin* is empty. The directory */tmp* is not removed. In the second example, the subdirectory *bin* is removed if it is empty. In the third example, the entire *apps/ar/bin* subdirectory structure is removed. First, *bin* is removed (only if it is empty), then *ar* is removed (only if it is empty), and then *apps* is removed (only if empty). The directory */tmp* is not removed. In the last example, all subdirectories named *SCCS* that reside in subdirectories in the current directory are removed.

The *rm* command with the *-r* (recursive) option is used to remove directories that have files or subdirectories in them. Unlike *rmdir*, which requires that subdirectories be empty, *rm -r* removes directories with their contents. Some examples follow.

```
# rm -r /tmp/libs
# rm -r /export/home/gsmith
# rm -r libs
```

In the first example, the directory */tmp/libs*, and all of its content (files and possibly more subdirectories with their own files or further subdirectories), is removed. The directory */tmp* is not removed. In the second example, the subdirectory *gsmith* (which is in the subdirectory */export/home*) is removed, along with all of its contents. In the last example, the subdirectory *libs* is removed.

CHAPTER SUMMARY

A pathname describes an absolute or relative location of a file or directory in a file system. An absolute pathname begins with a slash ("/"), while a relative pathname begins with the file or subdirectory name only.

In the C-Shell and Korn Shell, the path metacharacter *~userid* is expanded to mean the home directory of *userid*. In the Korn Shell, the path metacharacter ~+ (tilde plus) means the current working directory, while ~- (tilde hyphen) refers to the prior working directory.

The *pwd* command is used to display the current working directory. The *cd* command is used to change to another current working directory. The *ls* command lists the contents of a directory. The *ls* command can also be used to view details about a file or directory, including: owner, groupid, creation date and time, size, and permissions. The *file* command is used to determine what type of file a file is (e.g., program, shell script, text file, etc.).

New empty files can be created with the *touch* command. The *cp* command is used to copy one file to another. Files are renamed or moved with the *mv* command. The *rm* command is used to remove files.

The *cat* and *more* commands are used to display the contents of a file. The *cat* command shows all of a file's contents at once, while the *more* command shows one screen full at a time.

Subdirectories are created using the *mkdir* command. Like files, they are renamed and moved with the *mv* command. Empty subdirectories can be removed with the *rmdir* command; subdirectories with files in them must be removed with the *rm -r* command.

TEST YOURSELF

MULTIPLE CHOICE

1. Which two commands will transfer the contents of *file1* to *file2*? (Choose two)
   A. `mv file2 file1`
   B. `cp file1 file2; rm file1`
   C. `mv file1 file2`
   D. `cp file2 file1; rm file1`
   E. `cp file1 file2; mv file1`
   F. `copy file1 file2`

2. What is the purpose of the *rm -f* command?
   - A. It will follow directory trees looking for specified files.
   - B. It will remove files, write-protected or not.
   - C. It will remove files only, not directories.
   - D. It will remove files or directories, write-protected or not.

3. Your current working directory is */usr/local/g4*. Which command will move the directory */usr/local/lib* to */usr/local/g4/lib*?
   - A. `mv ../lib`
   - B. `mv ./lib g4`
   - C. `mv lib g4`
   - D. `mv ../local/lib ../g4`

4. Given:

   ```
   # mv /lib bin/
   ```

   What is the result?
   - A. The directory *bin/* is moved to the directory */lib*.
   - B. The directory *bin/* and its contents are moved to the directory */lib*.
   - C. The directory */lib* is moved to the directory *bin*.
   - D. The directory */lib* and its contents are moved to the directory *bin*.

5. What is the meaning of the *-i* option of the *rm* command?
   - A. *rm* prompts for confirmation before removing all of the files.
   - B. *rm* prompts for confirmation before removing each file.
   - C. *rm* shows which files would be removed, but does not actually remove them.
   - D. *rm* silently removes all of the files.

6. Given:

   ```
   # rmdir /g5
   ```

   What is the result on the directory */g5* containing files *log.txt* and *log6.txt*?
   - A. The contents of */g5* are removed.
   - B. The directory */g5* and its contents are removed interactively.
   - C. The directory */g5* and its contents are removed silently.
   - D. Nothing.

7. Given the dialogue:

```
# ls
log.txt          March.txt
# mv log.txt March.txt
```

What is the result of the *mv* command?

   A. The user is asked for confirmation before overwriting *March.txt*.
   B. The file *log.txt* is renamed *March.txt*.
   C. The contents of *log.txt* are copied to the file *March.txt* and *log.txt* removed.
   D. The file *log.txt* is assigned the same owner as the file *March.txt*.

8. Given the dialogue:

```
# ls -F
log.txt          March.txt          March/          /April
#
```

Which is true?

   A. This directory contains two files and two subdirectories.
   B. The subdirectories *March* and *April* are not empty.
   C. The subdirectories *March* and *April* are empty.
   D. The files *log.txt* and *March.txt* are empty.

9. Given:

```
grep ^624 goods.txt
```

What is the result?

   A. The first 624 lines of the file *goods.txt* are displayed.
   B. All lines containing the string `624` (only when found at the beginning of a line) in the file *goods.txt* are displayed.
   C. All lines containing the string `624` in the file *goods.txt* are displayed.
   D. All lines containing the string `^624` in the file *goods.txt* are displayed.

10. Which two of the following commands will successfully remove the directory */lib* and its contents? (Choose two)

    A. `rmdir /lib`

    B. `rm -rf /lib`

    C. `rm -f /lib/*;rmdir /lib`

    D. `rmdir -p /lib`

    E. `rmdir -p -s /lib`

FREE RESPONSE

11. What command is used to list files whose names begin with a period (".")?

12. What command is used to move the directory */lib* to */tmp*?

CHAPTER 7

vi Editor

After completing this chapter, you'll be able to meet the following Solaris Administration Exam objectives:

- List the keyboard sequences that are required to switch between the three modes of operation used by the vi editor.
- State the vi editor commands used to position and move the cursor, create and delete text, and copy or move text.
- Match the correct vi command sequences with their respective search and replace functions.

To fulfill these objectives, this chapter discusses:

- Starting the vi editor;
- vi modes;
- Exiting vi;
- Moving around the file;
- Text editing;
- Copying, inserting, searching, and replacing;

- Reading and writing files;
- Miscellaneous commands;
- Mapping new commands; and
- vi configuration.

7.1 Starting the vi Editor

The command used to start the vi editor is *vi [options] filename...*, where *filename* is a list of one or more files to edit. Some of the vi options are:

- *-s*. Suppress all interactive user feedback. This is useful when processing editor scripts.
- *-L*. List the name of all files saved as the result of an editor or system crash.
- *-r filename*. Edit filename after an editor or system crash. (Recovers the version of filename that was in the buffer when the crash occurred.)
- *-R*. Read-only mode; the *read-only* flag is set, preventing accidental overwriting of the file.
- *-v*. Start up in display editing state using vi. You can achieve the same effect by simply typing the *vi* command itself.
- *-V*. Verbose. When *ex* commands are read by means of standard input, the input will be echoed to standard error. This may be useful when processing *ex* commands within shell scripts.
- *-w n*. Set the default window size to *n* lines. This is useful when using the editor over a slow-speed line.
- *-x*. Encryption option. When used, vi simulates the *X* command of *ex* and prompts the user for a key. This key is used to encrypt and decrypt text using the algorithm of the *crypt* command. The *X* command makes an educated guess to determine whether text read is encrypted or not. The temporary buffer file is encrypted also, using a transformed version of the key typed in for the *-x* option. If an empty encryption key is entered (i.e., if the return key is pressed right after the prompt), the file will not be encrypted. This is a good way to decrypt a file that was erroneously encrypted with a mistyped encryption key, such as a backspace or undo key.
- *+ command* | *-c command*. Begin editing by executing the specified editor *command* (usually a search or positioning command).

If the file you specify does not exist, vi will create it for you. You must have write permission on any existing file you wish to edit and you must have write permission on the directory in which you wish to create a file.

After issuing the command to start vi, the screen will be cleared and you'll see the first 23 lines of the file (depending upon the size of the window). The bottom line of the screen will show the name of the file and its size. Figure 7-1 shows an example.

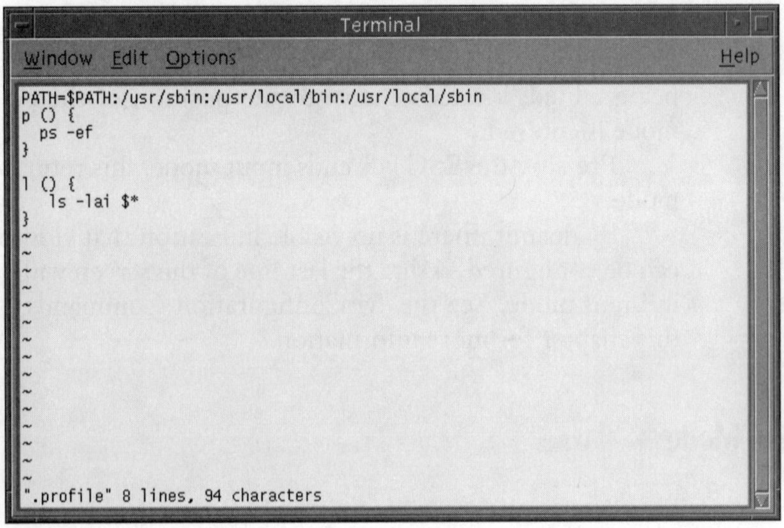

```
Terminal
Window  Edit  Options                                    Help
PATH=$PATH:/usr/sbin:/usr/local/bin:/usr/local/sbin
p () {
  ps -ef
}
l () {
  ls -lai $*
}
~
~
~
~
~
~
~
~
~
~
~
~
~
~
~
~
".profile" 8 lines, 94 characters
```

Figure 7–1 *The vi Editor*

Open files in read-only mode with the *view* command instead of the *vi* command. The syntax for view is *view filename...* .

Start vi in "beginner mode" with the *vedit* command instead of the *vi* command. When using *vedit* instead of vi, the *report flag* is set to *1*, the *showmode* and *novice* flags are set, and the *magic* flag is turned off. vi flags are discussed later in this chapter.

7.2 vi Modes

vi operates in three basic modes: *command*, *input*, and *last line*. Let's discuss each in detail.

Command Mode

This is the mode in effect when vi is started. In command mode, commands to move the cursor, entering text, or entering a vi command are permitted.

Most vi commands are single characters, typed wherever the cursor is located. vi commands are case-sensitive. Most are location-dependent, meaning they affect the file being edited at the location of the cursor when the command is entered.

Input Mode

Input mode is initiated by issuing one of the input mode commands. During input mode, any character typed will be inserted into the file being edited, located relative to the position of the cursor when input mode is entered.

Pressing the ESC key ends input mode; this returns vi to command mode.

By default, there is no visible indication that vi is in input mode. vi can be configured so that the last line of the screen will indicate that vi is in input mode. See the "vi Configuration Commands " section later in this chapter for more information.

Last Line Mode

Last line mode is initiated by typing the colon key (":") while in command mode. The cursor moves to the last line on the screen, where a variety of special vi commands can be entered. Last line mode is ended by completing the command or ended by pressing Ctrl-U then ESC (if any characters were entered in this mode), or by pressing ESC (if no characters were entered).

7.3 Exiting vi

Table 7.1 describes vi commands used to exit vi.

Table 7.1 *vi Exiting Commands*

KEY	DESCRIPTION
ZZ	write file and exit vi (if no changes were made, just exit)
:wqCR	write file and exit vi
:q!CR	quit vi without saving changes

7.4 Moving around the File

Table 7.2 lists the commands used to move the cursor and/or scroll through the file being edited.

Table 7.2 *Basic vi Cursor Movement Commands*

KEY	DESCRIPTION
(up arrow key), k	move cursor up one line
(down arrow key), j	move cursor down one line
(left arrow key), h	move cursor left one character
(right arrow key), l	move cursor right one character
^H, backspace	same as left arrow key
Space key	same as right arrow key
H	top line on screen
L	last line on screen
M	middle line on screen
^	first non-white-space character
CR	same as +
0	beginning of line
$	end of line

Advanced Moving around the File

Table 7.3 lists more commands used to move the cursor and scroll through the file being edited.

Table 7.3 *Advanced vi Cursor Movement Commands*

KEY	DESCRIPTION
+	next line on first non-white-space character
-	previous line on first non-white-space character
^F	forward one screen
^B	backward one screen
^D	scroll down one half screen

Table 7.3 *Advanced vi Cursor Movement Commands (Continued)*

KEY	DESCRIPTION
^U	scroll up one half screen
^E	scroll down one line
^Y	scroll up one line
n G	go to the beginning of line n
(	beginning of sentence
)	end of sentence
{	beginning of paragraph
}	end of paragraph
n	move to column n
w	forward a word
b	back a word
e	end of word
W	forward a blank-delimited word
B	back a blank-delimited word
E	end of a blank-delimited word

EXAM NOTES

THINK ABOUT IT . . .

Hey! I don't want to use my arrow keys—they are all the way over there, on the far side of the keyboard! Use the h, j, k, and l keys instead. They represent left, down, up, and right.

7.5 Text Editing

This section describes editing operations:

- Inserting text
- Commands while inserting text
- Deleting text
- Changing text

Inserting Text

Table 7.4 lists the commands used to insert text into the file being edited.

Table 7.4 *vi Insert Text Commands*

KEY	DESCRIPTION
a	append after cursor
A	append at end of line
i	insert before cursor
I	insert before first non-blank
o	open line below
O	open line above

Commands While Inserting Text

Table 7.5 lists the commands used while in insert mode.

Table 7.5 *vi Insertion Editing Commands*

KEY	DESCRIPTION
^H, backspace	erase last character entered
^W	erase last word entered
^U	erase this line of input
^Vchar	enter a nonprintable character (prepend with ^V)
^C	suspend insert mode
ESC	end insert mode, return to command mode

Deleting Text

Table 7.6 shows the commands used to delete text from the file being edited.

Changing Text

Table 7.7 lists the commands used to change text in the file being edited.

Table 7.6 *vi Delete Text Commands*

KEY	DESCRIPTION
X	delete character after cursor
X	delete character before cursor
Dw	delete word
dd	delete line
D	delete rest of line

Table 7.7 *vi Change Text Commands*

KEY	DESCRIPTION
rx	replace next character with *x*
C	change rest of line
cw	change rest of word

7.6 Copying, Inserting, Searching, and Replacing

This section describes editing operations:

- Copying text into buffers
- Inserting text from buffers
- Search and replace

Copying Text into Buffers

The commands listed in Table 7.8 are used to copy text in the file being edited. The commands beginning with double quotes (") are required when copying characters between files when editing more than one file

Table 7.8 *vi Copy Text Commands*

KEY	DESCRIPTION
yy	copy current line into buffer
yl	copy character after cursor into buffer
"xyy	copy current line into buffer *x*
"xyl	copy character after cursor into buffer *x*

at a time. These commands copy text into buffers read by commands in the next section, "Inserting Text from Buffers."

Inserting Text from Buffers

The commands shown in Table 7.9 are used to insert text into the file being edited. These commands insert text from buffers created by commands described in the previous section, "Copying Text into Buffers."

Table 7.9 *vi Insert Text Commands*

KEY	DESCRIPTION
p	insert contents of buffer after cursor
P	insert contents of buffer before cursor
"xp	insert contents of buffer *x* after cursor
"xP	insert contents of buffer *x* before cursor

The unnamed buffers in the two previous sections (the *yy*, *yl*, *p*, and *P* commands in "Copying Text into Buffers" and "Inserting Text from Buffers") are used to move text around a single file being edited. The named buffers (those beginning with "x in "Copying Text into Buffers" and "Inserting Text from Buffers") are used when moving text between two files being edited at the same time. You copy text with the "*xyy* or "*xyl* command, switch to another file, and then insert text with the "*xp* or "*xP* command.

Search and Replace

Table 7.10 lists the commands used to search for and/or replace text in the file being edited.

Table 7.10 *vi Search and Replace Commands*

KEY	DESCRIPTION
fx	Find next *x*
Fx	find previous *x*
tx	move to character after next *x*

Table 7.10 *vi Search and Replace Commands (Continued)*

KEY	DESCRIPTION
Tx	move to character after previous *x*
;	repeat last *f*, *F*, *t*, or *T*
'	repeat inverse of last *f*, *F*, *t*, or *T*
%	find matching (,), {, or }
/pat	go to next line matching pat
?pat	go to previous line matching pat
/pat/+n	go to nth line after matching pat
?pat ?-n	go to nth line before matching pat
n	Repeat last / or ?
N	Reverse last / or ?
Rtext	replace characters with *text* until ESC is pressed
:n,m s/old/new/gCR	change all occurrences of text "old" to text "new", starting at line n, ending at line m
:1,$ s/old/new/gCR	change all occurrences of text "old" to text "new", in entire file
:%s/old/new/gCR	change all occurrences of text "old" to text "new", in entire file

EXAM NOTES

THINK ABOUT IT . . .

What if you need to replace the slash character ("/") in a file? The "*s/old/new/*" notation will not work, since the slash character is a delimiter.

Use the question mark character when replacing the slash character. For example, if you need to replace every slash with an asterisk, the command would be "*s?/?*?*".

7.7 Reading and Writing Files

Table 7.11 describes vi commands used to read and write files being edited. See also the previous section, "Exiting vi."

Table 7.11 *vi Reading and Writing Files Commands*

KEY	DESCRIPTION
:wCR	write file, do not exit vi
:w!CR	write to file when file is read-only
:w filenameCR	write to *filename*, do not exit vi
:w! filenameCR	write to read-only *filename*, do not exit vi
:e!CR	discard changes, re-edit file
:e#CR	edit alternate file (when two or more were specified on the command line)
:e!#CR	edit alternate file, discard changes on current file (when two or more were specified on the command line)
:e filenameCR	edit *filename*
:r filenameCR	copy the contents of *filename* into current file

7.8 Miscellaneous Commands

Miscellaneous vi commands are listed in Table 7.12.

Table 7.12 *vi Miscellaneous Commands*

KEY	DESCRIPTION
u	undo last change
U	restore line
.	repeat last command
^	repeat last change
J	join lines
^L, ^R	clear and redraw
zCR	redraw window with current line at the top
z-CR	redraw window with current line at the bottom
z.CR	redraw window with current line at the middle
^G	show current line and file
:cmdCR	execute any valid ex or ed command
:shCR	run a command shell; upon exit, control returns to vi
:!cmdCR	run any valid UNIX command "cmd"; upon its exit, control returns to vi
:nCR	edit next file (when multiple files were specified in vi command)
:set showmode	tells vi to display when in insert or append mode

EXAM NOTES

THINK ABOUT IT . . .

Help! You cannot remember if you are in *insert* mode or not. How can you tell?

Press the ESC key. If you were in insert mode, you'll be placed in command mode. If you were in *last-line* mode, you will be placed in *command* mode unless you have typed in some characters on the command line.

EXAM NOTES

THINK ABOUT IT . . .

I need to edit two files, moving text from one to the other. How can I do this?

Open both files on the command line: *vi file1 file2.* Then, to "toggle" between the two files, press *:n.* To copy text from one file to the other, copy into and out of a "named" buffer: For instance, to copy one line of text into buffer "a", type *"ayy.* Then, toggle to the other file with *:n.* Then, to write the saved text into the other file, type *"ap.*

Numerals Before vi Commands

Most vi commands can be prepended with a number. For instance, the delete line command, *dd*, can be prepended with a number, such as *16dd*. This means delete 16 lines starting at this line.

The commands starting with :, /, or ? do not use this syntax.

7.9 Mapping New Commands

The *:map* command is used to create new commands or macros. *:map* allows you to create new commands, which is handy if you repeatedly perform certain operations. The syntax of the *:map* command is *:map n cmd*, where *n* is a letter, and *cmd* is a vi command.

If you wish the new command to contain a CR, you must press ^V before pressing CR when creating the new command.

Some examples follow.

```
:map g 1G^VCR
:map X 5dd
```

In the first example, the *g* key is mapped to the command used to move the cursor to the top of the file. In the second example, the letter *X* is used to delete five lines from a file.

7.10 vi Configuration Commands

vi has several configuration commands that are used to alter its operating characteristics. Some of these are shown in Table 7.13.

Table 7.13 *vi Configuration Commands*

COMMAND	DESCRIPTION
:set all	displays all options in effect for current vi session
:set showmodes (:set noshowmodes)	tells vi to display when in insert or append mode (do not show mode)
:set number (:set nonumber)	display line numbers (turn off line numbers)
:set wrapscan (:set nowrapscan)	go back to beginning of file when searching for text (stop at end of file when searching for text)

vi Configuration File

The configuration options shown in Table 7.13 can be placed in a file that takes effect every time you run vi. The configuration file name is *.exrc* and it must be placed in your home directory. An example *.exrc* file follows.

```
:set showmodes
:set wrapscan
:map g 1G^V^M
```

The first line sets "showmodes", meaning vi will display a message at the bottom of the screen when in insert or append mode. The second line sets "wrapscan", meaning vi will continue a text search at the top of a file after reaching the bottom of the file. The third line maps the "1G" command to the letter g.

Any valid *:set* or *:map* command can be placed in the *.exrc* file.

Chapter Summary

The commands used to start vi are *vi filename...*, *view filename...* (read-only), and *vedit filename...* (beginner mode). vi creates *filename* if it doesn't exist, if there are sufficient permissions to do so.

vi has three operating modes: command mode, input mode, and last-line mode.

In command mode, there are several commands available that move the cursor, delete, copy and paste text, and enter the other two modes. Numerals can precede most vi commands; these signal vi to execute the command that number of times (e.g., to delete a certain number of characters or lines).

In input mode, all characters typed on the keyboard are inserted into the file. There are a few key commands available in input mode, all having to do with editing what is being typed in. Pressing the ESC key ends input mode.

Last line mode is initiated by typing the colon key (":") while in command mode. Then, any of several vi commands can be entered, completed by pressing RETURN.

New commands can be created by mapping a key with the *:map* command.

vi can be configured with the *:set* command. A list of all available configuration commands can be viewed by entering the *:set all* command. vi configurations can be set permanently by creating an .exrc file.

Test Yourself

Multiple Choice

1. Which *vi* command is used to delete three lines?
   - A. `3dl`
   - B. `3dd`
   - C. `dldldl`
   - D. `3xl`

2. You are editing a file that you own and, when you try to save it, discover that it is read-only. What is the correct course of action?
   A. Abort vi.
   B. Enter the vi command `:chmod 666`.
   C. Enter the vi command `"s w!`.
   D. Enter the vi command `:w!`.

3. Given:

```
:1,80 s/644/755/g
```

   What is the result?
   A. In lines 1 through 80, substitute every occurrence of 644 with 755.
   B. In columns 1 through 80, substitute every occurrence of 644 with 755.
   C. In lines 1 through 80, substitute every occurrence of 755 with 644.
   D. In columns 1 through 80, substitute every occurrence of 755 with 644.
   E. Change the file permissions of the first 80 files in the current directory to 755.

4. Which command will start vi in "beginner" mode?
   A. `vedit filename`
   B. `vi -b filename`
   C. `viewedit filename`
   D. `vi -w filename`

5. What is the purpose of the *showmode* setting?
   A. It is used to show all vi settings.
   B. It determines whether vi will display file permissions.
   C. It determines whether vi will display which mode it is currently in.
   D. It is used to show all activated settings.

6. What is the purpose of the *:set all* command?
   A. It is used to show all vi settings.
   B. It determines whether vi will display file permissions.
   C. It is used to reset factory defaults.
   D. It is used to show all activated settings.

7. Which commands will deactivate the *wrapscan* setting?
   A. `:nowrapscan`
   B. `:set nowrapscan`
   C. `:unset wrapscan`
   D. `:set -wrapscan`

8. Given:

```
# vi +5dd log.txt
```

   What is the result?
   A. Edit the file *log.txt* in five days.
   B. Edit the file *log.txt* for five days.
   C. Create up to five backup copies when saving or exiting.
   D. The first five lines of the file are deleted, even before the vi session begins.

9. Given a vi session:

```
#ident  "@(#)networks   1.4     92/07/14 SMI"   /* SVr4.0 1.1   */
#
_
# The networks file associates Internet Protocol (IP) network numbers
# with network names.  The format of this file is:
#
#       network-name    network-number  nicknames . . .
#

#
# The loopback network is used only for intra-machine communication
#
loopback        127
```

```
#
# Internet networks
#
arpanet         10                  arpa    # Historical
~
~
~
~
~
                                                        OPEN MODE
```

Which is true?

A. vi is in input mode. The "a" or "A" command has been entered.
B. vi is in open mode. The "o" or "O" command has been entered.
C. vi is in input mode. The "o" or "O" command has been entered.
D. vi is in open mode. The "a" or "A" command has been entered.

10. Which four letter keys are used to move the cursor in command mode?

A. a, s, d, f
B. h, j, k, l
C. u, d, l, r
D. a, b, c, d

FREE RESPONSE

11. Enter the command used to turn on the showmodes vi setting.

12. You are editing the file *message.txt*. Enter the vi command to save it to the file *message.tmp*.

CHAPTER 8

Disks

After completing this chapter, you'll be able to meet the following Solaris Administration Exam objectives:

- Select the command used to add device configuration information for a new disk device without requiring a reboot of Solaris.
- Differentiate between the uses of a character (raw) disk (*/dev/rdsk*) and a block disk (*/dev/dsk*).
- Identify the correct usage of the *format* command.
- Select correct statements about the use of the menu selections for the *format* command.
- Select correct statements about the use of the menu selections for the *partition* subcommand under the *format* command.

To fulfill these objectives, this chapter discusses:

- Adding disks to a system;
- Disk devices; and
- The commands used to manage disks and file systems.

8.1 Adding Disks to a System

When a new disk device is added to a system, Solaris cannot access the device until Solaris' device tables have been rebuilt. There are several ways to accomplish this:

- Create the file */reconfigure* and reboot the system. When Solaris finds the */reconfigure file*, it will rebuild the system device tables.
- Reboot the system with the *reboot –r* command. (Note: This is *not* the preferred method since a *reboot* does not invoke the clean shutdown of daemons and application programs.) Upon reboot, Solaris will rebuild the system device tables.
- Shut down the system and boot with the *boot –r* Boot PROM command. Upon reboot, Solaris will rebuild the system device tables.
- Dynamically reconfigure the system device tables with the *devfsadm* command.

It is recommended that you back up the system prior to adding a new disk device to the system. A system malfunction or administrator error can cause existing disks to be reconfigured, resulting in data loss.

Adding a Device Dynamically Using the *devfsadm* Command

The *devfsadm* command is used to dynamically reconfigure system device tables without having to reboot the system. This can be especially useful in environments that have a poor tolerance for the down time usually associated with system reboots and hardware reconfiguration.

The *devfsadm* command does dynamically what a "*boot –r*" did in earlier versions of Solaris: It creates device files in */devices* and logical links in */dev* and loads any additional kernel drivers.

The syntax of the *devfsadm* command is *devfsadm [-C] [-c device_class] [-i driver_name] [-n] [-r root_dir] [-s] [-t table_file] [-v]*. The options for *devfsadm* are:

- *-C*. Cleanup mode. Prompts *devfsadm* to invoke cleanup routines that are not normally invoked to remove dangling logical links. If *-c* is also used, *devfsadm* only cleans up for the listed devices' classes.

- *-c device_class*. Restrict operations to devices of class *device_class*. Solaris defines the following values for *device_class*: *disk*, *tape*, *port*, *audio*, and *pseudo*. This option may be specified more than once to specify multiple device classes.
- *-i driver_name*. Configure only the devices for the named driver, *driver_name*. Example *driver_name*'s include: *sd* = SCSI disk; *st* = SCSI tape; and *pty* = pseudo terminal driver.
- *-n*. Do not attempt to load drivers or add new nodes to the kernel device tree.
- *-s*. Suppress any changes to */dev* or */devices*. This is useful with the *-v* option for debugging.
- *-t table_file*. Read an alternate *devlink.tab* file. *devfsadm* normally reads */etc/devlink.tab*.
- *-r root_dir*. Presume that the */dev* and */devices* directory trees are found under *root_dir*, not directly under root (/). No other use or assumptions are made about *root_dir*.
- *-v*. Print changes to */dev* and */devices* in verbose mode.

Examples of the *devfsadm* command follow.

```
# devfsadm -i sd
# devfsadm -c tape
# devfsadm -c disk -c tape -c pseudo
```

In the first example, *devfsadm* configures only those devices supported by the *sd* driver. In the second example, *devfsadm* configures only tape devices. In the third example, *devfsadm* configures disk, tape, and pseudo devices.

EXAM NOTES

THINK ABOUT IT . . .

You need to add another disk to the system, but you don't know what address to assign to it.

For simplicity we'll confine this example to a system with a single SCSI controller.

First you'll need to inventory your current disk devices. The *format* command will list what disks are on your system. But to be sure, shut your system down, perform a PROM reset, then perform a *probe-scsi* (these are covered in Chapter 3). Write down all of the used SCSI addresses. You can pick an unused address and assign that to your disk. You will have to refer to your disk hardware manual to see how to set the SCSI address for it.

8.2 Disk Devices

Raw and Block Device Interfaces

Each disk slice has two device interfaces associated with it—a "raw" device and a "block" device. These represent the two methods by which the system accesses a disk. Tools accessing the raw device read the device one character at a time, while tools accessing the block device read entire disk blocks at a time. These interfaces have file names in the */dev* directory associated with them. These file names are explained in the next section.

Device Interfaces File Names

Block device names reside in the */dev/dsk* directory, and raw device names reside in the */dev/rdsk* directory. An easy way to remember which is which is that "r" in rdsk means "raw disk."

A typical disk slice file name is */dev/dsk/c0t4d0s0*. The name *c0t4d0s0* means:

- c0—this is controller number 0
- t4—this is SCSI target number 4
- d0—this is SCSI disk number 0
- s0—this is slice number 0

For systems with only one SCSI controller, the controller number will always be zero. The target number is the address set by a switch on the back of the unit. The disk number refers to the SCSI logical unit number (LUN) for multidrive devices. For single-drive devices, this number is zero.

Another thing to remember is that, for example, */dev/dsk/c0t4d0s0* and */dev/rdsk/c0t4d0s0* refer to the same disk slice. The first is the disk slice's block device interface and the second is the slice's raw device interface.

Slice number 2 has a special arbitrary meaning—it represents the *entire* disk device.

Tools and Disk Interfaces Used

Different tools are designed to access one interface or the other—either the raw or the block device. Some examples of tools and which device type they use are shown in Table 8.1.

Table 8.1 *Disk Management Tools and Interfaces Used*

TOOL	DESCRIPTION	INTERFACE	COMMAND EXAMPLE
df	Show disk space consumption	block	df /dev/dsk/c0t2d0s4
fsck	Repair a file system	raw	fsck -p /dev/rdsk/c0t0d0s0
format	Format and partition a disk	raw	format /dev/dsk/c1t0d1s0
mount	Attach a file system to a directory	block	mount /dev/dsk/c1t3d0s0 /export/tools
newfs	Create a new file system	raw	newfs /dev/rdsk/c1t0d1s0
prtvtoc	Display disk partition information	raw	prtvtoc /dev/rdsk/c1t0d1s0

EXAM NOTES

THINK ABOUT IT . . .

You need to know which disk is which in your system. The internal disks don't have any visible SCSI address switches on them. What to do?

You will need to consult the hardware reference for your particular system. Some Sun SPARC systems assign internal disk SCSI addresses by their location—that is, which connector inside the system connects them.

As for the external drives, there is usually a visible switch on the back or bottom of the unit. Some units will need to be opened up, as the switches may only be inside (you should remove power before opening up any computer equipment).

In the worst case you may have a process of elimination on your hands. You might need to disconnect your disks (remember to label where they were connected so that you can return the system to its originally cabled state!) and reconnect them one at a time after running the PROM command *probe-scsi*. Once you discover the SCSI address of any unlabeled disk, put an external label on the disk so that you won't have to go through the pain again.

8.3 Formatting Disks

The *format* command is used to format and partition a disk device. The syntax of the *format* command is *format [options] devicename*, where *devicename* is a raw disk device name. The options available with the *format* command are:

- *-d disk-name*. Specify the disk to be acted upon.
- *-e*. Enable SCSI expert menu. This is not recommended for casual use.
- *-f command-file*. The interactive input for the *format* command comes from a *command-file* instead of from the keyboard.
- *-l log-file*. Log a transcript to the indicated *log-file*.
- *-m*. Enable extended messages. This is useful if an error occurs.
- *-M*. Enable extended and diagnostic messages.
- *-p partition-name*. Specify the partition table for the disk to be acted upon. The *–d* option must also be specified. The disk type must be specified with the *-t* option or already on the disk label.
- -. Silent. All of standard output is suppressed, but error messages are still displayed. This is usually used with the *-f* option.
- *-t disk-type*. Specify the *disk-type*. The *–d* option must also be used.
- *-x file*. Use the list of disks contained in *file*.

The *format* command is used to perform the following tasks:

- Perform a low-level format on the disk.
- Repair bad sectors on the disk.
- Run read/write tests on the disk.
- Create disk partitions.
- Remove disk partitions.
- List disk partitions.

The *format* command is interactive by default. After entering the *format* command, you will see the format prompt, where the following commands can be issued:

- *analyze*. Perform read, write, and compare tests.
- *backup*. Search for backup labels.
- *cache*. Enable, disable, and query the state of the write cache and the read cache. This menu item appears only when the *-e* option is specified, and is supported only on SCSI devices.

- *current*. Display the device name, the disk geometry, and the pathname to the current disk device.
- *defect*. Retrieve and print the disk's defect lists.
- *disk*. Choose the disk that will be used in subsequent operations (known as the *current* disk).
- *fdisk*. Run the *fdisk* program to create an fdisk partition for Solaris software (this is for Intel-based systems only).
- *format*. Format and verify the current disk. Note: This will destroy all data on the disk.
- *inquiry*. Display the vendor, product name, and revision level of the current disk.
- *label*. Write a new label to the current disk.
- *partition*. Create and modify slices. This brings up another interactive menu with its own commands described later in this section.
- *quit*. Exit the *format* menu.
- *repair*. Repair a specific block on the disk.
- *save*. Save new disk and slice information.
- *type*. Select (define) a disk type.
- *verify*. Read and display labels. Print information such as the number of cylinders, alternate cylinders, heads, sectors, and the partition table.
- *volname*. Label the disk with a new eight-character volume name.
- *!cmd*. Execute the *cmd* command, then return here.
- *?*. Display list of available commands.

The *format* program requires only the minimum number of characters to make the command unique. For instance, if you want to *partition* a disk, type *p* and RETURN. The *cache* and *current* commands require two letters apiece, so you would type *ca* or *cu*, respectively.

EXAM NOTES

THINK ABOUT IT . . .

Help! I formatted (low-level format) my disk, but I think I forgot to back up one of the file systems on it!

It's gone. There is no "undo" for a low-level format (nor for writing out a new partition table to the disk. Go slowly. Read the dialogues. Format is a powerful, yet destructive, tool. Mistakes can be costly.

Partition Submenu

The *partition* option brings up a submenu of available commands. These are:

- *0*—make a change to the '0' partition.
- *1*—make a change to the '1' partition.
- *2*—make a change to the '2' partition.
- *3*—make a change to the '3' partition.
- *4*—make a change to the '4' partition.
- *5*—make a change to the '5' partition.
- *6*—make a change to the '6' partition.
- *7*—make a change to the '7' partition.
- *select*—select a predefined table name.
- *modify*—modify a predefined partition table.
- *name*—give a name to the current table that can be used later.
- *print*—display the current partition table.
- *label*—write modified partition map and label to the disk.
- *!cmd*—execute *cmd* command, then return here.
- *?*—print this list of available commands.
- *quit*—quit and return to the format main command menu.

Here in the *partition* menu, *format* allows only the first letter (or two, as needed to eliminate ambiguities) of any command. For example, type *p* to display the current partition table.

If one of the partition numbers is specified in the partition menu, you'll be asked a series of questions about the partition. These are:

1. *format* asks for the *partition id*, which must be one of: *unassigned*, *boot*, *root*, *swap*, *usr*, *backup*, *stand*, *var*, *home*, or *alternates*. These labels are for your information only and do not have a bearing on the function or use of the partition.
2. Next, *format* asks for the *partition permission flags*, which must be one of:
   - *wm*—read-write, mountable (default)
   - *wu*—read-write, unmountable
   - *rm*—read-only, mountable
   - *ru*—read-only, unmountable
3. *format* now asks for the starting cylinder number for the partition.

4. *format* next asks for the size of the partition. Answer this in terms of blocks, cylinders, MB, or GB. The format for each is:
    - Cylinders. Append the size of the partition with a "c". As an example, for a partition with 500 cylinders, answer *500c*.
    - Blocks. Append the size of the partition with a "b". As an example, for a partition with 800 blocks, answer *800b*.
    - Megabytes. Append the size of the partition with an "m". As an example, for a partition with 900 megabytes, answer *900m*. Fractional sizes are allowed (e.g., 245.75).
    - Gigabytes. Append the size of the partition with a "g". As an example, for a partition with 4.5 gigabytes, answer *4.5g*.
5. You'll be returned to the partition submenu prompt. It is recommended that you next display the partition table with the *print* command (which can be entered as a *p*). Check the table carefully.
6. Once you are satisfied that the partition table is correct, you must write it to the disk with the *label* command (you can enter just *l*).
7. Format will analyze the proposed partition table and check for syntax errors, such as overlapping partitions, or partitions which exceed the size of the disk. If the partition map is valid, it will be written to the disk.

EXAM NOTES

THINK ABOUT IT . . .

You have a disk with four partitions. The first is presently used by a file system. You want to combine the remaining three partitions into a single partition and use it. How can this be done without destroying the existing partition?

First, back up the file system on that disk. If you make a mistake, you could destroy it.

Next, run the *format* program, and go to the *partition* submenu. Partition 0 is the one you want to keep, so you'll leave it alone. Partitions 1, 3, and 4 are the ones you want to combine into a new partition. Change the size of partitions 3 and 4 to zero cylinders. Now change the size of partition 1 to be that of 1, 3, and 4. Display the new partition table, and study it carefully before writing it to the disk. Make sure that partition 0 has not been changed.

Exit the *format* program. You should be able to remount the file system that uses partition zero.

Examples of disk formatting and changing a disk's partition table follow.

Formatting a Disk

This is an example of an actual disk format dialogue.

```
# format
Searching for disks...done

AVAILABLE DISK SELECTIONS:
       0. c0t1d0 <SUN2.1G cyl 2733 alt 2 hd 19 sec 80>
          /iommu@f,e0000000/sbus@f,e0001000/espdma@f,400000/
esp@f,800000/sd@1,0
       1. c0t3d0 <SUN1.05 cyl 2036 alt 2 hd 14 sec 72>
          /iommu@f,e0000000/sbus@f,e0001000/espdma@f,400000/
esp@f,800000/sd@3,0
       2. c0t4d0 <SUN1.05 cyl 2036 alt 2 hd 14 sec 72>
          /iommu@f,e0000000/sbus@f,e0001000/espdma@f,400000/
esp@f,800000/sd@4,0
Specify disk (enter its number): 2
selecting c0t4d0
[disk formatted]

FORMAT MENU:
        disk       - select a disk
        type       - select (define) a disk type
        partition  - select (define) a partition table
        current    - describe the current disk
        format     - format and analyze the disk
        repair     - repair a defective sector
        label      - write label to the disk
        analyze    - surface analysis
        defect     - defect list management
        backup     - search for backup labels
        verify     - read and display labels
        save       - save new disk/partition definitions
        inquiry    - show vendor, product and revision
        volname    - set 8-character volume name
        !<cmd>     - execute <cmd>, then return
        quit
format> format
Ready to format.  Formatting cannot be interrupted
and takes 19 minutes (estimated). Continue? yes
```

```
Beginning format. The current time is Mon Feb 26 06:21:54 2001

Formatting...
done

Verifying media...
        pass 0 - pattern = 0xc6dec6de
   2035/12/18

        pass 1 - pattern = 0x6db6db6d
   2035/12/18

Total of 0 defective blocks repaired.
format> quit
#
```

Changing the Partition Table

This is an example of an actual disk partition dialogue. A 1GB disk is partitioned into two equally sized partitions.

```
# format
Searching for disks...done

AVAILABLE DISK SELECTIONS:
       0. c0t1d0 <SUN2.1G cyl 2733 alt 2 hd 19 sec 80>
          /iommu@f,e0000000/sbus@f,e0001000/espdma@f,400000/
esp@f,800000/sd@1,0
       1. c0t3d0 <SUN1.05 cyl 2036 alt 2 hd 14 sec 72>
          /iommu@f,e0000000/sbus@f,e0001000/espdma@f,400000/
esp@f,800000/sd@3,0
       2. c0t4d0 <SUN1.05 cyl 2036 alt 2 hd 14 sec 72>
          /iommu@f,e0000000/sbus@f,e0001000/espdma@f,400000/
esp@f,800000/sd@4,0
Specify disk (enter its number): 2
selecting c0t4d0
[disk formatted]

FORMAT MENU:
        disk       - select a disk
        type       - select (define) a disk type
        partition  - select (define) a partition table
        current    - describe the current disk
        format     - format and analyze the disk
        repair     - repair a defective sector
```

```
        label       - write label to the disk
        analyze     - surface analysis
        defect      - defect list management
        backup      - search for backup labels
        verify      - read and display labels
        save        - save new disk/partition definitions
        inquiry     - show vendor, product and revision
        volname     - set 8-character volume name
        !<cmd>      - execute <cmd>, then return
        quit
format> partition

PARTITION MENU:
        0      - change `0' partition
        1      - change `1' partition
        2      - change `2' partition
        3      - change `3' partition
        4      - change `4' partition
        5      - change `5' partition
        6      - change `6' partition
        7      - change `7' partition
        select - select a predefined table
        modify - modify a predefined partition table
        name   - name the current table
        print  - display the current table
        label  - write partition map and label to the disk
        !<cmd> - execute <cmd>, then return
        quit
partition> print
Current partition table (original):
Total disk cylinders available: 2036 + 2 (reserved cylinders)

Part      Tag    Flag     Cylinders        Size            Blocks
  0       root    wm       0 - 1774      873.63MB    (1775/0/0) 1789200
  1       swap    wu    1775 - 2035      128.46MB    (261/0/0)   263088
  2     backup    wm       0 - 2035     1002.09MB    (2036/0/0) 2052288
  3 unassigned    wm       0                0        (0/0/0)          0
  4 unassigned    wm       0                0        (0/0/0)          0
  5 unassigned    wm       0                0        (0/0/0)          0
  6 unassigned    wm       0                0        (0/0/0)          0
  7 unassigned    wm       0                0        (0/0/0)          0

partition> 0
Part      Tag    Flag     Cylinders        Size            Blocks
  0       root    wm       0 - 1774      873.63MB    (1775/0/0) 1789200
```

```
Enter partition id tag[root]: alternates
Enter partition permission flags[wm]: wm
Enter new starting cyl[0]: 0
Enter partition size[1789200b, 1775c, 873.63mb, 0.85gb]: 1020c
partition> print
Current partition table (unnamed): ____
Total disk cylinders available: 2036 + 2 (reserved cylinders)

Part      Tag    Flag     Cylinders         Size            Blocks
  0 alternates    wm       0 - 1019      502.03MB    (1020/0/0) 1028160
  1       swap    wu    1775 - 2035      128.46MB    (261/0/0)   263088
  2     backup    wm       0 - 2035     1002.09MB    (2036/0/0) 2052288
  3 unassigned    wm       0               0         (0/0/0)          0
  4 unassigned    wm       0               0         (0/0/0)          0
  5 unassigned    wm       0               0         (0/0/0)          0
  6 unassigned    wm       0               0         (0/0/0)          0
  7 unassigned    wm       0               0         (0/0/0)          0

partition> 1
Part      Tag    Flag     Cylinders         Size            Blocks
  1       swap    wu    1775 - 2035      128.46MB    (261/0/0)   263088

Enter partition id tag[swap]: stand
Enter partition permission flags[wu]: wu
Enter new starting cyl[1020]: ____
Enter partition size[1023120b, 1015c, 499.57mb, 0.49gb]: 1016c
partition> print
Current partition table (unnamed): ____
Total disk cylinders available: 2036 + 2 (reserved cylinders)

Part      Tag    Flag     Cylinders         Size            Blocks
  0 alternates    wm       0 - 1019      502.03MB    (1020/0/0) 1028160
  1      stand    wu    1020 - 2035      500.06MB    (1016/0/0) 1024128
  2     backup    wm       0 - 2035     1002.09MB    (2036/0/0) 2052288
  3 unassigned    wm       0               0         (0/0/0)          0
  4 unassigned    wm       0               0         (0/0/0)          0
  5 unassigned    wm       0               0         (0/0/0)          0
  6 unassigned    wm       0               0         (0/0/0)          0
  7 unassigned    wm       0               0         (0/0/0)          0

label  - write partition map and label to the disk
partition> label
Ready to label disk, continue? yes

partition> print
Current partition table (unnamed): ____
Total disk cylinders available: 2036 + 2 (reserved cylinders)
```

```
Part      Tag    Flag     Cylinders         Size            Blocks
  0 alternates    wm       0 - 1019       502.03MB    (1020/0/0) 1028160
  1      stand    wu    1020 - 2035       500.06MB    (1016/0/0) 1024128
  2     backup    wm       0 - 2035      1002.09MB    (2036/0/0) 2052288
  3 unassigned    wm       0                 0        (0/0/0)          0
  4 unassigned    wm       0                 0        (0/0/0)          0
  5 unassigned    wm       0                 0        (0/0/0)          0
  6 unassigned    wm       0                 0        (0/0/0)          0
  7 unassigned    wm       0                 0        (0/0/0)          0

partition> quit

FORMAT MENU:
        disk       - select a disk
        type       - select (define) a disk type
        partition  - select (define) a partition table
        current    - describe the current disk
        format     - format and analyze the disk
        repair     - repair a defective sector
        label      - write label to the disk
        analyze    - surface analysis
        defect     - defect list management
        backup     - search for backup labels
        verify     - read and display labels
        save       - save new disk/partition definitions
        inquiry    - show vendor, product and revision
        volname    - set 8-character volume name
        !<cmd>     - execute <cmd>, then return
        quit
format> quit
#
```

In the foregoing example, the *format* command is invoked. *format* displays available disks and the list of available commands. The *partition* submenu is chosen; *format* displays the available *partition* subcommands. The *print* command tells format to display the current partition table.

Next, partition 0 (zero) is chosen. Its *tag* is changed to "alternates", and its size to 1020 cylinders. The partition table is displayed again with the *print* command. This is recommended to ensure that changes in the partition table are as intended.

Next, partition 1 is chosen, its tag changed to "stand", and its size set to 1016 cylinders. The partition table is again displayed with the *print* command.

Next, the new partition table is written to the disk using the *label* command. The partition table is again displayed with the *print* command.

Finally, format is exited with the *quit* command.

8.4 Creating, Tuning, and Checking File Systems

Creating File Systems with *newfs*

The *newfs* command is used to create file systems of type *ufs*. In its simplest form, all *newfs* needs to know is on which disk and partition the new file system needs to be created. There are, however, several options available for the administrator who wishes to create a file system with nonstandard configurations.

The *newfs* command is a friendly front-end to the *mkfs* command. *mkfs* is the program that actually creates a file system. It is easier to use the *newfs* command; the details of *mkfs* are not discussed in this book.

The syntax of the *newfs* command is *newfs [options] raw-device*, where *raw-device* is the raw device in the directory */dev/rdsk* in which the file system is to be created. The options for *newfs* are:

- *-N*. Print out the file system parameters that would be used in creating the file system without actually creating the file system.
- *-v*. Verbose. *newfs* prints out its actions, including the parameters passed to *mkfs*.
- *-c cgsize*. The number of cylinders per cylinder group (ranging from 16 to 256). The default is calculated by dividing the number of sectors in the file system by the number of sectors in a gigabyte, and then multiplying the result by 32. The default value will always be between 16 and 256. *mkfs* may override this value.
- *-f fragsize*. The smallest amount of disk space in bytes to allocate to a file. The values must be a power of two selected from the range 512 to the logical block size. If logical block size is 4096, legal values are 512, 1024, 2048, and 4096; if logical block size is 8192, 8192 is also a legal value. The default is 1024.
- *-i nbpi*. The number of bytes per inode. This specifies the density of inodes in the file system. The number is divided into the total size of the file system to determine the fixed number of inodes to

create. It should reflect the expected average size of files in the file system. If fewer inodes are desired, a larger number should be used; to create more inodes a smaller number should be given. The default for *nbpi* is as follows:

Disk size	*Density*
up to 1GB	2048
1GB–2GB	4096
2GB–3GB	6144
3GB+	8192

- *-m free*. The minimum percentage of free space to maintain in the file system (between 1% and 99%, inclusively). This space is off limits to normal users. Once the file system is filled to this threshold, only the superuser can continue writing to the file system. This parameter can be subsequently changed using the *tunefs* command. The default is [(64 MBytes/partition size) * 100], rounded down to the nearest integer and limited between 1% and 10%, inclusively.
- *-o space* | *time*. The file system can be instructed either to minimize the time spent allocating blocks or to minimize the space fragmentation on the disk. The default is *time*.
- *-s size*. The size of the file system in sectors. The default is to use the entire partition.

Some examples of *newfs* follow.

```
# newfs /dev/rdsk/c0t4d0s0
newfs: construct a new file system /dev/rdsk/c0t4d0s0: (y/n)? y
/dev/rdsk/c0t4d0s0: 1028160 sectors in 1020 cylinders of 14 tracks, 72
sectors 502.0MB in 64 cyl groups (16 c/g, 7.88MB/g, 3776 i/g)
super-block backups (for fsck -F ufs -o b=#) at: 32, 16240, 32448,
48656, 64864, 81072, 97280, 113488, 129696, 145904, 162112, 178320,
194528, 210736, 226944, 243152, 258080, 274288, 290496, 306704, 322912,
339120, 355328, 371536, 387744, 403952, 420160, 436368, 452576, 468784,
484992, 501200, 516128, 532336, 548544, 564752, 580960, 597168, 613376,
629584, 645792, 662000, 678208, 694416, 710624, 726832, 743040, 759248,
774176, 790384, 806592, 822800, 839008, 855216, 871424, 887632, 903840,
920048, 936256, 952464, 968672, 984880, 1001088, 1017296,
#
```

```
# newfs -m 1 /dev/rdsk/c0t4d0s0
newfs: construct a new file system /dev/rdsk/c0t4d0s0: (y/n)? y
/dev/rdsk/c0t4d0s0: 1028160 sectors in 1020 cylinders of 14 tracks, 72
sectors 502.0MB in 64 cyl groups (16 c/g, 7.88MB/g, 960 i/g)
super-block backups (for fsck -F ufs -o b=#) at: 32, 16240, 32448,
48656, 64864, 81072, 97280, 113488, 129696, 145904, 162112, 178320,
194528, 210736, 226944, 243152, 258080, 274288, 290496, 306704, 322912,
339120, 355328, 371536, 387744, 403952, 420160, 436368, 452576, 468784,
484992, 501200, 516128, 532336, 548544, 564752, 580960, 597168, 613376,
629584, 645792, 662000, 678208, 694416, 710624, 726832, 743040, 759248,
774176, 790384, 806592, 822800, 839008, 855216, 871424, 887632, 903840,
920048, 936256, 952464, 968672, 984880, 1001088, 1017296,
#
```

In the first example, a new file system is built on disk device */dev/rdsk/c0t4d0s0* with all default values. In the second example, a file system is built with only 1% of the file system reserved for root-only write access.

The output from *newfs* should be recorded and kept in a safe place. This is because the superblock values may be needed someday if the file system ever requires an emergency repair with *fsck*.

EXAM NOTES

THINK ABOUT IT . . .

You need to create a file system on a large disk. The file system needs to have more than the usual number of inodes because it will contain vast numbers of small files. Because the disk will contain small files, you want the fragment size (the minimum number of bytes allocated to a file) to be as small as possible (this allows for the greatest possible number of files in the file system). Finally, you want little, if any, extra space for root-only, since this file system will be used solely by end-user applications. How could you best configure this file system?

A smaller-than-default value for the *-i* option is needed. Next, the value for the *-f* option should be 512. Finally, the value for the *-m* option can be 1 or 0. An example command line for *newfs* would be:

```
newfs -i 40 -f 512 -m 1 /dev/rdsk/c1t3d0s1 .
```

Tuning File Systems with *tunefs*

The *tunefs* command is used to alter the characteristics of a file system after it has been built. The syntax of the *tunefs* command is *tunefs [options] raw-device|filesystem*, where *raw-device* is a device interface in the */dev/rdsk* directory, and *filesystem* is the file system's mount point as specified in */etc/vfstab*. Options for *tunefs* are:

- *-m minfree*. Specify the percentage of space held back from normal users; the minimum free space threshold. This value can be set to 0; however, up to a factor of three in throughput will be lost compared to the performance obtained at a 10% threshold. Note: If the value is raised above the current usage level, users will be unable to allocate files until enough files have been deleted to get under the higher threshold.
- *-o [space | time]*. Change optimization strategy for the file system. Setting to *space* will conserve space. Setting to *time* will organize file layout to minimize access time.

Some examples follow.

```
# tunefs -m 3 /dev/rdsk/c0t4d0s0
minimum percentage of free space changes from 5% to 3%
#

# tunefs -o time /export/home
optimization preference changes from time to space
#
```

In the first example, the minimum free space for the file system located in */dev/rdsk/c0t4d0s0* is changed from 5% to 3%. In the second example, optimization for the file system */export/home* is changed from time to space.

Checking File Systems with *fsck*

The *fsck* command is used to check the integrity of and repair a file system. The syntax of the *fsck* command is *fsck [options] raw-device*, where *raw-device* is a device interface in */dev/rdsk*. The options for *fsck* are:

- *-F FSType*. Specify the file system type on which to operate. Allowable values are *ufs*, *s5fs*, and *cachefs*.

- *-m*. Check but do not repair. This option checks that the file system is suitable for mounting, returning the appropriate exit status. If the file system is ready for mounting, *fsck* displays a message such as: *ufs fsck: sanity check: /dev/rdsk/c0t3d0s1 okay.*
- *-n* | *-N*. Assume a "no" response to all questions asked by *fsck*; do not open the file system for writing.
- *-V*. Echo the expanded command line but do not execute the command. This option may be used to verify and to validate the command line.
- *-y* | *Y*. Assume a "yes" response to all questions asked by *fsck*.
- *-o specific-options*. These *specific-options* can be any combination of the following separated by commas (with no intervening spaces). These options are valid with any file system type unless specified. Recall that file systems created in Solaris 8 are of type *ufs* by default. Ordinarily, options for other file system types will not apply.
  - *b=n*. Use block *n* as the superblock for the file system. Block 32 is always one of the alternate superblocks. Determine the location of other superblocks by running *newfs* with the *-Nv* options specified.
  - *f*. Force checking of file systems regardless of the state of their superblock clean flag.
  - *w*. Check writable file systems only.

Some examples of *fsck* follow.

```
# fsck /dev/rdsk/c0t3d0s6
** /dev/rdsk/c0t3d0s6
** Currently Mounted on /usr
** Phase 1 - Check Blocks and Sizes
** Phase 2 - Check Pathnames
** Phase 3 - Check Connectivity
** Phase 4 - Check Reference Counts
** Phase 5 - Check Cyl groups

FILE SYSTEM STATE IN SUPERBLOCK IS WRONG; FIX? n

29211 files, 506274 used, 178084 free (2260 frags, 21978 blocks,  0.3%
fragmentation)
#

# fsck -o b=32 /dev/rdsk/c0t4d0s0
Alternate super block location: 32.
```

```
** /dev/rdsk/c0t4d0s0
** Currently Mounted on
** Phase 1 - Check Blocks and Sizes
** Phase 2 - Check Pathnames
** Phase 3 - Check Connectivity
** Phase 4 - Check Reference Counts
** Phase 5 - Check Cyl groups
2 files, 9 used, 505350 free (14 frags, 63167 blocks,  0.0%
fragmentation)

***** FILE SYSTEM WAS MODIFIED *****
#

# fsck /dev/rdsk/c0t4d0s0
** /dev/rdsk/c0t4d0s0
BAD SUPER BLOCK: BAD VALUES IN SUPER BLOCK
USE AN ALTERNATE SUPER-BLOCK TO SUPPLY NEEDED INFORMATION;
eg. fsck [-F ufs] -o b=# [special ...]
where # is the alternate super block. SEE fsck_ufs(1M).
# fsck -y -o b=32 /dev/rdsk/c0t4d0s0
Alternate super block location: 32.
** /dev/rdsk/c0t4d0s0
** Currently Mounted on
** Phase 1 - Check Blocks and Sizes
1840700269 BAD I=3929
1840700269 BAD I=3929
1840700269 BAD I=3929
1840700269 BAD I=3929
1840700269 BAD I=3929
1840700269 BAD I=3929
1840700269 BAD I=3929
1840700269 BAD I=3929
1840700269 BAD I=3929
1840700269 BAD I=3929
EXCESSIVE BAD BLKS I=3929
CONTINUE?  yes

INCORRECT BLOCK COUNT I=3929 (22512 should be 352)
CORRECT?  yes

PARTIALLY TRUNCATED INODE I=7561
SALVAGE?  Yes

1840700269 BAD I=7561
1840700269 BAD I=7561
1840700269 BAD I=7561
1840700269 BAD I=7561
```

```
1840700269 BAD I=7561
1840700269 BAD I=7561
1840700269 BAD I=7561
1840700269 BAD I=7561
1840700269 BAD I=7561
1840700269 BAD I=7561
EXCESSIVE BAD BLKS I=7561
CONTINUE?  yes

INCORRECT BLOCK COUNT I=7561 (416 should be 352)
CORRECT?  yes

PARTIALLY TRUNCATED INODE I=7567
SALVAGE?  yes

1840700269 BAD I=7567
[remainder of output not shown]
#
```

In the first example, *fsck* checks a mount file system (*/usr*). One error was found, which has not been repaired. In the second example, an alternate superblock is specified and a file system repaired. In the third example, *fsck* determines that the superblock is bad. A second attempt is made, this time using block 32 as the superblock as well as the *-y* option (to answer "yes" to every query). Ultimately this file system could not be repaired; it had to be rebuilt with *newfs* and restored from backup.

Lost Files in *lost+found*

When *fsck* performs repairs on a damaged file system, *fsck* will salvage everything it can figure out. When a subdirectory becomes damaged, sometimes files that resided there are lost. *fsck* puts these files in the *lost+found* directory at the root of the file system.

The files in *lost+found* are named the same as their inode number. Sometimes there can be quite a few of these files. It can be difficult, if not impossible, to figure out where all of these files belong. There is a tool available that can help.

The *ff* command produces a list of files and their respective inode numbers. If you run the *ff* command regularly and save the output, this output might someday help you put a file system back together: You will be able to recover those files in lost+found, since the output of *ff* (run *before* the file system became corrupted!) will match every inode with its file or directory name.

An example *ff* command follows.

```
# ff /dev/dsk/c0t0d0s7
/dev/dsk/c0t0d0s7:
4       /.CPR
8384    /pete/.
176086  /gsmith/.
394076  /jhamid/.
5      /pete/seti/setiathome-2.4.sparc-sun-solaris2.6/README
6      /pete/seti/setiathome-2.4.sparc-sun-solaris2.6/README.xsetiathome
7      /pete/seti/setiathome-2.4.sparc-sun-solaris2.6/setiathome
8      /pete/seti/setiathome-2.4.sparc-sun-solaris2.6/xsetiathome
9      /pete/seti/setiathome-2.4.sparc-sun-solaris2.6/lock.sah
10     /pete/seti/setiathome-2.4.sparc-sun-solaris2.6/pid.sah
25160 /pete/src/PGP/pgp-6.5.8/man/man1/.
15     /pete/office52/share/fonts/type1/ariob___.pfa
16     /pete/office52/share/fonts/type1/ariob___.pfb
17     /pete/office52/share/fonts/type1/arion___.pfa
18     /pete/office52/share/fonts/type1/arion___.pfb
19     /pete/office52/share/fonts/type1/chevn___.pfa
20     /pete/office52/share/fonts/type1/chevn___.pfb
21     /pete/office52/share/fonts/type1/chevon__.pfa
22     /pete/office52/share/fonts/type1/chevon__.pfb
23     /pete/office52/share/fonts/type1/congb___.pfa
[remainder of output not shown]
```

In this example, the file system residing on device */dev/dsk/c0t0d0s7* is listed. The inode number for the file (or directory) *.CPR* is 4, the inode number for the file (or directory) *pete* is 8384, and so forth.

At the time of file system creation, the need to save the output from *newfs* cannot be overemphasized. In situations such as the third example, recovering a file system from alternate superblocks may be your only hope.

EXAM NOTES

THINK ABOUT IT . . .

You need to repair a file system but do not know which alternate superblocks are available. What, if anything, can be done?

You can run *newfs nn* on the file system, and try one of the alternate superblocks listed. But if the file system was built with nonstandard parameters, it is possible that one of the alternates you choose will not be a superblock at all, but a block containing ordinary data on the file system. Be prepared to restore the file system from backups.

CHAPTER SUMMARY

The Solaris device tables must be rebuilt before a newly added disk can be accessed. The device tables can be rebuilt by creating the file */reconfigure* and rebooting the system, or by booting the system with the *-r* option. The device tables can also be rebuilt by running the *cfgadm* command; this does not require a reboot.

Each disk has two device files associated with it. The first is associated with the system's block device interface and is found in the directory */dev/dsk*; the second is associated with the system's raw device interface and can be found in the directory */dev/rdsk*.

Disk device names are encoded with its SCSI controller and device numbers; for example, device *c0t4d0s6* means controller zero, target 4, device 0, slice 6.

Some tools, such as *df* and *mount*, access a disk's block device interface. Other tools, such as *fsck*, *format*, *newfs*, and *prtvtoc*, access a disk's raw device interface.

The *format* command is used to test, repair, and partition a disk. The format command's top-level menu commands are *analyze*, *backup*, *cache*, *current*, *defect*, *disk*, *fsck*, *format*, *inquiry*, *label*, *partition*, *quit*, *repair*, *save*, *type*, *verify*, *volname*, *!cmd*, and *?*. The *partition* command has a subcommand menu; its commands are *select*, *modify*, *name*, *print*, *label*, *~cmd*, *?*, as well as the numbers `0` through `7`.

The *newfs* command is used to create file systems. There is a variety of options available that determine the file system's physical characteristics, such as number of inodes, fragment size, logical block size, and so on. The output from *newfs* should be saved when creating new file systems.

The *tunefs* command is used to change some of the file system's performance characteristics after it has been created. Specifically, *tunefs* can be used to alter the rotational delay, minimum free blocks for root-only use, and optimization strategy.

The *fsck* command is used to interactively check and repair a damaged file system. A damaged file system can be salvaged using an alternate superblock. Depending upon the condition that caused the file system corruption, it may still be necessary to re-create the file system with *newfs* and restore it from backup.

TEST YOURSELF

MULTIPLE CHOICE

1. Which three of the following commands access a raw disk device? (Choose three)
   A. `df`
   B. `format`
   C. `mount`
   D. `prtvtoc`
   E. `newfs`
   F. `fsck`
2. Which five functions are performed by the *format* command? (Choose five)
   A. List disk partitions
   B. Create disk partitions
   C. View/change the SCSI address of a disk
   D. Run read/write tests on a disk
   E. Repair bad sectors on a disk
   F. Perform a low-level format of a disk
3. Which partition number represents an entire disk device?
   A. 0
   B. 1
   C. 2
   D. 7
4. Which three units of measure are NOT valid in the *format* command for determining the size of a partition? (Choose three)
   A. Cylinders
   B. Tracks
   C. Heads
   D. Blocks
   E. Megabytes
   F. Gigabytes
   G. Terabytes

5. When are overlapping disk partitions permitted?
   A. Only on disks greater than 2GB.
   B. Only on track boundaries.
   C. Only on cylinder boundaries.
   D. Never. Disk partitions may not overlap.
   E. Only on Ultra-SCSI disks.
6. Which option of the *fsck* command is used to specify an alternate superblock?
   A. a
   B. b
   C. s
   D. sb
7. What is the purpose of *format* command *partition id*?
   A. It helps the administrator recall the purpose of the partition. It is a label only and has no real influence on the partition.
   B. It binds the partition to a file system mount point. This prevents the partition from being mounted inappropriately.
   C. It binds the partition to a system's hostid. This prevents other systems from mounting the partition.
   D. It specifies the userid that is permitted to mount the partition as a file system.
8. What is the purpose of *label* command in the *format* command's *partition* submenu?
   A. The partition label is filled in (it is a free-form text field).
   B. The partition label is chosen from a list.
   C. The partition label is written to the disk.
   D. The partition map is written to the disk.
9. You are experiencing numerous disk errors on a specific disk device. What is the first step you should perform?
   A. Back up the file system and perform read and write tests.
   B. Reformat the disk. This will identify bad blocks and add them to the defect list so that the errors will not recur.
   C. Add the bad block(s) to the defect list with the repair command.
   D. Back up the file system, and repartition the disk, excluding the bad blocks.

10. What is the function of the "var" *partition id*?
    A. It binds the partition to the */var* file system so that it cannot be mounted in other locations.
    B. It helps the administrator recall that this partition contains the */var* file system.
    C. It reserves the partition for later use in the */var* file system.
    D. It identifies the partition as a variable-sized partition.

FREE RESPONSE

11. What is the command used to dynamically reconfigure the system device tables?

12. You have added a new disk device to the system. What file must you create to cause the system to rebuild the device tables at the next system reboot?

CHAPTER 9

File Systems

After completing this chapter, you'll be able to meet the following Solaris Administration Exam objectives:

- List the different types of file systems in the Solaris Operating Environment.
- State the effect of the commonly used options of the *mount* command.
- Differentiate between the purpose of the */etc/mnttab* and */etc/vfstab* files.
- Select correct statements about the intended purpose of the */etc*, */opt*, */usr*, */export*, and / (root) directories.
- List the steps required to access data on diskettes or CD-ROMs.
- Match the file types of regular files, directories, symbolic links, device files, and hard links to their respective functions.

To fulfill these objectives, this chapter discusses:

- File systems: types, use, and examples;

- File system structure: directories and the types of files found in file systems; and
- Mounting fixed and removable file systems using the *mount* command.

9.1 File System Types

The types of file systems used in Solaris are: UFS, S5FS, PCFS, HSFS, UDFS, NFS, TmpFS, CacheFS, LOFS, PROCFS, Mnttab, and XMEMFS. These file system types are grouped according to their use as follows.

- *Disk-based file systems.* These are file systems found on hard disks, floppy disks, CD-ROM, and DVD-ROM devices. The file system types used are UFS, S5FS, PCFS, HSFS, and UDFS.
- *Network-based file systems.* These are file systems that are accessible over a network. The only file system type used is NFS.
- *Virtual file systems.* These are memory-based file systems that are used to make available certain operating system kernel functions and facilities. Most virtual file systems do not use disk space (exceptions are noted). The file system types used are TmpFS, CacheFS, LOFS, PROCFS, Mnttab, and XMEMFS.

Each file system type is explained here.

UFS File System

UFS, or **U**NIX **F**ile **S**ystem, is the Solaris default file system type used on hard disks. Its roots are based in the Berkeley Fast File System released in BSD 4.3 Tahoe.

Although UFS is ordinarily the default file system, the default can be changed by editing the file */etc/defaults/fs* and substituting a new default file system type. The file */etc/defaults/fs* usually appears as follows:

```
LOCAL=ufs
```

S5FS File System

The S5FS file system is a UNIX System V file system used by PC versions of UNIX.

HSFS File System

The HSFS file system includes the High Sierra, Rock Ridge, and ISO 9660 file systems. The High Sierra file system was the first CD-ROM-based file system. The ISO 9660 file system is the first official version of the High Sierra file system. Rock Ridge is a set of extensions to ISO 9660 that present all UFS features except hard links. The HSFS file system is a read-only file system.

PCFS File System

The **PC** **F**ile **S**ystem (PCFS), is the format used on DOS-based diskettes. This provides the capability for Solaris to format, write, and read DOS diskettes.

UDFS File System

The **U**niversal **D**ata **F**ormat (UDF) file system is the industry standard used on **D**igital **V**ersatile **D**isc or **D**igital **V**ideo **D**isc (DVD) discs.

NFS File System

The **N**etwork **F**ile **S**ystem (NFS) is a client-server mechanism whereby a system, the NFS server, makes one or more of its physically resident file systems available for network access. One or more other systems, called NFS clients, access the server-based file system, over the network, *as though* it were physically resident locally.

CacheFS File System

The CacheFS file system is used to improve the performance of remote (i.e., NFS-based) file systems or slow local devices (e.g., CD-ROM, diskette, and DVD). When a file system is cached, the data read from the remote CD-ROM, diskette, or DVD is stored in a cache on the local system. The CacheFS file system consumes disk space on the local system.

TMPFS File System

The TMPFS file system is a memory-based file system. Its purpose is to create a very fast temporary storage facility to improve system performance. It is most commonly used as the basis for the */tmp* file system. Files stored in a TMPFS file system are not permanent; the entire contents of a TMPFS-based file system are lost when the system is shut down or rebooted.

TMPFS-based file systems consume system swap space; the system administrator must be mindful of this when configuring the size of available swap space on a system.

LOFS File System

The Loopback File System (LOFS) provides for the creation of a new virtual file system that is used to access files on a "real" file system via a different path. For instance, you could create a loopback file system based upon the */var* file system called */tmp/virtualvar*. Then, files and directories in */var* can also be accessed via */tmp/virtualvar*.

LOFS does not create an additional copy of a file system, but rather the *illusion* of an additional copy.

PROCFS File System

The Process File System (PROCFS) contains information about active processes on the system. Tools such as *ps* and the *proc* tools (such as *proc*, *pcred*, *pfiles*, and *pflags*) read data in */proc*.

Mnttab File System

The file */etc/mnttab* is really a mounted read-only file system containing information about other file systems that have been mounted by the system. In previous versions of Solaris, */etc/mnttab* was an ordinary file.

XMEMFS File System

The Extended Memory File System (XMEMFS) is a virtual file system used to manage and access large amounts of physical memory exceeding 4GB in size.

9.2 Solaris File Systems

File Systems and Their Function

By default the Solaris operating system contains several file systems, each with its own purpose. They are shown in the following. All are type UFS unless stated otherwise.

- */ (root)*—this is the top-most file system. Some notable subdirectories contained in the root file system include:
  - */etc*—Solaris operating system configuration files.
  - */dev* and */devices*—all hardware device interface files.
  - */mnt*—a convenient temporary file system mount point.
  - */cdrom*—CD-ROM directories appear here when a CD-ROM is mounted.
  - */floppy*—floppy directories appear here when a floppy disc is mounted.
  - */net*—mount point used by the automounter.
  - */kernel*—the Solaris kernel and device drivers.
- */usr*—all Solaris administrative and user tools, man pages, and user shells.
- */var*—system files which change dramatically through the life of the system, including spool files, log files, and operating system data files.
- */opt*—optional Solaris packages and third-party software.
- */proc*—the virtual process file system (PROCFS) containing information about active processes.
- */export/home*—users' home directories containing user files.
- */tmp*—temporary files stored in the TMPFS file system. Destroyed at reboot or shutdown.

Directories

A *directory* is an entity that contains zero or more files or other directories. A *subdirectory* is a directory that resides within a directory. The terms *directory* and *subdirectory* are nearly synonymous, except that the top-level directory would not be called a subdirectory.

Directories are explored more fully in Chapters 1 and 6.

File Types

The types of files used in Solaris are:

- Regular file—this is a file containing character data. This can include any type of data including plain readable text, an application program, a database file, or a core image.
- Directory—strictly speaking, a directory is a special type of file. It consists of pointers to the files and directories contained in the directory.
- Character device file—this is a special file that provides the representation of a hardware device, real or imaginary. Its primary characteristic is the presence of a "major number" and a "minor number," which follow a device numbering scheme that identifies devices. Character devices are those where individual characters can be written to and read from the device. Generally, all devices are character devices.
- Block device file—like the character device file, this is a file with major and minor numbers. Block devices are those where reads from and writes to the device are done in blocks of data (e.g., 512 bytes at a time) instead of one character at a time. Generally the only types of devices in this category are disks.
- FIFO file—also known as a "named pipe," this is a file used to buffer data being created by one process and read by one or more other processes.
- Door—this is a special file that provides access to an RPC caching mechanism.
- Socket—sometimes known as a "domain socket," this type of file exists to facilitate network communications between processes running on the same system.
- Symbolic link—this is not really a file at all, but a pointer to a file or directory. A symbolic link is most often used to provide "backward compatibility" for programs (or users) expecting to find a file or directory that has moved to a new location. The symbolic link magically routes read and write requests to the file's new location, transparently.

A file's type can be seen with the *ls -l* command. A file's type is indicated by the first character in the 10-character mode string. Table 9.1 shows these file types.

Table 9.1 `ls` *Command File Types*

FILE TYPE LETTER	FILE TYPE
-	Regular file
d	Directory
D	Door
l	Symbolic link
b	Block device
c	Character device
p	FIFO file
s	Domain socket

Some examples of *ls* output follow.

```
# ls -l zs@f,1100000:a
crw-rw-rw-   1 root     sys      29,  0 Apr 4  2000 zs@f,1100000:a
# ls -la SUNW,fdtwo@f,1400000:b
brw-rw-rw-   1 root     sys      36,  1 Apr 4  2000 SUNW,fdtwo@f,1400000:b
# ls -l .name_service_door
Dr--r--r--   1 root     root          0 Apr 5  2000 .name_service_door
# ls -l initpipe
prw-------   1 root     root          0 Mar 2 04:50 initpipe
# ls -ld lp
drwxrwxr-x   9 lp       lp          512 Apr 5  2000 lp
# ls -l resolv.conf
-rw-r--r--   1 root     other        35 Oct 4 05:33 resolv.conf
# ls -l hosts
lrwxrwxrwx   1 root     root         12 Apr 4  2000 hosts -> ./inet/hosts
#
```

In the first example, the file *zs@f,1100000:a* is a character device; its major number is 29, and its minor number is 0. In the second example, the file *SUNW,fdtwo@f,1400000:b* is a block device; its major and minor numbers are 36 and 1. In the third example, the file *.name_service_door* is a door. In the fourth example, the file *initpipe* is a FIFO. In the fifth example, the file *lp* is a directory. In the sixth example, the file *resolv.conf* is an ordinary file. In the last example, the file *hosts* is a symbolic link.

Inodes

An inode is the internal placeholder for a file. The inode contains all of the file's characteristics except for its name and contents. Strictly speaking, a file name is really a pointer to an inode. The characteristics of an inode include:

- *Inode number*—this is the unique number assigned to the inode. Inode numbers are unique within an individual file system, not on the entire system.
- *File mode*—the permission settings for the file.
- *File type*—regular file, character device, block device, FIFO, domain socket, door, or symbolic link.
- *File owner*—userid associated with the file.
- *File groupid*—groupid associated with the file.
- *Number of links*—the number of filenames associated with the inode. When the link count drops to zero, the inode is deleted.
- *Last access time*—date and time of last access.
- *Inode change time*—time of last update to the inode owner, group, permissions, and so on.
- *Last modification time*—date and time the file was last modified.
- *Disk block address(es)*—the starting block number in the file system where the contents of the file reside.
- *Locks*—an inode has several associated locks to protect its integrity and the file contents.

You can view a file's inode number with the *-i* option of the *ls* command. Here is an example:

```
# ls -il S80lp
   318933 -rwxr--r--   5 root     sys            460 Jan  5  2000 S80lp
#
```

In this example, we're looking at the single file *S80lp*. Its inode number is 318933. You can search for files by inode number with the *-inum* option of the *find* command. Here is an example.

```
# find . -inum 318933 -print
./init.d/lp
./rc0.d/K39lp
./rc1.d/K39lp
./rc2.d/S80lp
```

```
./rcS.d/K39lp
#
```

In this example, we are looking for all files with inode number 318933. Five files were found. Here are some characteristics of the files found in this example.

- The five file names (*./init.d/lp*, *./rc0.d/K39lp*, *./rc1.d/K39lp*, *./rc2.d/S80lp*, and *./rcS.d/K39lp*) all point to one physical file.
- If you edit one file, they all change because in reality there is only one file.
- You can create additional links to the file with the *ln* command.
- If you remove any one of the files, the rest will remain, and the one physical file will continue to exist.
- Only when you remove all of the files will the one physical file also cease to exist.

Creating Hard and Symbolic Links with the *ln* Command

The *ln* command is used to create both hard links and symbolic links to a file. The syntax of the *ln* command is *ln [options] source… target*, where *source* is an existing file name, and *target* is the pathname of the new link. If *target* is a file that already exists, it will be overwritten. The options for *ln* are:

- *-f*. Link files without questioning the user, even if the mode of target forbids writing. This is the default if the standard input is not a terminal.
- *-s*. Create a symbolic link. If the *-s* option is used with two arguments, *target* may be an existing directory or a nonexistent file. If target already exists and is not a directory, an error is returned. *source* may be any pathname and need not exist. If it exists, it may be a file or directory and may reside on a different file system from *target*. If *target* is an existing directory, a file is created in directory *target* whose name is *source* or the last component of *source*. This file is a symbolic link that references *source*. If *target* does not exist, a file with name *target* is created and it is a symbolic link that references *source*. If the *-s* option is used with more than two arguments, *target* must be an existing directory or an error will be returned. For each *source*, a link is created in *target* whose name is the last component of *source*; each new *source* is a

symbolic link to the original *source*. The *source* and *target* may reside on different file systems.

- *-n*. If the link is an existing file, do not overwrite the contents of the file. The *-f* option overrides this option.

Some examples follow.

```
# ln lp lp.sh
# ln -s cleanup /usr/local/bin/cleanup.sh
# ln -s fix.sh reload.sh suspend.sh /usr/local/admin
#
```

In the first example, a hard link to the existing file, *lp*, is created, called *lp.sh*. Both *lp* and *lp.sh* share the same inode. In the second example, a symbolic link to the file *cleanup* is created; the symbolic link will reside in */usr/local/bin* and be called *cleanup.sh*. In the last example, symbolic links to the three files *fix.sh*, *reload.sh*, and *suspend.sh* are created in the directory */usr/local/admin*.

9.3 Mounting Fixed File Systems

This section discusses the commands used to mount and view the status of mounted file systems, as well as some of the configuration and status files used.

The *mount* and *umount* Commands

The *mount* command is used to logically attach a file system residing on a disk partition to an existing directory. The syntax of the *mount* command is *mount [options] raw-device mount-point*, where *raw-device* is the name of the disk device in */dev/rdsk*, and *mount-point* is an existing directory.

The *umount* command is used to unmount a currently mounted file system.

The *mount* and *umount* commands share a common set of options; they are:

- *-F FSType*. Used to specify the *FSType* on which to operate. The *FSType* must be specified or must be determinable from */etc/vfstab*, or by consulting */etc/default/fs* or */etc/dfs/fstypes*.
- *-a [mount_points . . .]*. Perform *mount* or *umount* operations in parallel, when possible. If mount points are not specified, *mount*

will mount all file systems whose */etc/vfstab* "mount at boot" field is "yes." If mount points are specified, then */etc/vfstab* "mount at boot" field will be ignored. If mount points are specified, *umount* will unmount only those mount points. If none is specified, then *umount* will attempt to unmount all file systems in */etc/mnttab*, with the exception of certain system-required file systems: */*, */usr*, */var*, */var/adm*, */var/run*, */proc*, */dev/fd*, and */tmp*.

- *-f*. Forcibly unmount a file system. Without this option, *umount* does not allow a file system to be unmounted if a file on the file system is busy. Using this option can cause data loss for open files; programs that access files after the file system has been unmounted will get an error (EIO).
- *-p*. Print the list of mounted file systems in the */etc/vfstab* format. Must be the only option specified.
- *-v*. Print the list of mounted file systems in verbose format. Must be the only option specified.
- *-V*. Echo the complete command line, but do not execute the command. *umount* generates a command line by using the options and arguments provided by the user and adding to them information derived from */etc/mnttab*. This option should be used to verify and validate the command line.
- *-m*. Mount the file system without making an entry in */etc/mnttab*.
- *-g*. Globally mount the file system. On a clustered system, this globally mounts the file system on all nodes of the cluster. On a nonclustered system this has no effect (clusters are not discussed in this book).
- *-O*. Overlay mount. Allow the file system to be mounted over an existing mount point, making the underlying file system inaccessible. If a mount is attempted on a pre-existing mount point without setting this flag, the mount will fail, producing the error "device busy."
- *-r*. Mount the file system read-only.
- *-o*. Specify *FSType*-specific options in a comma-separated (without spaces) list of suboptions and keyword-attribute pairs for interpretation by the *FSType*-specific module of the command. Suboptions are:
  - *noatime*. By default, the file system is mounted with normal access time (*atime*) recording. If *noatime* is specified, the file

system will ignore access time updates on files, except when they coincide with updates to the *ctime* or *mtime*. This option reduces disk activity on file systems where access times are unimportant (e.g., a Usenet news spool). *noatime* turns off access time recording regardless of *dfratime* or *nodfratime*. UFS only.

- *dfratime* | *nodfratime*. By default, writing access time updates to the disk may be deferred (*dfratime*) for the file system until the disk is accessed for a reason other than updating access times. *nodfratime* disables this behavior. UFS only.
- *forcedirectio* | *noforcedirectio*. If *forcedirectio* is specified and supported by the file system, then for the duration of the mount forced direct I/O will be used. If the file system is mounted using *forcedirectio*, then data are transferred directly between user address space and the disk. If the file system is mounted using *noforcedirectio*, then data is buffered in kernel address space when data is transferred between user address space and the disk. *forcedirectio* is a performance option that benefits only from large sequential data transfers. The default behavior is *noforcedirectio*. UFS only.
- *intr* | *nointr*. Allow (do not allow) keyboard interrupts to kill a process that is waiting for an operation on a locked file system. The default is *intr*. UFS only.
- *largefiles* | *nolargefiles*. If *nolargefiles* is specified and supported by the file system, then for the duration of the mount it is guaranteed that all regular files in the file system have a size that will fit in the smallest object of type *off_t* supported by the system performing the mount. The mount will fail if there are any files in the file system not meeting this criterion. If *largefiles* is specified, there is no such guarantee. The default behavior is *largefiles*. If *nolargefiles* is specified, mount will fail for UFS if the file system to be mounted contained a large file (a file whose size is greater than or equal to 2GB) since the last invocation of *fsck* on the file system. The large file need not be present in the file system at the time of the mount for the mount to fail; it could have been created previously and destroyed. Invoking *fsck* on the file system will reset the file system state if no large files are present. After invoking *fsck*, a successful mount of the file system with *nolargefiles* specified indicates the absence of large files in the file system;

an unsuccessful mount attempt indicates the presence of at least one large file. UFS only.

- *logging* | *nologging*. If *logging* is specified, then logging is enabled for the duration of the mounted file system. Logging is the process of storing transactions (changes that make up a complete UFS operation) in a log before the transactions are applied to the file system. Once a transaction is stored, the transaction can be applied to the file system later. This prevents file systems from becoming inconsistent and eliminates the need to run *fsck*. And, because *fsck* can be bypassed, logging reduces the time required to reboot a system if it crashes or after an unclean halt. The default behavior is *nologging*. The log is allocated from free blocks on the file system, and is sized approximately 1MB per 1GB of file system, up to a maximum of 64MB. Logging can be enabled on any UFS, including root (/). The log created by UFS logging is continually flushed as it fills up. The log is totally flushed when the file system is unmounted or as a result of the *lockfs -f* command. UFS only.
- *m*. Mount the file system without making an entry in */etc/mnttab*. UFS only.
- *quota*. Quotas are turned on for the file system. UFS only.
- *remount*. Remounts a read-only file system as read-write (using the *rw* option). This option can be used only in conjunction with the *-f*, *logging*|*nologging*, *-m*, and *noatime* options. This option works only on currently mounted read-only file systems. UFS only.
- *rq*. Read-write with quotas turned on. Equivalent to *rw*, *quota*. UFS only.
- *ro* | *rw*. Read-only or read-write. Default is *rw* for UFS. *ro* is required for HSFS.
- *suid* | *nosuid*. Allow or disallow *setuid* execution. The default is *suid*. This option can also be used when mounting devices. UFS and HSFS only.
- *foldcase* | *nofoldcase*. Force uppercase characters in file names to lowercase when reading them from the file system. This is for compatibility with the previous behavior of PCFS. The default is *nofoldcase*. PCFS only.

Some examples of the *mount* and *umount* commands follow.

```
# mount /dev/dsk/c0t4d0s0 /export/home
# mount -o noatime,nosuid /dev/dsk/c1t0d0s2 /tools
# mount -p
/dev/dsk/c0t0d0s0 - / ufs - no rw,intr,largefiles,onerror=panic,suid,
dev=800000
/proc - /proc proc - no dev=2d80000
fd - /dev/fd fd - no rw,suid,dev=2e40000
mnttab - /etc/mnttab mntfs - no dev=2f40000
swap - /var/run tmpfs - no dev=1
swap - /tmp tmpfs - no dev=2
/dev/dsk/c0t0d0s7 - /export/home ufs - no rw,intr,largefiles,quota,
onerror=panic
,suid,dev=800007
# mount -v
/dev/dsk/c0t0d0s0 on / type ufs read/write/setuid/intr/largefiles/
onerror=panic/
dev=800000 on Thu Feb 22 20:46:25 2001
/proc on /proc type proc read/write/setuid/dev=2d80000 on Thu Feb 22
20:46:25 2001
fd on /dev/fd type fd read/write/setuid/dev=2e40000 on Thu Feb 22
20:46:27 2001
mnttab on /etc/mnttab type mntfs read/write/setuid/dev=2f40000 on Thu
Feb 22 20:46:29 2001
swap on /var/run type tmpfs read/write/setuid/dev=1 on Thu Feb 22
20:46:29 2001
swap on /tmp type tmpfs read/write/setuid/dev=2 on Thu Feb 22 20:46:31
2001
/dev/dsk/c0t0d0s7 on /export/home type ufs read/write/setuid/intr/
largefiles/quota/onerror=panic/dev=800007 on Thu Feb 22 20:46:31 2001
# mount -F HSFS -r /dev/dsk/c0t6d0s0 /cdrom
# umount /export/home
# umount /dev/dsk/c0t4d0s0
# umount -f /export/home
#
```

In the first example, the partition *c0t4d0s0* is mounted at the mount point */export/home*. In the second example, the partition *c1t0d0s2* is mounted at the mount point */tools*. Access times will not be updated in this file system, and no SUID commands can be run as SetUID. In the third example, the *mount* command shows, in */etc/vfstab* format, all currently mounted file systems. In the fourth example, the mount command shows, in verbose format, all currently mounted file systems. In the fifth example, a CD-ROM is mounted at the mount point */cdrom*. In the sixth example, the file system */export/home* is unmounted. In the seventh example, the file system mounted from partition *c0t4d0s0* is unmounted. In the eighth example, the file system */export/home* is forcibly unmounted.

EXAM NOTES

THINK ABOUT IT . . .

You need to temporarily mount the */export/tools* file system at a different location, because the */export* directory is unavailable.

You can mount the file system on the */mnt* directory. Get the name of the */export/tools* file system (e.g., */dev/rdsk/c1t0d0s2*) and issue the new *mount* command. For example:

```
# mount /dev/rdsk/c1t0d0s2 /mnt
```

Automatic File System Mounting at Boot Time

A system can be configured to automatically mount file systems at boot time. The */etc/vfstab* file is the configuration file that lists these file systems. The format of */etc/vfstab* is:

```
mount-device fsck-device mount-point Fstype fsck-pass
mount-at-boot mount-options
```

The fields are separated by a tab and/or one or more space. A "-" is used to indicate no entry in a field. Comment lines are prepended by a "#". Each of these fields is explained in the following.

- *mount-device*. The raw device (in */dev/rdsk*) to mount with the *mount* command.
- *fsck-device*. The character device (in */dev/dsk*) to check with the *fsck* command.
- *mount-point*. The location in the file system where the file system is to be attached.
- *FStype*. The type of file system (UFS, HSFS, NFS, etc.).
- *fsck-pass*. Whether the file system should be automatically checked at boot time. A nonzero numeric value signifies that the file system will be checked.

- *mount-at-boot*. Whether the file system should be automatically mounted at boot time (yes/no). This does not apply to the */proc* and *swap*, which are mounted at boot time anyway.
- *mount-options*. Any mount options passed to the *mount* command when the file system is mounted.

An example */etc/vfstab* file follows.

```
#device           device            mount          FS      fsck  mount    mount
#to mount         to fsck           point          type    pass  at boot  options
#
fd                -                 /dev/fd        fd      -     no       -
/proc             -                 /proc          proc    -     no       -
/dev/dsk/c0t0d0s1  -                -              swap    -     no       -
/dev/dsk/c0t0d0s0 /dev/rdsk/c0t0d0s0 /             ufs     1     no       -
/dev/dsk/c0t0d0s7 /dev/rdsk/c0t0d0s7 /export/home ufs 2    yes rq,quota
swap              -                 /tmp           tmpfs   -     yes      -
```

In this example *vfstab* file, the root ('/'), */export/home*, and */tmp* file systems are mounted at boot. The / and */export/home* file systems are *fsck*'d as well. The */export/home* file system is mounted with the *rq* and *quota* options.

Note that *fs*, *proc*, *swap*, and the */tmp* file system lack a *fsck*-device field. This is because these are all file systems that do not have a device that should be *fsck*'d.

The */etc/vfstab* File and the *mount* Command

When a file system is listed in the */etc/vfstab* file, that file system can be mounted by its mount point name alone. This is because the *mount* command will consult the */etc/vfstab* file for the device name and *mount* options. Note that when using the *mount* command manually, you will have to specify all desired mount options. An example *mount* command follows.

```
# mount /export/home
#
```

In this example, the */export/home* file system is mounted. The *mount* command find the mount device */dev/dsk/c0t0d0s7* in */etc/vfstab*.

Exam Notes

THINK ABOUT IT . . .

You have created a new file system in */dev/rdsk/c1t0d0s1* with the name */export/tools* and you want it to be automatically mounted at boot time.

Add the following entry to */etc/vfstab*.

```
/dev/dsk/c1t0d0s1   /dev/rdsk/c1t0d0s1   /export/tools ufs 2     yes     -
```

The */etc/mnttab* File

The */etc/mnttab* file contains a list of currently mounted file systems. The syntax of the */etc/mnttab* file is:

```
special mount_point fstype options time
```

The fields of */etc/mnttab* are:

- *special*. The name of the resource to be mounted. This is either the device name (for disk-based file systems) or a name for a virtual file system.
- *mount_point*. The pathname of the directory on which the file system is mounted.
- *fstype*. The file system type of the mounted file system.
- *options*. The mount options.
- *time*. The time at which the file system was mounted.

A typical */etc/mnttab* file follows.

```
/dev/dsk/c0t0d0s0     /    ufs  rw,intr,largefiles,onerror=panic,suid,de
v=800000          984164474
/proc   /proc    proc     dev=2d80000       984164474
fd      /dev/fd fd        rw,suid,dev=2e40000        984164476
mnttab  /etc/mnttab       mntfs    dev=2f40000        984164478
swap    /var/run          tmpfs    dev=1    984164478
swap    /tmp     tmpfs    dev=2    984164480
/dev/dsk/c0t0d0s7    /export/home    ufs rw,intr,largefiles,quota,onerror
=panic,suid,dev=800007  984164480
```

```
-hosts   /net     autofs  indirect,nosuid,ignore,nobrowse,dev=2fc0001
984164513
auto_home        /home   autofs   indirect,ignore,nobrowse,dev=2fc0002
984164513
-xfn     /xfn     autofs  indirect,ignore,dev=2fc0003      984164513
wallace:vold(pid442)    /vol     nfs      ignore,dev=3000002
984165551
```

Note that */etc/mnttab* is not literally a file, but a file system. In prior versions of Solaris, */etc/mnttab* was a file. But occasionally, entries in */etc/mnttab* would get "out of sync" with the true state of mounted file systems, so in Solaris 8 */etc/mnttab* was made a special file system. The only difference is that */etc/mnttab* is read-only and cannot be modified, even by root.

The *mountall* and *umountall* Commands

The *mountall* and *umountall* commands are used to mount and unmount multiple file systems. The syntax of the *mountall* command is *mountall [-F FSType] [-l| -r] [file_system_table]*; the syntax of the *umountall* command is *umountall [-k] [-s] [-F FSType] [-l| -r]* or *umountall [-k] [-s] [-h host]*. *mountall* will first run *fsck* on all file systems to be mounted. *mountall* and *umountall* check */etc/vfstab* and act only upon file systems specified to be automatically mounted at boot time. The options for the *mountall* and *umountall* commands are:

- *-F FSType*. Specify the *FSType* of the file system to be mounted or unmounted.
- *-h host*. Unmount all file systems listed in */etc/mnttab* that are remote-mounted from *host*. This option involves NFS, which is not covered in this book.
- *-k*. Use the *fuser -k mount-point* command. The *-k* option sends the SIGKILL signal to each process using the file. As this option spawns kills for each process, the kill messages may not show up immediately. There is no guarantee that *umountall* will unmount busy file systems, even if the *-k* option is specified.
- *-l*. Limit the action to local file systems. This option involves NFS, which is not covered in this book.
- *-r*. Limit the action to remote file system types. This option involves NFS, which is not covered in this book.
- *-s*. Do not perform the umount operation in parallel.

Some examples of the *mountall* and *umountall* command follow.

```
# mountall -F ufs
checking ufs filesystems
/dev/rdsk/c0t4d0s0: is clean.
/dev/rdsk/c0t1d0s7: is stable.
mount: /dev/dsk/c0t1d0s7 is already mounted, /export/home is busy,
        or the allowable number of mount points has been exceeded
# umountall
umount: /export/home busy
# umountall -k -F ufs
/export/home:       21335c 21336c
#
```

In the first example, all file systems of type UFS are mounted. From the messages displayed, we can infer that the */export/home* file system was already mounted, but that a file system that was not already mounted was mounted from device */dev/rdsk/c0t4d0s0*.

In the second example, an attempt was made to unmount all mounted UFS file systems. An error occurred; the */export/home* file system could not be unmounted because it was busy. In the third example, an attempt is made to forcibly unmount all UFS file systems. When the *-k* option is used, *umount* runs *fuser -k mount-point* and displays its output. Two processes, 21335 and 21336, had a file open somewhere in */export/home*.

9.4 Working with Removable File Systems

Mounting and Unmounting Removable Media without Volume Management

This section discusses the commands used to mount file systems on removable devices, such as floppy discs and CD-ROMs, when Volume Management is not running. Volume Management is discussed in a later section.

The *mount*, *umount*, *mountall*, and *umountall* commands, as well as the */etc/vfstab* and */etc/mnttab* files, all work with removable devices.

Some examples of *mount* and *umount* commands follow.

```
# mount -F pcfs /dev/diskette /floppy
# mount -F hsfs -o ro /dev/dsk/c0t6d0s0 /cdrom
#
```

In the first example, a PC format floppy diskette is mounted. In the second example, a CD-ROM is mounted.

Creating UFS File Systems on a Diskette

In addition to PC file systems—which allow Solaris systems to read and wrote PC-formatted diskettes—you can also create UFS file systems on diskettes.

To create a UFS file system on a diskette, the diskette must first be formatted with the *fdformat* command. The syntax of the *fdformat* command is *fdformat [-dDeEfHlLmMUqvx] [-b label] [-B filename] [-t dostype] [devname]*. Options for *fdformat* are:

- *-d*. Installs an MS-DOS file system and boot sector formatting. This is equivalent to the DOS *format* command or the *-t dos* option.
- *-D*. Formats a 720kb (3.5 inch) or 360kb (5.25 inch) double-density diskette (same as the *-l* or *-L* options). This is the default for double-density type drives. It is needed if the drive is a high- or extended-density type.
- *-e*. Ejects the diskette when done. (This feature is not available on all systems.)
- *-E*. Formats a 2.88MB (3.5 inch) extended-density diskette. This is the default for extended-density type drives.
- *-f*. Force. Do not ask for confirmation before starting format.
- *-H*. Formats a 1.44MB (3.5 inch) or 1.2MB (5.25 inch) high-density diskette. This is the default for high-density type drives; it is needed if the drive is the extended-density type.
- *-M*. Writes a 1.2MB (3.5 inch) medium-density format on a high-density diskette (use only with the *-t nec* option). This is the same as using *-m*. (This feature is not available on all systems.)
- *-U*. Performs umount on any file systems and then formats.
- *-q*. Quiet; do not print status messages.
- *-v*. Verifies each block of the diskette after the format.
- *-x*. Skips the format, and only writes a SunOS label or an MS-DOS file system.
- *-b label*. Labels the media with volume label. A SunOS volume label is restricted to eight characters. A DOS volume label is restricted to 11 uppercase characters.

- *-B filename*. Installs special boot loader in file name on an MS-DOS diskette. This option is meaningful only when the *-d* option (or *-t dos*) is also specified.
- *-t dos*. Installs an MS-DOS file system and boot sector formatting. This is equivalent to the DOS *format* command or the *-d* option.
- *-t nec*. Installs an NEC-DOS file system and boot sector on the disk after formatting. This should be used only with the *-M* option. (This feature is not available on all systems.)
- *devname*. Replaces *devname* with *rdiskette0* (systems without Volume Management) or *floppy0* (systems with Volume Management) to use the first drive or *rdiskette1* (systems without Volume Management) or *floppy1* (systems with Volume Management) to use the second drive. If *devname* is omitted, the first drive, if one exists, will be used. If *devname* is omitted, the default diskette drive, if one exists, will be used.

Some examples follow.

```
# fdformat -eH floppy0
Formatting 1.44 MB in /vol/dev/rdiskette0/unnamed_floppy
Press return to start formatting floppy.
..............................................................
#

# fdformat -v -b Tuesday floppy0
Formatting 1.44 MB in /vol/dev/rdiskette0/unnamed_floppy
Press return to start formatting floppy.
..............................................................
vvvvvvvvvvvvvvvvvvvvvvvvvvvvvvvvvvvvvvvvvvvvvvvvvvvvvvvvvvvvvvvvvvvvvvvvvvvvvvvv
#
```

In the first example, we're formatting a 1.44MB diskette and ejecting it when the formatting has completed. In the second example, the 1.44MB diskette formatting is being verified, and the label "Tuesday" is written to the diskette.

After formatting a diskette, it is possible to create a UFS file system on it with the *newfs* command. An example follows.

```
# newfs -v /dev/diskette
newfs: construct a new file system /dev/rdiskette: (y/n)? y
mkfs -F ufs /dev/rdiskette 2880 18 2 8192 1024 16 10 5 2048 t 0 -1 8 16
/dev/rdiskette: 2880 sectors in 80 cylinders of 2 tracks, 18 sectors
        1.4MB in 5 cyl groups (16 c/g, 0.28MB/g, 128 i/g)
```

```
super-block backups (for fsck -F ufs -o b=#) at:
 32, 640, 1184, 1792, 2336,
#
```

Next, the newly created file system can be mounted and used just like any other file system. An example *mount* command follows.

```
# mount /dev/diskette /mnt
# df /mnt
/mnt                (/dev/diskette     ):    2508 blocks      636 files
#
```

Ejecting Media

Floppy and CD discs are ejected with the *eject* command. The syntax of the *eject* command is *eject [options] device*. The options for the *eject* command are:

- *-d*. Display the name of the default device to be ejected.
- *-f*. Force the device to eject even if it is busy, if Volume Management is not running.
- *-n*. Display the nickname to device name translation table.
- *-p*. Do not try to call the *eject_popup* program.
- *-q*. Query to see if the media is present.

Some examples follow.

```
# eject -d
Default device is: /vol/dev/rdiskette0/unnamed_floppy
# eject cdrom
# eject floppy
WARNING: cannot unmount /dev/rdiskette, the file system is (probably)
busy
# eject -f floppy
WARNING: /dev/rdiskette has a mounted filesystem, ejecting anyway
#
```

In the first example, *eject* displays the default device, which in this case is the floppy drive. In the second example, the CD-ROM is ejected. In the third example, an attempt is made to eject the floppy; the eject is unsuccessful because there are one or more open files in the mounted file system (this error message can also indicate there is no diskette in the drive). In the fourth example, the floppy is forcibly ejected.

EXAM NOTES

THINK ABOUT IT . . .

You need to transfer several files from one Solaris system to another via diskette. Volume Management is not running on the system. What are the steps involved?

First, insert the diskette, then format the diskette with the *fdformat* command. Next, create a file system on the diskette with the *newfs* command. Next, mount the diskette with the *mount* command. Then, copy files to the mounted file system. Finally, eject the diskette with the *eject* command.

EXAM NOTES

THINK ABOUT IT . . .

You need to transfer files between a PC and a Solaris system using a DOS-formatted diskette. Volume Management is not running. What steps are involved?

First, insert the diskette and format it with the *fdformat -t dos* command. Next, mount the diskette with the *mount -F pcfs* command. Then, copy files to the diskette and eject it with the *eject* command.

9.5 Volume Management

Volume Management is a software cluster consisting of a daemon and a set of tools that make working with removable media much easier. The most notable characteristics of Volume Management are:

- CD-ROMs and diskettes are mounted automatically (or nearly so) when inserted.
- CD-ROMs and diskettes can be mounted by users lacking root privileges.

There are some other characteristics of Volume Management worth mentioning:

- All CD-ROM and diskette drive volumes can be accessed through the directory */vol/dev.* Specifically, CD-ROM device interfaces appear in */vol/dev/dsk/c0t6* (for block device access) and

/vol/dev/rdsk/c0t6 (for raw device access). Diskette interfaces are */vol/dev/diskette0* (block) and */vol/dev/rdiskette0* (raw); subsequent diskette devices are *diskette1* and *rdiskette1*, *diskette2*, and *rdiskette2*, and so forth.

- Volume Management uses convenient file system mount points. Specifically, diskettes are mounted onto the directory */floppy*, and CD-ROMs are mounted onto the directory */cdrom*.
- When Volume Management mounts a CD-ROM or diskette, it will be mounted to the directory */cdrom/cd-name* or */floppy/floppy-name*. But Volume Management also creates the generic aliases */cdrom/cdrom0* and */floppy/floppy0* to make scripts accessing these drives easier to write. Without this feature, any scripts or programs would have to first extract the media name (and hope it found the right one on systems with more than one CD or diskette drive!), a more complicated proposition.
- In addition to the raw and block device names mentioned earlier, Volume Management also provides some raw and block device aliases. For instance, */vol/dev/rdsk/c0t6/cd-name* also appears as */vol/dev/aliases/cdrom0*, and */vol/dev/rdiskette0/diskette-name* also appears as */vol/dev/aliases/floppy0*.
- On diskettes—or more commonly, CD-ROMs—with more than one file system (i.e., when the CD-ROM or diskette has more than one partition with a file system in each), Volume Management will automatically mount each file system found. By convention Volume Management creates subdirectories named s0 (slice zero), s1, s2, and so on. For instance, on a CD-ROM with two file systems, Volume Management will mount */cdrom/cdrom0/s0* and */cdrom/cdrom0/s1*, and present the devices */vol/dev/rdsk/c0t6/s0* and */vol/dev/rdsk/c0t6/s1*.

UFS file systems are not compatible across architectures. That is, a UFS file system created on a diskette on a SPARC system cannot be read by a system with IA architecture (and vice versa). Interchangeability between system architectures is not an intended feature of UFS. However, this limitation is not found with the CD-ROM ISO 9660 (High Sierra File System) format, which is readable by any system architecture. Compatibility with CD-ROMs with the ISO 9660 file system is seldom a problem.

When Volume Management encounters a CD-ROM with an ISO 9660 and a nonrecognizable UFS file system, it will ignore the nonrecognizable UFS file system but proceed and mount the recognized ISO 9660 file system using the slicing naming convention mentioned before this note.

Volume Management Daemon

The volume management daemon, *vold*, is started by the run control script */etc/rc2.d/S92volmgt*.

Mounting CD-ROMs with Volume Management

With Volume Management running, no special interaction is required. When the CD-ROM media is inserted into the drive, Volume Management automatically mounts all ISO 9660 and recognized UFS file systems.

Ejecting the CD-ROM (either with the *eject* command or by pressing the eject button) automatically unmounts the file system.

Mounting Diskettes with Volume Management

With Volume Management running, it is necessary to run the *volcheck* command after inserting a diskette. This is because diskette drives do not cause a hardware interrupt on the system when a diskette is inserted. No options are necessary for the *volcheck* command. If a diskette is in the drive, Volume Management will automatically mount all recognized file systems.

Ejecting the diskette with the *eject* command automatically unmounts the file system.

The syntax of the *volcheck* command is *volcheck [options] pathname*. Options for *volcheck* are:

- *-i secs*. Set the frequency of device checking to *secs* seconds. The default is two seconds. The minimum frequency is one second.
- *-t secs*. Check the named device(s) for the next *secs* seconds. The maximum number of seconds allowed is 28800, which is 8 hours. The frequency of checking is specified by *-i*. There is no default total time.
- *-v*. Verbose.
- *pathname*. The pathname of a media device.

Some examples of *volcheck* follow.

```
% volcheck
% volcheck /dev/diskette
```

```
% volcheck -v /dev/diskette
/dev/diskette has no media
% volcheck -v
/dev/diskette has media
% volcheck -i 10 -+28800
%
```

In the first example, *volcheck* checks all removable media drives. In the second example, *volcheck* checks only the diskette. In the third example, *volcheck* checks only the diskette; verbose mode indicates that no media is in the drive. The fourth example is similar to the third, except that media is in the drive. In the fifth example, all drives are checked every 10 seconds for 8 hours.

Table 9.2 illustrates the operational differences of mounting diskettes and CD-ROMs between systems with and without Volume Management.

Table 9.2 *Removable Media Comparison: without and with Volume Management*

STEP	WITHOUT VOLUME MANAGEMENT	WITH VOLUME MANAGEMENT
1	Insert media	Insert media
2	Become superuser	Run the *volcheck* command (diskettes only)
3	Determine location of the media device	
4	Create a mount point	
5	Mount the device with the *mount* command	
6	Exit superuser mode	
7	Read or write files on the media	Read or write files on the media
8	Become superuser	
9	Unmount the device with the *umount* command	
10	Eject media	Eject media
11	Exit superuser mode	

Volume Management Configuration

Volume management is configured with the */etc/vold.conf* and */etc/rmmount.conf* files. The default */etc/rmmount.conf* file is:

```
# @(#)rmmount.conf 1.10     00/02/14 SMI
#
# Removable Media Mounter configuration file.
#

# File system identification
ident hsfs ident_hsfs.so cdrom
ident ufs ident_ufs.so cdrom floppy rmdisk pcmem
ident pcfs ident_pcfs.so floppy rmdisk pcmem
ident udfs ident_udfs.so cdrom floppy rmdisk

# Actions
action cdrom action_filemgr.so
action floppy action_filemgr.so
action rmdisk action_filemgr.so

mount * hsfs udfs ufs -o nosuid
```

The default */etc/vold.conf* file is:

```
# @(#)vold.conf 1.25     99/11/11 SMI
#
# Volume Daemon Configuration file
#

# Database to use (must be first)
db db_mem.so

# Labels supported
label dos label_dos.so floppy rmdisk pcmem
label cdrom label_cdrom.so cdrom
label sun label_sun.so floppy rmdisk pcmem

# Devices to use
use cdrom drive /dev/rdsk/c*s2 dev_cdrom.so cdrom%d
use floppy drive /dev/rdiskette[0-9] dev_floppy.so floppy%d
use pcmem drive /dev/rdsk/c*s2 dev_pcmem.so pcmem%d forceload=true
# use rmdisk drive /dev/rdsk/c*s2 dev_rmdisk.so rmdisk%d

# Actions
insert dev/diskette[0-9]/* user=root /usr/sbin/rmmount
remount dev/diskette[0-9]/* user=root /usr/sbin/rmmount
insert dev/dsk/* user=root /usr/sbin/rmmount
remount dev/dsk/* user=root /usr/sbin/rmmount
eject dev/diskette[0-9]/* user=root /usr/sbin/rmmount
eject dev/dsk/* user=root /usr/sbin/rmmount
```

```
notify rdsk/* group=tty user=root /usr/lib/vold/volmissing -p

# List of file system types unsafe to eject
unsafe ufs hsfs pcfs udfs
```

CHAPTER SUMMARY

The file system types used by Solaris are disk-based (UFS, S5FS, PCFS, HSDS, and UDFS), network-based (NFS), and virtual (TmpFS, CacheFS, LOFS, PROCFS, Mnttab and XMEMFS).

The file systems found on a Solaris system are / (root), which contains the system kernel, configuration, and mount points for other file systems; */usr*, which contains tools, man pages, and shells; */var*, which contains log files, data files, and spool files; */opt*, which contains optional Solaris packages and third-party software; */proc*, which contains information about active processes; */export/home*, which contains user home directories; and */tmp*, which contains temporary files.

The file types used by Solaris are regular, directory, character device, block device, FIFO, door, socket, and symbolic link. A file's type can be determined with the *ls -l* command.

An inode is a file's internal placeholder. An inode contains all of the file's characteristics except for its name and contents. The inode includes the inode number, the file's permission settings, the file type (regular, directory, device, etc.), owner, groupid, last access time, last modification time, number of links, and a pointer to the first disk block where the file's contents can be found. A file's inode number can be viewed with the *ls -i* command.

Symbolic and hard links are created with the *ln* command.

File systems are mounted with the *mount* command, and unmounted with the *umount* command. The configuration file */etc/vfstab* contains a list of file systems that are automatically mounted at boot time. The */etc/mnttab* file contains a list of currently mounted file systems. The *mountall* and *umountall* commands are used to mount and unmount multiple file systems at once. All of these commands also work with removable media file systems.

UFS and PCFS file systems can be created on diskettes to facilitate the transfer of files between systems. A diskette is formatted with the *fdformat* command; a UFS file system is created on a floppy with the *newfs* command.

The *eject* command is used to eject removable media.

Volume Management simplifies the management of removable media by automatically mounting file systems and by presenting a consistent set of device names and mount points. The Volume Management configuration files are */etc/vold.conf* and */etc/rmmount.conf*.

TEST YOURSELF

MULTIPLE CHOICE

1. What is the purpose of the */etc/vfstab* file?
   A. It contains a list of virtual file systems to be mounted at boot time.
   B. It contains a list of virtual file systems configured on the system.
   C. It contains a list of file systems to be mounted at system boot time.
   D. It contains a list of currently mounted file systems.
2. What is the purpose of the */etc/mnttab* file?
   A. It contains a list of virtual file systems to be mounted at boot time.
   B. It contains a list of virtual file systems configured on the system.
   C. It contains a list of file systems to be mounted at system boot time.
   D. It contains a list of currently mounted file systems.
3. What option of the mount command is used to *mount* a PC-based file system?
   A. `-F PCFS`
   B. `-F PC`
   C. `-f PCFS`
   D. `-PCFS`

4. Which four are valid disk-based file system types? (Choose four)
   A. NFS
   B. DFS
   C. UFS
   D. S5FS
   E. HSFS
   F. ISO
   G. PCFS
5. Which command is used to forcibly unmount a file system?
   A. `unmount -f`
   B. `umount -f`
   C. `umount -F`
   D. `mount -un`
6. What is the purpose of the *fdformat* command?
   A. Format a floppy diskette.
   B. Partition a floppy diskette.
   C. Defragment a full disk.
   D. Create a FD file system.
7. What is required to create a DOS-format diskette on a Solaris system?
   A. Format the diskette with the *fdformat -d* command.
   B. Create a PCFS file system with the *newfs* command.
   C. Format the diskette with the *format* command.
   D. Mount the diskette with the *mount* command.

8. A software program reads and writes the data file */usr/local/data/sales.db*. A second software program needs to read the same file, but the program is expecting the pathname to be */export/data/sales.db*. The */usr* and */export* directories are in separate file systems. What is the best way for the second software program to be able to read the original data file?
   A. Create a shared inode with the *ln –si /export/data/sales.db* command.
   B. Create a hard link, */export/data/sales.db*, that points to */usr/local/data/sales.db*.
   C. Create a symbolic link, */export/data/sales.db*, that points to */usr/local/data/sales.db*.
   D. Create a shadow copy of */usr/local/data/sales.db* in the */export/data* directory.

9. Which statement about the PROCFS file system is true?
   A. It is not used on systems with more than 1G of main memory.
   B. It contains files containing information about active processes.
   C. It stores each process's stack and heap.
   D. It contains each user's procedure files.
   E. It is an image of the kernel's process table.

10. The directory */export/tools* contains the shell script *update.sh*. You mount a file system from another disk using the mount point */export/tools*. When you look for the file */export/tools/update.sh*, it is not found. Why?
   A. The file was moved to */export/tools/lost+found*.
   B. The root of the mounted file system does not contain a file called *update.sh*.
   C. The file *update.sh* was destroyed when its parent directory was used as a mount point.
   D. All files and directories in the original */export/tools* are hidden until the file system is unmounted.

FREE RESPONSE

11. What is the command used to mount a read-only file system from CD-ROM (when Volume Management is not running)?
12. What is the name of the file that contains a list of all mounted file systems?

CHAPTER 10

Backup and Recovery

After completing this chapter, you'll be able to meet these Solaris Administration Exam objectives:

- State the commands used to reduce the size of files and directories for storage to tape.
- Match listed backup, archive, and restore utilities to their respective functional capabilities.
- Identify the commands and steps required to back up a file system to tape.
- Identify the commands and steps required to restore a file system from tape.

To fulfill these objectives, this chapter discusses:

- Compressing files;
- Creating archive files;
- Backing up a system to tape; and
- Recovering from a backup tape.

10.1 Compressing Files

File compression refers to a technique used to store a file using a special encoding scheme that permits the file to consume less space. The reasons for compressing a file are:

- to conserve disk space;
- to save time transmitting the file over a slow medium (such as the Internet); and
- to reduce time needed to back up to tape or other slow device.

Several commands are available as standard in Solaris 8 to compress and decompress files. They are *compress/uncompress*, *zcat*, *gzip/gunzip*, *pack/unpack/pcat*, and *zip*. Each of these commands uses a different file name suffix when compressing files. Table 10.1 shows the commands and the suffixes used.

Each of the file compression commands are explained in this chapter.

compress and *uncompress*

The *compress* and *uncompress* commands are used to compress and uncompress files. The *compress* command creates a compressed file with the same name as the original file with a ".Z" suffix. The *uncompress* command reads a file with a ".Z" suffix and creates an uncompressed file without the ".Z" suffix. The syntax of the *compress* command is *compress [options] file...*, and the syntax of the *uncompress* command is *uncompress [options] file...* . The options for *compress* and *uncompress* are:

- *-c*. Write to the standard output; no files are changed and no .Z files are created. The behavior of the *zcat* command is identical to that of *uncompress -c*.
- *-f*. Force. When compressing, force compression of *file*, even if it does not actually reduce the size of the file, or if the corresponding

Table 10.1 *Compression Program File Suffixes*

SUFFIX	COMMANDS
.Z	*compress, uncompress, zcat*
.z	*pack, unpack, pcat*
.gz	*gzip, gunzip, gzcat*
.zip	*zip, unzip*

file.Z file already exists. If the *-f* option is not given, and the process is not running in the background, prompt to verify whether an existing *file.Z* file should be overwritten. When uncompressing, do not prompt for overwriting files. If the *-f* option is not given, and the process is not running in the background, prompt to verify whether an existing file should be overwritten. If the standard input is not a terminal and *-f* is not given, write a diagnostic message to standard error and exit with a status greater than 0.

- *-v.* Verbose. Write to standard error messages concerning the percentage reduction or expansion of each file.
- *-b bits.* Set the upper limit (in *bits*) for common substring codes. *bits* must be between 9 and 16 (16 is the default). Lowering the number of bits will result in larger, less-compressed files.
- *file*. A pathname of a file to be compressed. If *file* is - , or if no file is specified, the standard input will be used.

Some examples of the *compress* and *uncompress* commands follow.

```
# ls -l gcc.pkg
-rw-r--r--    1 root      other     4619147 Mar 12 05:43 gcc.pkg
# compress gcc.pkg
# ls -l gcc.pkg.Z
-rw-r--r--    1 root      other     1699229 Mar 12 05:43 gcc.pkg.Z
#

# compress -v gcc.pkg
gcc.pkg: Compression: 63.21% -- replaced with gcc.pkg.Z
#

# uncompress *.Z
#

# compress -c Tue.tar > /dev/rmt0
#
```

In the first example, the file *gcc.pkg* is listed with the *ls* command and then compressed. The *ls* command lists the size of the compressed file. In this example, the original file size was 4,619,147 bytes, and after compression was 1,699,229 bytes. In the second example, the file *gcc.pkg* is compressed with the *-v* option; compress states the percentage compression achieved. In the third example, all compressed files in the current directory are uncompressed. In the last example, the file *Tue.tar* is compressed, and the output written to the device */dev/rmt0*.

zcat

The *zcat* command is functionally identical to the *uncompress -c* command. That is to say, *zcat* uncompresses files compressed with the *compress* command and writes the output to standard output. The syntax of the *zcat* command is *zcat file...* , where *file* is a list of one or more files to uncompress.

Some examples follow.

```
# zcat Tue.tar.Z | tar tf -
./messages.0
./messages.1
./messages.2
./messages.3
#

# zcat sulog.Z | grep phil
#
```

In the first example, *zcat* uncompresses *Tue.tar.Z* and passes the uncompressed output to the *tar tf* – command, which reads the uncompressed data as its standard input. In the second example, *zcat* uncompresses *sulog.Z* and passes the output to the *grep phil* command.

EXAM NOTES

THINK ABOUT IT . . .

You need to compress a large file, but you find that there is insufficient room in the file system to do so (remember that the file system must have enough room for the file *and* its compressed copy). What can you do?

You could leave the file in place but create its compressed version in another file system. Say, for instance, that your large file is in */var,* and that you have enough room in */tmp* for the compressed copy. Use the command *compress -c file > /tmp/file.Z* to accomplish your task. Then, you could remove the original file from */var* and move its compressed version from */tmp* to */var.*

pack, unpack, and *pcat*

The *pack* and *unpack* commands are similar to *compress* and *uncompress*. The syntax of the *pack* command is *pack [-f] [-] file...* . The syntax of the *unpack* command is *unpack file...* . The syntax of the *pcat* command is *pcat file...* . Like *zcat*, the *pcat* command decompresses a file and writes to standard output. The options are:

- *-f*. Forces packing of *file*. This is useful for causing an entire directory to be packed even if some of the files will not benefit. Packed files can be restored to their original form using *unpack* or *pcat*.
- *file*. A pathname of a file to be *pack*ed, *unpack*ed, or *pcat*ed; *file* can include or omit the *.z* suffix.

Some examples follow.

```
# pack messages*
pack: messages: no saving - file unchanged
pack: messages.1: no saving - file unchanged
pack: messages.2: 34.6% Compression
pack: messages.3: 33.7% Compression

# pack -f messages*
pack: messages: 26.9% Compression
pack: messages.1: 28.8% Compression
pack: messages.2: 34.6% Compression
pack: messages.3: 33.7% Compression

# pcat messages.3.z | wc
    113    1516   10370

# unpack *z
#
```

In the first example, all files in the current working directory named *messages** are compressed. Note that two of the files found were not compressed (they were probably too small). In the second example, the same files are compressed—*pack* is forced to compress all files found. In the third example, the packed file *messages.3.z* is unpacked and counted with *wc*. In the fourth example, all files ending in "z" are unpacked.

gzip, *gunzip*, and *gzcat*

gzip, *gunzip*, and *gzcat* are freeware compression and decompression utilities included with Solaris.

The *gzip* command is used to compress one or more files. The *gunzip* command is used to decompress files. The *gzcat* command decompresses one or more files and writes the uncompressed file to standard output, similar to the *zcat* command.

The format of the *gzip* command is *gzip [-cdfhlLnNrtvV19] [-S suffix] [file ...]*. The syntax of the *gunzip* command is *gunzip [-cdfhlLnNrtvV19] [-S suffix] [file ...]*. The syntax of the *gzcat* command is *gzcat [-cdfhlLnNrtvV19] [-S suffix] [file ...]*. The options for these commands are:

- *-a*. ASCII text mode: Convert end-of-lines using local conventions. This option is supported only on some non-UNIX systems. For MS-DOS, CR-LF is converted to LF when compressing, and LF is converted to CR-LF when decompressing.
- *-c*. Write output on standard output; keep original files unchanged. If there are several input files, the output consists of a sequence of independently compressed members. To obtain better compression, concatenate all input files before compressing.
- *-d*. Decompress.
- *-f*. Force compression or decompression even if the file has multiple links or the corresponding file already exists, or if the compressed data is read from or written to a terminal. If the input data is not in a format recognized by *gzip*, and if the option *-c* is also given, copy the input data without change to the standard output: Let *gzcat* behave as *cat*. If *-f* is not given, and when not running in the background, *gzip* prompts to verify whether an existing file should be overwritten.
- *-l*. For each compressed file, list the following fields:
  - compressed size: size of the compressed file
  - uncompressed size: size of the uncompressed file
  - ratio: compression ratio (0.0% if unknown)
  - uncompressed_name: name of the uncompressed file

  The uncompressed size is given as *-1* for files not in *gzip* format, such as compressed .Z files. To get the uncompressed size for such a file, you can use:

  - gzcat file.Z | wc -c

In combination with the *-v* option, the following fields are also displayed:

- method: compression method
- crc: the 32-bit CRC of the uncompressed data
- date & time: time stamp for the uncompressed file

The compression methods currently supported are *deflate*, *compress*, *lzh* (SCO's *compress -H*) and *pack*. The CRC is given as ffffffff for a file not in gzip format. With *-n*, the uncompressed name, date, and time are those stored within the compressed file if present. With *-v*, the size totals and compression ratio for all files is also displayed, unless some sizes are unknown. With *-q*, the title and totals lines are not displayed.

- *-L*. Display the *gzip* license and quit.
- *-n*. When compressing, do not save the original file name and time stamp by default. (The original name is always saved if the name had to be truncated.) When decompressing, do not restore the original file name if present (remove only the *gzip* suffix from the compressed file name) and do not restore the original time stamp if present (copy it from the compressed file). This option is the default when decompressing.
- *-N*. When compressing, always save the original file name and time stamp; this is the default. When decompressing, restore the original file name and time stamp if present. This option is useful on systems that have a limit on file name length or when the time stamp has been lost after a file transfer.
- *-q*. Suppress all warnings.
- *-r*. Travel the directory structure recursively. If any of the file names specified on the command line are directories, *gzip* will descend into the directory and compress all the files it finds there (or decompress them in the case of *gunzip*).
- *-S .suf*. Use suffix *.suf* instead of *.gz*. Any suffix can be given, but suffixes other than *.z* and *.gz* should be avoided to avoid confusion when files are transferred to other systems. A null suffix forces *gunzip* to try decompression on all given files regardless of suffix, as in:
  - gunzip -S "" *

  Previous versions of *gzip* used the *.z* suffix. This was changed to avoid a conflict with the *pack* command.
- *-t*. Test. Check the compressed file integrity.

- *-v.* Verbose. Display the name and percentage reduction for each file compressed or decompressed.
- *-V.* Version. Display the version number and compilation options; then quit.
- *-1.* Fast. Indicates the fastest compression method (less compression).
- *-9.* Best. Indicates the slowest compression (best compression). The default is *-6* (biased toward high compression at expense of speed).

Some examples of *gzip*, *gunzip*, and *gzcat* follow.

```
# gzip messages*
#

# gzip -9 messages*
#

# gzip -l messages*
compressed  uncompr. ratio uncompressed_name
     4619     33235  86.1% messages.0
      331       798  62.1% messages.1
     5257     53162  90.1% messages.2
     2304     10370  78.0% messages.3
      212       521  64.4% messages
    12723     98086  87.0% (totals)
#

# gzip -lv messages*
method  crc      date  time  compressed uncompr. ratio uncompressed_name
defla c40c92e1 Mar 13 05:55        4619    33235  86.1% messages.0
defla 9f966462 Mar 13 05:55         331      798  62.1% messages.1
defla e5f23dc4 Mar 13 05:55        5257    53162  90.1% messages.2
defla a05c15b9 Mar 13 05:55        2304    10370  78.0% messages.3
defla 4ff702e7 Mar 13 05:55         212      521  64.4% messages
                                  12723    98086  87.0% (totals)
#

# gzip -r *log
#

# gzcat messages.3.gz | wc
     113     1516    10370
#
```

```
# gunzip *gz
#
```

In the first example, all files in the current working directory whose names begin with "messages" are compressed. The suffix *.gz* will be appended to the name of each compressed file. In the second example, all of the same files are compressed, except that *gzip* is instructed to use the best possible encryption algorithm (*-9* option). In the third example, *gzip* lists all compressed files with "messages" beginning their names. In the fourth example, *gzip* shows a long listing of the same compressed files (*-ly* option). In the fifth example, all files named "*log" in the current directory, as well as in all subdirectories, are compressed. In the sixth example, the file *messages.3.gz* is uncompressed and the output counted with the *wc* command. In the last example, all files compressed with *gzip* in the current directory are uncompressed.

EXAM NOTES

THINK ABOUT IT . . .

You need to compress some files to save space. Which compression program should be used?

This may depend on where these files might some day need to be uncompressed. The *compress* and *uncompress* programs are certainly easy to use, and they are found most everywhere, including older UNIX systems. *zip* might be a good choice if you need to be able to read the files on an MS-DOS system. Also, *zip* can create archives—a single compressed file containing several individual files.

Personal preference also matters. Use the compression program you like best, but think about where you may need to some day uncompress your files.

10.2 Creating Archive Files

File archiving is a technique used to store a collection of files within a single file. This allows you to take a "snapshot" of a number of files (including an entire file system) at once, in a manner that will allow you to extract one or more files from the archive later.

Several commands are available to archive files. They are *tar*, *cpio*, *zip/unzip*, and *jar*. Let's explore each of these commands.

tar

The *tar* command is used to create, extract, and work with archive files written in the tar format. Archive files in the tar format can be read by other UNIX systems, plus the MS-DOS pkzip program.

tar performs five major functions; they are:

1. Create a tar archive. The syntax of the *tar* command for creating an archive is:
   tar c [bBeEfFhiklnopPqvwX [0-7]] [block] [tarfile] [exclude-file] { -I include-file | -C directory | file | file}...
2. Replace a tar archive. New files are appended to the end of the archive. The syntax of the *tar* command for replacing a tar archive is:
   tar r [bBeEfFhiklnqvw [0-7]] [block] { -I include-file | -C directory | file | file}...
3. Update a tar archive. Named files are updated (if they are already in the tar archive), or appended to the archive. The syntax of the *tar* command for updating a tar archive is:
   tar u [bBeEfFhiklnqvw [0-7]] [block] [tarfile] file...
4. List the tar archive. The syntax of the *tar* command for listing a tar archive is:
   tar t [BefFhiklnqvX [0-7]] [tarfile] [exclude-file] { -I include-file | file}...
5. Extract one or more files from the tar archive. The syntax of the *tar* command for extracting from the tar archive is:
   tar x [BefFhiklmnopqvwX [0-7]] [tarfile] [exclude-file] [file]...

The options for *tar* are:

- *b*. Blocking factor. Used when reading or writing to raw magnetic archives (see *f* option). The block argument specifies the number of 512-byte tape blocks to be included in each read or write operation performed on the *tarfile*. The minimum is *1*; the default is *20*. The maximum value is a function of the amount of memory available and the blocking requirements of the specific tape device involved. The maximum cannot exceed 4194303.
- When a tape archive is being read from a raw magnetic tape, its actual blocking factor will be automatically detected provided that it is less than or equal to the nominal blocking factor (the value of the block argument, or the default value if the *b* option is not specified). If the actual blocking factor is greater than the nominal blocking factor, a read error will result.

- *B*. Block. Forces *tar* to perform multiple reads (if necessary) to read exactly enough bytes to fill a block. This option enables *tar* to work across the Ethernet, since pipes and sockets return partial blocks even when more data is coming. When reading from standard input, '-', this option is selected by default to ensure that *tar* can recover from short reads. This option is only relevant when *tarfile* is a raw magnetic tape.
- *e*. Error. Exit immediately with a positive exit status if any unexpected errors occur.
- *E*. Write a *tarfile* with extended headers. (Used with *c*, *r*, or *u* options; ignored with *t* or *x* options.) When a *tarfile* is written with extended headers, the modification time is maintained with a granularity of microseconds rather than seconds. In addition, file names no longer than 1024 characters that could not be archived without *E*, and file sizes greater than 8GB, are supported. The *E* flag is required whenever the larger files and/or files with longer names, or whose UID/GID (the numeric userid in */etc/passwd* and */etc/shadow*, and the numeric groupid in */etc/passwd* and */etc/group*) exceed 2097151, are to be archived, or if time granularity of microseconds is desired.
- *f*. File. Use the *tarfile* argument as the name of the tarfile. If *f* is specified, */etc/default/tar* is not searched. If *f* is omitted, *tar* will use the device indicated by the TAPE environment variable, if set; otherwise, it will use the default values defined in */etc/default/tar*. If the name of the *tarfile* is '-', *tar* writes to the standard output or reads from the standard input, whichever is appropriate. *tar* can be used as the head or tail of a pipeline. *tar* can also be used to move hierarchies with the command:

```
cd fromdir; tar cf - .| (cd todir; tar xfBp -)
```

- *F*. *tar* excludes all directories named *SCCS* and *RCS* from the tarfile.
- *FF*. *tar* excludes all directories named *SCCS* and *RCS*, all files with *.o* as their suffix, and all files named *errs*, *core*, and *a.out*.
- *h*. Follow symbolic links as if they were normal files or directories. Normally, *tar* does not follow symbolic links.
- *i*. Ignore directory checksum errors.
- *k size*. Require *tar* to use the *size* argument as the *size* of an archive in kilobytes. This is useful when the archive is intended

for a fixed-size device such as floppy disks. Large files are then split across volumes if they do not fit in the specified size.

- *l*. Link. Output error message if unable to resolve all links to the files being archived. If *l* is not specified, no error messages are printed.
- *m*. Modify. The modification time of the file is the time of extraction. This option is valid only with the *x* option.
- *n*. The file being read is a nontape device. Reading of the archive is faster since *tar* can randomly seek around the archive.
- *o*. Ownership. Assign to extracted files the user and group identifiers of the user running the program, rather than those on tarfile. This is the default behavior for users other than root. If the *o* option is not set and the user is root, the extracted files will take on the group and user identifiers of the files on tarfile. The *o* option is valid only with the *x* option.
- *p*. Restore the named files to their original modes, and Access Control Lists (ACLs) if applicable, ignoring the present umask. This is the default behavior if invoked as superuser with the *x* option specified. If superuser, SetUID, and sticky information are also extracted from the archive, restored files are restored with their original owners and permissions, rather than owned by root. When this option is used with the *c* option, ACLs are created in the tarfile along with other information. Errors will occur when a tarfile with ACLs is extracted by previous versions of *tar*.
- *P*. Suppress the addition of a trailing "/" on directory entries in the archive.
- *q*. Stop after extracting the first occurrence of the named file. *tar* will normally continue reading the archive after finding an occurrence of a file.
- *v*. Verbose. Output the name of each file preceded by the option letter. With the *t* option, *v* provides additional information about the tarfile entries. The listing is similar to the format produced by the *-l* option of the *ls* command.
- *w*. What. Output the action to be taken and the name of the file, then await the user's confirmation. If the response is affirmative, the action is performed; otherwise, the action is not performed. This option cannot be used with the *t* option.
- *X*. Exclude. Use the *exclude-file* argument as a file containing a list of relative pathnames for files (or directories) to be excluded

from the tarfile when using the options *c*, *x*, or *t*. Be careful of trailing white spaces. Also beware of leading white spaces, since, for each line in the excluded file, the entire line (apart from the newline) will be used to match against the initial string of files to exclude. Multiple *X* options may be used, with one *exclude-file* per option. In the case where included files (see *-I include-file* option) are also specified, the excluded files take precedence over all included files. If a file is specified in both the exclude-file and the include-file (or on the command line), it will be excluded.

- *[0-7]*. Select an alternative drive on which the tape is mounted. The default entries are specified in */etc/default/tar*. If no digit or *f* option is specified, the entry in */etc/default/tar* with digit "0" is the default.
- *-I include-file*. Opens *include-file* containing a list of files, one per line, and treats it as if each file appeared separately on the command line. Be careful of trailing white spaces. Also beware of leading white spaces, since, for each line in the included file, the entire line (apart from the newline) will be used to match against the initial string of files to include. In the case where excluded files (see the *X* option) are also specified, they take precedence over all included files. If a file is specified in both the exclude-file and the include-file (or on the command line), it will be excluded.
- *-C directory file*. Performs a *chdir* operation on directory and performs the *c* (create) or *r* (replace) operation on *file*. Use short relative pathnames for *file*. If *file* is ".", archive all files in the directory. This option enables archiving files from multiple directories not related by a close common parent.
- *file*. A pathname of a regular file or directory to be archived (when the *c*, *r*, or *u* options are specified), extracted (*x*) or listed (*t*). When *file* is the pathname of a directory, the action applies to all of the files and (recursively) subdirectories of that directory.
- *tarfile*. The *tar* command archives and extracts files to and from a single file called a *tarfile*. *Tarfile* can be a magnetic tape file (such as */dev/rmt0*), or it can be any ordinary file.
- *exclude-file*. See the *X* option.

Some examples of the *tar* command follow.

```
# tar cvf m.tar messages*
a messages 99K
a messages.0 33K
```

```
a messages.1 1K
a messages.2 52K
a messages.3 11K
# tar tf m.tar
messages
messages.0
messages.1
messages.2
messages.3
# tar tvf m.tar
-rw-r--r--   0/1   101376 Mar 16 09:00 2001 messages
-rw-r--r--   0/1    33235 Mar 10 05:08 2001 messages.0
-rw-r--r--   0/1      798 Mar  3 07:12 2001 messages.1
-rw-r--r--   0/1    53162 Feb 22 21:00 2001 messages.2
-rw-r--r--   0/1    10370 Feb 17 20:43 2001 messages.3
#
```

```
# cd /etc
# tar cEf /tmp/etc.tar .
tar: ./.name_service_door is not a file. Not dumped
# tar tvf /tmp/etc.tar
drwxr-xr-x   0/3        0 Mar 11 03:10 2001 .
drwxr-xr-x   0/3        0 Mar  7 14:24 2001 ./default
-r--r--r--   0/3      803 Nov 10 17:13 1999 ./default/sys-suspend
-r-xr-xr-x   0/2       12 Apr  4 21:49 2000 ./default/cron
-r--r--r--   0/3      210 Apr  4 21:49 2000 ./default/devfsadm
-r--r--r--   0/3     2826 Apr  4 21:49 2000 ./default/dhcpagent
-r--r--r--   0/2       10 Apr  4 21:49 2000 ./default/fs
-r--r--r--   0/3      367 Jun  1 05:45 2000 ./default/inetinit
-r--r--r--   0/3     1183 Apr  4 21:49 2000 ./default/kbd
-r--r--r--   0/2      576 Apr  4 21:49 2000 ./default/nfslogd
-r--r--r--   0/3       74 Apr  4 21:49 2000 ./default/passwd
-r--r--r--   0/3      526 Apr  4 21:49 2000 ./default/tar
-r--r--r--   0/3       16 Apr  4 21:49 2000 ./default/utmpd
-r-xr-xr-x   0/0      624 Apr  4 22:17 2000 ./default/init
-r--r--r--   0/3     1722 Apr  4 21:49 2000 ./default/login
[ remainder of output not shown ]
#
```

```
# tar cvf /tmp/bkp.tar -I /tmp/includefiles
a ./etc/passwd 1K
a ./etc/shadow 1K
a ./etc/group 1K
a ./etc/hosts symbolic link to ./inet/hosts
a ./etc/netmasks symbolic link to ./inet/netmasks
a ./etc/networks symbolic link to ./inet/networks
```

```
a ./etc/default/passwd 1K
# cat /tmp/includefiles
./etc/passwd
./etc/shadow
./etc/group
./etc/hosts
./etc/netmasks
./etc/networks
./etc/default/passwd
# cd /tmp
# tar xvf bkp.tar ./etc/group
tar: blocksize = 14
x ./etc/group, 325 bytes, 1 tape blocks
# ls -l /tmp/etc
total 16
-rw-r--r--   1 root     sys          325 Feb  9 04:34 group
#

# tar cf - /var/adm | compress > /tmp/varadm.tar.Z
# ls -l /tmp/varadm.tar.Z
-rw-r--r--   1 root     other     109669 Mar 16 10:05 /tmp/varadm.tar.Z
# zcat /tmp/varadm.tar.Z | tar tf -
/var/adm/
/var/adm/log/
/var/adm/passwd/
/var/adm/streams/
/var/adm/aculog
/var/adm/spellhist
/var/adm/utmpx
/var/adm/wtmpx
/var/adm/sm.bin/
/var/adm/acct/
/var/adm/acct/fiscal/
/var/adm/acct/nite/
/var/adm/acct/sum/
/var/adm/sa/
/var/adm/messages
[ remainder of output not shown ]
#

# cd /var/adm; tar cf - . | (cd /export/tools;tar xpf -)
#
```

In the first example, the tar archive *m.tar* is created; it consists of the files named *messages.** in the current directory. The archive is listed in short format (*tar tf*) , then in long format (*tar tvf*).

In the second example, the tar archive */tmp/etc.tar* is created, which consists of all files in */etc*. Incidentally, the file *.name_service_door*, which is a door file, is not backed up. Next, the archive is listed in long format.

In the third example, the tar archive *bkp.tar* is created; it consists of files listed in the file */tmp/includefiles*. Next, after *cd*'ing to */tmp*, the file */etc/group* is restored. Because the files listed in */tmp/includefiles* began with a "./" instead of just a "/", the file */etc/group* could be restored to any location, in this case */tmp*. Were the files in */tmp/includefiles* to begin with a "/", *tar* would have been able to restore files only back to their original locations.

In the fourth example, all files in the directory */var/adm* are written to a tar archive. In this example, *tar* writes its tar archive to standard output instead of to a file. The standard output is piped to the *compress* command, which writes its own standard output to the file */tmp/varadm.tar*.Z. This is a common technique for building a compressed tar archive. Next, the compressed archive is piped from the *zcat* command to *tar*; so in this case *tar* is reading its input from standard input (signified by the "-"). *tar* lists the contents of this archive to standard output.

In the fifth example, the contents of the directory */var/adm* is copied to the directory */export/logs*.

Examples of *tar* writing to and reading from tapes will appear in later sections in this chapter.

EXAM NOTES

THINK ABOUT IT . . .

You need to restore a file from a tar archive, but you want to restore the file to an alternate location (e.g., */tmp*) because you do not want to overwrite the production version of the file. How should you proceed?

First, list the table of contents of the archive. If the directory names begin with a dot, then you will be able to restore any files to any desired location by just *cd*'ing to */tmp* and extracting files from the tar archive. If, however, the directory names begin with a slash, you will be able to restore these files only to their original location. But there is still an alternative.

You could temporarily rename the existing directory where your present files reside. Then, create a new directory with the original name. Restore the backed-up files to the original directory name. Now you have a directory with your present files, and another with your backed-up files restored. (Note that if the files in these directories are currently being used, renaming the in-use directory is not such a good idea.)

cpio

The *cpio* command is used to create, extract, and work with archive files written in the cpio format. Archive files in the cpio format can be read by many other UNIX systems.

cpio performs three functions; they are:

1. Copy in. *cpio* creates an archive. The syntax of the *cpio* command for creating an archive is:
   cpio -i [bBcdfkmPrsStuvV6] [-C bufsize] [-E file] [-H header] [-I file [-M message]] [-R id] [pattern]...
2. Copy out. *cpio* reads from an archive. The syntax of the *cpio* command for reading from an archive is:
   cpio -o [aABcLPvV] [-C bufsize] [-H header] [-O file [-M message]]
3. Pass. *cpio* is used to copy the contents of one directory to another directory. The syntax of the *cpio* command for copying a directory is:
   cpio -p [adlLmPuvV] [-R id] directory

The options for *cpio* include:

- *-i*. Extracts files from the standard input.
- *-o*. Reads the standard input to obtain a list of pathnames and copies those files onto the standard output.
- *-p*. Reads the standard input to obtain a list of pathnames of files. This is used to copy those files to another location on the system.
- *-a*. Resets access times of input files after they have been copied. Access times are not reset for linked files when *cpio -pla* is specified (mutually exclusive with *-m*).
- *-A*. Appends files to an archive. The *-A* option requires the *-O* option. Valid only with archives that are files, or that are on floppy diskettes or hard disk partitions.
- *-b*. Reverses the order of the bytes within each word (use only with the *-i* option). This is usually used when trying to read a cpio archive that was created on a non-Solaris UNIX system.
- *-B*. Blocks input/output 5120 bytes to the record. The default buffer size is 8192 bytes when this and the *-C* options are not used. *-B* does not apply to the pass option; *-B* is meaningful only with data directed to or from a tape drive; for example, */dev/rmt/0m*.
- *-c*. Reads or writes header information in ASCII character form for portability. There are no UID or GID restrictions associated

with this header format. Use this option between SVR4-based machines, or the *-H odc* option between unknown machines. The *-c* option implies the use of expanded device numbers, which are supported only on SVR4-based systems. Use *-H odc* to transfer files between SunOS 4 or Interactive UNIX and the Solaris 8 operating environment.

- *-C bufsize*. Blocks input/output *bufsize* bytes to the record, where *bufsize* is replaced by a positive integer. The default buffer size is 8192 bytes when this and *-B* options are not used. (*-C* does not apply to the pass option; *-C* is meaningful only with data directed to or from a tape drive.)
- *-d*. Creates directories as needed. Used with the *-o* option.
- *-E file*. Specifies an input file (*file*) that contains a list of file names to be extracted from the archive (one file name per line).
- *-f*. Copies in all files except those in patterns.
- *-H header*. Reads or writes header information in *header* format. Always use this option or the *-c* option when the origin and the destination machines are different types (mutually exclusive with *-c* and *-6*). Valid values for header are:
  - *bar*. *bar* head and format. Used only with the *-i* option.
  - *crc* | *CRC*. ASCII header with expanded device numbers and an additional per-file checksum. There are no UID or GID restrictions associated with this header format.
  - *odc*. ASCII header with small device numbers. This is the IEEE/P1003 Data Interchange Standard *cpio* header and format. It has the widest range of portability of any of the header formats. It is the official format for transferring files between POSIX-conforming systems. Use this format to communicate with SunOS 4 and Interactive UNIX. This header format allows UIDs and GIDs up to 262143 to be stored in the header.
  - *tar* | *TAR*. *tar* header and format. This header format allows UIDs and GIDs up to 2097151 to be stored in the header.
  - *ustar* | *USTAR*. IEEE/P1003 Data Interchange Standard tar header and format. This header format allows UIDs and GIDs up to 2097151 to be stored in the header. Files with UIDs and GIDs greater than 2097151 will be archived with the UID and GID of 60001. To transfer a large file (> 8GB), the header format can be tar/TAR, ustar/USTAR, or odc only.

- *-I file*. Reads the contents of *file* as an input archive. Avoids having to use "<" to specify the tape drive containing the archive. If *file* is a tape drive, and the current medium has been completely read, replace the medium and press RETURN to continue to the next medium. This option is used only with the *-i* option.
- *-k*. Attempts to skip corrupted file headers and I/O errors that may be encountered. If you want to copy files from a medium that is corrupted or out of sequence, this option lets you read only those files with good headers. (For cpio archives that contain other cpio archives, encountered errors may cause *cpio* to terminate prematurely. *cpio* will find the next good header, which may be one for a smaller archive, and terminate when the smaller archive's trailer is encountered.) Used only with the *-i* option.
- *-l*. Whenever possible, links files rather than copying them. (Usable only with the *-p* option.)
- *-L*. Follows symbolic links. The default is not to follow symbolic links.
- *-m*. Retains previous file modification time. This option is ineffective on directories that are being copied (mutually exclusive with *-a*).
- *-M message*. Defines a *message* to use when switching media. When you use the *-O* or *-I* options and specify a character special device, you can use this option to define the message that is printed when you reach the end of the medium. A "%d" can be placed in message to print the sequence number of the next medium needed to continue.
- *-O file*. Directs the output of *cpio* to *file*. Avoids use of ">" to specify the output device. If *file* is a tape or diskette and the current medium is full, replace the medium and type RETURN to continue to the next medium. Use only with the *-o* option.
- *-P*. Preserves ACLs. If the option is used for output, existing ACLs are written along with other attributes to the standard output. ACLs are created as special files with a special file type. If the option is used for input, existing ACLs are extracted along with other attributes from standard input. The option recognizes the special file type. Note that errors will occur if a cpio archive with ACLs is extracted by previous versions of *cpio* that do not recognize the ACL. This option should not be used with the *-c* option, as ACL support may not be present on all systems, and hence is not portable. Use ASCII headers for portability.

- *-r*. Interactively renames files. If the user types a carriage return alone, the file is skipped. If the user types a ".", the original pathname will be retained. (Not available with *cpio -p*.)
- *-R id*. Reassigns ownership and group information for each file to userid (*id* must be a valid login ID from */etc/passwd*). This option is valid only for the superuser.
- *-s*. Swaps bytes within each halfword. This is typically used when trying to read a cpio archive that was created on a non-Solaris UNIX system.
- *-S*. Swaps halfwords within each word. This is typically used when trying to read a cpio archive that was created on a non-Solaris UNIX system.
- *-t*. Prints a table of contents of the input. No files are extracted from the archive (mutually exclusive with *-V*).
- *-u*. Copies unconditionally (normally, an older file will not replace a newer file with the same name).
- *-v*. Verbose. Prints a list of file names. When used with the *-t* option, the table of contents looks like the output of an *ls -l* command.
- *-V*. Special verbose. Prints a dot for each file read or written. Useful to assure the user that *cpio* is working without printing out all file names.
- *-6*. Processes a UNIX System Sixth Edition archive format file. Use only with the *-i* option (mutually exclusive with *-c* and *-H*).
- *directory*. A pathname of an existing *directory* to be used as the target of *cpio -p*.
- *pattern*. Expressions making use of a pattern-matching notation similar to that used by the Bourne Shell for file name pattern matching, and similar to regular expressions. The following metacharacters are defined:
  - *. Matches any string, including the empty string.
  - ?. Matches any single character.
  - [. . .]. Matches any one of the enclosed characters. A pair of characters separated by "-" matches any symbol between the pair (inclusive), as defined by the system default collating sequence. If the first character following the opening "[" is a "!", the results are unspecified.
  - !. means "not". (For example, the !abc* pattern would exclude all files that begin with abc.)

In patterns, metacharacters ?, *, and [. . .] match the slash (/) character, and backslash (\) is an escape character. Multiple cases of pattern can be specified and if no pattern is specified, the default for pattern is * (i.e., select all files). Each pattern must be enclosed in double quotes; otherwise, the name of a file in the current directory might be used.

Examples of *cpio* commands follow.

```
# find . -print | cpio -od -O /tmp/etc.cpio
4576 blocks
#

# cat /tmp/etc.cpio | cpio -iduV
..................................................
..................................................
..................................................
..................................................
..................................................
..................................................
..................................................
..................................................
..................................................
..................................................
..................................................
..................................................
.........
4576 blocks
#

# cat /tmp/etc.cpio | cpio -iadu "group" "default/*"
4576 blocks
#

# ls *db | cpio -odV > /tmp/db.cpio
.....
20447 blocks
#

# cpio -it -I /tmp/etc.cpio
.
default
default/sys-suspend
default/cron
default/devfsadm
default/dhcpagent
default/fs
```

```
default/inetinit
default/kbd
default/nfslogd
default/passwd
default/tar
default/utmpd
default/init
default/login
default/su
default/power
default/dhcp
TIMEZONE
autopush
[ remainder of output not shown ]
#

# cpio -itv -I /tmp/etc.cpio
drwxr-xr-x  40 root   sys       0 Mar 11 03:10 2001, .
drwxr-xr-x   2 root   sys       0 Mar  7 14:24 2001, default
-r--r--r--   1 root   sys     803 Nov 10 17:13 1999, default/sys-suspend
-r-xr-xr-x   1 root   bin      12 Apr  4 21:49 2000, default/cron
-r--r--r--   1 root   sys     210 Apr  4 21:49 2000, default/devfsadm
-r--r--r--   1 root   sys    2826 Apr  4 21:49 2000, default/dhcpagent
-r--r--r--   1 root   bin      10 Apr  4 21:49 2000, default/fs
-r--r--r--   1 root   sys     367 Jun  1 05:45 2000, default/inetinit
-r--r--r--   1 root   sys    1183 Apr  4 21:49 2000, default/kbd
-r--r--r--   1 root   bin     576 Apr  4 21:49 2000, default/nfslogd
-r--r--r--   1 root   sys      74 Apr  4 21:49 2000, default/passwd
-r--r--r--   1 root   sys     526 Apr  4 21:49 2000, default/tar
-r--r--r--   1 root   sys      16 Apr  4 21:49 2000, default/utmpd
-r-xr-xr-x   1 root   root    624 Apr  4 22:17 2000, default/init
-r--r--r--   1 root   sys    1722 Apr  4 21:49 2000, default/login
-r--r--r--   1 root   sys     703 Apr  4 21:49 2000, default/su
-r--r--r--   1 root   sys    1232 Jan  5 16:00 2000, default/power
-rw-r--r--   1 root   sys      65 Sep 29 04:34 2000, default/dhcp
lrwxrwxrwx   1 root   root     14 Apr  4 21:49 2000, TIMEZONE -> ./
default/init
lrwxrwxrwx   1 root   root     16 Apr  4 21:49 2000, autopush -> ../sbin
/autopush
[ remainder of output not shown ]
#

# find . -print|cpio -pdm /export/etc
4242 blocks
#
```

In the first example, the *find* command is used to create a list of all files and directories in the current working directory; the standard output from *find* is piped to the standard input of *cpio*, which creates the archive file *etc.cpio*.

In the second example, *cpio* restores all files and directories in the */tmp/etc.cpio* archive. The *-V* option causes *cpio* to print a single "." when it has restored each file.

In the third example, the file group and all files in the directory *default* are restored from the cpio archive */tmp/etc.cpio*. The access times for restored files are preserved since the *-a* option is used.

In the fourth example, all files named **db* are written to the cpio archive */tmp/db.cpio*.

In the fifth example, the files in the archive */tmp/etc.cpio* are listed in short format.

In the sixth example, all of the files in the archive */tmp/etc.cpio* are listed in long (*ls -l*) format.

In the seventh example, the entire contents of the current working directory (".") are copied to the directory */export/etc*.

EXAM NOTES

THINK ABOUT IT . . .

You need to restore some files from a cpio archive to a different location so that you can examine some of the backed-up files offline. How is this done?

First, list the archive contents with the *cpio -it* command to ensure that the pathnames stored in the archive begin with a "./". Then, change to another directory (e.g., */tmp*) and restore the files there with the *cpio -idum* command.

EXAM NOTES

THINK ABOUT IT . . .

You have a tar archive that contains files you need to restore. But your *tar* program has a problem. All you have is *cpio*. Is there anything you can do?

Yes. You can use the *-H tar* option of the *cpio* command to read the tar archive. An example command line would be: *cpio -iduH tar < archive.tar.*

zip and *unzip*

zip and *unzip* are freeware compression programs included with Solaris. *zip* files are interchangeable with *zip* files on other UNIX and non-UNIX platforms. In addition to compressing individual files, *zip* can also create collections of compressed files called zip archives.

The *zip* command is used to compress, and archive individual files and groups of files. The *unzip* command is used to uncompress and extract from archive files. The syntax of the *zip* command is:

zip [-AcdDeEfFghjklLmoqrRSTuvVwXyz@$] [-b path] [-n suffixes] [-t mmddyyyy] [-tt mmddyyyy] [zipfile [file1 file2 ...]] [-xi list]

The syntax of the *unzip* command is:

unzip [-Z] [-cflptuvz[abjnoqsCLMVX$]] file[.zip] [file(s) ...] [-x xfile(s) ...] [-d exdir]

The options for *zip* are:

- *-b path*. Use the specified *path* for the temporary zip archive. For example:

  ```
  zip -b /tmp stuff *
  ```

  will put the temporary zip archive in the directory */tmp*, copying over *stuff.zip* to the current directory when done. This option is useful only when updating an existing archive, and the file system containing this old archive does not have enough space to hold both old and new archives at the same time.
- *-c*. Add one-line comments for each file. File operations (adding, updating) are done first, and the user is then prompted for a one-line comment for each file. Enter the comment followed by RETURN, or just RETURN for no comment.
- *-d*. Remove (delete) entries from a zip archive. For example:

  ```
  zip -d foo foo/tom/junk foo/harry/\* \*.o
  ```

  will remove the entry *foo/tom/junk*, all of the files that start with *foo/harry/*, and all of the files that end with *.o* (in any path). Note that shell pathname expansion has been inhibited with backslashes, so that zip can see the asterisks, enabling *zip* to match on the contents of the zip archive instead of the contents of the current directory.

- *-D*. Do not create entries in the zip archive for directories. Directory entries are created by default so that their attributes can be saved in the zip archive. The environment variable ZIPOPT can be used to change the default options. For example, under UNIX with sh:

```
ZIPOPT="-D"; export ZIPOPT
```

(The variable ZIPOPT can be used for any option except *-i* and *-x* and can include several options.) The option *-D* is a shorthand for *-x* "*/" but the latter cannot be set as default in the ZIPOPT environment variable.

- *-f*. Replace (freshen) an existing entry in the zip archive only if it has been modified more recently than the version already in the zip archive; unlike the update option (*-u*) this will not add files that are not already in the zip archive. For example:

```
zip -f foo
```

This command should be run from the same directory that the original *zip* command was run, since paths stored in zip archives are always relative.

Note that the time zone environment variable TZ should be set according to the local time zone in order for the *-f*, *-u*, and *-o* options to work correctly. The reasons behind this are somewhat subtle but have to do with the differences between the UNIX format file times (always in GMT) and most of the other operating systems (always local time) and the necessity to compare the two. A typical TZ value is "MET-1MEST" (Middle European Time with automatic adjustment for "summertime" or Daylight Savings Time).

- *-F*. Fix the zip archive. This option can be used if some portions of the archive are missing. It is not guaranteed to work, so you *must* back up the original archive first.
- *-FF*. The compressed sizes given inside the damaged archive are not trusted and *zip* scans for special signatures to identify the limits between the archive members. The single *-F* is more reliable if the archive is not excessively damaged; for example, if it has only been truncated, so try this option first.

Neither the *-F* or *-FF* option will recover archives that have been incorrectly transferred in ASCII mode instead of binary. After the repair, the *-t* option of *unzip* may show that some files have a bad CRC. Such files cannot be recovered; you can remove them from the archive using the *-d* option of *zip*.

- *-g*. Grow (append to) the specified zip archive, instead of creating a new one. If this operation fails, *zip* attempts to restore the archive to its original state. If the restoration fails, the archive might become corrupted. This option is ignored when there's no existing archive or when at least one archive member must be updated or deleted.
- *-h*. Display the zip help information (this also appears if *zip* is run with no arguments).
- *-i files*. Include only the specified *files*, as in:

```
zip -r foo . -i \*.c
```

which will include only the *files* that end in *.c* in the current directory and its subdirectories. *zip* does not allow recursion in directories other than the current one. The backslash avoids the shell file name substitution, so that the name matching is performed by *zip* at all directory levels. Also consider:

```
zip -r foo  . -i@include.lst
```

which will include only the files in the current directory and its subdirectories that match the patterns in the file *include.lst*.

- *-j*. Store just the name of a saved file (not its path), and do not store directory names. By default, *zip* will store the full path.
- *-J*. Strip any prepended data (e.g., a SFX stub) from the archive.
- *-k*. Attempt to convert the names and paths to conform to MS-DOS, store only the MS-DOS attribute (just the user write attribute from UNIX), and mark the entry as made under MS-DOS (even though it was not); for compatibility with older versions of pkunzip under MS-DOS, which cannot handle certain names such as those with two dots.
- *-l*. Translate the UNIX end-of-line character LF into the MS-DOS convention CRLF. This option should not be used on binary files. This option can be used on UNIX if the zip file is intended for pkunzip under MS-DOS. If the input files already contain CRLF, this option adds an extra CR. This ensures that

unzip -a on UNIX will get back an exact copy of the original file and undo the effect of *zip -l*.

- *-ll*. Translate the MS-DOS end-of-line CRLF into UNIX LF. This option should not be used on binary files. This option can be used on MS-DOS if the zip file is intended for *unzip* under UNIX.
- *-L*. Display the *zip* license.
- *-m*. Move the specified files into the zip archive; actually, this deletes the target directories/files after making the specified zip archive. If a directory becomes empty after removal of the files, the directory is also removed. No deletions are done until *zip* has created the archive without error. This is useful for conserving disk space, but is potentially dangerous so it is recommended to use it in combination with *-T* to test the archive before removing all input files.
- *-n suffixes*. Do not attempt to compress files named with the given *suffixes*. Such files are simply stored (0% compression) in the output zip file and zip doesn't waste its time trying to compress them. The *suffixes* are separated by either colons or semicolons. For example:

```
zip -rn .Z:.zip:.tiff:.gif:.snd  foo foo
```

  will copy everything from *foo* into *foo.zip*, but will store any files that end in .Z, *.zip*, *.tiff*, *.gif*, or *.snd* without trying to compress them (image and sound files often have their own specialized compression methods). By default, *zip* does not compress files with extensions in the list *.Z:.zip:.zoo:.arc:.lzh:.arj*. Such files are stored directly in the output archive. The environment variable ZIPOPT can be used to change the default options. For example, under UNIX with *csh*:

```
setenv ZIPOPT "-n .gif:.zip"
```

  To attempt compression on all files, use:

```
zip -n : foo
```

  The maximum compression option *-9* also attempts compression on all files regardless of extension.
- *-o*. Set the "last modified" time of the zip archive to the latest (oldest) "last modified" time found among the entries in the zip

archive. This can be used without any other operations, if desired. For example:

```
zip -o foo
```

will change the last modified time of *foo.zip* to the latest time of the entries in *foo.zip*.

In this case, all the files and directories in *foo* are saved in a zip archive named *foo.zip*, including files with names starting with ".", since the recursion does not use the shell's file name substitution mechanism.

If you wish to include only a specific subset of the files in directory *foo* and its subdirectories, use the *-i* option to specify the pattern of files to be included. You should not use *-r* with the name ".*", since that matches ".." which will attempt to zip up the parent directory (probably not what was intended).

- *-R*. Travel the directory structure recursively starting at the current directory; for example:

```
zip -R foo *.c
```

In this example, all the files matching **.c* in the tree starting at the current directory are stored into a zip archive named *foo.zip*.

- *-t mmddyyyy*. Do not operate on files modified prior to the specified date, where *mm* is the month (0–12), *dd* is the day of the month (1–31), and *yyyy* is the year. For example:

```
zip -rt 12072000 infamy foo
```

will add all the files in *foo* and its subdirectories that were last modified on or after December 7, 2000, to the zip archive *infamy.zip*.

- *-tt mmddyyyy*. Do not operate on files modified after or at the specified date, where *mm* is the month (0–12), *dd* is the day of the month (1–31), and *yyyy* is the year. For example:

```
zip -rtt 11301999 infamy foo
```

will add all the files in *foo* and its subdirectories that were last modified before the November 30, 1999, to the zip archive *infamy.zip*.

- *-T.* Test the integrity of the new zip file. If the check fails, the old zip file is unchanged and (with the *-m* option) no input files are removed.
- *-u.* Replace (update) an existing entry in the zip archive only if it has been modified more recently than the version already in the zip archive. For example:

  ```
  zip -u stuff *
  ```

  will add any new files in the current directory and update any files that have been modified since the zip archive *stuff.zip* was last created/modified (note that *zip* will not try to pack *stuff.zip* into itself when you do this).

  Note that the *-u* option with no arguments acts like the *-f* (freshen) option.
- *-v.* Verbose mode or print diagnostic version information. Normally, when applied to real operations, this option enables the display of a progress indicator during compression and requests verbose diagnostic information about zipfile structure oddities.

  When *-v* is the only command-line argument, and *stdout* is not redirected to a file, a diagnostic screen is printed. In addition to the help screen header with program name, version, and release date, some pointers to the Info-ZIP home and distribution sites are given. Then, it shows information about the target environment (compiler type and version, OS version, compilation date, and the enabled optional features used to create the *zip* executable.
- *-x files.* Explicitly exclude the specified files; for example:

  ```
  zip -r foo foo -x \*.o
  ```

  which will include the contents of *foo* in *foo.zip* and exclude all the files that end in *.o*. The backslash avoids the shell file name substitution, so that the name matching is performed by zip at all directory levels.

  Also:

  ```
  zip -r foo foo -x@exclude.lst
  ```

  will include the contents of *foo* in *foo.zip* and exclude all the files that match the patterns contained in the file *exclude.lst*.

- *-X*. Do not save extra file attributes (UID/GID and file times).
- *-y*. Store symbolic links as such in the zip archive instead of compressing and storing the file referred to by the link.
- *-z*. Prompt for a multiline comment for the entire zip archive. The comment is ended by a line containing just a period, or an end of file (^D). The comment can be taken from a file; for example:

```
zip -z foo < foowhat
```

- *-#*. Regulate the speed of compression using the specified digit *#*, where *-0* indicates no compression (store all files), *-1* indicates the fastest compression method (less compression), and *-9* indicates the slowest compression method (optimal compression, ignores the suffix list). The default compression level is *-6*.
- *-@*. Take the list of input files from standard input, one file name per line.

The options for *unzip* are:

- *-a*. Converts text files. Ordinarily all files are extracted exactly as they are stored (as "binary" files). The *-a* option causes files identified by *zip* as text files (those with the "t" label in zipinfo listings, rather than "b") to be automatically extracted as such, converting line endings, end-of-file characters, and the character set itself as necessary. (For example, UNIX files use line feeds [LFs] for end-of-line [EOL] and have no end-of-file [EOF] markers; Macintoshes use carriage returns [CRs] for EOLs; and most PC operating systems use CR+LF for EOLs and control-Z for EOF. In addition, IBM mainframes and the Michigan Terminal System use EBCDIC rather than the more common ASCII character set, and NT supports Unicode.) Note that *zip*'s identification of text files is by no means perfect; some "text" files may actually be binary and vice versa. *unzip* therefore prints "[text]" or "[binary]" as a visual check for each file it extracts when using the *-a* option.
- *-aa*. Force all files to be extracted as text, regardless of the supposed file type.
- *-b*. Treat all files as binary (no text conversions).
- *-B*. Save a backup copy of each overwritten file with a tilde appended (e.g., the old copy of "foo" is renamed to "foo~"). This is similar to the default behavior of emacs in many locations.

- *-c*. Extract files to stdout. This option is similar to the *-p* option except that the name of each file is printed as it is extracted, the *-a* option is allowed, and ASCII-EBCDIC conversion is automatically performed if appropriate. This option is not listed in the *unzip* usage screen.
- *-C*. Match file names case insensitively. *unzip*'s philosophy is "you get what you ask for." Because some file systems are fully case sensitive (notably those under the UNIX operating system) and because both zip archives and *unzip* itself are portable across platforms, *unzip*'s default behavior is to match both wildcard and literal filenames case sensitively. That is, specifying *makefile* on the command line will match only "makefile" in the archive, not "Makefile" or "MAKEFILE" (and similarly for wildcard specifications). Since this does not correspond to the behavior of many other operating/file systems (e.g., OS/2 HPFS, which preserves mixed case but is not sensitive to it), the *-C* option may be used to force all file name matches to be case insensitive. In the earlier example, all three files would then match "makefile" (or "make*", or similar). The *-C* option affects files in both the normal file list and the excluded-file list (xlist).
- *-d exdir*. An optional directory *exdir* to which to extract files. By default, all files and subdirectories are extracted to the current directory; the *-d* option allows extraction to an arbitrary directory. This option need not appear at the end of the command line; it is also accepted before the zipfile specification (with the normal options), immediately after the zipfile specification, or between the file(s) and the *-x* option. The option and directory may be concatenated without any white space between them, but note that this may cause normal shell behavior to be suppressed. In particular, "-d ~" (tilde) is expanded by UNIX C-Shells into the name of the user's home directory, but "-d~" is treated as a literal subdirectory "~" of the current directory.
- *-f*. Freshen existing files; that is, extract only those files that already exist on disk and that are newer than the disk copies. By default *unzip* queries before overwriting, but the *-o* option may be used to suppress the queries.
- *-j*. Junk paths. The archive's directory structure is not re-created; all files are deposited in the extraction directory (by default, the current one).

- *-l*. List archive files (short format). The names, uncompressed file sizes and modification dates, and times of the specified files are printed, along with totals for all files specified. In addition, the zipfile comment and individual file comments (if any) are displayed. If a file was archived from a single-case file system (e.g., the old MS-DOS FAT file system) and the *-L* option was given, the file name is converted to lowercase and is prefixed with a caret (^).
- *-L*. Convert to lowercase any file name originating on an uppercase-only operating system or file system. Depending on the archiver, files archived under single-case file systems (VMS, old MS-DOS FAT, etc.) may be stored as all-uppercase names; this can be ugly or inconvenient when extracting to a case-preserving file system such as OS/2 HPFS or a case-sensitive one such as UNIX.

  By default *unzip* lists and extracts such file names exactly as they're stored (excepting truncation, conversion of unsupported characters, etc.); this option causes the names of all files from certain systems to be converted to lowercase.
- *-M*. Pipe all output through an internal pager similar to the *more* command. At the end of a screen full of output, *unzip* pauses with a "--More--" prompt; the next screen full may be viewed by pressing the ENTER (RETURN) key or the spacebar. *unzip* can be terminated by pressing the "q" key and, on some systems, the ENTER/RETURN key. Unlike UNIX's *more*, there is no forward-searching or editing capability. Also, *unzip* doesn't notice if long lines wrap at the edge of the screen, effectively resulting in the printing of two or more lines and the likelihood that some text will scroll off the top of the screen before being viewed. On some systems the number of available lines on the screen is not detected, in which case *unzip* assumes the height is 24 lines.
- *-n*. Never overwrite existing files. If a file already exists, skip the extraction of that file without prompting. By default *unzip* queries before extracting any file that already exists; the user may choose to overwrite only the current file, overwrite all files, skip extraction of the current file, skip extraction of all existing files, or rename the current file.
- *-o*. Overwrite existing files without prompting. This is a dangerous option, so use it with care.

- *-p*. Extract files to stdout. Nothing but the file data is sent to stdout, and the files are always extracted in binary format, just as they are stored (no conversions).
- *-t*. Test archive files. This option extracts each specified file in memory and compares the CRC (cyclic redundancy check, an enhanced checksum) of the expanded file with the original file's stored CRC value.
- *-u*. Update existing files and create new ones if needed. This option performs the same function as the *-f* option, extracting (with query) files that are newer than those with the same name on disk, and in addition it extracts those files that do not already exist on disk.
- *-v*. Be verbose or print diagnostic version info. *-v* has two purposes: When a zipfile is specified with no other options, *-v* lists archive files verbosely, adding to the basic *-l* information the compression method, compressed size, compression ratio, and 32-bit CRC. When no zipfile is specified (i.e., the complete command is simply "*unzip –v*"), a diagnostic screen is printed. In addition to the normal header with release date and version, *unzip* lists the home Info-ZIP ftp site and where to find a list of other ftp and non-ftp sites; the target operating system for which it was compiled, as well as (possibly) the hardware on which it was compiled, the compiler and version used, and the compilation date; and any special compilation options that might affect the program's operation. *-v* also works in conjunction with other options (e.g., *-t*) to produce more verbose or debugging output; this is not yet fully implemented but will be in future releases.
- *-x xfile...* . An optional list of archive members to be excluded from processing. Since wildcard characters match directory separators ("/"), this option may be used to exclude any files that are in subdirectories. For example,

  ```
  unzip foo *.[ch] -x */*
  ```

  would extract all C source files in the main directory, but none in any subdirectories. Without the *-x* option, all C source files in all directories within the zipfile would be extracted.
- `-z`. Display only the archive comment.

Some examples of the *zip* and *unzip* commands follow.

```
# zip /tmp/messages messages*
  adding: messages (deflated 89%)
  adding: messages.0 (deflated 91%)
  adding: messages.1 (deflated 86%)
  adding: messages.2 (deflated 62%)
  adding: messages.3 (deflated 90%)
#

# zip -f /tmp/messages
#

# zip -f /tmp/messages
freshening: messages (deflated 89%)
#

# zip -R /tmp/etc.zip *
  adding: default/cron (stored 0%)
  adding: default/fs (stored 0%)
  adding: default/passwd (deflated 5%)
  adding: default/tar (deflated 48%)
  adding: default/init (deflated 39%)
  adding: default/dhcp (stored 0%)
  adding: TIMEZONE (deflated 39%)
  adding: autopush (deflated 52%)
  adding: cfgadm (deflated 53%)
  adding: clri (deflated 54%)
  adding: crash (deflated 56%)
  adding: cron (deflated 67%)
  adding: dcopy (deflated 54%)
  adding: dhcp/inittab (deflated 71%)
  adding: ff (deflated 54%)
  adding: fmthard (deflated 53%)
  adding: format (deflated 57%)
  adding: fs/hsfs/mount (deflated 52%)
  adding: fs/nfs/mount (deflated 56%)
  adding: fs/ufs/mount (deflated 52%)
  adding: fsck (deflated 55%)
[ remainder of output not shown ]
#

# zip -z /tmp/adm
enter new zip file comment (end with .):
This is a copy of /var/adm archived on March 19, 2001.
The files in this archive can be restored into /tmp for examination
```

```
if necessary.
.
#

# zip -d adm.zip messages.2
deleting: messages.2
#

# zip -T /tmp/adm
test of /tmp/adm.zip OK
#

# unzip -l adm
Archive:  adm.zip
This is a copy of /var/adm archived on March 19, 2001.
The files in this archive can be restored into /tmp for examination
if necessary.
 Length    Date     Time    Name
 ------    ----     ----    ----
     67  02-22-01  04:40   vold.log
 101656  03-16-01  09:44   messages.0
  33235  03-10-01  05:08   messages.1
  53162  02-22-01  21:00   messages.3
 203264  03-16-01  09:01   m.tar
      0  04-04-00  21:49   aculog
      0  04-04-00  21:49   spellhist
   3720  03-20-01  05:21   utmpx
 557256  03-20-01  05:21   wtmpx
  37418  03-20-01  05:24   messages
   6946  03-20-01  05:24   sulog
  28084  03-20-01  05:21   lastlog
 ------                    -------
1024808                    12 files
#

# unzip -v adm
Archive:  adm.zip
This is a copy of /var/adm archived on March 19, 2001.
The files in this archive can be restored into /tmp for examination
if necessary.
 Length  Method   Size  Ratio   Date     Time    CRC-32    Name
 ------  ------   ----  -----   ----     ----    ------    ----
     67  Stored     67    0%  02-22-01  04:40  c1aa3b7c   vold.log
 101656  Defl:N   9231   91%  03-16-01  09:44  36d8b0d0   messages.0
  33235  Defl:N   4590   86%  03-10-01  05:08  c40c92e1   messages.1
  53162  Defl:N   5228   90%  02-22-01  21:00  e5f23dc4   messages.3
 203264  Defl:N  16575   92%  03-16-01  09:01  f3821869   m.tar
```

```
      0  Stored        0   0%  04-04-00  21:49  00000000   aculog
      0  Stored        0   0%  04-04-00  21:49  00000000   spellhist
   3720  Defl:N      283  92%  03-20-01  05:21  5b266ece   utmpx
 557256  Defl:N    19386  97%  03-20-01  05:21  5fdc82b0   wtmpx
  37418  Defl:N     4254  89%  03-20-01  05:24  3c296d6e   messages
   6946  Defl:N     1180  83%  03-20-01  05:24  11de0f5d   sulog
  28084  Defl:N      153 100%  03-20-01  05:21  3a9c5ba4   lastlog
 ------           ------  ---                              -------
1024808            60947  94%                              12 files
#

# unzip adm.zip
Archive:  adm.zip
This is a copy of /var/adm archived on March 19, 2001.
The files in this archive can be restored into /tmp for examination
if necessary.
 extracting: vold.log
replace messages.0? [y]es, [n]o, [A]ll, [N]one, [r]ename: A
  inflating: messages.0
  inflating: messages.1
  inflating: messages.3
  inflating: m.tar
 extracting: aculog
 extracting: spellhist
  inflating: utmpx
  inflating: wtmpx
  inflating: messages
  inflating: sulog
  inflating: lastlog
#

# unzip adm.zip sulog
Archive:  adm.zip
This is a copy of /var/adm archived on March 19, 2001.
The files in this archive can be restored into /tmp for examination
if necessary.
  inflating: sulog
#
```

In the first example, the zip archive */tmp/messages.zip* is created, consisting of all files in the current directory named *messages**. In the second example, the same zip archive is refreshed; note that the lack of output means no refreshing took place. In the third example, however, refreshing *did* take place, since the file *messages* had changed since the previous refresh.

In the fourth example, the zip archive */tmp/etc.zip* is created. It consists of all files in the current working directory, plus all subdirectories and their contents.

In the fifth example, a three-line comment is added to the zip archive */tmp/adm.zip*. Note that this comment appears in subsequent listings of this archive in later examples.

In the sixth example, the file *messages.2* is removed from the zip archive *adm.zip*. In the seventh example, the zip archive */tmp/adm* is tested for integrity.

In the eighth example, the zip archive *adm.zip* is listed (short list); in the ninth example, the same archive is listed again (long list).

In the tenth example, all files in the *adm.zip* archive are extracted into the current working directory. In the eleventh example, only the file *sulog* is extracted from the *adm.zip* archive—again into the current working directory.

jar

The *jar* command is used to create, extract, and work with archive files written in the jar format. Archive files in the jar format can be read by many other UNIX systems. The syntax of the *jar* and *tar* commands are quite similar. One noted difference is that *jar* also compresses its archives. The syntax of the *jar* command is *jar [cfMmotv] [x file] [manifest-file] destination input-file [input-files]*. The options for the *jar* command are:

- *c*. Creates a new or empty archive on the standard output.
- *f*. The second argument specifies a jar file to process. In the case of creation, this refers to the name of the jar file to be created (instead of on stdout). For table or extract, the second argument identifies the jar file to be listed or extracted.
- *M*. Do not create a manifest file for the entries. A manifest file is a separate file that contains a list of files in the jar archive.
- *m*. Includes manifest information from specified pre-existing manifest file. Example use:

```
jar cmf myManifestFile myJarFile *.class
```

You can add special-purpose name-value attribute headers to the manifest file that aren't contained in the default manifest.

Examples of such headers would be those for vendor information, version information, package sealing, and headers to make *jar*-bundled applications executable. This feature is specific to Java object packaging that is outside the scope of this book.

- *o*. Store only, without using zip compression.
- *t*. Lists the table of contents from standard output.
- *v*. Generates verbose output on stderr.
- *x file*. Extracts all files, or just the named files, from standard input. If *file* is omitted, then all files are extracted; otherwise, only the specified file or files are extracted.

Some examples of the *jar* command follow.

```
# jar cf /tmp/log.jar .
#

# jar cvf /tmp/log.jar .
added manifest
adding: log/ (in=0) (out=0) (stored 0%)
adding: passwd/ (in=0) (out=0) (stored 0%)
adding: streams/ (in=0) (out=0) (stored 0%)
adding: aculog (in=0) (out=0) (stored 0%)
adding: spellhist (in=0) (out=0) (stored 0%)
adding: utmpx (in=4092) (out=321) (deflated 92%)
adding: wtmpx (in=526008) (out=18568) (deflated 96%)
adding: sm.bin/ (in=0) (out=0) (stored 0%)
adding: acct/ (in=0) (out=0) (stored 0%)
adding: acct/fiscal/ (in=0) (out=0) (stored 0%)
adding: acct/nite/ (in=0) (out=0) (stored 0%)
adding: acct/sum/ (in=0) (out=0) (stored 0%)
adding: sa/ (in=0) (out=0) (stored 0%)
adding: messages (in=101656) (out=9286) (deflated 90%)
adding: vold.log (in=67) (out=69) (deflated -2%)
adding: sulog (in=6501) (out=1127) (deflated 82%)
adding: lastlog (in=28084) (out=148) (deflated 99%)
adding: messages.0 (in=33235) (out=4590) (deflated 86%)
adding: messages.1 (in=798) (out=302) (deflated 62%)
adding: messages.2 (in=53162) (out=5228) (deflated 90%)
adding: messages.3 (in=10370) (out=2275) (deflated 78%)
#

# jar tvf /tmp/log.jar
     0 Fri Mar 16 14:06:46 PST 2001 META-INF/
    68 Fri Mar 16 14:06:46 PST 2001 META-INF/MANIFEST.MF
     0 Tue Apr 04 21:49:08 PDT 2000 log/
```

```
     0 Tue Apr 04 21:49:08 PDT 2000 passwd/
     0 Tue Apr 04 21:49:08 PDT 2000 streams/
     0 Tue Apr 04 21:49:48 PDT 2000 aculog
     0 Tue Apr 04 21:49:48 PDT 2000 spellhist
  4092 Fri Mar 16 09:32:58 PST 2001 utmpx
526008 Fri Mar 16 09:32:58 PST 2001 wtmpx
     0 Tue Apr 04 22:12:38 PDT 2000 sm.bin/
     0 Tue Apr 04 22:39:50 PDT 2000 acct/
     0 Tue Apr 04 22:39:50 PDT 2000 acct/fiscal/
     0 Tue Apr 04 22:39:50 PDT 2000 acct/nite/
     0 Tue Apr 04 22:39:50 PDT 2000 acct/sum/
     0 Tue Apr 04 22:39:50 PDT 2000 sa/
101656 Fri Mar 16 09:44:46 PST 2001 messages
    67 Thu Feb 22 04:40:58 PST 2001 vold.log
  6501 Fri Mar 16 09:42:34 PST 2001 sulog
 28084 Fri Mar 16 09:32:58 PST 2001 lastlog
 33235 Sat Mar 10 05:08:42 PST 2001 messages.0
   798 Sat Mar 03 07:12:34 PST 2001 messages.1
 53162 Thu Feb 22 21:00:36 PST 2001 messages.2
 10370 Sat Feb 17 20:43:10 PST 2001 messages.3
#

# jar vx messages < /tmp/log.jar
extracted: messages
#

# jar vxf /tmp/log.jar
   created: META-INF/
 extracted: META-INF/MANIFEST.MF
   created: log/
   created: passwd/
   created: streams/
  inflated: aculog
  inflated: spellhist
 extracted: utmpx
 extracted: wtmpx
   created: sm.bin/
   created: acct/
   created: acct/fiscal/
   created: acct/nite/
   created: acct/sum/
   created: sa/
 extracted: messages
 extracted: vold.log
 extracted: sulog
 extracted: lastlog
```

```
extracted: messages.0
extracted: messages.1
extracted: messages.2
extracted: messages.3
#
```

In the first example, the jar archive */tmp/log.jar* is created, consisting of all files in the current working directory. In the second example, the same jar archive is created with verbose output. In the third example, the same jar archive is displayed in verbose format. In the fourth example, the file *messages* is extracted in verbose format. In the fifth example, all files are extracted from */tmp/log.jar* in verbose format.

10.3 Backing Up a System to Tape

This section describes tape drive devices, the *mt* command, and methods used to back up files and directories to tape. The *tar*, *cpio*, and *jar* archive commands, discussed in the previous section, are used here.

Tape Devices

Before you can begin backing up your system you need to be familiar with your tape backup devices. Because there are so many different types, makes, and models of tape drives, only some generalities will be discussed here.

Tape device names are found in the directory */dev/rmt*. The naming convention for tape devices and common features is:

```
/dev/rmt/Xabn
```

where *X* is the device number. The first drive on the system is *0*, the second is *1*, and so forth, up to 7 drives per SCSI controller. *A* is the optional density, where *l* = low, *m* = medium, *h* = high, *u* = ultra, and *o* = compressed. The *b* is for optional Berkeley (SunOS4.x) support. The *n* is for no rewind. Ordinarily, after a program writes to a tape, the tape will rewind back to the beginning. If the no-rewind device is written to instead, the tape will stop after writing.

Note that not all combinations of device name options will be present for each tape device. Some devices may have other options that are not discussed here.

Some example tape device names follow.

```
/dev/rmt/0
/dev/rmt/1n
/dev/rmt/0on
```

The first example signifies the first tape drive, default density. The second example signifies the second tape drive with the no-rewind option. The third example signifies the first tape drive with compression and no rewind.

The *mt* Command

The *mt* command is used to position magnetic tapes. The syntax of the *mt* command is *mt [-f tapename] command... [count]*. The options for *mt* are:

- *-f tapename*. tapename is a tape drive's raw device name. If *-f tapename* is not specified, the environment variable TAPE is used. If TAPE does not exist, *mt* uses the device */dev/rmt/0n*.
- *command*. This is one of the following tape positioning commands:
  - *eof* | *weof*. Write *count* EOF marks at the current position on the tape.
  - *fsf*. Forward space over *count* EOF marks. The tape is positioned on the first block of the file.
  - *fsr*. Forward space *count* records.
  - *bsf*. Back space over *count* EOF marks. The tape is positioned on the beginning-of-tape side of the EOF mark.
  - *bsr*. Back space *count* records.
  - *nbsf*. Back space *count* files. The tape is positioned on the first block of the file. This is equivalent to *count+1 bsf*s followed by one *fsf*.
  - *asf*. Absolute space to *count* file number. This is equivalent to a *rewind* followed by an *fsf count*.
  - *eom*. Space to the end of recorded media on the tape. This is useful for appending files onto previously written tapes. If *count* is specified, it is ignored; the command is performed only once.

- *rewind*. Rewind the tape. If *count* is specified, it is ignored; the command is performed only once.
- *offline* | *rewoffl*. Rewind the tape and, if appropriate, take the drive unit offline by unloading the tape. If *count* is specified, it is ignored; the command is performed only once.
- *status*. Print status information about the tape unit. If *count* is specified, it is ignored; the command is performed only once.
- *retension*. Rewind the cartridge tape completely, then wind it forward to the end of the reel and back to the beginning of the tape to smooth out tape tension. If *count* is specified, it is ignored; the command is performed only once.
- *reserve*. Allow the tape drive to remain reserved after closing the device. The drive must then be explicitly released. If *count* is specified, it is ignored; the command is performed only once.
- *release*. Re-establish the default behavior of releasing at close. If *count* is specified, it is ignored; the command is performed only once.
- *forcereserve*. Break the reservation of the tape drive held by another host and then reserve the tape drive. This command can be executed only with superuser privileges. If *count* is specified, it is ignored; the command is performed only once.
- *erase*. Erase the entire tape. Erasing a tape may take a long time depending on the device and/or tape. Refer to the device-specific manual for time details. If *count* is specified, it is ignored; the command is performed only once.

- *count*. This is an optional field that signifies how many times that command is to be carried out.

Some examples of the *mt* command follow.

```
# mt -f /dev/rmt/0n fsf 2
# mt -f /dev/rmt/1n rewind
# mt retension
# mt eof 1
```

In the first example, the tape */dev/rmt/0n* is forward spaced over the next two EOF marks. In the second example, tape */dev/rmt/1n* is rewound. In the third example, the tape (specified in the TAPE environment variable, or the drive */dev/rmt/0n*) is retensioned. In the fourth example, one EOF mark is written on the tape (specified in the TAPE environment variable, or the drive */dev/rmt/0n*).

EXAM NOTES

THINK ABOUT IT . . .

Each day you perform eight backups to a single tape using the no-rewind device. Four backups run in the morning, four in the afternoon, and then the tape is removed and another one loaded in its place.

After the four morning backups, an operator restored some files from one of the morning backups. Now you need to reposition the tape so that the afternoon backups will start at the right place. How would you do this?

Since we don't know the position of the tape now, the best thing to do is rewind it with the *mt rewind* command. Then, we move the tape forward to the end of the fourth backup with the *mt fsf 4* command. Then, the tape will be in the right position when the afternoon backups begin.

ufsdump and *ufsrestore*

The *ufsdump* and *ufsrestore* commands are used to back up and restore files from tape. The syntax of the *ufsdump* command is *ufsdump [options] [arguments] files_to_dump*. The syntax of the *ufsrestore* command is *ufsrestore i | r | R | t | x [abcdfhlmostvyLT] [archive_file] [factor] [dumpfile] [n] [label] [timeout] [filename]...* . Options for *ufsdump* are:

- *0–9*. The "dump level." All files specified by *files_to_dump* that have been modified since the last ufsdump that was performed with a dump level lower than the current ufsdump are copied to the *dump_file* destination (normally a magnetic tape device). For instance, if a "level 2" dump was done on Monday, followed by a "level 4" dump on Tuesday, a subsequent "level 3" dump on Wednesday would contain all files modified or added since the "level 2" (Monday) backup. A "level 0" dumps copies of the entire file system to the *dump_file*.
- *a archive_file*. Archive a dump table of contents in the specified *archive_file* to be used by *ufsrestore* to determine whether a file is in the dump file that is being restored.

- *b factor*. Specify the blocking *factor* for tape writes. The default is 20 blocks per write for tapes of density less than 6250 BPI (bytes per inch). The default blocking *factor* for tapes of density 6250 BPI and greater is 64. The default blocking *factor* for cartridge tapes (*c* option) is 126. The highest blocking *factor* available with most tape drives is 126. Note: The blocking factor is specified in terms of 512-byte blocks, for compatibility with *tar*.
- *c*. Cartridge. Set the defaults for cartridge instead of the standard 1/2-inch reel. This sets the density to 1000 BPI and the blocking factor to 126. Since *ufsdump* can automatically detect the end of the media, only the blocking parameter normally has an effect. When cartridge tapes are used, and this option is not specified, *ufsdump* will slightly miscompute the size of the tape. If the *b*, *d*, *s*, or *t* options are specified with this option, their values will override the defaults set by this option.
- *d bpi*. Tape density. Not normally required, as *ufsdump* can detect the end of the media. This parameter can be used to keep a running tab on the amount of tape used per reel. The default density is 6250 BPI except when the *c* option is used for cartridge tape, in which case it is assumed to be 1000 BPI per track. Typical values for tape devices are 6250 BPI for 1/2-inch tape, and 1000 BPI for 1/4-inch cartridge.
- *D*. Dump to diskette.
- *f dump_file*. Use *dump_file* as the file to dump to, instead of */dev/rmt/0*. If *dump_file* is specified as "-", dump to standard output.

  If the name of *dump_file* is of the form *machine:device*, the dump is done from the specified machine over the network using *rmt*. Since *ufsdump* is normally run by root, the name of the local machine must appear in the */.rhosts* file of the remote machine. If the file is specified as *user@machine:device*, *ufsdump* will attempt to execute as the specified user on the remote machine. The specified user must have a *.rhosts* file on the remote machine that allows the user invoking the command from the local machine to access the remote machine.
- *l*. Autoload. When the end of the tape is reached before the dump is complete, take the drive offline and wait up to two minutes for the tape drive to be ready again. This gives autoloading (stackloader) tape drives a chance to load a new tape. If the drive is ready within two minutes, continue. If it is not, *ufsdump* will prompt for another tape and wait.

- *L string*. Sets the tape label to *string*, instead of the default *none*. *string* may be no more than 16 characters long. If it is longer, it is truncated and a warning printed; the dump will still be done. The tape label is specific to the *ufsdump* tape format, and bears no resemblance to IBM or ANSI-standard tape labels.
- *n*. Notify all operators in the *sys* group that *ufsdump* requires attention by sending messages to their terminals, in a manner similar to that used by the *wall* command. Otherwise, such messages are sent only to the terminals (such as the console) on which the user running *ufsdump* is logged in.
- *o*. Offline. Take the drive offline when the dump is complete or the end of the media is reached, then rewind the tape or eject the diskette. In the case of some autoloading 8mm drives, the tape is removed from the drive automatically. This prevents another process—which might rush in to use the drive—from inadvertently overwriting the media.
- *s size*. Specify the *size* of the volume being dumped to. Not normally required, as *ufsdump* can detect the end of the media. When the specified *size* is reached, *ufsdump* waits for you to change the volume. *ufsdump* interprets the specified size as the length in feet for tapes and cartridges, and as the number of 1024-byte blocks for diskettes. The values should be a little smaller than the actual physical size of the media (e.g., 425 for a 450-foot cartridge). Typical values for tape devices depend on the *c* option, for cartridge devices, and the *D* option for diskettes:

  1/2-inch tape—2300 feet
  60MB 1/4-inch cartridge—425 feet
  150MB 1/4-inch cartridge—700 feet
  diskette—1422 blocks (corresponds to a 1.44MB diskette)
- *S*. Size estimate. Determine the amount of space needed to perform the dump without actually doing it, and display the estimated number of bytes it will take. This is useful with incremental dumps to determine how many volumes of media will be needed.
- *t tracks*. Specify the number of tracks for a cartridge tape. Not normally required, as *ufsdump* can detect the end of the media. The default is nine tracks. The *t* option is not compatible with the *D* option. Values for Sun-supported tape devices are:

  60MB 1/4-inch cartridge—9 tracks
  150MB 1/4-inch cartridge—18 tracks

- *T time_wait[hms]*. Sets the amount of time to wait for an autoload command to complete. This option is ignored unless the *l* option has also been specified. The default waiting period is two minutes. Specify time units with a trailing *h* (for hours), *m* (for minutes), or *s* (for seconds). The default unit is minutes.
- *u*. Update the dump record. Add an entry to the file, */etc/dumpdates*, for each file system successfully dumped that includes the file system name, date, and dump level.
- *v*. After each tape or diskette is written, verify the contents of the media against the source file system. If any discrepancies occur, prompt for new media, then repeat the dump/verification process. The file system must be unmounted. This option cannot be used to verify a dump to standard output.
- *w*. Warning. List the file systems that have not been backed up within a day. This information is gleaned from the files */etc/dumpdates* and */etc/vfstab*. When the *w* option is used, all other options are ignored. After reporting, *ufsdump* exits immediately.
- *W*. Warning with highlight. Similar to the *w* option, except that the *W* option includes all file systems that appear in */etc/dumpdates*, along with information about their most recent dump dates and levels. File systems that have not been backed up within a day are highlighted.
- *files_to_dump*. Specifies the files to dump. Usually it identifies a whole file system by its raw device name (e.g., */dev/rdsk/c0t3d0s6*). Incremental dumps (levels 1–9) of files changed after a certain date only apply to a whole file system. Alternatively, *files_to_dump* can identify individual files or directories. All named directories that may be examined by the user running *ufsdump*, as well as any explicitly named files, are dumped. This dump is equivalent to a level 0 dump of the indicated portions of the file system, except that */etc/dumpdates* is not updated even if the *-u* option has been specified. In all cases, the files must be contained in the same file system, and the file system must be local to the system where *ufsdump* is being run. *files_to_dump* is required and must be the last argument on the command line.

Exactly one of the following options is required for *ufsrestore*.

- *i*. Interactive. After reading in the directory information from the media, *ufsrestore* invokes an interactive interface that allows you to browse through the dump file's directory hierarchy and select individual files to be extracted. This is explained in detail later in this chapter.

- *r*: Recursive. Restore the entire contents of the dumped file system into the current directory (which should be the top level of the file system). To completely restore a file system, use this function letter to restore the level 0 dump, and again for each incremental dump. Although this function letter is intended for a complete restore onto a clear file system, if the file system contains files not on the dump, they are preserved.
- *R*. Resume restoring. *ufsrestore* requests a particular volume of a multivolume set from which to resume a full restore (see the *r* function letter). This allows *ufsrestore* to start from a checkpoint when it is interrupted in the middle of a full restore.
- *t*. Table of contents. List each file name that appears on the media. If no file name argument is given, the root directory is listed. This results in a list of all files on the media, unless the *h* function modifier is in effect. The table of contents is taken from the media or from the specified archive file, when a function modifier is used. This function modifier is mutually exclusive with the *x* and *r* function letters.
- *x*. Extract the named files from the media. If a named file matches a directory whose contents were written onto the media, and the *h* modifier is not in effect, the directory is recursively extracted. The owner, modification time, and mode are restored (if possible). Existing files are overwritten and a warning is given. If no file name argument is given, the root directory is extracted. This results in the entire tape being extracted unless the *h* modifier is in effect. Use the *x* option to restore partial file system dumps, as they are (by definition) not entire file systems.

Options for *ufsrestore* are:

- *a archive_file*. Read the table of contents from *archive_file* instead of the media. This function modifier can be used in combination with the *t*, *i*, or *x* function letters, making it possible to check whether files are on the media without having to mount the media. When used with the *x* and interactive (*i*) function letters, it prompts for the volume containing the file(s) before extracting them.
- *b factor*. Specify the blocking factor for tape reads. For variable-length SCSI tape devices, unless the data were written with the

default blocking factor, a blocking factor at least as great as that used to write the tape must be used; otherwise, an error will be generated. Note that a tape block is 512 bytes. Refer to the man page for your specific tape driver for the maximum blocking factor.

- *c.* Convert the contents of the media in 4.1BSD format to the new ufs file system format.
- *d.* Turn on debugging output.
- *f dump_file.* Use *dump_file* instead of */dev/rmt/0* as the file to restore from. Typically *dump_file* specifies a tape or diskette drive. If *dump_file* is specified as "-", *ufsrestore* reads from the standard input. This allows *ufsdump* and *ufsrestore* to be used in a pipeline to copy a file system:

```
ufsdump 0f - /dev/rdsk/c0t0d0s7 | (cd /home;ufsrestore xf -)
```

If the name of the file is of the form *machine:device*, the restore is done from the specified machine over the network using *rmt*. Since *ufsrestore* is normally run by root, the name of the local machine must appear in the */.rhosts* file of the remote machine. If the file is specified as *user@machine:device*, *ufsrestore* will attempt to execute as the specified user on the remote machine. The specified user must have a *.rhosts* file on the remote machine that allows the user invoking the command from the local machine to access the remote machine.

- *h.* Extract or list the actual directory, rather than the files that it references. This prevents hierarchical restoration of complete subtrees from the tape.
- *l.* Autoload. When the end of the tape is reached before the restore is complete, take the drive offline and wait up to two minutes (the default, see the *T* option) for the tape drive to be ready again. This gives autoloading (stackloader) tape drives a chance to load a new tape. If the drive is ready within two minutes, continue. If it is not, prompt for another tape and wait.
- *L label.* The *label* that should appear in the header of the dump file. If the labels do not match, *ufsrestore* issues a diagnostic and exits. The tape label is specific to the *ufsdump* tape format, and bears no resemblance to IBM or ANSI-standard tape labels.
- *m.* Extract by inode numbers rather than by file name to avoid regenerating complete pathnames. Regardless of where the files

are located in the dump hierarchy, they are restored into the current directory and renamed with their inode number. This is useful if only a few files are being extracted.

- *o*. Take the drive offline when the restore is complete or the end of the media is reached and rewind the tape, or eject the diskette. In the case of some autoloading 8mm drives, the tape is removed from the drive automatically.
- *s n*. Skip to the *n*th file when there are multiple dump files on the same tape. For example, the command:

```
ufsrestore xfs /dev/rmt/0hn 5
```

  would position you to the fifth file on the tape when reading volume 1 of the dump. If a dump extends over more than one volume, all volumes except the first are assumed to start at position 0, no matter what *s n* value is specified.

  If *s n* is specified, the backup media must be at BOT (beginning of tape). Otherwise, the initial positioning to read the table of contents will fail, as it is performed by skipping the tape forward n-1 files rather than by using absolute positioning. This is because on some devices absolute positioning is very time consuming.
- *T timeout [hms]*. Sets the amount of time to wait for an autoload command to complete. This option is ignored unless the *l* option has also been specified. The default timeout period is two minutes. The time units may be specified as a trailing *h* (hours), *m* (minutes), or *s* (seconds). The default unit is minutes.
- *v*. *ufsrestore* displays the name and inode number of each file it restores, preceded by its file type.
- *y*. Do not ask whether to abort the restore in the event of tape errors. *ufsrestore* tries to skip over the bad tape block(s) and continue as best it can.

Some examples of *ufsdump* and *ufsrestore* are:

```
# ufsdump 0f /dev/rmt/0 /export/home
  DUMP: Writing 32 Kilobyte records
  DUMP: Date of this level 0 dump: Tue Apr 17 20:21:27 2001
  DUMP: Date of last level 0 dump: the epoch
  DUMP: Dumping /dev/rdsk/c0t0d0s7 (wallace:/export/home) to /dev/rmt/1.
  DUMP: Mapping (Pass I) [regular files]
  DUMP: Mapping (Pass II) [directories]
```

```
    DUMP: Estimated 2121734 blocks (1036.00MB).
    DUMP: Dumping (Pass III) [directories]
    DUMP: Dumping (Pass IV) [regular files]
    DUMP: 68.11% done, finished in 0:04
    DUMP: Tape rewinding
    DUMP: 2121598 blocks (1035.94MB) on 1 volume at 1207 KB/sec
    DUMP: DUMP IS DONE
#

# ufsdump 0f root@wallace:/dev/rmt/1n /var/adm
    DUMP: Writing 32 Kilobyte records
    DUMP: Date of this level 0 dump: Tue Apr 17 20:46:04 2001
    DUMP: Date of last level 0 dump: the epoch
    DUMP: Dumping /dev/rdsk/c0t0d0s0 (grommit:/) to wallace:/dev/rmt/1n.
    DUMP: Mapping (Pass I) [regular files]
    DUMP: Mapping (Pass II) [directories]
    DUMP: Estimated 2586 blocks (1.26MB).
    DUMP: Dumping (Pass III) [directories]
    DUMP: Dumping (Pass IV) [regular files]
    DUMP: 2558 blocks (1.25MB) on 1 volume at 1424 KB/sec
    DUMP: DUMP IS DONE
#
```

In the first example, *ufsdump* performs a full backup of file system */export/home* to tape */dev/rmt/0*. In the second example, *ufsdump* performs a full backup of the directory */var/adm* from the system *grommit*, over the network to the system *wallace* on the no-rewind tape device */dev/rmt/1n*. For the second example to work, the system *wallace* must have a */.rhosts* file with the following entry in it:

```
grommit root
```

ufsrestore *Interactive Mode*

ufsrestore has an interactive mode that lets you interactively browse a *ufsdump* archive and select files to restore. The interactive environment resembles the shell. The commands available in interactive mode are:

- *add [filename]*. Add the named file or directory to the list of files to extract. If a directory is specified, add that directory and its files (recursively) to the extraction list (unless the *h* option is in effect).
- *cd directory*. Change to *directory* (within the dump file).
- *delete [filename]*. Delete the current directory, or the named file or directory, from the list of files to extract. If a directory is

specified, delete that directory and all its descendants from the extraction list (unless the *h* option is in effect). The most expedient way to extract a majority of files from a directory is to add that directory to the extraction list and then delete specific files to omit.

- *extract*. Extract all files on the extraction list from the dump media. *ufsrestore* asks which tape volume the user wishes to mount. The fastest way to extract a small number of files is to start with the last volume and work toward the first. If *s n* is given on the command line, volume 1 will automatically be positioned to file *n* when it is read.
- *help*. Display a summary of the available commands.
- *ls [directory]*. List files in *directory* or the current directory, represented by a "." (period). Directories are appended with a "/" (slash). Entries marked for extraction are prefixed with a "*" (asterisk). If the verbose option is in effect, inode numbers are also listed.
- *marked [directory]*. Like *ls*, except only files marked for extraction are listed.
- *pager*. Toggle the pagination of the output from the *ls* and *marked* commands. The pager used is that defined by the PAGER environment variable, or more if that environment variable is not defined. The PAGER environment variable may include white-space-separated arguments for the pagination program.
- *pwd*. Print the full pathname of the current working directory.
- *quit*. *ufsrestore* exits immediately, even if the extraction list is not empty.
- *setmodes*. Prompts: set owner/mode for "."). Type *y* for *yes* to set the mode (permissions, owner, times) of the current directory (".") into which files are being restored equal to the mode of the root directory of the file system from which they were dumped. Normally, this is what you want when restoring a whole file system, or restoring individual files into the same locations from which they were dumped. Type *n* for *no* to leave the mode of the current directory unchanged. Normally, this is what you want when restoring part of a dump to a directory other than the one from which the files were dumped.
- *setpager command*. Sets *command* to use for paginating output instead of the default or that inherited from the environment.

The *command* string may include arguments in addition to the command itself.

- *verbose*. Toggle the status of the *v* modifier. While *v* is in effect, the *ls* command lists the inode numbers of all entries, and *ufsrestore* displays information about each file as it is extracted.
- *what*. Display the dump header on the media.

An example *ufsrestore* interactive dialogue follows.

```
# ufsrestore if /dev/rmt/0n
ufsrestore > ls
.:
 etc/
ufsrestore > cd etc
ufsrestore > add passwd shadow group
ufsrestore > cd rc3.d
ufsrestore > ls
./etc/rc3.d:
 README            S50apache        X76snmpdx
 S15nfs.server     X34dhcp          X77dmi
ufsrestore > add S50apache
ufsrestore > ls
./etc/rc3.d:
 README           *S50apache        X76snmpdx
 S15nfs.server     X34dhcp          X77dmi
ufsrestore > marked
./etc/rc3.d:
*S50apache
ufsrestore > cd ..
ufsrestore > marked
./etc:
*group   *passwd  *rc3.d/  *shadow
ufsrestore > extract
You have not read any volumes yet.
Unless you know which volume your file(s) are on you should start
with the last volume and work towards the first.
Specify next volume #: 1
set owner/mode for '.'? [yn] y
ufsrestore > quit
#
```

In this example, after starting *ufsrestore*, we see the *ufsrestore* interactive prompt. The *ls* command shows that there is a single directory, */etc*. After *cd*'ing to */etc*, we add the files *passwd*, *shadow*, and *group* to be restored. Then, after changing to the directory *rc3.d*, we add another file to restore, *S50apache*. An *ls* in this directory shows that *S50apache* is marked to be restored (note the asterisk before the name).

In this directory, the *marked* command lists the current working directory, *./etc/rc3.d*, as well as *S50apache*. After *cd*'ing up one directory, the *marked* command lists all files marked for extraction.

After entering the *extract* command, *ufsrestore* asks for the volume number, and then asks if the permissions for the current directory should be set to those saved in the ufsdump backup. Then interactive mode is exited with the *quit* command.

tar and *cpio*

Just as *tar* and *cpio* can be used to create disk archives, they can also be used to create archives on magnetic tape. Some examples of *tar* and *cpio* are shown here.

```
# tar cvf /dev/rmt/0 .
a ./ 0 tape blocks
a ./autofs 119 tape blocks
a ./cachefs 609 tape blocks
a ./fifofs 60 tape blocks
a ./hsfs 122 tape blocks
a ./lofs 43 tape blocks
a ./mntfs 36 tape blocks
a ./nfs 660 tape blocks
a ./procfs 396 tape blocks
a ./sockfs 215 tape blocks
a ./specfs 80 tape blocks
a ./tmpfs 105 tape blocks
a ./ufs 575 tape blocks
a ./udfs 334 tape blocks
# cd /tmp
# tar tf /dev/rmt/0
./
./autofs
./cachefs
./fifofs
./hsfs
./lofs
./mntfs
./nfs
./procfs
```

```
./sockfs
./specfs
./tmpfs
./ufs
./udfs
# tar tvf /dev/rmt/1
drwxr-xr-x   0/3        0 Dec 13 05:46 2000 ./
-rwxr-xr-x   0/3    60800 Jan  8 17:51 2000 ./autofs
-rwxr-xr-x   0/3   311496 Jan  8 17:51 2000 ./cachefs
-rwxr-xr-x   0/3    30360 Jan  8 17:51 2000 ./fifofs
-rwxr-xr-x   0/3    62240 Jan  8 17:51 2000 ./hsfs
-rwxr-xr-x   0/3    22016 Jan  8 17:51 2000 ./lofs
-rwxr-xr-x   0/3    18288 Jan  8 17:51 2000 ./mntfs
-rwxr-xr-x   0/3   337616 Jan  8 17:51 2000 ./nfs
-rwxr-xr-x   0/3   202328 Dec  8 22:00 2000 ./procfs
-rwxr-xr-x   0/3   109808 Jan  8 17:51 2000 ./sockfs
-rwxr-xr-x   0/3    40768 Jan  8 17:51 2000 ./specfs
-rwxr-xr-x   0/3    53608 Jan  8 17:51 2000 ./tmpfs
-rwxr-xr-x   0/3   294208 Jan  8 17:51 2000 ./ufs
-rwxr-xr-x   0/3   170656 Jan  8 17:51 2000 ./udfs
# ls|cpio -ovdumc -O /dev/rmt/1
acct
aculog
lastlog
log
m.tar
messages
messages.0
messages.1
messages.2
messages.3
passwd
sa
sm.bin
spellhist
streams
sulog
utmpx
vold.log
wtmpx
2191 blocks
# cpio -it -I /dev/rmt/1
acct
aculog
lastlog
log
```

```
m.tar
messages
messages.0
messages.1
messages.2
messages.3
passwd
sa
sm.bin
spellhist
streams
sulog
utmpx
vold.log
wtmpx
2191 blocks
# cpio -ivt -I /dev/rmt/1
drwxrwxr-x   5 adm    adm          0 Apr  4 22:39 2000, acct
-rw-------   1 uucp   bin          0 Apr  4 21:49 2000, aculog
-r--r--r--   1 root   root     28084 Apr 17 04:54 2001, lastlog
drwxr-xr-x   2 adm    adm          0 Apr  4 21:49 2000, log
-rw-r--r--   1 root   other   203264 Mar 16 09:01 2001, m.tar
-rw-r--r--   1 root   other    74414 Apr 17 21:19 2001, messages
-rw-r--r--   1 root   other     1241 Apr  6 05:04 2001, messages.0
-rw-r--r--   1 root   other      553 Mar 31 07:46 2001, messages.1
-rw-r--r--   1 root   other    47437 Mar 24 13:58 2001, messages.2
-rw-r--r--   1 root   other   101656 Mar 16 09:44 2001, messages.3
drwxr-xr-x   2 adm    adm          0 Apr  4 21:49 2000, passwd
drwxrwxr-x   2 adm    sys          0 Apr  4 22:39 2000, sa
drwxr-xr-x   2 root   sys          0 Apr  4 22:12 2000, sm.bin
-rw-rw-rw-   1 root   bin          0 Apr  4 21:49 2000, spellhist
drwxr-xr-x   2 root   sys          0 Apr  4 21:49 2000, streams
-rw-------   1 root   root      7908 Apr 16 20:39 2001, sulog
-rw-r--r--   1 root   bin       4092 Apr 17 04:54 2001, utmpx
-rw-r--r--   1 root   root        67 Feb 22 04:40 2001, vold.log
-rw-r--r--   1 adm    adm     650628 Apr 17 05:18 2001, wtmpx
2191 blocks
#
```

In the first example, a tar archive is created on device */dev/rmt/1*. Next, the current directory is set to */tmp*, and the tape archive listed in short format, then in long format.

Next, a *cpio* backup is performed, and the files backed up are displayed. Next, the *cpio* backup archive is listed, first in short format, and then in long format.

EXAM NOTES

THINK ABOUT IT . . .

Given the choices available for compressing a tape backup, which is best?

The options available are: (1) use the tape drive's hardware compression, (2) back up a compressed archive of files, and (3) back up an archive of compressed files.

Option 1 will take the least amount of computer resources, since the compression will be performed by the hardware. But you should first know how many other tape drives in your organization also have the same hardware compression capability in case you have to perform a file or system recovery. If your system with the compressing tape drive (or the drive itself) fails, you will be forced into a scenario offering few choices.

Option 2 is easy to implement. Using *tar* as an example, you would do something similar to this: *tar cvf - /directory | compress > /dev/rmt/0.*

Option 3 is almost as easy to implement. Using *tar* again as an example, you would do something like this:

```
compress /directory/*; tar cvf /dev/rmt/0 /directory
```

A possible pitfall with this option is that you must have sufficient disk space to compress the files—and you will have to curtail access to the files while they are compressed (another option would be to create compressed copies of the files in another directory, leaving the original files intact).

At sites where hardware compression is unavailable, you are facing Options 2 or 3. Option 2 seems easier to implement, but there is one caveat: A read error on the tape will render the entire backup unreadable. This is because compress will abort if it cannot read the entire backup error-free. With Option 3, a read error on the tape will render the one backed-up file unreadable, but other files on the tape can be recovered.

To conclude, hardware compression is desirable as long as most or all of your drives support it. If not, then Option 3 might be the next best choice, since the unlikely event of a tape read error will affect one file and not the entire backup.

10.4 Recovering a System from a Backup Tape

This section describes the steps used to restore files from a backup tape. Examples of *ufsrestore*, *tar*, and *cpio* are shown here.

```
# ufsrestore xf /dev/rmt/1 /var/adm/messages
You have not read any volumes yet.
Unless you know which volume your file(s) are on you should start
with the last volume and work towards the first.
Specify next volume #: 1
set owner/mode for '.'? [yn] n
#

# tar xvf /dev/rmt/1 ./autofs ./lofs
x ./autofs, 60800 bytes, 119 tape blocks
x ./lofs, 22016 bytes, 43 tape blocks
#

# cpio -iv "messages.2" < /dev/rmt/1
messages.2
2191 blocks
#
```

In the first example, the file */var/adm/messages* is restored from a ufsdump archive. In the second example, the files *autofs* and *lofs* are restored from a tar archive. Finally, in the third example, the file "*messages.2*" is recovered.

Chapter Summary

There are several tools available for compressing files. They are (1) *compress*, *uncompress*, and *zcat*; (2) *pack*, *unpack*, and *pcat*; (3) *gzip*, *gunzip*, and *gzcat*; and (4) *zip* and *unzip*.

The *compress* command compresses individual files, and can also write a compressed file to standard output. The *uncompress* command decompresses files compressed with the *compress* command, and can read compressed data from standard input. The *zcat* command decompresses files and writes the file output to standard output. Files compressed with the compress command will by default have the .Z suffix.

The *pack* command compresses individual files. The *unpack* command decompresses files compressed with the *pack* command. Like *zcat*, the *pcat* command decompresses files compressed with pack and writes to standard output.

The *gzip* command compresses individual files, and can write to standard output. The *gunzip* command decompresses files compressed with *gzip*. The *gzcat* command decompresses files compressed with *gzip* and writes to standard output. *gzip*, *gunzip*, and *gzcat* are freeware public domain tools.

The tools available for archiving files and collections of files are *tar*, *cpio*, *zip/unzip*, and *jar*. Each of these tools can create archive files on disk. Archives written in tar and cpio formats are generally readable on other types of UNIX systems that have tar and cpio. Although each of these tools creates archives in its own unique format, cpio can read tar archives, and zip archives can be read on MS-DOS systems that have the pkzip or WinZip programs. Zip and unzip are freeware public domain tools.

Tape device names are found in */dev/rmt*; the syntax for tape device names is */dev/rmt/Xabn*, where *X* is the tape drive number, *a* is the optional density, *b* is for Berkeley/SunOS 4 compatibility, and *n* is for no rewind.

The *mt* command is used to manage and position a magnetic tape. The common subcommands are used to rewind a tape, retension a tape, and move the tape forward and backward.

The *ufsdump* program is used to back up file systems to tape. The *ufsrestore* program restores files from tape. *ufsrestore* has an interactive mode where a backup archive can be browsed and files selected for restore.

The *tar* and *cpio* tools are used to create backup tapes. The syntax for *tar* and *cpio* writing to backup tape is identical to the syntax for creating disk-based archive files; the only difference is that the destination for *tar* or *cpio* is a tape device name instead of an archive file name.

TEST YOURSELF

MULTIPLE CHOICE

1. Which is NOT a characteristic of the *cpio –p* command?
   A. Copies all files including named pipes.
   B. Copies files and/or directories to another location.
   C. Copies all files except named pipes.
   D. Preserves ACLs.

2. Which command correctly extracts the file *main.c* from the tar archive *prog.tar*?
   A. `tar xf prog.tar main.c`
   B. `tar xf main.c prog.tar`
   C. `tar -xf main.c prog.tar`
   D. `tar xf main.c < prog.tar`

3. You need to view the contents of the third tar archive on a magnetic tape. You are unsure of the tape's current position. Which will properly position the tape and read the archive?
   A. `mt rewind;tar t;mt fsf 3`
   B. `mt rewind; mt fsf 3; tar t`
   C. `tar tp 3`
   D. `mt fsf 3;tar t`

4. Which four statements about cpio are true? (Choose four)
   A. cpio can write tar archives.
   B. cpio can read tar archives.
   C. cpio archives can be read by other UNIX systems.
   D. Like zip, cpio can optionally compress an archive that it creates.
   E. cpio can back up device special files.
   F. cpio can create a multi-tape archive.
   G. cpio's *-f* option is used to freshen an archive.

5. Which two command sequences compress a tar archive? (Choose two)
   A. `tar cf - . | compress > backup.tar`
   B. `tar cCf backup.tar .`
   C. `compress backup.tar`
   D. `tar cf - . ; compress > backup.tar`
   E. `tar cZf backup.tar .`

6. You need to restore a file *prog.c* from a zip archive *b.zip* to a new location, */tmp*. Which command performs this?
   A. `zip -x archive.zip prog.c -d /tmp`
   B. `unzip prog.c archive.zip -d /tmp`
   C. `unzip -l /tmp archive.zip prog.c`
   D. `unzip archive.zip prog.c -d /tmp`

7. Which two methods allow you to choose the tape device the *tar* command should use without specifying a tape device name in the command? (Choose two)
   A. Define the tape device in the TAPE environment variable.
   B. Define the tape device in */etc/default/tar.*
   C. Define the tape device in the ARCHIVE environment variable.
   D. `tar` cannot write to a tape device unless it is explicitly stated in the command line.

8. What is the purpose of a no-rewind tape device?
   A. It is used for continuous-loop tape cartridges that cannot be rewound.
   B. It is used for tapes that are written only in the forward direction.
   C. It permits multiple archives to be written to the tape, one after the other.
   D. It permits random access to the tape.

9. You need to compress a large file, but the file system in which it resides has insufficient room to compress it. Which two are valid options? (Choose two)
   A. Compress the file in place with the *compress -n* (no temporary file) command.
   B. Write the compressed output to another file system using the *compress -c* command.
   C. Copy the file to a larger file system, compress it there, and copy the compressed file back to the original file system.
   D. Split the file into small pieces, compress the pieces, then concatenate the pieces back together.
   E. First pack the file to purge the holes, and then compress it.

10. Given:

```
# tar cf - . | (cd /tmp; tar xf -)
```

What is the result?

A. The contents of the current working directory are moved to the */tmp* directory.
B. The contents of the current working directory are copied to the */tmp* directory.
C. A listing of the current working directory is copied to the */tmp* directory.
D. Tar archives in the current working directory are restored to the */tmp* directory.

FREE RESPONSE

11. Specify the command used to restore the entire contents of a tape backed up with *ufsbackup*. Assume that the tape drive is */dev/rmt/0*.
12. Specify the command used to read the table of contents of a compressed tar archive named *root.tar.Z*.

CHAPTER 11

Security

After completing this chapter, you'll be able to meet the following Solaris Administration Exam objectives:

- List command sequences used to display or modify file and directory permissions.
- Differentiate the effect of selected umask values on the permissions assigned to newly created files and directories.
- List in sequence the steps to create, modify, and delete access control lists (ACLs) on files.

To fulfill these objectives, this chapter discusses:

- Displaying file and directory permissions;
- Changing file and directory permissions;
- Umask;
- File and directory access control lists; and
- Finding files and directories with permission attributes.

11.1 File and Directory Permissions

This section describes the concepts behind file and directory ownership and how things work (or don't work) with regard to permissions.

Each file and directory on a system has exactly one owner—that is, a username associated with it. Also, each file and directory has a groupid; in other words, a group (from the */etc/group* file) associated with it.

A file or directory has permission codes assigned to it that specify what the owner may do with the file. These permissions codes are: read, write, and execute. A file or directory can have any or all of these permission codes assigned to the owner; in fact, the file or directory can have none of these permissions assigned to the owner. That's right—a file or directory can have permissions such that the owner can neither read, write, nor execute it.

The same permission codes are also assigned to the groupid: read, write, and execute. None, any, or all codes in any combination are allowed.

A file or directory has a third set of permission codes. These are permissions for what we call "other" or "world." These permissions determine the access permissions for users who are neither the owner, nor are they a member of the groupid associated with the file. The same permission codes apply for other—read, write, and execute—in any combination.

Working with File Permissions

This section describes all of the things a user is allowed to do with a file depending upon its ownership, groupid, and permission settings.

A user is allowed to read a file if:

- The user is the owner and the owner is allowed to read the file.
- The user is a member of the file's associated group and the group is allowed to read the file.
- The user is not the owner, not a member of the file's associated group, and "other" is allowed to read the file.

A user is allowed to write to a file if:

- The user is the owner and the owner is allowed to write to the file.
- The user is a member of the file's associated group and the group is allowed to write to the file.
- The user is not the owner, not a member of the file's group, and "other" is allowed to write to the file.

A user is allowed to execute the file if:

- The user is the owner and the owner is allowed to execute the file.
- The user is a member of the file's associated group and the group is allowed to execute the file.
- The user is not the owner, not a member of the file's group, and "other" is allowed to execute the file.

For files that are, for example, data files and not executable programs, the execute permission is meaningless. Still, the user will be allowed to *attempt* to execute such a file, but the operating system will recognize that the file is not a program and will not execute it.

When a user is allowed to read a file, he or she can do any of the following:

- Copy the contents of the file to another file.
- Edit the file with vi or other text-editing program (the user will not be allowed to save changes unless he or she also has write permissions).
- Print the file.
- Read the file with any program or tool.

When a user is allowed to write a file, he or she can do any of the following:

- Add data to the file.
- Remove data from the file.
- Remove *all* data from the file.
- Change data in the file.

When a user is allowed to execute a file, she or he can *attempt* to execute it. If it is in fact an executable file, the operating system will load it into memory and execute it.

Notice that we never mentioned anything about creating or removing files. This is because those functions depend upon the permissions of the directory in which those operations would take place. These are described in the next section.

Files with SetUID and SetGID Permissions

When an executable file has the SetUID permission set, a process that runs by executing this file is granted access based on the owner of the file (usually root), rather than the user who is running the executable file. This allows a user to access files and directories that are normally available only to their owner.

When an executable file has the SetGID permission set, the process's effective groupid (GID) is changed to the group owner of the file, and a user is granted access based on permissions granted to that group.

Working with Directory Permissions

This section describes all of the things that a user is allowed to do with a directory depending upon its ownership, groupid, and permission settings.

When a user is allowed to read a directory, this means her or she is allowed to list the contents of the directory with the *ls* command, or with any other tool that is used to read a directory's contents.

When a user is allowed to write to a directory, this means:

- The user may add files or subdirectories to the directory.
- The user may remove files or subdirectories from the directory, including those not owned by the user.

When a user has execute permissions on a directory, this means:

- The user may *cd* to the directory.
- The user may *cd* to a subdirectory in the directory (provided the subdirectory has adequate permissions).
- The user may read from, write to, or execute files in the directory, provided the files themselves have the proper permissions.

If a subdirectory has only the execute permission set, this means that the user can *cd* to it, *cd* through it, but the user may not list the contents of the directory or place anything in it.

Directories with Sticky Bit Permissions

When a directory has the sticky bit permission set, the directory's rule for file deletion changes. Without the sticky bit set, the read-write permissions are sufficient to add or remove objects in the directory. The rules are:

- A file or subdirectory may be removed by the owner.
- A file or subdirectory may be removed by the owner of the directory containing the object.

- A file or subdirectory may be removed by a user—not the owner, but who has write permissions to the object.
- The superuser may remove any object.

The */tmp* and */var/tmp* directories are typically set with global read/write/execute permissions, plus the sticky bit. This means that all users may create files in these directories, but—as stated earlier—only the owner of a file or directory may remove it.

Directories with SetUID and SetGID Permissions

When a directory has the SetGID permission set, then any file or directory subsequently created there will have its groupid set to the groupid of the directory, not the groupid of the user creating it.

Setting the SetUID permission on a directory has no effect.

EXAM NOTES

THINK ABOUT IT . . .

You need to create a "drop box" directory where users can deposit and pick up files. You don't want users to be able to see what files are in the directory, but you want users to be able to create files there and to pick them up only if they know the exact name of the file. You also do not want users to be able to delete or overwrite other users' files. Can this be done?

Yes. Create a directory with write, execute, and sticky bit, but no read access. Users may deposit files for collection by the system administrator. They may pick up files provided they know their exact name. They will not be able to overwrite each other's files. Make sure that any files you place in the directory for collection are read only (*chmod* 444).

11.2 Displaying File and Directory Permissions

The *ls -l* command is used to display the ownership and permissions of a file or directory. The *ls –l* command displays a 10-character permission string, the owner, groupid, and other information about files and directories listed. The 10-character permission string is described here.

- The first character may be one of the following:
  - *d*—the entry is a directory
  - *D*—the entry is a door
  - *l*—the entry is a symbolic link
  - *b*—the entry is a block special file
  - *c*—the entry is a character special file
  - *p*—the entry is a fifo (or "named pipe") special file
  - *s*—the entry is a domain socket
  - -—the entry is an ordinary file
- The next nine characters are grouped in three sets of three characters each. The first three refer to the owner's permissions; the next three to permissions of others in the group owner of the file; and the last three to all others. Within each set, the three characters indicate permission for read, to write, and execute, respectively. The character after permissions is the access control lists (ACL) indication. A plus sign ("+") is displayed if there is an ACL associated with the file. ACLs are discussed later in this chapter.
- Some special indicators can appear within the nine characters described earlier. They are:
  - *s*. When in the position normally occupied by an *x* for owner's execute permission, this indicates the SetUID and execute permissions are turned on. When in the position normally occupied by an *x* for group execute permission, this indicates the SetGID and execute permissions are turned on.
  - *S*. When in the position normally occupied by an *x* for owner's execute permission, this is an undefined state where SetUID permission it turned on, but execute is turned off.
  - *l*. Found in the position normally occupied by an *x* for group execute permission, this indicates the mandatory file locking permission is turned on, the SetGID permission is on, and the group execution permission is off.
  - *t*. Found in the position normally occupied by an *x* for other execute permission, this indicates the sticky bit and execute permissions are turned on.
  - *T*. Found in the position normally occupied by an *x* for other execute permission, this indicates the sticky bit permission is

turned on, but other execute permission is turned off. This is an undefined state.

Some examples follow.

```
# ls -l flag
-rw-r--r--   1 gsmith   staff            0 Mar 27 05:27 flag
# ls -l /bin/passwd
-r-sr-sr-x   3 root     sys         101744 Jan  5  2000 /bin/passwd
# ls -ld /tmp
drwxrwxrwt   5 root     sys            269 Mar 28 03:30 /tmp
# ls -l /dev/null
lrwxrwxrwx   1 root     other           27 Apr  4  2000 /dev/null -> ../
devices/pseudo/mm@0:null
# ls -lL /dev/null
crw-rw-rw-   1 root     sys         13,  2 Mar 27 05:25 /dev/null
#
```

In the first example, the file *flag* is owned by user *gsmith*, and its groupid is *staff*. This is an ordinary file (indicated by the first character being a "–").

In the second example, the file */bin/passwd* is also an ordinary file. It is owned by *root*, and its groupid is sys. Owner, group, and others may read and execute the file. The SetUID and SetGID permissions are turned on (indicated by the "s" in the owner and group execute permission positions).

In the third example, the directory */tmp* is a directory. It is owned by *root*, and its groupid is *sys*. Global read, write, and execute permissions are set, as is the sticky bit permission (indicated by the "t" in the last position).

In the fourth example, the file */dev/null* is a symbolic link (indicated by the "l" in the first position).

In the fifth example, the *ls -L* option is used, which tells *ls* to list a file referenced by a symbolic link, rather than the symbolic link itself. The file */dev/null* is a character special file with global read and write permissions.

11.3 Changing File and Directory Permissions

This section describes the commands used to change the ownership and permissions of files and directories.

The *chown* Command

The *chown* command is used to change the owner of a file. The syntax of the *chown* command is *chown [-fhR] owner [: group] file...* . The options for *chown* are as follows:

- *-f*. Do not report errors.
- *-h*. If the file is a symbolic link, change the owner of the symbolic link. Without this option, the owner of the file referenced by the symbolic link is changed.
- *-R*. Recursive. *chown* descends through the directory, and any subdirectories, setting the ownership ID as it proceeds. When a symbolic link is encountered, the owner of the target file is changed (unless the *-h* option is specified), but no recursion takes place.
- *owner[:group]*. A userid and optional groupid to be assigned to file. The *owner* portion of this option must be a username from the user database or a numeric userid. Either specifies a userid to be given to each file named by *file*. If a numeric *owner* exists in the user database as a username, the userid number associated with that username will be the userid. Similarly, if the *group* portion of this option is present, it must be a group name from the group database or a numeric groupid. Either specifies a groupid to be given to each file. If a numeric group operand exists in the group database as a group name, the groupid number associated with that group name will be used as the groupid.
- *file*. A pathname of one or more files (or directories) whose userid is to be modified.

Some examples of the *chown* command follow.

```
# chown gsmith /export/home/gsmith
# chown -R gsmith:staff /export/home/gsmith
# chown 0 /etc/defaultrouter
#
% chown gsmith /etc/hosts
chown: /etc/hosts: Not owner
% chown gsmith .profile
chown: .profile: Not owner
%
```

In the first example, the ownership of directory */export/home/gsmith* is changed to user *gsmith*. In the second example, the ownership of the directory */export/home/gsmith*—and all files and subdirectories found there—is changed to *gsmith*. In the third example, the ownership of */etc/defaultrouter* is changed to user number 0 (root).

In the fourth example, a nonroot user attempts to change the ownership of */etc/hosts* to *gsmith*. *chown* returns an error message, indicating that the user attempting this does not own */etc/hosts*.

In the last example, a nonroot user attempts to change the ownership of *.profile* (a file that this user does own) to *gsmith*. The error message in this case indicates that a nonroot user may not change the ownership of a file.

The operating system has a configuration option that restricts ownership changes. When this option is in effect, the owner of a file is prevented from changing the ownerid of the file, even a file owned by that user. Only the superuser can arbitrarily change ownerids whether or not this option is in effect. This option is set by including the following line in */etc/system*:

```
set rstchown = 1
```

To disable this option, include the following line in */etc/system*:

```
set rstchown = 0
```

This option is enabled by default.

The *chgrp* Command

Similar to the *chown* command, the *chgrp* command is used to change the groupid for a file or directory. The syntax of the *chgrp* command is *chgrp [-fhR] group file...* . Options for *chgrp* are:

- *-f*. Force. Do not report errors.
- *-h*. If the file is a symbolic link, change the group of the symbolic link. Without this option, the group of the file referenced by the symbolic link is changed.
- *-R*. Recursive. *chgrp* descends through the directory, and any subdirectories, setting the specified groupid as it proceeds. When a symbolic link is encountered, the group of the target file is changed (unless the *-h* option is specified), but no recursion takes place.
- *group*. A group name from the group database or a numeric groupid. Either specifies a groupid to be given to each file named

by one of the file operands. If a numeric group option exists in the group database as a group name, the groupid number associated with that group name is used as the groupid.

- *file*. A pathname of a *file* whose groupid is to be modified.

Some examples follow.

```
# chgrp staff addresses.txt
# chgrp -R dvlp /export/tools
# chgrp 3 /etc/passwd
#
% chgrp sys .profile
chgrp: .profile: Not owner
%
```

In the first example, the file *addresses.txt* is set to groupid *staff*. In the second example, the directory */export/tools*—and all files and directories contained there—are changed to group *dvlp*. In the third example, the file */etc/passwd* is changed to group number 3. In the last example, a nonroot user attempts to change the groupid of the file *.profile* to *sys*. This is unsuccessful because the user is not a member of the group *sys*.

The operating system has a configuration option that restricts ownership changes. When this option is in effect, the owner of the file may change the group of the file only to a group to which the owner belongs. Only the superuser can arbitrarily change ownerids, whether or not this option is in effect. To set this configuration option, include the following line in */etc/system*:

```
set rstchown = 1
```

To disable this option, include the following line in */etc/system*:

```
set rstchown = 0
```

This option is enabled by default.

The *chmod* Command

The *chmod* command is used to change permission settings on a file.

chmod has two forms—absolute mode and symbolic mode. These represent two different notations that are used to change file permissions. The syntax of the *chmod* command in absolute mode is *chmod [-fR] <absolute-mode> file...* . The options for *chmod* in absolute mode are:

- *-f*. Force. *chmod* will not complain if it fails to change the mode of a file.
- *-R*. Recursively descend through directory arguments, setting the mode for each file as described earlier. When symbolic links are encountered, the mode of the target file is changed, but no recursion takes place.

Absolute *mode* is specified using octal numbers:

```
chmod nnnn file . . .
```

where *n* is a number from 0–7. An absolute mode is constructed from the mathematical sum of any of the following modes:

- 4000—Set userid on execution.
- 20#0—Set groupid on execution if # is 7, 5, 3, or 1. Enable mandatory locking if # is 6, 4, 2, or 0.
- 1000—Turn on the sticky bit.
- 0400—Allow read by owner.
- 0200—Allow write by owner.
- 0100—Allow execute by owner.
- 0700—Allow read, write, and execute by owner.
- 0040—Allow read by group.
- 0020—Allow write by group.
- 0010—Allow execute by group.
- 0070—Allow read, write, and execute by group.
- 0004—Allow read by others.
- 0002—Allow write by others.
- 0001—Allow execute by others.
- 0007—Allow read, write, and execute by others.

The SetGID bit cannot be set (or cleared) in absolute (numeric) mode; it must be set (or cleared) in symbolic mode (described later in this section).

Some examples follow.

```
# chmod 644 .profile
# chmod 750 setcomp
# chmod 4755 expire
```

In the first example, the file *.profile* is set to permissions 644 (read and write by owner, read-only for group and others). In the second example, file *setcomp* is set to permissions 750 (read, write, and execute by owner, read and execute for group, and no permissions for others). In the third example, file *expire* is set to permissions 4755 (SetUID, read, write, and execute for owner, read and execute for group and others).

The syntax of the *chmod* command in symbolic mode is *chmod [-fR] <symbolic-mode-list> file....* The options for *chmod* in symbolic mode are:

- *-f.* Force. *chmod* will not complain if it fails to change the mode of a file.
- *-R.* Recursively descend through directory arguments, setting the mode for each file as described earlier. When symbolic links are encountered, the mode of the target file is changed, but no recursion takes place.

symbolic-mode-list is a comma-separated list (with no intervening whitespace) of symbolic mode expressions of the form:

```
[who] operator [permissions]
```

Operations are performed in the order given. Multiple permissions letters following a single operator cause the corresponding operations to be performed simultaneously.

- *who*—zero or more of the characters *u*, *g*, *o*, and *a*, which specify whose permissions are to be changed or assigned:
  - *u*. Sets user's permissions.
  - *g*. Sets group's permissions.
  - *o*. Sets others' permissions.
  - *a*. Sets all permissions (user, group, and other).

If *who* is omitted, it defaults to *a*, but the setting of the file mode creation mask (discussed later in this chapter) is taken into account. When who is omitted, *chmod* will not override the restrictions of your user mask.

- *operator*—either +, –, or =, which signify how permissions are to be changed.
  - +. Add permissions. If *permissions* is omitted, nothing is added. If who is omitted, add the file mode bits represented by *permissions*, except for those with corresponding bits in the file mode

creation mask. If *who* is present, add the file mode bits represented by the *permissions*.

- –. Take away permissions. If *permissions* is omitted, do nothing. If *who* is omitted, clear the file mode bits represented by *permissions*, except for those with corresponding bits in the file mode creation mask. If *who* is present, clear the file mode bits represented by *permissions*.
- =. Assign permissions absolutely. If *who* is omitted, then (a) clear all file mode bits; if *who* is present, then clear the file mode bits represented by *who*; and (b) add the file mode bits represented by *permissions*, except for the those with corresponding bits in the file mode creation mask. If *permissions* is omitted, do nothing else. If *who* is present, add the file mode bits represented by *permissions*. Unlike other symbolic operations, = has an absolute effect in that it resets all other bits represented by *who*. Omitting *permissions* is useful only with = to take away all permissions.

- Permission—any compatible combination of the following letters:
  - *r.* Read permission.
  - *w.* Write permission.
  - *x.* Execute permission.
  - *l.* Mandatory locking.
  - *s.* SetUID or SetGID.
  - *t.* Sticky bit.
  - *u, g, o.* Indicate that *permission* is to be taken from the current user, group, or other mode, respectively.

Some examples follow.

```
# chmod o+x clear.sh
# chmod a+r users.txt
# chmod go-x run.sh
# chmod go=r,u+x form.sh
#
```

In the first example, execute permissions are added for others for the file *clear.sh*. In the second example, read permissions are added for all users for the file *users.txt*. In the third example, execute permissions are removed from group and others for the file *run.sh*. In the last example, read permissions only are assigned to group and others, and execute permission added for owner, for the file *form.sh*.

After changing ownership or permissions for a file, you should verify results by listing the file's permissions with the *ls -l* command.

EXAM NOTES

THINK ABOUT IT . . .

How can you prevent ordinary users from using the *su* command to become root?

There are two ways. First, of course, the root password must be carefully guarded and frequently changed. But more importantly, it is possible to prevent ordinary users from being able to execute the *su* command at all.

Create a new group for system administrators; for this example it will be called *sysadmin*. Add the appropriate users to the new *sysadmin* group using *admintool* or by editing the */etc/group* file.

Change the permissions on */usr/bin/su* as follows. First, change its groupid to sysadmin. Next, make sure that the read and execute permissions for group are turned on. Next, remove the read and execute bits for other.The commands would be:

```
chgrp sysadmin /usr/bin/su
chmod 550 /usr/bin/su
```

The *umask* Command

The *umask* command sets or displays the file mode creation mask. This affects the initial permissions set for subsequently created files and directories.

umask uses the same type of numbering scheme that the *chmod* command uses in numeric mode. The *umask* value is a three-digit octal number: The first digit is for user, the second for group, and the third for other. The *umask* value contains the permissions that are *omitted* from a subsequently created file or directory.

When the *umask* value is changed, the change takes effect only for the life of the session. In the case of a Windows environment where the user has several windows open, setting a *umask* value in a window takes effect only in that window. To make a change more persistent, a *umask* command should be placed in the user's *.cshrc* or *.profile* file.

For review, the octal permission values are:

- 1—execute
- 2—write
- 4—read

Consider this example. A user's *umask* value is 027. This means:

- No permissions are omitted for user.
- Write permissions are omitted for group.
- All permissions are omitted for others.

A file that the user creates will have the permissions 640. That is, the user will be able to read and write the file, group members will be able to read the file, and others will have no permissions at all.

An easy way to understand this is that the permissions for created files will always be the numeric value 666 minus the *umask* value. Using this example,

```
666
-027
----
640
```

In this subtraction we don't "carry." In the one's column, 6 minus 7 equals 0.

Now let's look at some real examples.

```
# umask 027
# umask
27
# touch foo
# ls -l foo
-rw-r--r--   1 gsmith   staff          0 Mar 29 05:42 foo
# umask 777
# touch bar
# ls -l bar
----------   1 gsmith   staff          0 Mar 29 05:43 bar
# umask 000
# touch footoo
# ls -l footoo
-rw-rw-rw-   1 gsmith   staff          0 Mar 29 05:44 footoo
#
```

In this example, the *umask* is set to 027 and then displayed. *umask* does not display a leading zero if its value is less than 100. The file *foo* is created and its permissions displayed. It symbolic permissions are `-rw-r--r--`, which numerically is 644.

Next, the *umask* is set to 777, meaning subsequently created files will have no permissions. This is borne out as the file *bar* is created and listed: It has no permissions.

Finally, the *umask* is set to 000, meaning subsequently created files will have all permissions. This is evident when the file *footoo* is created: All users have read and write access to the file.

umask *and Directories*

umask similarly determines the permissions of subsequently created directories. Numerically, we subtract the umask from 777 to determine a directory's permission. For example,

```
 777
-027
----
 750
```

In this example, a *umask* of 027 will result in any created directories having permission 750. Let's look at some more real examples.

```
# umask 022
# umask
22
# mkdir foo
# ls -ld foo
drwxr-xr-x   2 gsmith   staff          512 Mar 29 05:54 foo
# umask 027
# mkdir bar
# ls -ld bar
drwxr-x---   2 gsmith   staff          512 Mar 29 05:55 bar
# umask 000
# mkdir footoo
# ls -ld fubar
drwxrwxrwx   2 gsmith   staff          512 Mar 29 05:56 footoo
#
```

In this example, the *umask* is set to 022 and the directory *foo* created. Its permissions are, numerically, 755; which, when subtracted from 777, is 022.

Next, the *umask* is changed to 027 and the directory *bar* created. Its permissions are 750.

Finally, the *umask* is changed to 000 and the directory *footoo* created. It has wide-open permissions.

Each shell has a built-in *umask* command, and there is also a *umask* command in */usr/bin*.

EXAM NOTES

THINK ABOUT IT . . .

Can you prevent users from setting their own *umask* value?

It depends. If users have access to a shell prompt, then they can change their *umask* value for that shell, and potentially for everything they do if they can edit or overwrite their *.profile* (or *.cshrc*, *.login*, or *.kshrc*) file.

If a user has no access to a shell prompt, then it is possible to prevent a user from being able to change their *umask*.

If a user can execute other commands on the system, then the */usr/bin/umask* command needs to be removed or its permissions changed so that users cannot execute it.

11.4 File and Directory Access Control Lists

The reality of today's larger and more complex environments has exceeded the ability for the user/group/other to keep up. Exceptions to file or directory access rules are in some cases too difficult—or impossible—to manage.

Access control lists can be used to set permissions for user, group, and other, as well as specific users and groups not included in the original user/group categories.

This section describes the tools used to work with access control lists.

Setting Access Control Lists

The *setfacl* command is used to change access control list (ACL) settings for files and directories. The syntax of the *setfacl* command is *setfacl [-r] -s acl_entries file*, *setfacl [-r] -md acl_entries file*, or *setfacl [-r] -f acl_file file*. The options for *setfacl* are:

- *-s acl_entries*. Set a file's ACL. All old ACL entries are removed and replaced with the newly specified ACL. The entries need not be in any specific order. They will be sorted by the command before being applied to the file.
- *-m acl_entries*. Add one or more new ACL entries to the file, and/or modify one or more existing ACL entries on the file. If an entry already exists for a specified UID or GID, the specified permissions will replace the current permissions. If an entry does not exist for the specified UID or GID, an entry will be created.
- *-d acl_entries*. Delete one or more entries from the file. The entries for the file owner, the file group owner, and others may not be deleted from the ACL. Note that deleting an entry does not necessarily have the same effect as removing all permissions from the entry.
- *-f acl_file*. Set a file's ACL with the ACL entries contained in the file named *acl_file*. The same constraints on specified entries hold as with the *-s* option. The entries are not required to be in any specific order in the file. Also, if you specify a dash "-" for, standard input is used to set the file's ACL.
- *-r*. Recalculate the permissions for the ACL mask entry. The permissions specified in the ACL mask entry are ignored and replaced by the maximum permissions necessary to grant the access to all additional user, file group owner, and additional group entries in the ACL. The permissions in the additional user, file group owner, and additional group entries are left unchanged.
- *acl_entries*. An ACL entry consists of the following fields separated by colons.
  - *entry_type*. Type of ACL entry on which to set file permissions. For example, *entry_type* can be user (the owner of a file) or *mask* (the ACL mask).
  - *uid* or *gid*. Username or user identification number. Or, group name or group identification number.

- *perms*. Represents the permissions that are set on *entry_type*. *perms* can be indicated by the symbolic characters *rwx* or a number (the same permissions numbers used with the *chmod* command).

The following are valid ACL entries:

- *u[ser]::perms*. File owner permissions.
- *g[roup]::perms*. File group owner permissions.
- *o[ther]:perms*. Permissions for users other than the file owner or members of file group owner.
- *m[ask]:perms*. The ACL mask. The mask entry indicates the maximum permissions allowed for users (other than the owner) and for groups. The mask is a quick way to change permissions on all the users and groups.
- *u[ser]:uid:perms*. Permissions for a specific user. For *uid*, you can specify either a username or a numeric UID.
- *g[roup]:gid:perms*. Permissions for a specific group. For *gid*, you can specify either a group name or a numeric GID.

A directory may contain "default" ACL entries. If a file or directory is created in a directory that contains default ACL entries, the newly created file will have permissions generated according to the intersection of the default ACL entries and the permissions requested at creation time. The *umask* will not be applied if the directory contains default ACL entries. If a default ACL is specified for a specific user (or users), the file will have a regular ACL created; otherwise, only the mode bits will be initialized according to the intersection described earlier. The default ACL should be thought of as the maximum discretionary access permissions that may be granted. The syntax for "default" ACL entries follow.

- *d[efault]:u[ser]::perms*. Default file owner permissions.
- *d[efault]:g[roup]::perms*. Default file group owner permissions.
- *d[efault]:o[ther]:perms*. Default permissions for users other than the file owner or members of the file group owner.
- *d[efault]:m[ask]:perms*. Default ACL mask.
- *d[efault]:u[ser]:uid:perms*. Default permissions for a specific user. For *uid*, you can specify either a username or a numeric UID.
- *d[efault]:g[roup]:gid:perms*. Default permissions for a specific group. For *gid*, you can specify either a group name or a numeric GID.

Displaying Access Control Lists

The *getfacl* command is used to list a file's ACL. The syntax of the *getfacl* command is *getfacl [-ad] file...* . The options for *getfacl* are:

- *-a.* Display the file name, the file owner, the file group owner, and the ACL of *file*.
- *-d.* Display the file name, the file owner, the file group owner, and the default ACL of *file*, if it exists.
- *file.* The pathname of a regular file, special file, or named pipe.

Some examples of *setfacl* and *getfacl* follow.

```
# setfacl -s u::rw-,g::rw-,o:--- foo
# ls -l foo
-rw-rw----   1 gsmith   staff          0 Mar 30 05:34 foo
# getfacl foo

# file: foo
# owner: gsmith
# group: staff
user::rw-
group::rw-              #effective:rw-
mask:rw-
other:---
# setfacl -m u:pete:rwx foo
# ls -l foo
-rw-rw----+  1 gsmith   staff          0 Mar 30 05:34 foo
# getfacl foo

# file: foo
# owner: gsmith
# group: staff
user::rw-
user:pete:rwx           #effective:rw-
group::rw-              #effective:rw-
mask:rw-
other:---
# getfacl foo | setfacl -f - bar
# mkdir xdir
# setfacl -s u::rwx,g::r-x,o:r-x xdir
# setfacl -m d:u::rwx,d:g::r-x,d:o:r-x,d:m:r-x xdir
# setfacl -m d:u:pete:rwx xdir
# getfacl xdir

# file: xdir
```

```
# owner: gsmith
# group: staff
user::rwx
group::r-x                    #effective:r--
mask:rw-
other:r-x
default:user::rwx
default:user:pete:rwx
default:group::r-x
default:mask:r-x
default:other:r-x
# touch xdir/test
# getfacl xdir/test

# file: xdir/test
# owner: gsmith
# group: staff
user::rw-
user:pete:rwx                 #effective:r--
group::r--                    #effective:r--
mask:r--
other:r--
#
```

In the first example, initial user/group/other ACL settings are applied to the file *foo*. A look at *foo* with *ls -l* shows there is no true ACL—this first command could have been done with *chmod*. *getacl* shows the settings so far.

Next, *setfacl* is used to give user *pete* read/write/execute access to *foo*. Another look with *ls -l* shows there is now an ACL applied to the file (notice the "+" after the permission string). *getfacl* shows the new entry for user *pete*. The mask value displayed, *rw-*, restricts the actual permissions granted to user *pete*. To the right of user *pete* permissions is the effective (actual) permission, *rw-*. Although *setfacl* was used to grant user *pete rwx* permissions, the mask value of *rw-* reduces *pete*'s permissions to *rw-*.

Next, access control list settings for the file *foo* are applied to the file *bar* using a *getfacl | setfacl* command.

The example continues with a directory *xdir*. First, ordinary permissions, then default settings, are applied. Default settings determine access to the file by users and groups who are not given special permissions. A default setting is applied that specifies that user *pete* has read/write/execute access to any file or directory created in the directory *xdir*. Because the ACL mask value is *rw-*, the group permission, *r-x*, is effectively reduced to *r--*.

Next, the file *test* is created in the subdirectory *xdir*, and the ACL for test is displayed, confirming the presence of the special access configured for user *pete*. Because the ACL mask value is *r--*, the permission granted to *pete*, *rwx*, is effectively reduced to *r--*.

Working with Access Control Lists

Only the UFS file system supports ACLs. If you back up and then restore files with ACLs to file systems that do not support ACLs, the ACLs will be lost.

When archiving files with ACLs, use *tar*'s *p* option to preserve and restore ACLs. Similarly, *cpio*'s *-p* option must be used to preserve ACLs. *ufsdump* and *ufsrestore* automatically preserve ACLs.

EXAM NOTES

THINK ABOUT IT . . .

What if you need everyone in a group *except* for one user to have access to a file? How is that done?

Easily! Using *chmod* or *setfacl*, assign appropriate permissions to the group. Then, using *setfacl*, assign "---" (not read, not write, and not execute) permissions to the specific user. Here is an example command line:

```
setfacl -m u::chas:---
```

11.5 Finding Files and Directories with Permission Attributes

This section describes how the *find* command can be used to locate files and directories that have particular permission attributes.

The *find* command can be used to locate files on a system having specific permission settings. The syntax of the *find* command is *find directory expression*, where *directory* is the place where find should start searching and *expression* is one or more of the following:

- *-user username*. Search for files owned by *username*; *username* can be the actual username or the numeric userid.

- *-group groupname*. Search for files owned by *groupname*; *groupname* can be the actual group name or the numeric groupid.
- *-perm [-]mode*. The *mode* argument is used to represent file mode bits. The format is identical to the symbolic mode used by the *chmod* command.

  If the hyphen is omitted, the primary will evaluate as true when the file permission bits exactly match the value of the resulting template. Otherwise, if *mode* is prefixed by a hyphen, the primary will evaluate as true if at least all the bits in the resulting template are set in the file permission bits.
- *-perm [-]onum*. True if the file permission flags exactly match the octal number *onum* as used by the *chmod* command numeric syntax. If *onum* is prefixed by a minus sign ("-"), only the bits that are set in *onum* are compared with the file permission flags, and the expression evaluates true if they match.
- *-name filename*. Search for files named *filename*.
- *-print*. Find will list all files found matching criteria.
- *-exec command {} \;*. Execute *command* with the located file or files as arguments to *command*.
- *-type x*. Find files of type *x*, where *x* is one of: *f* (ordinary file), *d* (directory), *b* (block special file), *c* (character special file), *D* (door), *l* (symbolic link), *p* (named pipe), or *s* (socket).

Some examples of the *find* command are:

```
# find /export/home -perm u=rwx,g=rx,o=rx -print
# find /tmp -perm 750 -exec ls -la {} \;
```

In the first example, *find* will list all files in or below the directory */export/home* with *u=rwx*, *g=rx*, *o=rx* permissions. In the second example, *find* will locate all files with 750 permissions in the directory */tmp* and perform an *ls -la* on each file found.

The *find* command cannot search for files with specific ACL permissions.

EXAM NOTES

THINK ABOUT IT . . .

You need to find all files with a particular groupid that have write permissions for the group and remove those write permissions. How can this be done on a single command line?

Two commands are needed: *find* and *chmod*.The *find* command with the *-type*, *-group*, and *-perms* options will be used to locate the correct files; the *chmod* command will be used to change those permissions. Here is an example command line:

```
find . -type f -group engr -perm -g=r -exec chmod g-w () \;
```

CHAPTER SUMMARY

Each file and directory on a system is assigned an owner and groupid. A combination of *read*, *write*, and *execute* permissions are assigned to each file and directory for the category *owner*, *group*, and *other* users. Permissions on a file determine who can read and write to the file and, if the file is an executable program, who can execute it. Permissions on a directory determine who can search and view its contents, as well as whether files or directories can be added to or removed from the directory.

Executable files with SetUID permissions will run as though they were run as the file's owner. Similarly, executable files with SetGID permissions will run as though they were run as the file's group.

Directories with the SetGID permission cause subsequently created files or directories within that directory to inherit the groupid of the directory rather than the groupid of the user creating the file or directory.

When a directory has the sticky bit permission set, only owners of files in that directory may remove their files, even if the directory has global read/write/execute permissions.

The *ls -l* command is used to display details about a file's or directory's ownership and permissions.

The *chown* command is used to change the owner of a file. Similarly, the *chgrp* command is used to change the groupid of a file. The *chmod* command is used to change the permission settings (read, write, and execute for each of owner, group, and other) for a file or directory. The *chown* command uses both a numeric and a symbolic syntax.

The *umask* is a value that determines the initial permissions assigned to any file or directory that is created. The *umask*, expressed in numeric form similar to *chmod*'s numeric syntax, lists the settings that will be omitted from a subsequently created file or directory.

An advanced access control list (ACL) feature exists where additional access control permissions can be assigned to a user or group for any file or directory. The *setfacl* command is used to set access control permissions, and the *getfacl* command reads and displays these permissions.

The *find* command can be used to find files or directories with specific permission settings, as well as files with specific owners and group ids.

TEST YOURSELF

MULTIPLE CHOICE

1. What is the purpose of the *chmod* command?
   - A. It is used to change file permissions.
   - B. It is used to change file modes.
   - C. It is used to set the umask.
   - D. It is used to view the umask.
2. Given the access control list:

```
# file: foo
# owner: gsmith
# group: staff
user::rwx
group::rwx                    #effective:rwx
mask:rwx
other:rw-
default:user::r--
default:user:pete:r-x
default:user:1002:---
default:group::r--
default:mask:---
default:other:---
```

which four statements are correct? (Choose four)

A. *foo* is a file.
B. *foo* is a directory.
C. A file created in this directory will have *r--r-----* permissions.
D. User *pete* has read and execute privileges for *foo*.
E. This output was created by the *getfacl* command.
F. This output was created by the *setfacl* command.

3. Given the output:

```
drwx---r-x+  2 gsmith   staff        512 Mar 31 04:49 xdir
```

which three statements are correct? (Choose three)

A. *xdir* is a directory.
B. *xdir* is a file.
C. The groupid *staff* has no access to *xdir*.
D. User *gsmith* is not the owner of *xdir*.
E. The "+" signifies there is additional information available about permissions to access *xdir*.

4. What is the function of *umask*?

A. It determines whether a user can access a file or directory.
B. It determines the initial permissions of a subsequently created file or directory.
C. It is used to change the permissions of existing files and directories.
D. It is not used in Solaris; it has been replaced with Access Control Lists.

5. Given:

```
# umask 027
# mkdir test
#
```

what will be the permissions of test?

A. `----w-rwx`
B. `027`
C. `rw-r-----`
D. `rwxr-x---`

6. Given:

```
# umask 027
# cat > test
^D
#
```

what will be the permissions of `test`?

   A. `----w-rwx`
   B. `027`
   C. `rw-r-----`
   D. `rwxr-x---`

7. Which command is used to change the groupid of a file or directory?

   A. `chmod`
   B. `chgrp`
   C. `chown -g`
   D. `chmod -g`

8. Given:

```
chmod 2644 bowman
```

what is the effect?

   A. Mandatory file locking is set for file *bowman*.
   B. SetGID on execution is set for file *bowman*.
   C. SetUID on execution is set for file *bowman*.
   D. The sticky bit is set for file *bowman*.

9. Which command does the same thing as `chmod 641 login.sh`?

   A. `chmod u=rw,g=x,o=r login.sh`
   B. `chmod u+rw,g+r,o+x login.sh`
   C. `chmod u=rw,g=r,o=x login.sh`
   D. `chmod u-rw,g-r,o-x login.sh`

10. What is the effect of the SetUID permission on a directory?
    A. Users can change the permissions of any files they own that reside in the directory, regardless of the permissions on the directory itself.
    B. All subsequently created files will inherit the groupid of the directory instead of the groupid of its creator.
    C. All subsequently created files will inherit the userid of the directory instead of the userid of its creator.
    D. Nothing—this is an undefined condition.

FREE RESPONSE

11. What command is used to display an access control list?
12. What command is used to recursively change the groupid of a directory?

CHAPTER 12

Remote Administration

After completing this chapter, you'll be able to meet the following Solaris Administration Exam objectives:

- State the command to perform remote system operations such as remote login, remote copy, and remote shell commands.
- State the subcommands that are used by the ftp utility to transfer files between a local system and a remote system.

To fulfill these objectives, this chapter discusses:

- The commands used to execute commands remotely and to log in to another system over the network;
- The commands used to copy files from one system to another; and
- Remote administration configuration and access control.

12.1 Remote Sessions

Two commands, *telnet* and *rlogin*, give you the capability of logging in to another system on the network.

telnet Command

The *telnet* command is used to initiate a character-based session on another system on the network. The syntax of the *telnet* command is *telnet [-8ELcdr] [-e escape_char] [-l user] [-n tracefile] host [port]]*. The options for *telnet* are:

- *-8*. Specifies an eight-bit data path. Negotiating the telnet binary option is attempted for both input and output.
- *-c*. Disables the reading of the user's *.telnetrc* file. (See the *toggle skiprc* command in the *telnet* man page.)
- *-d*. Sets the initial value of the *debug* toggle to TRUE.
- *-e escape_char*. Sets the initial escape character to *escape_char*. *escape_char* may also be a two-character sequence consisting of '^' followed by one character. If the second character is '?', the delete character is selected. Otherwise, the second character is converted to a control character and used as the escape character. If the escape character is the null string (i.e., *-e* ""), it is disabled.
- *-e*. Stops any character from being recognized as an escape character. This effectively prevents the ability to enter telnet's command mode.
- *-l user*. When connecting to a remote system that understands the ENVIRON option, then *user* will be sent to the remote system as the value for the ENVIRON variable USER.
- *-L*. Specifies an eight-bit data path on output. This causes the BINARY option to be negotiated on output.
- *-n tracefile*. Opens *tracefile* for recording trace information. See the *set tracefile* command in this section.
- *-r*. Specifies a user interface similar to *rlogin*. In this mode, the escape character is set to the tilde (~) character, unless modified by the *-e* option. The *rlogin* escape character is only recognized when it is preceded by a carriage return. In this mode, the *telnet* escape character, normally '^]', must still precede a *telnet* command. The *rlogin* escape character can also be followed by '.\r' or

'^Z', and, like *rlogin*, closes or suspends the connection, respectively. This option is an uncommitted interface and may change in the future.

- *host*. This is the name or IP address of the remote system to which the *telnet* session is to be established.
- *port*. Specifies the TCP/IP port number to connect to on the remote system. If not specified, *telnet* will connect to port 23.

Telnet has two operating modes: input mode and command mode. While in command mode, *telnet* will display the command mode prompt:

```
telnet>
```

While in command mode, any of the following commands are available:

- *open [-l user] [host [port]]*. Opens a connection to the named *host*. If no port number is specified, *telnet* will attempt to contact a telnet server at the default port (23). The host specification may be either a host name or an IP address. The *-l* option passes the *user* as the value of the ENVIRON variable USER to the remote system.
- *close*. Closes any open *telnet* session and exit *telnet*. An EOF (in command mode) will also close a session and exit.
- *quit*. Same as *close*.
- *s*. Suspends *telnet*. This command works only when the user is using a shell that supports job control, such as sh.
- *status*. Shows the current status of *telnet*. This includes the peer one is connected to, as well as the current mode.
- *display [argument...]*. Displays all, or some, of the *set* values.
- *? [command]*. Gets help. With no arguments, *telnet* prints a help summary. If a command is specified, *telnet* will print the help information for just that command.
- *send argument...* . Sends one or more special character sequences to the remote host. The following are the arguments that can be specified (more than one *argument* may be specified at a time):
  - *escape*. Sends the current telnet *escape* character (initially ^]).
  - *brk* | *break*. Sends the telnet brk (break) sequence, which may have significance to the remote system.

    - *ec*. Sends the telnet ec (erase character) sequence, which erases the last character entered.
    - *?*. Prints out help information for the *send* command.
- *set argument [value] | unset argument*. Sets any one of a number of *telnet* variables to a specific value. The special value "off" turns off the function associated with the variable. The values of variables may be interrogated with the *display* command. If *value* is omitted, the value is taken to be true, or "on." If the *unset* form is used, the value is taken to be false, or "off." The variables that may be specified are:
    - *echo*. This is the value (initially ^E) that, when in "line by line" mode, toggles between local echoing of entered characters for normal processing and suppressing echoing of entered characters; for example, entering a password.
    - *escape*. This is the telnet *escape* character (initially ^]) that enters telnet command mode when connected to a remote system.
    - *quit*. If *telnet* is in localchars mode and the quit character is typed, a telnet BRK sequence (see *send, brk*) is sent to the remote host. The initial value for the *quit* character is taken to be the terminal's *quit* character.
    - *tracefile*. This is the file to which the output, generated when the *netdata* or the *debug* option is TRUE, will be written. If *tracefile* is set to "-", then tracing information will be written to standard output (the default).
    - *?*. Displays the legal *set* and *unset* commands.
- *logout*. Sends the telnet *logout* option to the remote side. This command is similar to a *close* command. However, if the remote side does not support the *logout* option, nothing happens. If the remote side does support the *logout* option, this command should cause the remote side to close the telnet connection. If the remote side also supports the concept of suspending a user's session for later reattachment, the *logout* argument indicates that the remote side should terminate the session immediately.

In most cases, telnet returns to input mode after a command has completed. Thus, to execute several commands in a row, it is usually necessary to press the escape sequence (which is *Ctrl-]* by default) to return to command mode.

While in input mode, all characters typed are transmitted to the remote system.

An example telnet dialogue follows.

```
# telnet grommit
Trying 192.168.0.35...
Connected to grommit.
Escape character is '^]'.

SunOS 5.7

login: pete
Password: ********
Last login: Sun Apr  1 06:09:19 from wallace
Sun Microsystems Inc.   SunOS 5.7       Generic October 1998
You have new mail.
grommit% ^]
telnet> status
Connected to grommit.
Operating in single character mode
Catching signals locally
Remote character echo
Escape character is '^]'.
^]
telnet> display options
won't show option processing.
     DO   ECHO
     DO   SUPPRESS GO AHEAD
     WILL TERMINAL TYPE
     WILL NAWS
     WILL NEW-ENVIRON

^]
telnet> display
will flush output when sending interrupt characters.
won't send interrupt characters in urgent mode.
won't skip reading of ~/.telnetrc file.
won't map carriage return on output.
will recognize certain control characters.
won't turn on socket level debugging.
won't print hexadecimal representation of network traffic.
won't print user readable output for "netdata".
won't show option processing.
won't print hexadecimal representation of terminal traffic.

echo            [^E]
escape          [^]]
rlogin          [off]
```

```
tracefile        "(standard output)"
flushoutput      [^O]
interrupt        [^C]
quit             [^\]
eof              [^D]
erase            [^?]
kill             [^U]
lnext            [^V]
susp             [^Z]
reprint          [^R]
worderase        [^W]
start            [^Q]
stop             [^S]
forw1            [off]
forw2            [off]
ayt              [^T]

grommit% ps
   PID TTY       TIME CMD
  4404 pts/0     0:00 csh
grommit% who
pete        pts/0        Apr  5 05:01    (wallace)
grommit% ^]
telnet> logout
Connection closed by foreign host.
#
```

In this example, a telnet session is opened to the system *grommit*, and is logged in as user *pete*. After pressing the telnet escape sequence (the sequence default is ^]); it does not literally display in a user session, but is shown here to signify when it has been entered), the status command is entered, followed by the *display* options and *display* commands. Next, a few shell commands are entered (*ps* and *who*). Finally, we return to telnet command mode and issue a *logout* command. Note that you can just type *exit* or *^D* to log out of a remote session.

rlogin Command

The *rlogin* command is similar to the *telnet* command in that it is used to establish a login session on another system. The primary similarities and differences between *rlogin* and *telnet* are shown in Table 12.1.

The syntax for the *rlogin* command is *rlogin [-8EL] [-ec] [-l username] hostname*. The options for *rlogin* are:

Table 12.1 *Comparison of* telnet *and* rlogin

CHARACTERISTIC	TELNET	RLOGIN
Command mode	Command mode with a rich set of commands available.	No command mode.
Access control	User must always supply userid and password to log in.	If permissions are granted with *~/.rhosts* or */etc/hosts.equiv*, user *may* be able to log in without having to furnish a password.

- *-8*. Pass eight-bit data across the network instead of seven-bit data.
- *-ec*. Specify a different escape character, *c*, for the line used to disconnect from the remote host.
- *-E*. Stop any character from being recognized as an escape character.
- *-l username*. Specify a different *username* for the remote login. If you do not use this option, the remote *username* used is the same as your local *username*.
- *-L*. Allow the rlogin session to be run in "litout" mode.
- *hostname*. The remote machine on which *rlogin* establishes the remote login session.

Lines that you type which start with the tilde character are "escape sequences" (the escape character can be changed using the *-e* option):

- ~. . Disconnect from the remote host. This is not the same as a logout, because the local host breaks the connection with no warning to the remote end.
- *~susp*. Suspend the login session (only if you are using a shell with Job Control). *susp* is your "suspend" character, usually CTRL-Z.
- *~dsusp*. Suspend the input half of the login, but output will still be seen (only if you are using a shell with Job Control). *dsusp* is your "deferred suspend" character, usually CTRL-Y.

rlogin is one of the "*r* commands"; the others are *rsh* and *rexec*, which are discussed later in this chapter. All of the *r* commands use an access control mechanism that is discussed in the section "Remote Administration Access Control" later in this chapter.

Some example *rlogin* dialogues follow.

```
wallace% rlogin grommit
Password: ********
Last login: Fri Apr  6 05:38:40 from wallace
Sun Microsystems Inc.   SunOS 5.7       Generic October 1998
You have new mail.
grommit% ps
   PID TTY       TIME CMD
  7522 pts/0     0:00 csh
grommit% exit
grommit% logout
Connection closed.
wallace% rlogin grommit -l stuan
Password: ********
Last login: Mon Apr  9 04:09:43 from wallace
Sun Microsystems Inc.   SunOS 5.7       Generic October 1998
$ who am i
stuan      pts/1        Apr  9 04:12    (wallace)
$ ~.
Closed connection.
wallace%
```

In the first example, an rlogin session is opened on the system *grommit*. Since no username is issued, *rlogin* assumes that the username on *grommit* is the same as that on *wallace*. After supplying the account's password on *grommit*, the shell prompt appears. After running *ps*, the session logs out with the *exit* command.

The second example is an rlogin session to *grommit* under the username *stuan*. Then, after running *who am i*, this session abruptly exits with the ~. sequence.

Remote accounts may grant permission for remote logins to execute. In such cases, the remote user will not be prompted for a password. If no permission is granted, the remote login will not proceed until the account's password is supplied. This is discussed fully in the following section.

EXAM NOTES

THINK ABOUT IT . . .

On system A, you opened a telnet session to system B, and from there you opened a telnet session to system C. Now you need to forcibly disconnect the B-to-C telnet session. When you press the escape sequence, which telnet are you talking to?

When you press the escape sequence (usually Ctrl-]), you are talking to the "nearest" telnet, in this case the A-to-B session.

Here is how to get the B-to-C telnet session into command mode. In the local telnet session, send the escape sequence, then at the command line you send the break sequence to the next telnet session, then send a "quit" after that. Here is a sample dialogue:

```
# ^]
telnet> send escape
telnet> quit
#
```

In this example, after pressing *^]*, the A-to-B *telnet* prompt appears. After typing *send escape*, the B-to-C *telnet* prompt appears. That is the one we *quit*, leaving us at system B.

122 Remote Commands

Remote commands can be issued to a system over a network with the *rsh* command. The syntaxes of the *rsh* command are *rsh [-n] [-l username] hostname command* and *rsh hostname [-n] [-l username] command*. There is no functional difference between these two syntaxes. The options for *rsh* are:

- *-l username*. Use *username* as the remote username instead of the local username. In the absence of this option, the remote *username* is the same as the local *username*.
- *-n*. Redirect the input of *rsh* to */dev/null*. This is sometimes needed to avoid unintended interactions between *rsh* and the shell that invokes it. For example, if you are running *rsh* and invoke a *rsh* in the background without redirecting its input away from the terminal, it will block even if no reads are posted by the remote command. The *-n* option will prevent this.
- *hostname*. The remote system on which *command* is to be performed. *hostname* can be a system name or IP address.
- *command*. The *command* to be executed on the specified *hostname*.

If no *command* is specified, *rsh* performs an rlogin to *hostname*. Some examples follow.

```
wallace% rsh grommit uptime
  4:37am  up 10:58,  1 user,  load average: 0.01, 0.00, 0.01
wallace% rsh preston -l stuan df /
```

```
/                      (/dev/dsk/c0t3d0s0 ):  222752 blocks    82767 files
wallace% rsh noodle -l gsmith
Last login: Mon Apr  9 04:39:12 from wallace
Sun Microsystems Inc.   SunOS 5.7       Generic October 1998
$ exit
wallace%
```

In the first example, the *uptime* command is executed on the system *grommit*. In the second example, the command *df /* is executed on the system *preston* as userid *stuan*. In the third example, an *rsh* is executed on system *noodle* as userid *gsmith*. Because no command is specified, an rlogin is invoked and a shell prompt displayed. The shell is terminated with the *exit* command.

Remote accounts must explicitly grant permissions for remote commands to execute. This is discussed fully in the following section.

rsh can accept input from standard input and send output to standard output. Some examples follow.

```
wallace% rsh grommit ps -ef|grep mail
    root  238   1  0 17:41:34 ?        0:00 /usr/lib/sendmail -bd -q15m
wallace% cat /etc/netmasks | rsh preston "cat > /etc/netmasks"
wallace% tar cf - . | rsh noodle "cd /tmp/;tar xf -"
wallace%
```

In the first example, the command *ps -ef* is executed on the system *grommit*. The output from the *ps* command run on *grommit* becomes standard input for the *grep* command, which is executed on the system *wallace*.

In the second example, the command *cat /etc/netmasks* is executed locally. The contents of the file */etc/netmasks* becomes the standard input for the remote command *cat > /etc/netmasks*. Double quotes are placed around the entire remote command to force it to execute remotely. Otherwise, the "*> /etc/netmasks*" would execute on the local system instead of on the remote system.

In the third example, a tar archive is created and written to standard output. This is directed to the remote commands on the system *noodle* "*cd /tmp*" and "*tar xf –*". This effectively copies the contents of the local directory to */tmp* on *noodle*.

Remote commands that use shell metacharacters (input and output redirection and pipes) should be tested carefully to ensure that you get the desired results.

EXAM NOTES

THINK ABOUT IT . . .

You need to write a script that logs the amount of free space on the remote system *pinky*. What command(s) need to be used?

Use the *rsh* command to perform a *df* on the remote system and store the results on a file on the local system. For example, the command could be:

```
rsh pinky df -kl >> pinkylog
```

In this example, the command *df -kl* is performed on the system *pinky*, and the results appended to the local logfile *pinkylog*.

12.3 Remote File Copy

The *rcp* and *ftp* commands are used to copy files from one system to another. Let's take a look at each.

rcp Command

The *rcp* (remote copy) command is used to copy one or more files from one system to another. The syntaxes of the *rcp* command is *rcp [-p] filename1 filename2* and *rcp [-pr] filename... directory*. The first syntax is used to copy individual files from one system to another, while the second syntax is used to copy one or more files—or complete directories—from one system to another. The options for *rcp* are explained here.

- *-p*. Attempt to give each copy the same modification times, access times, modes, and ACLs if applicable as the original file.
- *-r*. Copy each subtree rooted at file name; in this case the destination must be a directory.

- *filename*. Each *filename* is either a remote file of the form *hostname:path*, or a local file name (without the ":").
- *directory*. Each *directory* is either a remote directory of the form *hostname:path*, or a local directory name (without the ":").

Examples of the *rcp* command follow.

```
# rcp /etc/netmasks grommit:/etc
# rcp -r /export/tools preston:/export/tools
#
```

In the first example, the file */etc/netmasks* is copied to the remote system *grommit* in the directory */etc*. In the second example, the entire contents of the directory */export/tools* is copied to the system *preston*.

rcp can also perform "third party" copies; *rcp* running on system "A" can have files on system "B" copied to system "C". An example follows.

```
# rcp root@preston:/etc/netmasks root@grommit:/etc
#
```

In this example, the file */etc/netmasks* on system *preston* is copied to the directory */etc* on the system *grommit*. The *rcp* can be run from another system (neither *preston* nor *grommit*).

Remote accounts must explicitly grant permissions for remote copies to execute. This is discussed fully in the following section.

ftp Command

The *ftp* (file transfer protocol or file transfer program) command is used to copy files from one system to another. Running the *ftp* command starts a command interpreter that is used to set session parameters and request file copy operations. The syntax of the *ftp* command is *ftp [-dgintv] [-T timeout] [hostname]*. The options for *ftp* are:

- *-d*. Enables debugging.
- *-i*. Turns off interactive prompting during multiple file transfers.

- *-n*. Does not attempt "auto-login" upon initial connection. If auto-login is not disabled, *ftp* checks the *.netrc* file in the user's home directory for an entry describing an account on the remote machine. If no entry exists, *ftp* will prompt for the login name of the account on the remote machine (the default is the login name on the local machine), and, if necessary, prompts for a password and an account with which to log in.
- *-T timeout*. Enables global connection timer, specified in seconds (decimal). The timer is reset when anything is sent to the server on the control connection, and disabled while the client is prompting for user input. On the data connection, timeouts rely on TCP and may only timeout on network outages between the client and server. It may not timeout, for instance, if the server is waiting for an NFS server.
- *-v*. Shows all responses from the remote server, as well as report on data transfer statistics. This is turned on by default if *ftp* is running interactively with its input coming from the user's terminal.
- *hostname*. The name or IP address of a remote host to which an ftp session is to be started.

When ftp is started, the *ftp* command interpreter is started and the *ftp* prompt displayed:

```
ftp>
```

The following commands can be issued to the command interpreter:

- *! [command]*. Runs *command* as a shell command on the local machine. If no command is given, invoke an interactive shell.
- *append local-file [remote-file]*. Appends file *local-file* to the file *remote-file* on the remote machine. If *remote-file* is not specified, the local file name is used, subject to alteration by any *ntrans* or *nmap* settings. File transfer uses the current settings for "representation type," "file structure," and "transfer mode."
- *ascii*. Sets the "representation type" to "network ASCII." This is the default type. See the *type* command.
- *binary*. Sets the "representation type" to "image." See the *type* command.
- *bye*. Terminates the ftp session with the remote server and exits ftp. An EOF (typing *^D*) will also terminate the session and exit.
- *cd remote-directory*. Changes the working directory on the remote machine to *remote-directory*.

- *close*. Terminates the ftp session with the remote server, and returns to the command interpreter. Any defined macros are erased.
- *delete remote-file*. Deletes the file *remote-file* on the remote machine.
- *debug*. Toggles debugging mode. When debugging is on, *ftp* prints each command sent to the remote machine, preceded by the string ->.
- *disconnect*. A synonym for *close*.
- *get remote-file [local-file]*. Retrieves the *remote-file* and stores it on the local machine. If the local file name *local-file* is not specified, it is given the same name it has on the remote machine, subject to alteration by the current *case*, *ntrans*, and *nmap* settings. The current settings for "representation type," "file structure," and "transfer mode" are used while transferring the file.
- *hash*. Toggles hash-sign (#) printing for each data block transferred. The size of a data block is 8192 bytes.
- *help [command]*. Prints an informative message about the meaning of *command*. If no argument is given, *ftp* prints a list of the known commands.
- *lcd [directory]*. Changes the working directory on the local machine. If no directory is specified, the user's home directory is used.
- *ls [remote-directory | -al] [local-file]*. Prints an abbreviated listing of the contents of a directory on the remote machine. If *remote-directory* is left unspecified, the current working directory is used.

  The *-a* option lists all entries, including those that begin with a dot (.), which are normally not listed. The *-l* option lists files in long format, giving mode, number of links, owner, group, size in bytes, and time of last modification for each file. If the file is a special file, the size field instead contains the major and minor device numbers rather than a size. If the file is a symbolic link, the file name is printed followed by "" and the pathname of the referenced file.

  If no local file is specified, or if *local-file* is -, the output is sent to the terminal.
- *mdelete remote-files*. Deletes the *remote-files* on the remote machine.

- *mdir remote-files local-file*. Like *dir*, except multiple remote files may be specified. If interactive prompting is on, *ftp* will prompt the user to verify that the last argument is indeed the target local file for receiving mdir output.
- *mget remote-files*. Expands *remote-files* on the remote machine and performs a *get* for each file name thus produced. See the man page for the *glob* command for details on the file name expansion. Resulting file names will then be processed according to *case*, *ntrans*, and *nmap* settings. Files are transferred into the local working directory, which can be changed with *lcd directory*; new local directories can be created with *! mkdir directory*.
- *mkdir directory-name*. Makes a directory on the remote machine.
- *mput local-files*. Expands wildcards in the list of local files given as arguments and performs a *put* for each file in the resulting list. See the man page for the *glob* command for details of file name expansion. Resulting file names will then be processed according to *ntrans* and *nmap* settings.
- *open host [port]*. Establishes a connection to the specified host ftp server. An optional port number may be supplied, in which case, *ftp* will attempt to contact an ftp server at that *port*. If the *auto-login* option is on (default setting), *ftp* will also attempt to automatically log the user in to the ftp server.
- *prompt*. Toggles interactive prompting. Interactive prompting occurs during multiple file transfers to allow the user to selectively retrieve or store files. By default, prompting is turned on. If prompting is turned off, any *mget* or *mput* will transfer all files, and any *mdelete* will delete all files.
- *put local-file [remote-file]*. Stores a file *local-file* on the remote machine. If *remote-file* is left unspecified, the local file name is used after processing according to any *ntrans* or *nmap* settings in naming the remote file. File transfer uses the current settings for "representation type," "file structure," and "transfer mode."
- *pwd*. Prints the name of the current working directory on the remote machine.
- *quit*. A synonym for *bye*.
- *recv remote-file [local-file]*. A synonym for *get*.
- *rename from to*. Renames the file *from* on the remote machine to have the name *to*.

- *rmdir directory-name*. Deletes the directory *directory-name* on the remote machine.
- *send local-file [remote-file]*. A synonym for *put*.
- *status*. Show the current status of *ftp*.
- *user user-name [password] [account]*. Identify yourself to the remote ftp server. If the password is not specified and the server requires it, *ftp* will prompt the user for it (after disabling local echo). If an account field is not specified, and the ftp server requires it, the user will be prompted for it. If an account field is specified, an *account* command will be relayed to the remote server after the login sequence is completed if the remote server did not require it for logging in. Unless *ftp* is invoked with "auto-login" disabled, this process is done automatically on initial connection to the ftp server.
- *? [command]*. A synonym for *help*.

An example ftp session follows.

```
# ftp grommit
Connected to grommit.
220 grommit FTP server (SunOS 5.7) ready.
Name (grommit:pete): root
331 Password required for root.
Password: ********
230 User root logged in.
ftp> lcd /var/adm
Local directory now /var/adm
ftp> cd /tmp
250 CWD command successful.
ftp> mkdir logs
257 MKD command successful.
ftp> pwd
257 "/tmp" is current directory.
ftp> cd logs
250 CWD command successful.
ftp> bin
200 Type set to I.
ftp> mput *
mput acct? ^C
Continue with mput? n
ftp> prompt
Interactive mode off.
ftp> mput *
acct: not a plain file.
200 PORT command successful.
```

```
150 Binary data connection for admcronenv (192.168.0.34,32888).
226 Transfer complete.
local: admcronenv remote: admcronenv
73 bytes sent in 0.00066 seconds (107.36 Kbytes/s)
200 PORT command successful.
150 Binary data connection for lastlog (192.168.0.34,32889).
226 Transfer complete.
local: lastlog remote: lastlog
28084 bytes sent in 0.0013 seconds (21359.64 Kbytes/s)
log: not a plain file.
200 PORT command successful.
150 Binary data connection for m.tar (192.168.0.34,32890).
226 Transfer complete.
local: m.tar remote: m.tar
203264 bytes sent in 0.17 seconds (1136.13 Kbytes/s)
[ remainder of output not shown ]
ftp> quit
221 Goodbye.
#
```

In this example, an ftp session is opened to the remote system *grommit*, and logged in as *root*. The local directory is changed to */var/adm*, and the remote directory changed to */tmp*. On the remote system, the subdirectory *logs* (under */tmp*) is created. Then, after listing the remote current directory (*/tmp*), we change to the subdirectory *logs*. Next, transfer mode is changed to *binary* (in anticipation of the need to transfer binary files later on in this session).

Then, the command to send all files in the local directory is issued (*mput **). *ftp* prompts for the first file (*acct*), at which point the transfer is aborted with a *^C*. Interactive mode is turned off with the *prompt* command. Then, the *mput* * command is reissued. Since interactive mode is off, *ftp* transfers all files in the current local directory. The ftp session is closed with the *quit* command.

EXAM NOTES

THINK ABOUT IT . . .

Periodically, you need to transfer batches of files from one system to another. Is there an easy way to do this?

Your task could be made easier if, instead of transferring large numbers of files, you instead create a single archive file and transfer that instead. This has the added advantage of preserving file ownership and permissions, and it is simply easier to transfer a single file over the network.

Create a tar archive to contain the files you need to transfer. Then send the tar archive file over the network with *ftp* or *rcp*, and then restore the tar archive on the destination system.

12.4 Remote Login Access Control

This section describes access control mechanisms used by *telnet* and *rlogin* to determine whether ordinary users and root may log in remotely.

/etc/default/login File

A setting in the */etc/default/login* file is used to control whether root can log in remotely or whether it must log in only on the system console. If the CONSOLE setting is set, then root can log in only on the system console. If the CONSOLE setting is commented or absent, then root can log in over the network with *rlogin* or *telnet*.

If the CONSOLE setting is set, then it will appear as follows in */etc/default/login*:

```
CONSOLE=/dev/console
```

Here is a sample dialogue where the CONSOLE setting is set.

```
# telnet grommit
Trying 192.168.0.35...
Connected to grommit.
Escape character is '^]'.

SunOS 5.7

login: root
Password: ********
Not on system console
Connection closed by foreign host.
#
```

EXAM NOTES

THINK ABOUT IT . . .

You want to increase security at your site by preventing root logins over the network (by setting */etc/default/login*). But how does an administrator become root when necessary?

The administrator should log into the target system using his or her own userid, and then *su* to root afterwards.

/etc/nologin File

The */etc/nologin* file is used to control whether users may log in to the system.

If */etc/nologin* is present, no login attempts will be allowed, and the contents of */etc/nologin* will be displayed to any user trying to log in. It is generally useful to place in */etc/nologin* some message explaining why the system is unavailable.

Root is exempt from the effects of */etc/nologin*.

A sample dialogue follows.

```
# cat > /etc/nologin
The system will be going down at 10am today for maintenance.  It should
be back up within an hour. We apologize for the inconvenience.
^D
#

% telnet grommit
Trying 192.168.0.35...
Connected to grommit.
Escape character is '^]'.

SunOS 5.7

login: pete
Password: ********
The system will be going down at 10am today for maintenance.  It should
be back up within an hour.  We apologize for the inconvenience.
Connection closed by foreign host.
%
```

In this example, the file */etc/nologin* is created on the system *grommit*. Then, in another session, a user attempts to log in to *grommit*. The message created in */etc/nologin* is displayed and the login attempt terminated.

125 Remote Administration Access Control

This section describes the access control mechanism used by the "*r* commands" (*rlogin*, *rsh*, and *rcp*) described earlier in this chapter.

Two configuration files are used to determine whether an inbound *rlogin*, *rsh*, or *rcp* is permitted to run on a system without being challenged for a password. They are */etc/hosts.equiv*, and *.rhosts*. Each is explained in more detail in the following.

Because each of the three *r* commands runs somewhat differently, Table 12.2 describes the behavior of each with regard to permissions.

/etc/hosts.equiv File

The configuration file */etc/hosts.equiv* contains permission entries for inbound *r* commands. The system administrator manages this file. The format for entries in this file is explained later in this section.

.rhosts File

The configuration file *.rhosts* contains the same type of permission entries for inbound *r* commands. The primary difference between */etc/hosts.equiv* and *.rhosts* is that a *.rhosts* file resides in a user's home directory and is maintained by the user. Thus, each user has some degree of control whether an inbound remote command may execute using his or her identity without having to supply the user's password.

The format for entries in *.rhosts* is explained later in this section.

Format of /etc/hosts.equiv *and* .rhosts

The format of */etc/hosts.equiv* and *.rhosts* consists of individual positive and negative entries, each of which either grants or denies password-less access for an individual user, an individual system, or combinations therein.

Table 12.2 *r Commands Permissions*

COMMAND	PERMISSION GRANTED	PERMISSION DENIED
rlogin	Login permitted, password not required.	Login permitted, password required.
rsh	Remote command permitted, password not required.	Remote command permitted, password required.
rcp	Remote copy permitted.	Remote copy denied.

Each entry occupies one line in the file. Table 12.3 shows the format for entries.

/etc/hosts.equiv *and* .rhosts *Search Order*

The system first checks */etc/hosts.equiv*, and then the *.rhosts* file in the home directory of the local user who is requesting access. Authentica-

Table 12.3 /etc/hosts.equiv *and* .rhosts *Format*

FORM	DESCRIPTION
hostname	Users from the named host are trusted. That is, they may access the system with the same username as they have on the remote system without having to supply a password. This form may be used in both the */etc/hosts.equiv* and *.rhosts* files.
hostname username	The named user from the named host can access the system. This form may be used in individual *.rhosts* files to allow remote users to access the system as a different local user. If this form is used in the */etc/hosts.equiv* file, the named remote user will be allowed to access the system as *any* local user.
+	This will allow a user from any remote host to access the system with the same username.
+ username	This entry will allow the named user from any remote host to access the system.
hostname +	This will allow any user from the named host to access the system as the local user.
- hostname	This will disallow all access from the named host.
hostname -username	This disallows access by the named user only from the named host.

tion succeeds when a matching positive entry is found. Authentication will fail when the first matching negative entry is found, or if no matching entries are found in either file. If both negative and positive entries appear in a file, the one that appears first will prevail.

The exception to this rule is that if the inbound *r* command requests the userid *root*, then only the root *.rhosts* (i.e., */.rhosts*) file is checked.

The system checks */etc/hosts.equiv* for lines in the following order:

1. +
2. +@ netgroup (netgroups are not covered in the Part I or Part II exams)
3. -@ netgroup
4. - hostname
5. hostname

The system checks a *.rhosts* file for lines in the following order:

1. +
2. +@ netgroup
3. -@ netgroup
4. - hostname
5. hostname

The system will ignore the *.rhosts* file if it is not owned by the user.

EXAM NOTES

THINK ABOUT IT...

Given the following */etc/hosts.equiv*

```
wallace phil
wallace +
wallace - dave
```

and given the following *.rhosts* in user *dave* home directory

```
wallace
```

what will the outcome be of an inbound *rlogin* from the system *wallace* for userid *dave*? What about an inbound *rcp* request?

An inbound *rlogin* will first check */etc/hosts.equiv,* and when it reaches the *wallace +* entry, the *rlogin* will proceed without a password challenge. The entry *wallace – dave* will not be considered, since a succeeding entry is found immediately before it. The *.rhosts* file is not consulted, since an answer was found in */etc/hosts.equiv.*

An inbound *rcp* request is permitted as well.

What if the *wallace – dave* entry precedes the *wallace +* entry?

The inbound *rlogin* will challenge for dave's password. The inbound *rcp* will fail.

CHAPTER SUMMARY

The *telnet* command is used to initiate a character-based session on a remote system. A username and password are required to log in to the remote system. *telnet* can be placed into command mode in order to change its operating characteristics using a rich set of available commands.

The *rlogin* (remote login) command is also used to initiate a character-based session on a remote system. *rlogin* has no command mode, but an *rlogin* session can still be forcibly terminated if necessary.

Commands can be executed on a remote system using the *rsh* (remote shell) command. The output from the remote command will be sent back to the local system. The *rsh* command can be placed in the middle of a stream, accepting standard input from the output from another command, and similarly its output can be piped into the input to another command.

Files and entire directories can be copied form one system to another using the *rcp* command. *rcp* can also initiate third-party copies between two other systems.

The *ftp* command is used to copy files between systems. *ftp* uses a command interpreter and has a rich set of commands used to copy files individually or in batches.

The CONSOLE setting in the */etc/default/login* configuration file determines whether root may log in via a *telnet* or *rlogin* session, or whether it may only log in at the system console. The */etc/nologin* file is used to prevent subsequent logins; any text placed in the file */etc/nologin* will be displayed to users trying to log in. It can be useful to place the reason for the login restriction in the file.

The */etc/hosts.equiv* and *.rhosts* files are used to determine which usernames will accept inbound *R*-commands (*rlogin*, *rcp*, *rsh*) without having to supply the password. Each user may maintain his or her own *.rhosts* file, which is placed in his or her home directory.

TEST YOURSELF

MULTIPLE CHOICE

1. What command in telnet's command mode will return to session mode?
   A. `resume`
   B. `cont`
   C. `continue`
   D. just press CR to return to session mode
2. What is the purpose of the *rsh* command?
   A. Start a restricted shell on a remote system.
   B. Execute an arbitrary command on a remote system.
   C. Start a shell on a remote system, bypassing login.
   D. Start a restricted shell on the local system.
3. Which four are valid *telnet* subcommands? (Choose four)
   A. `open`
   B. `bye`
   C. `line`
   D. `swap`
   E. `send`
   F. `status`
4. Which two are used to transfer files between systems? (Choose two)
   A. `ftp`
   B. `rcp`
   C. `rcopy`
   D. `telnet`
   E. `rsh`
   F. `move`

5. You have initiated a remote login session with another system with the *rlogin* command. Now you need to forcibly terminate the session. Which key sequence will accomplish this?
   A. `Ctrl-]`
   B. `^]`
   C. `~.`
   D. `~quit`
6. Which command is used to log in to a remote system?
   A. `login`
   B. `telnet`
   C. `rtelnet`
   D. `logrem`
7. Which two commands use */etc/hosts.equiv*? (Choose two)
   A. `telnet`
   B. `rlogin`
   C. `rcp`
   D. `rexec`
   E. `rcopy`
   F. `ftp`
   G. `resh`
8. What is the purpose of the *.rhosts* file?
   A. It specifies which users on which hosts are allowed to access an account without having to supply its password.
   B. It specifies which users are allowed to access an account without having to supply its password.
   C. It specifies which remote hosts are allowed to access an account without having to supply its password.
   D. It specifies which systems a user may log in to without having to supply a password.

9. Given the */etc/hosts.equiv* file:

```
mustard -walker
spinach george
+ herbert
mustard
```

which statement is true?

   A. User *herbert* may rlogin to this system, from any system on the network except *mustard*.
   B. All users on the system *spinach* may rlogin to this system; only the user *george* is required to supply his password.
   C. All users on the system *mustard* may rlogin to this system without having to supply their password.
   D. All users on the system *mustard*, except *walker*, may rlogin to this system without having to supply their password.

10. What is the purpose of the */etc/nologins* file?
   A. It prevents remote users from logging in to the system; its contents state the reason.
   B. It prevents remote users from logging in to the system.
   C. It contains a list of invalid rlogin attempts.
   D. It prevents root from logging in except from the console.

FREE RESPONSE

11. Specify the command used to copy the entire */etc* directory to the system *rookie*.

12. Specify the *ftp* command used to copy all files from a remote directory.

APPENDIX 

Answers

A.1 Chapter 1: System Concepts

1. A is correct. The SIGTERM signal is signal number 15.
2. C and D are correct.
3. D is correct. MANPATH lists which directories are searched for man pages.
4. B, C, and E are correct. A is incorrect because the "/5" signifies the number of lightweight processes—it is not part of the command line itself. Higher numbers in the PRI column signify higher priority.
5. A is correct. *prstat -p15489* will show process number 15489 continuously. The *ps -fp15489* is a valid command, but will show the status of this process only one time. *prstat -L 15489* is not a valid syntax. *prstat -P 15489* shows the status of processes whose parent is process 15489.
6. A, C, E, and I are correct.
7. A, D, and G are correct. Daemons run in the background, are usually started at boot time, and have their standard (STDIN, STDOUT, STDERR) file descriptors closed. They do not necessarily run as root, nor do they run at a different priority. They are not necessarily bound to a CPU.
8. C is correct. A relative pathname does not start with a slash ("/"). A and B are absolute pathnames. D is an invalid pathname.

9. B is correct. A and D are incorrect because the userid in the output is root, not daemon. The syntax of C is incorrect.
10. A is correct. The *-U* option of the *pkill* command is used to kill processes associated with a particular userid. The *-n* option matches commands (processes other than those owned by lp might be killed). The *-x* option does not use an optional argument. The *-t* option kills processes associated with a particular terminal.
11. "*kill -HUP 1512*" or "*kill -1 1512*" is correct. The syntax of the *kill* command is *kill [signal] processid*, where *signal* is symbolic or numeric. The numeric value for the SIGHUP signal is 1.
12. "*man -s4 passwd*" is correct. The passwd file (and all other files) is discussed in man pages section 4. The "*man passwd*" command will display information about the *passwd* command.

A.2 Chapter 2: Installation

1. B is correct. The *-d* option causes *patchadd* to not save backout information. The *patchrm* command is used to delete patches. Patch status is displayed with *patchadd -p*.
2. D is correct. The *pkgchk -v pkgname* command lists all files and directories in *pkgname*. The *pkginfo -l* command does not list files contained in a package. B is incorrect because "bnu" is not the name of the package.
3. B is correct.
4. A, B, D, and G are correct. The collision rate and MAC address are irrelevant.
5. A, D, and E are correct. There are no "upgrade" CDs.
6. C is correct. *patchadd -p* or *showrev -p* are used to show installed patch information. There are no "permanently installed" software packages or partially installed patches.
7. B is correct. *pkginfo -x* is used to show patch information. *pkginfo -v* is used to display information about a specific version of a package. *pkgchk -i* is used to check packages listed in a text file.
8. A is correct. *patchadd -p* shows installed patches, not patches that should be installed. Obsoleted patches do not need to be removed. *patchadd -p* (nor any other command) does not indicate whether this is a required patch.
9. C is correct.
10. A is correct. B is not the best answer, because there is no mention of backing up the system. C is incorrect because there is no *reboot --*

-upgrade command. D is incorrect because it is not necessary to partition the boot disk.

11. *pkginfo -l* or *pkginfo -x* are correct. Both show packages and their versions.
12. *patchadd -d 109545-03* is correct. The *-d* option is used to install a patch without backout information.

A.3 Chapter 3: The Boot PROM

1. B is correct. The *devalias* PROM command is used to set device aliases. These last until the next system reset or power cycle. The *nvalias* PROM command is used to make permanent changes to device aliases.
2. C is correct. The *nvalias* PROM command is used to make permanent changes to device aliases.
3. D and E are correct. The correct syntaxes for setting PROM configuration variables are *setenv variable value* and *eeprom [variable[=value]]*.
4. C is correct. The correct sequence is to first see if the system responds to a Stop A on the console, and if that is ineffective, then to power-cycle and boot the system.
5. A is correct. The *security-mode* configuration variable determines which commands are allowed without having to supply the PROM password.
6. A, B, C, and E are correct. D is incorrect, because the PROM's settings are preserved when the system is reset or power-cycled.
7. B is correct. Because *auto-boot?* is *false*, the system will stop at the Boot PROM prompt at powerup. The *boot* command will boot the system from the boot-device, in case *disk*.
8. D is correct. The correct syntax is *eeprom [variable [=value]]*. Allowable examples of the *eeprom* command are: *eeprom*, *eeprom auto-boot?*, *eeprom auto-boot?=true*.
9. D is correct. The *nvalias* command is used so that the new device alias will not be destroyed at the next system reset or power cycle. Since this device is booted from only in emergencies, the boot-device variable is not changed.
10. B is correct. Answers C and D are also true, but B is the best answer. The *security-mode* variable has nothing to do with PROM audit logging (there is no such thing as PROM audit logging).
11. *setenv boot-device net* or *eeprom boot-device=net* are correct.
12. *setenv boot device disk3* or *eeprom boot-device=disk3* are correct.

A.4 Chapter 4: Initialization and Shutdown

1. C is correct. The entry that determines default run level is the initdefault entry in */etc/inittab*. The entry reads "`is:3:initdefault:`" and the 3 determines that the system's default run level is 3.
2. A, C, and D are correct. The *who -r* command is used to view the current run level. *init -r* and *takedown* are not valid commands.
3. B is correct. The *-r* option, when it follows the double-hyphen delimiter ("- -"), is passed to the PROM's boot program.
4. A is correct. The *-s* boot flag boots the system to single-user mode (run level "s").
5. D is correct. */dev/null* is the correct response when */etc/system* is corrupted, incorrect, or missing.
6. B is correct. The syntax of the *halt* and *poweroff* commands are the same. The only difference is that the *poweroff* command also removes system power after halting the system.
7. C is correct. Answer B (*shutdown -i5 -g0*) gives users no opportunity to log off. Answers A and D are incorrect because of improper command syntax.
8. A is correct. The system's run level follows the words "run level" in *who -r* output.
9. D is correct. The system's previous run level is the last item in *who -r* response.
10. C is correct. A is incorrect because the *initdefault* entry is not in */etc/system*. B and D are incorrect—they are the wrong course of action.
11. *shutdown –i5* or *init 5* is correct. Run level 5 is the shutdown and powerdown run state. Although the *poweroff* command also removes power, it is not considered a graceful shutdown.
12. *-d* is correct. This is the option to force a crash dump before rebooting.

A.5 Chapter 5: User Administration

1. A is correct.
2. B is correct. The *useradd –D skel_dir=/etc/skel* command sets */etc/skel* as the default skeleton file directory. When the *useradd* command is used to create accounts, files such as *.profile* will be copied from */etc/skel* to the new user's home directory.

3. C is correct. *find* is used to search for files matching specific criteria.
4. A is correct. The *rusers* command is used to list which users are logged on to remote machines.
5. A, D, and H are correct. *-exec* is used to specify a command to execute on the result list. *-user* is used to specify a particular owner of a file. *-print* is used to display the output to the screen.
6. B is correct. The fourth field determines the user's primary group ID. The user's secondary groupids are determined by the */etc/group* file.
7. D is correct. This is determined in the */etc/group* file, which is not shown.
8. C is correct. The group *staff* has a password, which the user will have to supply when entering the *newgrp* command.
9. D is correct. The letters NP mean "No Password." No password entered could possibly encrypt to the string "NP."
10. B is correct. All of the accounts would have unique passwords, although from a system perspective they are the same account, since their userids are the same.
11. *useradd* is correct. The *useradd* command is used to add new user accounts, or to change the *useradd* command defaults.
12. *find -user* is correct. The scenario states that we need to find all files owned by a user that was removed. You would have to determine the numeric ID of the user, and then construct a complete command line similar to the following:

```
find / -user 1002 -print
```

A.6 Chapter 6: Files and Directories

1. B and C are correct. The syntax of *mv* is *mv source target*.
2. B is correct. The *-f* option specifies that files are to be removed regardless of permissions (provided they are owned by the user deleting them).
3. A is correct.
4. D is correct. The directory */lib*, and its contents, are moved to the subdirectory *bin/*. What we do not know is the absolute location of *bin/* (not that it matters in this case).
5. B is correct. The *-i* option is the "interactive" option; *rm* asks for confirmation before removing each file.

6. D is correct. The *rmdir* command does not remove a directory that is not empty.
7. C is correct. When the *source* and *target* are both files, and if *target* already exists, it is overwritten by the contents of *source*. Further, the file *source* is removed.
8. A is correct. From the dialogue shown it cannot be determined whether the directories or files are empty.
9. B is correct. *grep* displays all lines in the file *goods.txt* that begin with the string “624”.
10. B and C are correct. A, D, and E are incorrect because *rmdir* does not remove empty directories.
11. *ls -a* is correct.
12. *mv /lib /tmp* is correct.

A.7 Chapter 7: vi Editor

1. B is correct. The command to delete a line is *dd*; prepending a *3* tells vi to delete three lines.
2. D is correct.
3. A is correct. The structure of the *search-and-replace* command is *:startline,endline s/oldtext/newtext/g*.
4. A is correct. *vedit* runs vi in beginner mode. *viewedit* and *vi –b* are both invalid. *vi -w* is used for nonstandard screen sizes.
5. C is correct. The *showmodes* setting determines whether vi will display which mode it is currently in.
6. A is correct. *:set all* is used to display all current settings.
7. B is correct. Settings are turned off with the *:set nosetting* command.
8. D is correct. The *+command* option is used to execute *command* after starting vi.
9. C is correct. The message “OPEN MODE” at the bottom of the screen indicates that the *o* or *O* command has been entered, which puts vi into input mode.
10. B is correct. The h, j, k, and l keys represent left, down, up, and right.
11. *:set showmode* is correct.
12. *:w message.tmp* is correct. This is the format used to save the edited file to another file name.

A.8 Chapter 8: Disks

1. B, D, and F are correct. The *fsck*, *format*, *newfs*, and *prtvtoc* commands access a raw disk device. The *df* and *mount* commands access a block disk device.
2. A, B, D, E, and F are correct. C is incorrect, because *format* does not view or change SCSI addresses.
3. C is correct. Slice (or partition) number 2 represents the entire disk device.
4. B, C, and G are correct. The only valid units of measure for partition sizes are cylinders, blocks, megabytes, and gigabytes.
5. D is correct. Disk partitions may never overlap.
6. B is correct. The *-o b=n* option is used in *fsck* to specify an alternate superblock.
7. A is correct. *partition id* is informational only and has no influence on how the partition is used.
8. D is correct. The *label* command causes new partition information to be written to the disk.
9. A is correct. Before performing any disk tests or operations, all data must be backed up. After testing the disk, bad blocks may be added to the defect list.
10. B is correct. The *partition id* is an informational label only.
11. "*devfsadm*" is correct.
12. "/reconfigure" is correct.

A.9 Chapter 9: File Systems

1. C is correct. */etc/vfstab* is the file containing file systems to be mounted at boot time.
2. D is correct. */etc/mnttab* is the file containing currently mounted file systems.
3. A is correct. The *-F file-system-type* option of the *mount* command is used to specify the type of file system to be mounted.
4. C, D, E, and G are correct. NFS is a network file system type. DFS and ISO are not valid file system types.
5. B is correct. The *-f* option of the *umount* command is used to forcibly unmount a file system.
6. A is correct.
7. A is correct. Formatting the diskette with the *fdformat -d* command is all that is needed to create a DOS-format diskette.

8. C is correct. A symbolic link, */export/data/sales.db* that points to */usr/local/data/sales.db*, will cause file input/output to */export/data/sales.db* to actually be carried out on the original file, */usr/local/data/sales.db*. A is incorrect because there is no such thing as a shared inode. D is incorrect because there is no such thing as a shadow copy. B is incorrect because hard links cannot reference a file in another file system.
9. B is correct. A is incorrect because system memory size has nothing to do with the PROCFS file system. C, D, and E are incorrect because PROCFS does not perform the stated functions.
10. D is correct. Files and directories in a directory used as a mount point are hidden until the file system is unmounted.
11. *mount –F hsfs –o ro /dev/dsk/c0t6d0s0 /cdrom* is correct. These are the minimum elements required to mount a CD-ROM.
12. */etc/mnttab* is correct. This file contains a list of all mounted file systems.

A10 Chapter 10: Backup and Recovery

1. C is correct. The *cpio -p* command preserves ACLs, copies device files, and is used to copy files and directories to another location.
2. A is correct. The format of a basic extract command is *tar xf tar-archive file-to-extract*. *tar* does not precede options with a hyphen.
3. B is correct. Because the position of the tape is unknown, it must first be rewound (*mt rewind*). Then, the tape must be advanced to the third archive (*mt fsf 3*). Only then can the correct archive be read.
4. B, C, E, and F are correct. *cpio* can read tar archives with the *-H tar* option, but *cpio* cannot create tar archives. *cpio* archives can be interchanged between different UNIX systems, and it can create multi-tape archives. *cpio* has no compression or freshen options.
5. A and C are correct. *tar* lacks a compression option, so a tar archive must be compressed separately. The tar archive can be compressed as it is created (answer A) or after it is created (answer C). Answer D is incorrect because of faulty syntax.
6. D is correct. The format for restoring a file to an alternate location is *zip ziparchive file-to-extract -d location*. Answers A, B, and C have incorrect syntax.
7. A and B are correct. *tar* will write to the tape device defined by the TAPE environment variable or in the file */etc/default/tar*.

8. C is correct. The no-rewind device does not rewind after a file is written to it. Other tape devices automatically rewind after a file is written to it.
9. B and C are correct. The only viable options are to move the file to a larger file system, or write the compressed output to another file system.
10. B is correct. This is the command used to copy the contents of a directory to */tmp*.
11. *ufsrestore xf /dev/rmt/0* is correct.
12. *zcat root.tar.Z | tar tf -* or *uncompress -c root.tar.Z | tar tf -* is correct.

A11 Chapter 11: Security

1. A is correct. *chmod* is used to change permission settings on files and directories.
2. B, C, D, and E are correct. A is incorrect; we know *foo* is a file because of the presence of *default* ACL entries. This output was generated by the *getfacl* command.
3. A, C, and E are correct. *xdir* is a directory; group permissions are "---" which signifies that the groupid *staff* has no access to *xdir*. Username *gsmith* does own the directory. The "+" signifies the presence of an Access Control List (ACL), which contains additional information about who has what access to *xdir*.
4. B is correct. *umask* determines the value of subsequently created files and directories.
5. D is correct.
6. C is correct.
7. B is correct. The *chgrp* command changes the groupid for a file or directory.
8. A is correct. When the group permission is 2, 4, or 6, mandatory file locking is set on the file.
9. C is correct.
10. D is correct. This is an undefined condition.
11. *getfacl* is correct.
12. *chgrp –R* is correct.

A12 Chapter 12: Remote Administration

1. D is correct. There is no command to resume session mode; just press return at the *telnet>* prompt to return to it.

2. B is correct. *rsh* is the remote shell command used to run a command on another system.
3. A, C, E, and F are correct. *bye* and *swap* are not valid telnet commands.
4. A and B are correct. There is no *rcopy* command; *telnet* is a session program that does not transfer files; *rsh* is a remote shell program; there is no *move* command.
5. C is correct. "~." is the connection sequence used to forcibly close a telnet connection.
6. B is correct. *telnet* is used to log in to another system. *login* is used to log in to the local system. *rtelnet* and *logrem* are not valid commands.
7. B and C are correct. Only the valid *R* commands (*rlogin*, *rcp*, *rsh*) use */etc/hosts.equiv*.
8. A is correct. The *.rhosts* file contains a list of users on which systems are allowed to log into this system without having to supply a password. Answers B and C are not correct, since each answer specifies only users and hosts, respectively.
9. D is correct. A is incorrect: User *herbert* may rlogin from any system. B is incorrect: Only user *george* on the system *spinach* may *rlogin*. C is incorrect, because of the negative entry *–walker*.
10. A is correct. */etc/nologins* prevents remote logins; its contents state why. It is not a logfile, and it has nothing to do with root logging in at the console.
11. *rcp -r /etc rookie:/etc* is correct.
12. *mget* * is correct.

APPENDIX B

Examination Objectives

The objectives in Table B.1 define the scope of material covered by the Sun Certified System Administrator for Solaris 8 Operating Environment Exam, Part I.

Table B.1 *Examination Objectives*

Objective Section	Objective	Covered in Chapter
System Concepts	Match selected system administration terms to their respective definitions: daemons, shell, file system, kernel, operating system.	1
	Define the effect of using various main command options when viewing online manual pages.	
Process Control	List the commands that display information for all active processes on the system.	1
	State the effect of sending a specified signal to a process.	
	List the commands used to terminate an active process.	

Table B.1 *Examination Objectives (Continued)*

Objective Section	Objective	Covered in Chapter
Installation	Describe the sequence of steps required to perform the Solaris 8 Operating Environment software installation on a networked standalone system.	2
	Identify the function of the following package administration commands: *pkgadd*, *pkginfo*, *pkgchk*, and *pkgrm*.	
	Identify the steps required to install a patch, verify which patches are currently installed, and remove a patch using the *patchadd*, *patchrm*, or *showrev* commands.	
The Boot Prom	State or recognize the combination of actions required to interrupt a nonresponsive system.	3
	State the command strings used to manipulate custom device aliases.	
Initialization and Shutdown	Match the Solaris run levels to their intended functions.	4
	State the function of the following files or directories and the relationships between them: */etc/inittab*, */etc/init.d*, */etc/rc#* (where # falls in the range of 0 to 6, or S), or */etc/rc#.d* (where # falls in the range of 0 to 6, or S).	
	Identify the commands used to change the run level of a system to a specified state.	
The Boot Process	Match the boot command options to their respective functions.	4
	Select the command that reports the current run level of a Solaris system.	
	Given a sample run control directory, differentiate between the basic activity in a script whose name begins with an uppercase S and a script whose name begins with an uppercase K.	
User Administration	Identify the following login procedures: Log in to a system, log out of a system, and change login passwords.	5
	State the command used to identify which users are currently logged into the system.	
	State the steps required to create user accounts on the local system using the admintool utility.	
	State the command syntax to add, modify, or delete user / group accounts on the local system with the *useradd*, *groupadd*, *usermod*, *groupmod*, *userdel*, or *groupdel* commands.	
	Given a user's login shell, list the shell initialization files used to set up a user's work environment at login.	

Table B.1 *Examination Objectives (Continued)*

Objective Section	Objective	Covered in Chapter
Basic Command Syntax	Using absolute or relative pathnames, select valid command strings to move between specified points within a given directory tree.	6
	Select the metacharacter combinations necessary to construct pathname abbreviations for access to files and directories within the directory tree.	
	State the commands needed to list the contents of directories and determine the file types within a directory.	
	List the commands used to create or remove directories.	
	State the commands used to copy, create, rename, or remove files.	
Security	Identify how to search for regular expressions in the contents of one or more files.	6
	List command sequences used to display or modify file and directory permissions.	11
	Differentiate the effect of selected umask values on the permissions assigned to newly created files and directories.	
	List in sequence the steps to create, modify, and delete Access Control Lists (ACLs) on files.	
Editor	List the keyboard sequences that are required to switch between the three modes of operation used by the vi editor.	7
	State the vi editor commands used to position and move the cursor, create and delete text, and copy or move text.	
	Match the correct vi command sequences with their respective search and replace functions.	
Disk Configuration	Select the command used to add device configuration information for a new disk device without requiring a reboot of Solaris.	8
	Differentiate between the uses of a character (raw) disk (*/dev/rdsk*) and a block disk (*/dev/dsk*).	
Format	Identify the correct usage of the *format* command.	8
	Select correct statements about the use of the menu selections for the *format* command.	
	Select correct statements about the use of the menu selections for the partition subcommand under the *format* command.	

Table B.1 *Examination Objectives (Continued)*

Objective Section	Objective	Covered in Chapter
File Systems	List the different types of file systems in the Solaris Operating Environment.	9
	State the effect of the commonly used options of the *mount* command.	
	Differentiate between the purpose of the */etc/mnttab* and */etc/vfstab* files.	
	Select correct statements about the intended purpose of the */etc*, */opt*, */usr*, */export*, and / (the root) directories.	
	List the steps required to access data on diskettes or CD-ROMs.	
Files and Directories	Match the file types of regular files, directories, symbolic links, device files, and hard links to their respective functions.	9
	State the commands used to reduce the size of files and directories for storage to tape.	10
Backup and Recovery	Match listed backup, archive, and restore utilities to their respective functional capabilities.	10
	Identify the commands and steps required to back up a file system to tape.	
	Identify the commands and steps required to restore a file system from tape.	
Remote Connection	State the command to perform remote system operations such as remote login, remote copy, and remote shell commands.	12
	State the subcommands that are used by the ftp utility to transfer files between a local system and a remote system.	

APPENDIX C

Sample Pre-Test Agreement

This is a sample of the agreement to which all Solaris Certification exam takers must assent before taking the exam. The agreement consists of definitions of personal responsibility, testing regulations, nondisclosure, exam userid/ password, and privacy. This is followed by three questions asked of the exam taker, which are also included here.

For more information on exam terms and conditions, please read the Preface.

CERTIFICATION CANDIDATE PRE-TEST AGREEMENT

THIS AGREEMENT GOVERNS ALL SUN CERTIFICATION TESTS. YOU MUST CLICK "I AGREE" ON QUESTION 1 BELOW TO TAKE THE TEST.

THE TEST WILL STOP IF YOU CLICK "I DO NOT AGREE" ON QUESTION 1.

A. *Personal Responsibility*. I agree that all work submitted by me in satisfaction of certification requirements (for example, test taking, submission of exercises, etc.) shall be entirely my own. I will neither: (a) provide or accept improper assistance; nor (b) use unauthorized materials (collectively "Misconduct") in attempting to satisfy certification requirements. I understand that if Sun determines that I have engaged in Misconduct, Sun may revoke any certifications and rights previously granted to me, and may prohibit me from any further participation in the Certification Program.

B. *Testing Regulations*. In taking any test, I will comply with all testing regulations including but not limited to testing regulations governing the materials that I may bring into the testing area and/or refer to during the test. After completing any test, I will return all testing materials to the test administrator. I understand that I must wait at least two (2) weeks before trying to re-take any test, and that I may not take any test more than three (3) times within any calendar year without written permission from the Sun Certification Program Manager.

C. *Nondisclosure*. I understand and agree that the content of all tests and any test materials are proprietary and confidential information of Sun, and I agree not to disclose or share any of the content of these materials. In addition, I shall not ask for, write (in any media), publish, or otherwise disclose any test questions or answers.

D. *User ID and Password*. I understand and agree that I will receive a user ID to access the Sun Candidate database (the "Database"). I understand that I must create my own password to the Database the first time that I access the Database. I understand and agree that the user ID is confidential and proprietary information of Sun and/or its authorized vendors. I understand and agree that I am responsible for any and all activities resulting from any use of the user ID issued to me in conjunction with my password. I agree that in the event I believe that the user ID or password has been stolen, used by unauthorized persons or otherwise compromised, I will immediately notify Sun by sending an email to: who2contact@central.sun.com.

E. *Data Privacy*. Sun Microsystems respects your desire for privacy. Sun will collect, store, process, and use data collected from this test in order to process and validate your test, mail you the results of your test and certification documents if you pass, and to contact you with test satisfaction inquiries. The information collected will not be distributed outside Sun. However Sun may share your personal data with those companies with which Sun has contracted to perform some of these testing services for the purposes listed above. Sun will comply with the provisions and principles of the applicable data protection legislation and makes every effort to contract with companies that also value data protection and meet Sun's standards. Data may be transferred from your location to Sun or its affiliated companies in other countries. Test information provided to Sun in this context will be gathered by Prometric and transmitted to a secure, password-protected, database controlled by Sun's authorized vendors and accessible by authorized persons only. Your information will be stored only for the length of time necessary to complete the process listed above and in compliance with related record retention regulations.

You may request a copy of your personal data in Sun's records or update your personal information by email, fax or in writing; to do so, please refer to the URL regarding Sun's Privacy Policy on your score sheet at the end of your examination.

Question 1: BY CLICKING THE "I AGREE" BUTTON BELOW YOU STATE THAT YOU HAVE READ AND UNDERSTAND THIS AGREEMENT, THAT YOU AGREE TO BE BOUND BY ITS TERMS AND CONDITIONS, AND THAT YOU AGREE THAT SUN MAY COLLECT, STORE, PROCESS AND USE YOUR DATA IN ACCORDANCE WITH THE SECTION ENTITLED "DATA PRIVACY," ABOVE.

{I Agree}

{I Do Not Agree}

If you press this button, the test will stop.

{Are you Sure you want to stop the Test?}

{Yes, I want to stop the Test}

If you press this button the test will stop and you may obtain a refund of your money by following the directions printed on the score sheet.

{No, I want to go back to the Pre-Test Agreement}

[If the Candidate presses this button, return Candidate to the beginning of the Agreement]

[The following questions will be asked only if the Candidate answers "I Agree" to the previous question]

YOU MAY TAKE THE TEST IF YOU CLICK "I DO NOT AGREE" ON QUESTIONS 2 & 3.

Question 2: Sun may use my address or other contact information to contact me by email, fax, letter or telephone regarding product announcements, program information, events, or other related Sun activities. (You may take the Test even if you press "I Do Not Agree").

{I Agree}

{I Do Not Agree}

Question 3: Sun may share my address or other contact information with other companies to have them contact me by email, fax, letter or telephone regarding product announcement, program information, events, or other related Sun activities. (You may take the Test even if you press "I Do Not Agree).

{I Agree}

{I Do Not Agree}

APPENDIX D

Sun Certification Program Policy on Candidate Misconduct

This appendix contains Sun's policy on candidate misconduct. For more information on exam terms and conditions, please refer back to the Preface. Because terms and conditions are likely to change over time, please refer to Sun's Certification Web site for the latest available information.

The Sun Certification Program (the "Certification Program") is designed to recognize personal knowledge and skill with respect to particular technologies. Sun has created a series of certification tests designed to objectively measure individual knowledge and skill with respect to a technology. The credential conferred by the Certification Program delivers its greatest value to you only as long as the Test is secure and continues to operate as a measure of personal knowledge and skill. Sun requires every candidate for Sun Certification to assist in maintaining the integrity and security of the Tests.

All candidates for Sun Certification are required to read and click through the Candidate Pre-Test Agreement immediately prior to taking a Sun Certification Test, denoting the candidate's agreement that all work submitted by the candidate in satisfaction of certification requirements (for example, test taking, submission of exercises, etc.) shall be entirely that of the Candidate. Read sample Candidate Pre-Test Agreement. Candidates may neither: (a) provide or accept improper assistance; nor (b) use unauthorized materials in attempting to satisfy certification requirements.

Sun requires all candidates to comply with all testing regulations imposed by Sun or its test administration vendor, in connection with taking a Sun Certification Test. Sun has a 2-week minimum waiting period before a candidate may attempt to re-take any test. In addition, a candidate may not attempt to take a test more than three (3) times within any calendar year without written permission from the Sun Certification Program Manager.

The content of all tests and test materials are proprietary and confidential information of Sun. Candidates may not disclose or share any of the content of these materials; nor may candidates ask for, write (in any media), publish, or otherwise disclose any test questions or answers.

Candidates may not forge certificates, misuse their user ID or password in the Sun Certification Candidate Database, or misrepresent themselves as Sun Certified. Sun may revoke any Sun Certified status or other rights previously conferred on any candidate, and may permanently bar candidates from participating in the Sun Certification Program, if Sun determines that a candidate has engaged in any misconduct with respect to the Sun Certification Program, including, but not limited to the prohibited conduct outlined in this policy.

APPENDIX E

Supplemental Information

This appendix contains additional materials on Solaris commands. The sections in this appendix are:

- User Interfaces
- Using the System
- Entering Individual Commands and Options
- Command Syntax in the Reference Manual
- Commands
- Configuration Files

E.1 User Interfaces

The user interface refers to the software used to communicate with the user. The system sends information to the user through the monitor and speaker; the user sends information to the system through the keyboard and mouse.

There are two types of user interfaces: character and graphical. Their descriptions follow.

Character User Interfaces

The character interface takes keyboard input from the user to communicate with the system (a few "nonprintable" characters—by nonprintable characters I mean characters like line feeds, ^C, Tabs, etc.—are also used). Only the keyboard and monitor are used in character interfaces.

The Shell

The shell is the primary character-interface program. The shell is a part of the operating system, accepting user-issued commands and displaying command results. The three most popular shells supplied with Solaris are the Bourne Shell, the C-Shell, and the Korn Shell. Chapter 5 describes these shells in detail.

Graphical User Interfaces

The graphical interface uses visually enhanced features. These features include windows and the ability to "point" to different parts of the screen. With the proper software, a user can view and even draw pictures using a graphical interface. In addition to the keyboard and monitor, the mouse is also used in the graphical interface; it is used to "point" to and "select" items on the screen.

Although the graphical interface provides several tools that can be used to manage the system, a shell interface is also provided so that a user can interact with the system using a character interface. This is necessary since many of the administrative tools used in Solaris are character oriented.

Solaris provides two graphical user interfaces: OpenWindows and the Common Desktop Environment, or CDE. CDE is described in the next section. While OpenWindows is still provided with Solaris, it may not be included in future releases.

E.2 Using the System

Logging In and Logging Out of the System

Any user wishing to use the system must first log in by entering his or her userid and password at the login prompt. The userid and password are supplied by the system administrator.

On systems using a character interface, the login prompt resembles the following:

```
SunOS 5.8
login: gsmith
Password: ********
Last login: Fri Nov 17 15:04:48 from spica
Sun Microsystems Inc. SunOS 5.8 Generic February 2000
You have mail.
$
```

Figure E-1 illustrates the login prompt on systems using a graphical interface.

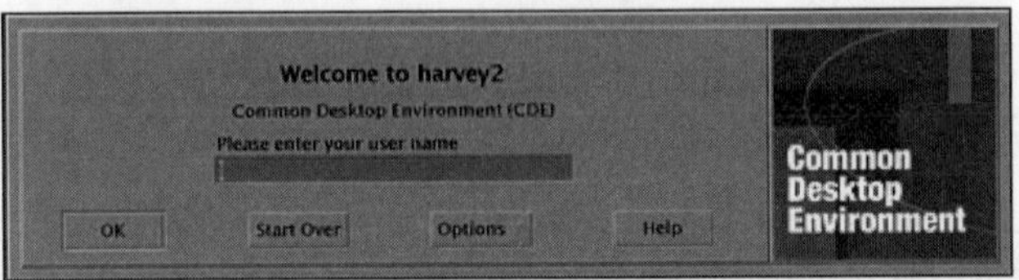

Figure E–1 *Graphical Interface Login Screen*

Interacting with the Character Environment

After logging in to a character environment system, you will see a shell prompt that the UNIX administrator has set up for you. This prompt may be as simple as a dollar sign ("$"), a pound sign ("#"), or it may be more elaborate, perhaps showing your userid, the system name, and/or your current working directory.

At the prompt, you can enter any valid UNIX command. The results of that command will be displayed to the screen unless you "redirect" the output of that command elsewhere (see Chapter 6 for details on redirection).

Entering Basic Commands

Entering commands is as easy as typing them in and reading the output. A short sample session is shown here.

```
# uname -a
SunOS wallace 5.8 Generic sun4u sparc SUNW,Ultra-1
# date
Wed Nov 22 05:55:15 PST 2000
# df -k
```

```
Filesystem             kbytes    used   avail capacity  Mounted on
/dev/dsk/c0t0d0s0     1897375 1240304  600150    68%    /
/proc                       0       0       0     0%    /proc
fd                          0       0       0     0%    /dev/fd
mnttab                      0       0       0     0%    /etc/mnttab
swap                   595112       8  595104     1%    /var/run
swap                   595112       8  595104     1%    /tmp
/dev/dsk/c0t0d0s7     1653183  734286  869302    46%    /export/home
# ps -l
 F S   UID    PID   PPID  C PRI NI     ADDR     SZ   WCHAN TTY     TIME CMD
 8 R   0      365    363  0  51 20 707ec778    131         pts/2   0:00 sh
#
```

PAGING OUTPUT WITH THE *more* COMMAND

Commands that produce many lines of output can be "paged" through the *more* command. This pauses the output after every full screen so that each page can be read as needed. Paging output is especially useful on today's fast systems that can produce output far faster than we can read it.

To page output with *more*, append the characters "| more" to the end of a command. An example follows.

```
$ ls -l|more
total 27540
-r-xr-xr-x   1 root     bin        20796 Jan  5  2000 acctcom
-r-xr-xr-x  38 root     bin         5256 Jan  5  2000 adb
-r-xr-xr-x   1 root     bin        10172 Jan  5  2000 addbib
-r-s--x--x   1 root     sys       341204 Jan 14  2000 admintool
-r-xr-xr-x  17 root     bin          131 Jan  5  2000 alias
-r-xr-xr-x   1 root     bin        14912 Jan  5  2000 aliasadm
-r-xr-xr-x   1 root     bin          441 Jan  5  2000 amiadmin
-r-xr-xr-x   1 root     bin          438 Jan  5  2000 amicert
-r-xr-xr-x   1 root     bin          447 Jan  5  2000 amicertify
-r-xr-xr-x   1 root     bin          448 Jan  5  2000 amidecrypt
-r-xr-xr-x   1 root     bin          448 Jan  5  2000 amiencrypt
-r-xr-xr-x   1 root     bin          453 Jan  5  2000 amikeystore
-r-xr-xr-x   1 root     bin          585 Jan  5  2000 amilogin
-r-xr-xr-x   1 root     bin          591 Jan  5  2000 amilogout
-r-xr-xr-x   1 root     bin          441 Jan  5  2000 amisign
-r-xr-xr-x   1 root     bin          447 Jan  5  2000 amiverify
-rwxr-xr-x   1 bin      bin        19832 Dec 16  1999 apm
lrwxrwxrwx   1 root     other         24 Apr  4  2000 appletviewer ->
../java/bin/appletviewer
-rwxr-xr-x   1 root     bin         9004 Jan  5  2000 apptrace
-r-xr-xr-x   4 root     bin        28900 Jan  5  2000 apropos
```

```
--More--
-rwxr-xr-x   1 root     bin        9004 Jan  5  2000 apptrace
-r-xr-xr-x   4 root     bin       28900 Jan  5  2000 apropos
-r-xr-xr-x   1 root     bin         944 Jan  5  2000 arch
-r-xr-xr-x   1 root     bin        6368 Jan  5  2000 asa
-rwsr-xr-x   1 root     sys       36320 Jan  5  2000 at
-rwsr-xr-x   1 root     sys       13796 Jan  5  2000 atq
-rwsr-xr-x   1 root     sys       12756 Jan  5  2000 atrm
-rwxr-xr-x   1 root     staff    213052 Dec  3  1999 audioconvert
-rwxr-xr-x   1 root     staff    108084 Dec  3  1999 audioplay
-rwxr-xr-x   1 root     staff     26344 Dec  3  1999 audiorecord
-r-xr-xr-x   1 root     bin        7416 Jan  5  2000 auths
-r-xr-xr-x   2 root     bin       85828 Jan  5  2000 awk
-r-xr-xr-x   1 root     bin        6344 Jan  5  2000 banner
-r-xr-xr-x   1 root     bin         901 Jan  5  2000 basename
-r-xr-xr-x   1 root     bin      516392 Jan  5  2000 bash
-r-xr-xr-x   1 root     bin         321 Jan  5  2000 batch
-r-xr-xr-x   1 root     bin       25600 Jan  5  2000 bc
-rwxr-xr-x   1 root     bin       10160 Jan  5  2000 bdiff
-r-xr-xr-x   1 root     bin       23776 Jan  5  2000 bfs
-r-xr-xr-x  17 root     bin         131 Jan  5  2000 bg
-r-xr-xr-x   3 root     bin       23936 Jan  5  2000 bunzip2
-r-xr-xr-x   1 root     bin       16884 Jan  5  2000 busstat
-r-xr-xr-x   3 root     bin       23936 Jan  5  2000 bzcat
-r-xr-xr-x   3 root     bin       23936 Jan  5  2000 bzip2
--More--

-r-xr-xr-x   1 root     bin         944 Jan  5  2000 arch
-r-xr-xr-x   1 root     bin        6368 Jan  5  2000 asa
-rwsr-xr-x   1 root     sys       36320 Jan  5  2000 at
-rwsr-xr-x   1 root     sys       13796 Jan  5  2000 atq
-rwsr-xr-x   1 root     sys       12756 Jan  5  2000 atrm
-rwxr-xr-x   1 root     staff    213052 Dec  3  1999 audioconvert
-rwxr-xr-x   1 root     staff    108084 Dec  3  1999 audioplay
-rwxr-xr-x   1 root     staff     26344 Dec  3  1999 audiorecord
-r-xr-xr-x   1 root     bin        7416 Jan  5  2000 auths
-r-xr-xr-x   2 root     bin       85828 Jan  5  2000 awk
-r-xr-xr-x   1 root     bin        6344 Jan  5  2000 banner
-r-xr-xr-x   1 root     bin         901 Jan  5  2000 basename
-r-xr-xr-x   1 root     bin      516392 Jan  5  2000 bash
-r-xr-xr-x   1 root     bin         321 Jan  5  2000 batch
-r-xr-xr-x   1 root     bin       25600 Jan  5  2000 bc
-rwxr-xr-x   1 root     bin       10160 Jan  5  2000 bdiff
-r-xr-xr-x   1 root     bin       23776 Jan  5  2000 bfs
-r-xr-xr-x  17 root     bin         131 Jan  5  2000 bg
-r-xr-xr-x   3 root     bin       23936 Jan  5  2000 bunzip2
```

```
-r-xr-xr-x   1 root     bin         16884 Jan  5  2000 busstat
-r-xr-xr-x   3 root     bin         23936 Jan  5  2000 bzcat
-r-xr-xr-x   3 root     bin         23936 Jan  5  2000 bzip2
--More--
(remainder of output suppressed)
```

At each "--More--" prompt, pressing the spacebar causes another screen full of output to be displayed. Other commands that can be used in *more* include:

- RETURN. Scrolls one more line of output.
- *b*. Scrolls back one screen full.
- *d*. Scroll forward one half a screen full instead of an entire screen full.
- *v*. Edit with the vi editor (works only if more is displaying a file, not output from a command).
- */text*. Search for "text"; *more* scrolls forward and stops if string "text" is found.
- *q*. Quit.

CONTROL CHARACTERS

There are some special control characters that are useful in the character environment. They include:

- ^U. This is used to erase what you have typed in the command line (provided you haven't pressed Enter yet). This might be easier than pressing the Backspace key, especially if you have typed in a lot of characters. The notation "^U" is shorthand for pressing and holding the Ctrl key, then pressing U, then releasing both keys.
- ^C. This is used to stop the execution of a command that is running. Pressing ^C will not "undo" what the command has already done, but it will prevent further execution. For instance, if you enter a command to remove several files and you press ^C, any files which have already been removed will not be "unremoved," but any files which have not yet been removed will still not be removed.
- ^S. This is used to temporarily halt the output from a command. This was more useful when terminals connected to UNIX systems (and the systems themselves) were much slower than they are today. Many commands produce output so quickly that it is

impossible to press ^S before all of the output has scrolled by. But for commands that produce output slowly (such as writing files to tape), this is still helpful.

- ^Q. This is used to resume the output from a command when ^S has been pressed.

Interacting with the Common Desktop Environment (CDE)

Figure E-2 shows an example CDE screen that appears when a new user logs in for the first time. If the local UNIX administrator has made changes to the environment, of course, the screen will appear different.

Let's explore the components of the CDE Environment shown in Figure E-2.

Front Panel

The Front Panel is the "dashboard" for the CDE environment. It gives you point-and-click and drag-and-drop access to the majority of

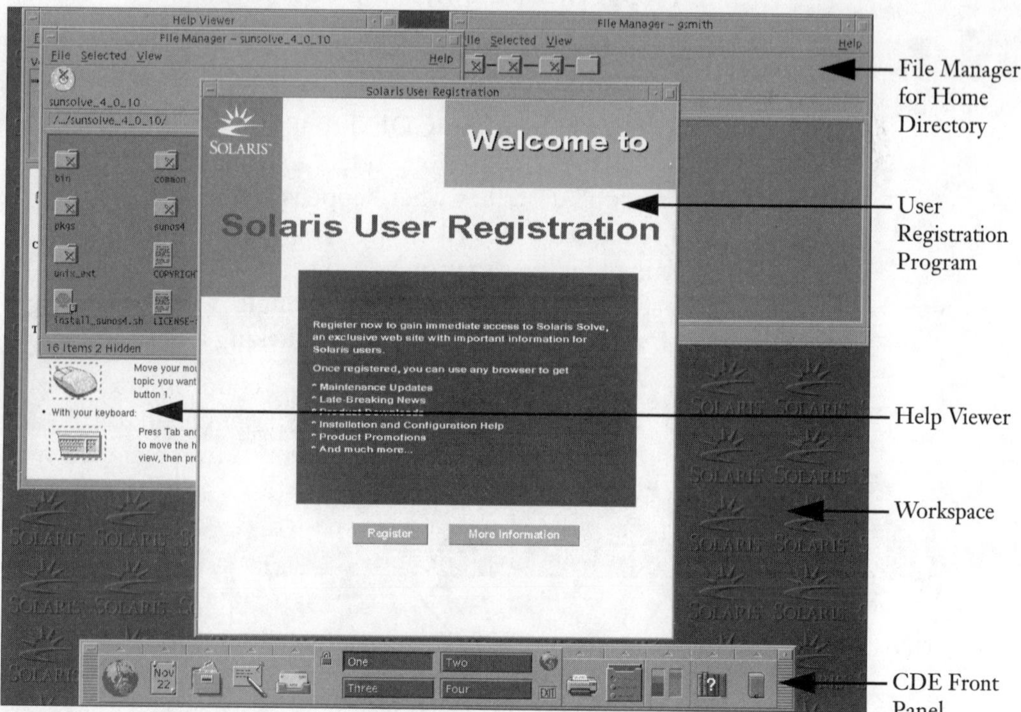

Figure E–2 *Representation of the CDE Environment*

applications on your system; it allows you to switch workspaces; and it displays information such as time and date, printer status, and so on. You can customize your Front Panel to include your favorite applications, and you can move or minimize the Front Panel.

The Front Panel enables you to run the common actions on the Main Panel with one click of the mouse, and you can activate the 30 or so other controls on the subpanels with two clicks of the mouse. Controls are grouped logically into subpanels, making them easier to find.

Many controls on the Front Panel act as "drop zones" that carry out actions on files and text, often interpreting the required action by looking at the file contents. For instance, if you drop a mail message on the activity drop zone (spinning globe) it opens the message in Mailer, but if you drop a text file on the same drop zone, it opens the file in Text Editor. Front Panel is also fully Web-aware, running the Web browser when you drop bookmark files, URL text, or HTML files on appropriate drop zones.

Many controls on the Front Panel also act as indicators, displaying time and date, print and mail status, workstation performance, and so on.

The CDE Front Panel is shown in Figure E-3.

Subpanels

The controls and subpanels in the CDE Front Panel are explained in Table E.1. In this table, "Click Action" refers to a single right-click on the item; "Drop Action" describes what happens when a file is dropped on the item; and "Indicator" describes any variations in appearance and the meaning explained by the variation.

Clicking a subpanel tab (the small rectangle with the triangle shown in Figure E-3) will open that subpanel. Clicking it again will close

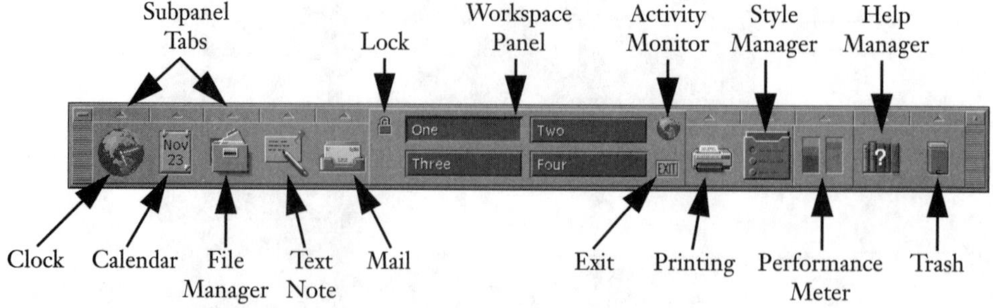

Figure E–3 *Detailed View of the CDE Front Panel*

Table E.1 *CDE Controls and Subpanels*

CONTROL	SUBPANEL	CLICK ACTION	DROP ACTION	INDICATOR
Workspace Buttons	None	Switch to Workspace; rename Workspace	None	Indicates current Workspace
Lock	None	Locks window; must be unlocked with password	None	None
Exit	None	Exits CDE, logs off	None	None
Activity Monitor	None	Displays a "Go" action dialogue box	Runs action, depending upon the type of file dropped	Spins to indicate system activity
Clock	Links	Opens the default Web browser	None	Current time
Calendar	Cards	Opens the Calendar program	Dropping an appointment file adds appointment to calendar	Current date
File Manager	Files	Opens File Manager, viewing home directory	Dropping a folder opens a File Manager view of that folder	None
Text Note	Applications	Opens Text Editor program	Dropped file or text put on the Workspace	None
Mailer	Mail	Opens Mail program	Dropped item attached to a new message window	Changes if new mail is waiting
Printing	Personal printers	Status of default printer displayed	Dropped file printed on default printer	None
Style Manager	Tools	Opens the Style Manager program	None	None
Performance Meter	Hosts	Opens the Performance Meter program	Opens the Performance Meter for the hostname dropped	CPU and disk activity
Help Manager	Help	Opens the Help application	Dropping a master volume file (*.sdl) opens a Help Viewer window with that help volume	None
Trash	Trash	Opens the Trash Can viewer, showing contents	None	Empty or not empty

the subpanel. Figure E-4 demonstrates the CDE Front Panel with the Mail and Hosts subpanels opened.

Workspace Menu

In addition to the programs listed in all of the CDE subpanels, there is also a Workspace Menu. This is another feature of the CDE that lets you select programs to run.

To start the Workspace menu, move the mouse pointer over the Workspace and right-click the mouse to bring up the Workspace menu. Many of the menu choices lead to submenus that list programs that you can run. The top-level workspace menu is shown in Figure E-5.

Figure E–4 *CDE Subpanels*

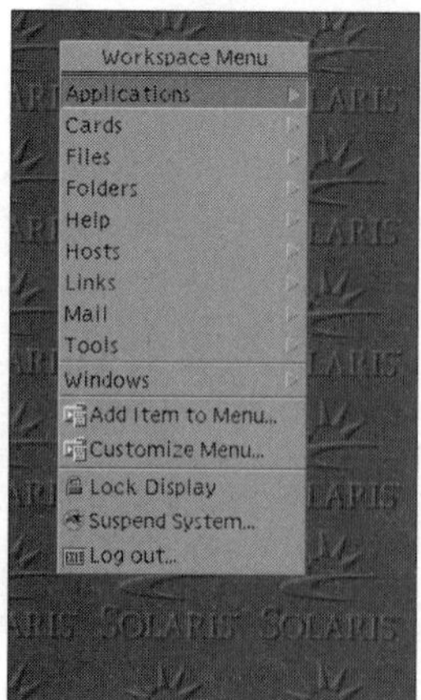

Figure E–5 *The CDE Workspace Menu*

Windows and Icons

The two primary items on a CDE screen are windows and icons. Figure E-6 shows an example of a CDE screen with windows and icons.

A *window* is a rectangle on the screen containing information related to a process. The process communicates with the user through the window by showing the user information. A Web browser, text editor, and clock are examples of processes that use windows to communicate with the user. All windows in CDE have controls that are used to resize, move, or close them. A window with its controls is shown in Figure E-7.

Table E.2 outlines each of the controls pictured in Figure E-7.

An icon results when a window is minimized. An icon is a space-saving representation of the window. Minimizing a window to an icon does not stop the program running in the window; everything in the window is intact, just "put away" until it is needed later.

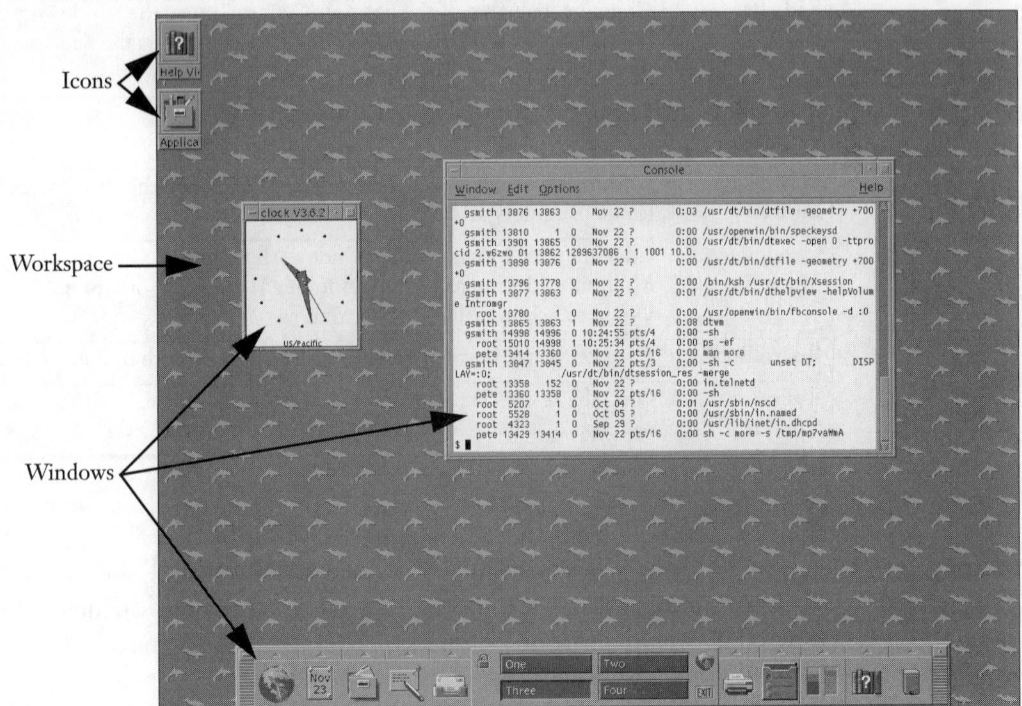

Figure E–6 *CDE Screen with Windows and Icons*

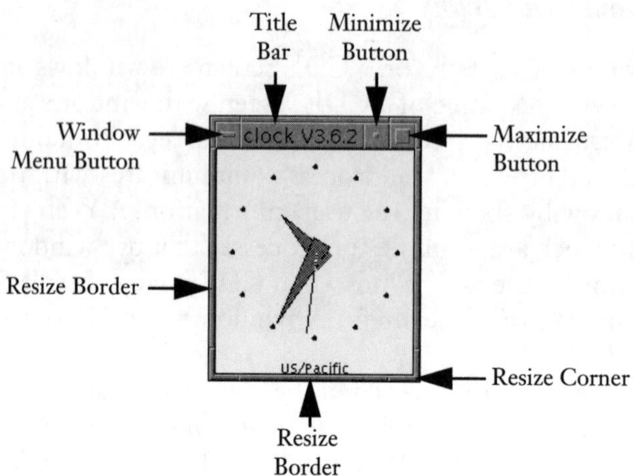

Figure E–7 *Windows and Their Controls*

Table E.2 *Explanation of CDE Window Controls*

CONTROL	DESCRIPTION
Title Bar	Contains the name of the program. You can move the window by dragging the Title Bar. Clicking the Title Bar brings the window into focus.
Minimize Button	Clicking once minimizes the window to an icon.
Maximize Button	Clicking once maximizes the window so that it fills the entire screen (some programs disable this capability).
Window Menu Button	Clicking once brings up the Window Menu, where you can select Minimize, Maximize, Occupy Another Workspace, or Close. Double-clicking will close the window.
Resize Border	Drag the resize border to change the height or width of the window.
Resize Corner	Drag the resize corner to change the height and width of the window.

FOCUS

One window is said to be in "focus," and all others out of focus. This allows CDE to determine, for instance, into which window to insert characters when you type characters on the keyboard.

Depending on your settings, a window will come into focus either when you click on it (the default), or when you move the mouse pointer over it. Also, your settings may dictate that the window in focus will jump to the "front" (in front of any other windows which may be blocking it), or it may be partially hidden behind other windows that are in front of it.

The window in focus will have a different color border, to visually differentiate it from all other windows.

If you refer back to Figure E-2 you will see that the User Registration window is in focus. Its border, in particular the title bar, is visibly darker than other windows on the screen.

CUSTOMIZING CDE

The CDE Desktop Controls menu is used to customize the screen appearance and system behavior. This menu is found on the CDE front panel, as illustrated in Figure E-8.

- Extras. The Extras option contains several advanced features such as restoring, reloading, and updating resources, editing the *Dtwmrc* file (a text file containing your desktop window manager settings), and getting information about windows on the screen.

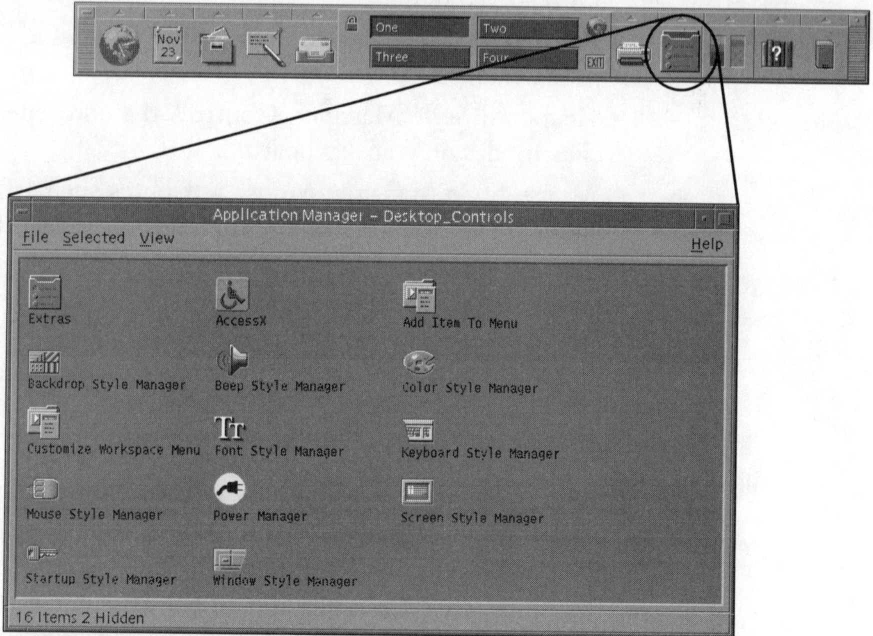

Figure E–8 *CDE Desktop Controls*

- AccessX. AccessX is a set of extensions to CDE that make it easier for the disabled to use the system. Some of the features that can be controlled include sticky keys, mouse keys, slow keys, and toggle keys. Sticky keys, mouse keys, slow keys, and toggle keys are features added to facilitate ease of use by disabled persons, according to the Americans with Disabilities Act.
- Add Item to Menu. Provides an easy way to add a program to the Workspace Menu.
- Backdrop Style Manager. Allows you to change the pattern or color for the backdrop (also known as the Workspace).
- Beep Style Manager. Permits changes to the pitch, duration, and volume of beep tones.
- Color Style Manager. Controls the color maps used on the system. This is important if you don't have a 24-bit frame buffer, or if you run applications that use their own color maps. In extreme cases, a phenomenon called "color flashing," occurs when there are not enough colors in the color maps for everything that is currently running on the system.
- Customize Workspace Menu. Lets you edit all items in the Workspace menu.
- Font Style Manager. Controls which fonts and sizes appear on your windows.
- Keyboard Style Manager. Controls the autorepeat and audible-click modes on your keyboard.
- Mouse Style Manager. Mouse attributes such as right- and left-handedness, double-click speed, and pointer acceleration are set here.
- Power Manager. This controls the Solaris Power Management settings, including power-saving modes and autoshutdown.
- Screen Style Manager. Sets the screen saver mode and auto-screen lock timer.
- Startup Style Manager. This setting controls whether the current CDE session should be continued upon next login, and whether CDE should confirm logout when the user presses the exit button.
- Window Style Manager. This control window focuses behavior and whether the icon should be placed on the workspace or in a special icons window.

E.3 Entering Individual Commands and Options

Most of the time you'll enter one command at a time on the command line.

Command Syntax

A *command* consists of the name of the command, plus any specific options and arguments. A command *option* is used to specify a particular optional behavior or result that differs from the command's default. *Arguments* refer to any additional information that is supplied on the command line.

Command options follow the name of the command itself. Options are usually preceded by a hyphen ("-"); for example, the "e" option on a command would be written "-e". Options can usually be grouped together after a single hyphen; for example, "-efm".

Entering Multiple Commands on a Single Command Line

More than one command may be entered on the command line. Separate commands by the semicolon (";"). An example follows.

```
# uptime;id;date
  5:16am  up 61 day(s), 9:21, 2 users, load average: 0.00, 0.00, 0.01
uid=100(pete) gid=4(adm)
Sat Nov 11 05:16:00 PST 2000
#
```

In this example, the *uptime* command, followed by the *id* command, followed by the *date* command, are all entered on one line. The output for these commands is displayed, one after the other, in the same order as the commands.

Directing Input and Output

It is often necessary to send the output of a command to a file instead of to the screen. Similarly, it is easy to direct a command to read its input from a file instead of from the command line.

Before we get to some examples, some terms need to be defined. These are standard input, standard output, and standard error.

- *Standard input* is the input supplied to a command.
- *Standard output* is the normal output generated by a command.
- *Standard error* is the error output generated by a command.

One more thing before we can show those examples of directing input and output: We need to look at the symbols that are used. They are defined in Table E.3.

Here are some examples.

```
ps -ef > procdata
lp < file.txt
df >> disklog
cat filename 2> file-errors
ruptime > up.txt 2>&1
```

In the first example, the output of the *ps -ef* command is sent to the file *procdata*. In the second example, the *lp* command gets its input from the file *file.txt*. In the third example, the output from the *df* command is appended to the file *disklog*. In the fourth example, standard error output is sent to the file *file-errors*. In the last example, output and errors from the *ruptime* command are sent to the file *up.txt*.

Table E.3 *File Redirection Symbols*

SYMBOL	DESCRIPTION
<	Accept input for a command from a file instead of from standard input.
>	Direct standard output from a command to a file. If the file does not exist, it will be created. If the file does exist, its contents will be overwritten.
>>	Direct standard output from a command to a file. If the file does not exist, it will be created. If the file does exist, its contents will be preserved, and new output from the command appended to it.
2>	Direct standard error from a command to a file. If the file does not exist, it will be created. If the file does exist, its contents will be overwritten.
2>&1	Direct standard error to the same target as standard output.

Now that we've discussed standard input and output, we can go to the next topic, command pipelining.

Command Pipelining

Command pipelining refers to the ability to link commands together. By this we mean that the output of one command can be sent directly to the input of another command, and the output of that command sent to the input of the next, and so forth. Consider this example without pipelining.

```
# who > users.txt
# grep acct < users.txt > acctusers.txt
# sort < acctusers.txt > sortedusers.txt
# lp < sortedusers.txt
```

With command pipelining, these commands can be put together into a single, simpler, command line like this:

```
# who | grep acct | sort | lp
#
```

In the this example, the output from the *who* command is sent to the input to the *grep acct* command, whose output is sent to the input of the *sort* command, whose output is sent to the *lp* command.

Another nice thing about command pipelining is that there are no intermediate files to clean up afterwards.

E.4 Command Syntax in the Reference Manual

The Solaris reference manual (commonly known as "man pages") uses a specific notation to represent command options and arguments. This notation is explained in Table E.4.

Table E.4 *Command Syntax Notation*

SYMBOL	MEANING
[ ]	Brackets. The option or argument enclosed in these brackets is optional. If the brackets are omitted, the argument must be specified.
. . .	Ellipses. Several values can be provided for the previous argument, or the previous argument can be specified multiple times, for example, "filename . . .".
|	Separator. Only one of the arguments separated by this character can be specified at a time.
{ }	Braces. The options and/or arguments enclosed within braces are interdependent, such that everything enclosed must be treated as a unit.

Consider this example. Here is the syntax for the hypothetical *abc* command.

```
/usr/bin/abc -r|-R [-fip] source_dir... target_dir
```

In this example, the complete path for the *abc* command is */usr/bin/abc*. You are required to use either the *-r* or the *-R* option. You *may* use any combination of the *-f*, *-i*, or *-p* options—or none at all. You *must* furnish one or more source directories (noted by "source_dir"), separated by spaces. You *must* specify a target directory (noted by "target_dir").

Here are some valid examples of this command.

```
/usr/bin/abc -rf /home/joe /tmp
/usr/bin/abc -R /usr/local/lib /export/usr/lib
/usr/bin/abc -RP /var/adm /var/log /tmp/log
```

E.5 Commands

Adding a Disk Device Dynamically Using the *cfgadm* Command

The *cfgadm* command is used to dynamically reconfigure system device tables without having to reboot the system. This can be especially useful in environments that have a poor tolerance for the downtime resulting from system reboots.

The following procedure is an illustration showing how a disk device is added to a SCSI bus. We will add a disk to SCSI bus c1.

1. Back up the system to tape.
2. List the SCSI buses on the system with the *cfgadm –l* command. For example,

```
# cfgadm -l
    Ap_Id            Type          Receptacle    Occupant      Condition
    c0               scsi-bus      connected     configured    unknown
    c1               scsi-bus      connected     configured    unknown
#
```

In this example, the system has two SCSI buses, called c0 and c1.

3. List the devices on the SCSI buses with the *cfgadm -al* command. For example,

```
# cfgadm -al
    Ap_Id            Type          Receptacle    Occupant      Condition
    c0               scsi-bus      connected     configured    unknown
    c0::dsk/c0t0d0   disk          connected     configured    unknown
```

```
     c0::rmt/0        tape         connected    configured   unknown
     c1               scsi-bus     connected    configured   unknown
     c1::dsk/c1t3d0   disk         connected    configured   unknown
#
```

Here, there are two devices on the SCSI bus c0: a disk device at address c0t0d0 and a tape device; SCSI bus c1 has a single disk device at address c1t3d0.

4. Set the address for your new disk device to that of an unused address. In this example, address 3 is in use. Set the address for the new disk to address 4. Do not connect the new disk device yet.
5. Add the SCSI device to the bus with the *cfgadm-x* command. For example,

```
# cfgadm -x insert_device c1
Adding device to SCSI HBA: /devices/sbus@1f,0/SUNW,fas@1,8800000
This operation will suspend activity on SCSI bus: c1
Continue (yes/no)? y
SCSI bus quiesced successfully.
It is now safe to proceed with hotplug operation.
#
```

6. IO activity on the SCSI bus is now suspended. Connect the new device to the bus and power it up. Then you may now answer the following query:

```
Enter y if operation is complete or n to abort (yes/no)? y
```

7. Verify that the device has been added with the *cfgadm –al* command:

```
# cfgadm -al
Ap_Id            Type         Receptacle   Occupant     Condition
c0               scsi-bus     connected    configured   unknown
c0::dsk/c0t0d0   disk         connected    configured   unknown
c0::rmt/0        tape         connected    configured   unknown
c1               scsi-bus     connected    configured   unknown
c1::dsk/c1t3d0   disk         connected    configured   unknown
c1::dsk/c1t4d0   disk         connected    configured   unknown
#
```

8. Note the new entry—the last item in the example list above. It is now safe to use the device.

whoami Command

The *whoami* command displays the current user name. Users frequently using this command should put */usr/ucb* in their PATH. An example follows.

```
$ whoami
mark
$
```

id Command

The *id* command is similar to the *whoami* command, except that it reveals more information, including UID and groupids. Examples follow.

```
$ id
uid=100(pete) gid=4(adm)
$ id -a
uid=100(pete) gid=4(adm) groups=4(adm),10(staff)
$
```

The *id -a* command also shows all of the groups for which the user is a member.

E.6 Configuration Files

The */etc/default* directory contains several configuration files that are used to define default behavior for a number of commands. The files contained in */etc/default* are:

- *cron*. Contains an entry that determines whether cron writes to the logfile */var/cron/log*, as well as the default PATH for jobs started by cron.
- *devfsadm*. Used to configure default settings for *devfsadm* command.
- *dhcp*. Settings for dhcp server.
- *dhcpagent*. Settings for dhcp client.
- *fs*. Setting for default file system type.
- *inetinit*. Contains TCP_STRONG_ISS setting that governs the TCP initial sequence number generation parameters.

- *init*. Miscellaneous system settings such as time zone and locale values.
- *kbd*. Keyboard settings such as keyclick.
- *login*. Contains login settings that govern whether root is allowed to log in remotely, if logins require a password, default umask, and so on.
- *nfslogd*. Contains some NFS server settings.
- *passwd*. Password aging and length settings.
- *power*. Power management settings.
- *su*. Location of su log, initial PATH used by root, whether su's are logged by syslog.
- *tar*. Parameters for various tape devices.
- *sys-suspend*. Contains user(s) with permission to execute sys-suspend
- *utmpd*. Settings for utmpd daemon.

APPENDIX F

Additional Resources

This appendix contains suggestions for readers who wish to learn more about Solaris.

Bialaski, Tom. *Solaris Guide for Windows NT Administrators.* Palo Alto, CA: Sun Microsystems Press and Upper Saddle River, NJ: Prentice Hall PTR. 1999.

Cockcroft, Adrian, and Richard Pettit. *Sun Performance and Tuning: Java and the Internet.* Palo Alto, CA: Sun Microsystems Press and Upper Saddle River, NJ: Prentice Hall PTR. 1998.

Gregory, Peter H. *Solaris Security.* Palo Alto, CA: Sun Microsystems Press and Upper Saddle River, NJ: Prentice Hall PTR. 1999.

Mauro, Jim, and Richard McDougall. *Solaris Internals: Core Kernel Architecture.* Palo Alto, CA: Sun Microsystems Press and Upper Saddle River, NJ: Prentice Hall PTR. 2000.

Sobell, Mark G. *A Practical Guide to Solaris.* Reading, MA: Addison Wesley Longman. 1999.

Stringfellow, Stan, Miroslav Klivansky, and Michael Barton. *Backup and Restore Practices for Sun Enterprise Servers.* Palo Alto, CA: Sun Microsystems Press and Upper Saddle River, NJ: Prentice Hall PTR. 2000.

Winsor, Janice A. *Solaris 8 System Administrator's Reference Guide.* Palo Alto, CA: Sun Microsystems Press and Upper Saddle River, NJ: Prentice Hall PTR. 2000.

———. *Solaris System Administrator's Guide,* 3d ed. Palo Alto, CA: Sun Microsystems Press and Upper Saddle River, NJ: Prentice Hall PTR. 2000.

———. *Solaris Advanced Administrator's Guide,* 3d ed. Palo Alto, CA: Sun Microsystems Press and Upper Saddle River, NJ: Prentice Hall PTR. 2000.

Wong, Brian L. *Configuration and Capacity Planning for Solaris Servers.* Palo Alto, CA: Sun Microsystems Press and Upper Saddle River, NJ: Prentice Hall PTR. 1997.

All Sun documentation is available online at http://docs.sun.com/.

Patches are available online at http://sunsolve.sun.com.

Information on other Sun Microsystems Press books is available online at http://www.sun.com/books.

INDEX

G

H

I

J

K

L

M

Q

R

S

GET READY!

Congratulations on taking control of your career! With Sun certification, you can enjoy the benefits of increased job opportunities, greater career advancement potential, and more professional respect.

The first step in preparing for exams is discovering what you need to know. The next step is discovering what you don't. To help you measure your skills and understand any gaps, Sun offers online skills assessments. They'll help you focus your energies on learning the skills that can lead to certification. Online skills assessments are available at: http://suned.sun.com/USA/solutions/assessments.html.

GET SET!

Preparation is the key to success, and this study guide is a good first step. However, our years of experience have taught us that few people learn in exactly the same way. So we've created innovative learning solutions that can augment this guide, including:

Learning Solutions: Delivered via the Sun Web Learning Center, Sun's innovative eLearning solutions include Web-based training, online mentoring, ePractice exams, and the benefits of a community of like-minded people. Available by subscription, eLearning solutions from Sun give you anywhere, anytime learning—providing the flexibility you need to prepare according to your schedule, at your pace. You can visit the Sun Web Learning Center at http://suned.sun.com/WLC.

Practice Exams: Also available through the Sun Web Learning Center, ePractice exams are practice tools that can help you prepare for Sun's Java platform certifications. The questions in the ePractice exams are written in the same format as the certification tests, helping acquaint you with the style of the actual certification exams. You get immediate results and recommendations for further study, helping you prepare and take your certification tests with more confidence. You can register for ePractice exams at http://suned.sun.com/US/wlc/.

Instructor-Led Training: Sun's expert instructors provide unparalleled learning experiences designed to get you up to speed quickly. Available at over 200 Sun locations worldwide or at your facility, instructor-led courses provide learning experiences that will last a lifetime.

Self-Paced CD-ROM-based Training: Using JavaTutor, our CD-ROM-based learning solutions help you prepare for exams on your own terms, at your own pace, in a dynamic environment. After you're certified, they'll serve as perfect reference tools.

GO!

After you take your exams and become certified, go ahead and celebrate. For more information, visit: http://suned.sun.com.

Your road is wide open. Enjoy the journey.